WE NEVER SAID GOOD-BYE

Memoirs of a Bombardier from World War II

By

Jack I. Moore

CGM Publishing, New York

WE NEVER SAID GOOD-BYE by Jack I. Moore
Copyright © 2011 by Jack I. Moore

Published by CGM, New York

Library of Congress Control Number: 2013932573

Hardcover ISBN: 978-0-9889450-2-9
Paperback ISBN: 978-0-9889450-1-2
E-pub ISBN: 978-0-9889450-3-6
Kindle ISBN: 978-0-9889450-4-3

First Edition: March, 2013

Printed in the United States of America.
10 9 8 7 6 5 4 3 2 1

WWW.WENEVERSAIDGOODBYE.COM

For Emily

TABLE OF CONTENTS

GREENHOUSE IN THE SKY

My wife and I were flying home to Minneapolis from Fort Meyers, Florida; and it seemed to take forever. In a burst of economic wisdom, we had decided to attach ourselves to the cargo of a "less expensive" flight. The decision was not shrewd in as much as it involved three hours in a jet propelled, high flying sardine can. It's predominant feature was a passenger section obviously designed for very slender and youthfully flexible travelers. We were, however, presented with an excellent sight line to the back of the seat just ahead and were welcome to view four inches of the right wing through one of the tiny side windows which functioned, presumably, to ease the trauma of anxious customers teetering on the raw edge of claustrophobia.

My bride of forty-five years and I exchanged glances of understanding; adapt or go mad. She buckled her seat belt, ignoring the earnest young flight attendant who was, at the top of her voice, coaching us on the best method of inflating life rafts in the event of an emergency landing during our flight over the drought stricken midwestern United States.

The click of my wife's seat belt signaled our decision; we would adapt. We must brace for one hundred eighty crawling minutes dedicated to squirming, wiggling, checking and rechecking our watches.

None of this was, in the least, surprising. It was assumed that our money-saving entry fee would not provide for creature comforts beyond those afforded cattle on the way to market. As realists, we held no expectation of pheasant under glass when the ladies in snappy blue jackets flaunting glistening silver wings forced their way down the narrow aisle to deal out plastic smiles and white boxes of anonymous sandwiches.

My wife was not visibly affected. As always she was quick to cope. A brief rummaging in her carry-on bag produced a book. It was titled *Chicken Soup For Golfers*. An omnivorous reader, she would be completely absorbed until the last page was finished or the wheels of the plane touched the runway; whichever came first. If "finished" came first, she would close the book, turn to me and say, "You have that look. What are you thinking about? I hope not one of your wild ideas like saving a couple of dollars by riding in this torture chamber."

Actually, I was letting my mind wander. We had reached our altitude. What a shame to travel so far and so high above such interesting places and be able to see nothing. I sighed and told myself softly, "I wish I had my greenhouse." My wife did not raise her eyes from the book. She may have heard my mumbling. If so, the subject would come up later, not while she was reading. In any event, she would not be disturbed, only curious. Still, I wondered why some adventurous aircraft manufacturer had not considered the promotional value of a glass-bottomed jet, or even a couple of floor-to-ceiling windows toward the back of the fuselage.

Suddenly, my musing was jolted by the charge of a very heavy gentleman with a very red face thumping from side to side of the narrow aisle, banging against the arms of seats in a desperate dash for the rest room, a truly amazing sight. It furnished a brief, unexpected but pleasantly bizarre side show. The effect on our fellow passengers was immediate and positive. Necks had been craned, pulse rates increased. People actually regarded one another and nodded or smiled. Unfortunately, the incipient community spirit perished at birth and the jet engines once again sneaked into our consciousness, humming their melancholy and monotonous refrain. In his own fashion, the kidney inspired sprinter had demonstrated that something to see or do can blow away abject boredom and gloom as effectively as dry martinis or checks in the mail; sometimes even faster.

When I had my 'greenhouse' there were always interesting things to see; things that crept into my memory to stay forever. Who knows what we might be savoring at this very minute if it was possible to see more than a tiny swatch of sky from the cabin of a jet-liner?

In the world below were famous rivers, Civil War battlefields, birthplaces of presidents; unique and wonderful sights that were ours for the taking; scenes to please our eyes and burrow deeply into our memories; facts that could be exaggerated for our neighbors on warm summer evenings around the pool. We might have watched a mighty river meander along getting wider and meaner as it swallows tributaries from all directions, hammering at dams and overflowing levees; you know you're looking at a power greater than man when you see that! We might have stared down at the top of a rolling forest fire, watched it lick at defenseless trees with the tongue of a thousand dragons. Could anyone forget such a majestic tragedy?

There we were, high in the sky. Who knows what we were

passing over at that particular moment? It might be someplace or something never to be forgotten. It could happen. It happened to me. A view that lasted less than a minute but will never truly fade. It haunts me and from time to time, when triggered by a newspaper article or a picture on the wall it returns full force. It zings into focus in living color and full-bodied stereophonic sound to recreate bitterness and anguish as vivid and painful as at that first glance so many years before.

Back then there was a war going on and most young men wanted to enlist in one branch of the service or another. Waiting around to be drafted, probably into the infantry, was not a promising alternative. My choice was the United States Army Air Corps. Eventually, that meant finding oneself in pre-flight school at Santa Ana, California and being subjected to a physical that lasted about two weeks. The eye examination consumed three or four of those days and was an important part of the procedure that would determine how remaining days, weeks, months, or years of a military career were to be lived.

The exact figures were an army secret; but our guess, when we had our bull sessions later, was that about 30% to 50% of the Lucky Lindy "wannabes" who arrived with us were "washed out" and sent to aerial gunnery school or wherever live bodies were needed within the Army Air Corps. The others of us became aviation cadets and were classified for pilot, navigation, or bombardier training. My Army Air Corps physical exam revealed eyes that were both 20/15, about the same as Ted Williams, good enough to pick up the stitches on a fast curveball. That was it, I would train as a bombardier. It would not have been typical of the Army to inquire whether I was pleased or felt another form of endeavor might better tickle my fancy.

Those were the days when the bombardier on a large, long-range bomber must have excellent eyesight. These days, military flyers guide their missiles with radar and other mind-boggling technology.

Pilots are their own bombardiers and the last thing they need is a glass cage on the front of the fuselage with some twenty year old kid kneeling over a bombsight, relying on figures he calculated from a cardboard "computer."

But those are not these days; these are those days. There can be no question that in those days a "pickle aimer" had to be able to see everything, had to be able to pick up the IP (initial point) where the bomb run started, had to be able to follow the target in the bombsight to adjust the cross hairs again and again until the lines crossed and it was "bombs away!" It was for that very reason they put shiny glass noses on long range bombers and why I was obliged to spend about 700 combat hours floating high above the Pacific with a view as unobstructed as from the basket of a hot air balloon. With the exception of certain unavoidable disturbances caused by enemy fighter planes or anti-aircraft guns, it was the best seat in the house. The crew called it "the greenhouse." I called it "*my* greenhouse."

My greenhouse was on the nose of a B-24 Liberator bomber belonging to the 7th Air Force, 38th Bomb Squadron, 30th Bomb Group based on the island of Saipan in the Central Pacific Marianas Chain. Our arrival there in September 1944 followed by a few days the announcement from Marine headquarters that the island was "secured." We soon learned that the term "secured" meant the other guys were beaten but not necessarily finished. For a couple of weeks, our sleep was punctuated by the rapid fire clack, clack, clack of Marines rooting enemy soldiers from their hiding places in the hills and forest above our squadron area.

They belonged to the 1st Marine Division. Later, when our squadron moved into Quonset huts down on the beach, their area was next to ours. We got to know many of them quite well and noticed they were busy preparing for something; no one doubted it would be

Iwo Jima. They were young guys like us, loaded with souvenirs and ready to trade. A pint of rum could barter for enough stuff to decorate a good-sized family room if a person had a way to get it back to the States. Some of the "gyrenes," as we called them, or "Jar Heads," as they sometimes called themselves, were veterans of two or three bloody landings in other places as well as Saipan. One of the Marine outfits we came to know better than others were the Fifth JASCO. Their job during an invasion landing was to go in first and put down the wires for communications. To a man, we hoped they would never have to invade Iwo.

We flew a few easy missions to start out; positioned down below the lead ship, surrounded on all sides by crews that had some idea of what they were doing. We were officially in combat but our mothers need not have worried. As for me, the bombardier, I was given the complicated task of opening the bomb bay doors when so ordered, watching the open bomb bays of the lead airplane and, when the bombs started falling from that one, reaching up with my left hand and pulling the salvo lever back, thereby releasing the bombs from our plane. I caught on to it in no time at all. However, our missions soon became much more difficult.

The arrival of the 20th Air Force created a need for parking space and a long runway for their giant B-29's. They found it on Saipan by taking over our runway and stationing many of the planes on Tinian, which was visible across the bay. Our pilots had to use a shorter runway with a fifty-foot cliff to get over at the end. Everything heated up. The clock had started moving toward one of the most courageous episodes in the history of our nation.

No one had to tell us that the B-29s were having trouble. It was rumored that their engines were overpowered. One morning, standing in our chow line, we were dumbfounded to watch three or four of them in succession struggle off the ground, falter and crash into the bay. We heard that, on some missions, more than half the B-29s taking off aborted and had to return to their base without reaching the target.

In the beginning, they bombed the Japanese from high altitude and results were not considered satisfactory. As a result, Bomber Command ordered low level attacks on Tokyo and other heavily defended targets. Great damage was delivered to the targets but losses of crews and aircraft were not acceptable. Part of the difficulty was that many planes and crews as well as wounded personnel, went down unnecessarily for lack of an emergency landing area between Saipan and Japan. Iwo Jima, at approximately the midway point between the B-29's home base and the Japanese homeland would be the answer if it could be taken.

The B-29's needed help. Pressure at high levels of command must have been sizzling. Our 7th Air Force B-24s began hitting Iwo often and hard and, one day, as we approached the IP (initial point) to start our bomb run on Airfield Number Two, we were treated to the sight of mammoth fighting ships of the U.S Navy totally encircling the small island. Among them were the A-1 heavy weights, battle ships and cruisers.

Our information was that the thunderous shelling continued day and night. The guns, aimed squarely at the center of the island, indicated the bombardment had merely been interrupted and the usual afternoon barrage would be resumed as soon as we dropped our bombs and were out of the way. Our mission was unopposed, a "milk run." Even the 120s in the volcano were silent. We dropped our bombs and headed for home. It seemed impossible that any fighting force could be concealed on the moonscape that had just passed beneath my greenhouse.

The Marines had already left for somewhere. Approaching Saipan on the way home from Iwo just a few days previous, I peered down from my greenhouse through broken clouds not expecting to see anything more interesting than white caps. Suddenly, as we punched through the gloomy overcast, there it was an armada of troop transports moving ever so slowly, almost reluctantly. What would be going through the minds of the men down there whose futures had been put on hold? They were my age. How long did they expect to live? How much time will they have now? For some perhaps a few days or a week. Some will be lucky. In combat you need luck. I picture the mothers and fathers, the sisters and brothers, girl-friends and wives who will be receiving telegrams of doom. They don't see these gray-shrouded sea-going hearses stealing away in the twilight shadows. I pray that an invasion will be called off or that they will find no Japanese on the island; at least not enough to stand and fight. I know these are hollow wishes but I want to believe it will be one or the other.

A few mornings later, on the chalkboard in front of the operations tent, our crew is listed to lead a mission. The destination is not shown, only the times of briefing, trucks to the flightline, start engine time, and takeoff time.

Take off time is listed as 2400 hours, midnight. I look at Henry Janeski our first pilot and we raise our eyebrows. It means we will have to get upstairs and into formation by the light of the moon, if there is a moon. In England it was not unusual to form up in blinding fog or the shank of the evening. However, they had special planes and equipment such as fluorescent lighting on the wings and fuselage of the flight leader. In addition, they had practiced and developed tactics for the job.

Since we are a lead crew, Janeski and I attend a special briefing before the general briefing for all the crews. They tell us the mission is to Iwo Jima. We have been there so often that we are tempted to ask, "What else is new?" We don't ask it because this one is different. We are not starting for Iwo at midnight just to get there in time for breakfast. We are told that we must put our bombs on the island by 0700 hours (7 a.m.). H-Hour, the time when the landing will start, is 0800 hours (8 a.m.). We are also told that we will be going in at deck level which means I will be using a little hand held wire contraption called a five-and-dime-store aimer instead of the usual bombsight. The rate of closure at deck level will be much too fast for the sophisticated Norden.

We will be on our nineteenth mission, more than half of the number required to complete our tour and go home. On the truck riding to the flight line, I sit next to Erwin Makowsky, my best buddy, a bombardier on Carl Lee's crew, also flight leaders. Mack and I graduated from advanced bombardier school at Deming, NM in the class of 44-2. By the luck of the draw, we kept turning up at the same places. Conversation on the trucks going to the flightline for a mission was rare. However, on this occasion, Mack tapped me on the shoulder and said, "You know, Jack I., we're going to be old men before our time if we keep this kind of thing up." I nodded agreement and returned to my own thoughts which were thousands of miles away in Minneapolis, Minnesota. It might be the middle of winter, but I would have happily trudged a hundred miles through the snow barefooted to be there right then.

The truck dumps us off at the hardstand where our B-24, *Wild Ass Ride*, is parked. Jan gets us up in the sky without any trouble and each crew-member stands at a window or sits in a turret watching for wing lights emerging from the dark. Somehow, our wingmen join us in formation and we head for Iwo. It is an uneventful flight and toward morning we spot Minami Rock which is our rendezvous point. Our squadron drifts together and we prepare to pick up the IP to start the bomb run. We have been maintaining radio silence but, now, Jan's voice crackles over the intercom.

"Pilot to crew. We have a message not to drop our bombs. The Navy says it's too close to H-Hour. Take a look down there right now, you guys. Pray for the gyrines on those boats. We're heading for home." I had a clear but brief look at the troopships. Second-rate sea-going hotels, for transients only, ready and waiting to send their frightened, courageous guests into an arena a thousand times more cruel than any inhuman entertainment devised by any Caesar. Have you ever awakened in the morning not being certain of seeing the next sunset? If you have shared that experience you will be able to understand the waves of sadness that washed over me. I didn't want it to happen, wanted to call out to someone to stop the horror before it began.

Live men were waiting in those boats; young men in the prime of life. My mind did not want to accept the fact that, before we were safely back at Saipan, hundreds of them would be dead or ruined for life. This was real. Right now they were as alive as anyone on earth was; breathing, praying, looking one last time at pictures of their wives or sweethearts. Our B-24 quickly left the island behind.

We tried to get Tokyo Rose on the radio but she was playing strange music as often happened. I left the greenhouse, crawled down the tunnel and climbed up to the flight deck. Janeski and Phil Gaines, our co-pilot, were sitting quietly, looking out the window at some tall cumulus clouds. Nobody felt like talking so I went back to the greenhouse and stared down at the ocean. We still held out some hope that the Japanese might not be able to resist the invasion.

The flight was quiet and uneventful. Jan put us down softly at Saipan and we hustled back to our Quonset where there was a radio.

It was now several hours since we left Iwo so we felt there might be something to report. There was. We were told that the Marines had gained a foothold on the island and were proceeding toward Mount Surabachi. Almost in unison, we asked, "Where's Mount Surabachi?" We decided the press must have found a name for the volcano, our despised volcano, the home of 120mm anti-aircraft guns that could be wheeled out of a cave and fill the sky with flak at the start of every bomb run. It is safe to say that, in the 38th bomb squadron, the word 'volcano' was never pronounced without a preceding unprintable modifier.

Three days later, we boarded a well-upholstered C-54 that was used to fly USO entertainers around the Pacific. We had been granted a two-week rest leave at Hickam Field in Hawaii. Our crew of ten were the only people on the plane who were not ambulatory cases from the battle at Iwo. They were a plane load of very happy people who had received famous "million dollar" wounds, the kind that were not too serious but bad enough to get the soldier home and out of the fray. They would live; they were going home. There were bandages and crutches, burns and broken bones but, for them, the war was over, they were free to dream.

At the first opportunity, I slipped into an empty seat next to one of the Marines and asked how it was going up there. He said it was bad, very bad. I asked about the 5th JASCO, the wire layers. He said they had trouble because the volcanic ash made it impossible to dig a foxhole; the holes refilled themselves as quickly as they were dug out. I didn't want to ask the next question, but I did. "Well," I told him, "I knew some of those guys. How did they come out?"

He turned his head and gazed out the window. Clearly, it was difficult for him to answer. "Seventy-five percent," he said, "Seventy-five percent casualties in the first fifteen minutes." For some reason we both felt unworthy to be alive.

That was all a long time ago and I might have gotten it out of my head by now but the pictures and statues of Marines installing the flag up on top of the volcano have become so famous that they pop up everywhere. One glance and I'm back in my greenhouse feeling the same sadness as the day it all happened. I was there, I saw it, saw the battleships, saw the troop transports leave Saipan, saw them again only an hour before the Marines hit the beach, saw it all through my greenhouse window. Those young Marines were the bravest people on earth and they deserved better than to die on that God forsaken island.

They deserved much better.

The wheels of our plane hit the runway with a loud thump. My wife has closed her book and is giving me her once over look, a quick inspection to determine if I need a haircut or have spaghetti on my shirt. "Are you feeling all right?" she asks "How long since you've had your eyes checked?"

"My eyes are fine." I tell her.

"Well," she says, "Your eyes are all watery and puffy. It looks like eyestrain to me. I'll get an appointment for you for next week."

"I guess that would be all right." I see no point in arguing about it. Eyestrain is eyestrain; even if it only occurs when the patient sees a picture of the flag raising on Iwo Jima and is transported back to his greenhouse in the sky.

CHAPTER 1

THE ESSENCE OF GOING AWAY

Today is Sunday, January 31, 1943 and an icy winter wind whistles around the corners of my grandparent's house. I wonder if sometime I might pray to hear that mournful song again. In less than an hour I will deliver my future, as requested, to the United States Army Air Corps. I will go where they send me, do what they tell me, and someday, God willing, be welcomed back home to the blare of trumpets and shy smiles from grateful young ladies. However the date of my return is neither specified nor guaranteed.

Because I have been ordered to report to the Federal Building at 800 hours (8 a.m.), my mother and I and my grandma have risen early and will attend 6:00 o'clock mass at St. Lawrence church where I was baptized and made my first communion. We will drive there in the dark. The weather is cold and blustery even by the standard of a Minnesota winter. The temperature is zero and my mother and I are forced to chisel a layer of rime ice off the widows before we can see well enough to drive. A cold moon lights footprints in the snow and ruts in the road.

The church is not crowded. The entire roster of worshippers includes the three of us, a few nurses from the night shift at nearby St. Andrews hospital and four, half-frozen young soldiers. I guess they have stopped on the way home from wherever they were trying to squeeze a few hours of enjoyment from a relentless and blustery Saturday evening. It is now six in the morning so wherever they were, the boys made an evening of it.

They are shivering in spite of being bundled in heavy GI overcoats. I wonder if they might have run into car trouble. The odds are less than fifty/fifty that a car will start if left outside on a night like this in Minnesota. It is probably self-preservation rather than religious zeal that has put them in church at this odd hour. Their faces are shiny red. Runny noses force them to use the back of their gloves for handkerchiefs. Otherwise, they wring their hands and rub them together in an effort to restart circulation.

My nose, which is not running, detects that the gentlemen are well fortified with anti-freeze. I don't want to stare at them but, in twenty-four hours, that will be me in a khaki outfit and I will be a long way from home. I wonder who they are and where they're from. The only military base near Minneapolis and St Paul is ancient Fort Snelling, which was built in 1820 to serve as a lookout over the Minnesota River during an Indian uprising. In normal times it serves as a polo field and induction office for new recruits, but not even the Minnesota National Guard trains there.

My guess is that they must be home on leave after basic training. Their GI overcoats cover any chevrons that might be on the sleeves of their uniforms. I notice no unit patches on the sleeves or shoulders of the coats themselves. The men are certainly not officers and probably are all privates, which means they haven't been in the service long enough to earn any stripes or bars.

I'm a bit surprised they show no interest in the nurses just a couple of pews away. Undoubtedly the cold and snow have sapped their interest in any project other than getting home alive. All evidence points to a balky engine. If so, they are in a tight spot. Even if a person knew who to call, it can take hours to get someone to come out and start your car on a morning like this. I should offer some assistance but it's out of the question. We will have just enough time to plow our way back home, eat breakfast, and hurry downtown to report as ordered. These soldiers could be on furlough, returning from overseas or might be new recruits with only one day longer in service than I will have at this time tomorrow. My conscience tells me to offer some help. They will need it; there's no doubt about that. I don't see what I can do. I certainly can't afford to be late reporting for duty. I have no choice except to turn my back and leave them in the snow. It seems like a cowardly way to start a military career. I feel rotten about it, but that's the way it is in this man's army. I'm learning a good lesson. It's the same one I saw on my dad's face the morning he left for Louisiana with the National Guard knowing our family would be disrupted. When duty calls, the decision has already been made.

The priest turns toward the congregation and holds up the host for the consecration. We are at the most solemn time of the mass. Grandma sits quietly, listening to the priest chanting in Latin, not understanding any of the words but knowing exactly what they mean. She is tiny and has struggled against asthma most of her adult life but love and compassion give her strength. Her name is Julia and she is often called when a neighbor falls ill or, in the Irish tradition, a family summons her to hold the head of the sick and dying. When there is a death in the neighborhood, the bereaved family often invites my Grandma Julia to sit with them through the night in a candle lit room where the body rests.

She and Grandpa raised five sons and a daughter, my mother. It is seldom mentioned that they lost a son and daughter at ages five and seven. Her compassion is genuine.

Grandma loves to play cards and is a very sharp player. Name your game: five-card draw, five-card stud, seven-card stud, Racehorse Smear, Hearts, Old Maid, Five Hundred, or her favorite, fifty-two pickup, which she plays endlessly with little folks on the block who don't know any other games, but really enjoy her lemonade.

During the summer, my friends and I play some serious poker on the front porch and Grandma often comes out and joins the action. She always asks, "Can I get in?" and sits down without waiting for an answer. She makes herself comfortable on the porch swing, pulls a shawl over her shoulders and proceeds to clean us all out. We use candy instead of chips or money. The candy is called "sixers," because the caramels are six for a nickel. When she has scraped up the last pot and won all the sixers, she gives us back our candy and goes into the house to make us some lemonade. Everybody loves Grandma Flavin.

I don't know if I'm half-asleep or partly awake. My thoughts are far from the church, the voice of the priest drifts up and down. I know some Latin and usually read along from a missal, which has Latin and English side by side. This morning I have not even opened the book.

Six a.m. mass is never very long. Soon the priest gives us a blessing and we say a Hail Mary together as he kneels at the foot of the altar. As expected, getting home is a slow and slippery ride. Visibility is bad and it's difficult to dodge around the snowbirds that have been left parked in the street. In spite of everything, we arrive back home with enough time for a big breakfast and a chance to wonder why life has changed so much in such a short time.

The kitchen is warm and filled with the pungent odor of eggs frying, hot coffee brewing and bacon sizzling. My mother is tending the stove, silently. Grandma Flavin is puttering with the toaster.

I had visited my two brothers, Bob and Bill, and sister, Pat, at bedtime last evening. It pulled at my heart a bit to say goodbye instead of goodnight. Now they are sleeping soundly upstairs. Grandpa Flavin did not join us. I understand and am certain he has an important reason. I'm sure he doesn't want me to see him cry. He is the smartest, wittiest man I ever knew but he is all Irish, a son of parents who fled the great potato famine in the suffocating hold of an overcrowded sailing ship. Irish men are sentimental and weep more easily than their women, but they'll run and hide rather than admit it or, much less, show it in front of the whole world. I idolize Grandpa Flavin. All of my uncles have married and moved away; Grandpa and I are now the men of the house and I'm his chauffeur.

Grandpa owns a 1938 Plymouth that he purchased brand new. Oddly enough, he has never learned to drive an automobile and has no interest in doing so. Occasionally, he asks me to take him to Stanley's, a small bar on Nicollet Island. He likes to put his foot on the rail, order a beer and chat with his old friend Stanley. I have a bottle of orange pop and, sometimes, a few nickels to play in the pinball machine. After one beer, we head back home. The rest of the time I am able to use the car as I want. Grandpa has a humorous answer, usually with an Irish twist, to fit any situation but, today, he will be keeping his thoughts to himself. I understand, I know he's proud of what I'm doing. I have no doubt that he will have someone else, probably my mother, driving him to Stanley's where he will be passing the word that his grandson,

Jack, is winning the war single handed. "Hell of a kid," he will tell, Stanley. "Played a little baseball, too. Made the freshman team over at the 'U'."

My mother's given name is Perigo but everyone calls her "Paree." She is not happy about the war, and for good reason. Her husband is already in combat in North Africa facing General Rommel, the legendary "Desert Fox," on battlefields with strange names such as Kasserine Pass. Dad is a captain in the field artillery of the 34th Division, inducted with the Minnesota National Guard when President Roosevelt began putting a citizen army together in the summer of 1940. Now my mother must say goodbye to her oldest son and she is not ready to accept another mole in what had once been a beautiful garden of roses.

Unexpectedly, almost overnight, our family structure has been shattered. A thirty-eight year old man with a wife and four children is not in danger of being called into service by the draft board. However, my dad, Howard I. Moore, was a man who enlisted in the Navy three times at the age of fifteen during World War I. According to Grandma Moore, she hurried down to the Navy recruitment office the first two times and pulled him home by the nose. The third time, it was a case of "three strikes and you're in." The Navy said, "If he wants to join up that bad, you might as well let him stay." They taught him Morse code and how to handle a telegraph machine. After that, they put him on a small boat in the West Indies and he served as a radio operator right up until the armistice.

When the war ended, he joined the National Guard and remained in it; loyally attending training camp, patrolling during labor uprisings, and lending a hand when natural disasters visited the area. He felt, sincerely, that he could not desert "the guard" now, when he was needed. My mother did not share his philosophy but, in her customary fashion, prepared to make the best of it.

The 34th Division was ordered to Camp Claiborne in Louisiana for training and the family followed, all except me. I am a freshman at the University of Minnesota and it was decided that I should stay with my grandparents, the Flavin side of the family. That was fine with me. I have many friends in the neighborhood and often stayed at Grandma's house on weekends even before the family went south. It is just a short walk to the University.

My mother rented a house in a town called Bunkie, Louisiana close enough to camp for Dad to be able to visit when time would permit. My brothers and sister enrolled in school in Bunkie. The United States had not yet entered the war, but already our lives were changed forever. Not long after the attack on Pearl Harbor, the 34th division was sent to Fort Dix, in Trenton, New Jersey. My mother and the rest of the family returned home but, since Mom had sold our former house, they joined me at Grandma and Grandpa's where there was plenty of room.

We wonder about the meaning of the move to Fort Dix but quickly learn that it had been a large embarkation point for troops being sent to Europe in the First World War. It seems certain that the 34th Division will be one of the first contingents to follow in the footsteps of the doughboys that won "the war to end all wars" less than twenty years ago. Upon hearing that news, my mother announced that she and I would be taking a trip on a Greyhound bus, a 24 hour ride, straight through to Trenton, New Jersey to spend a few days with Dad.

Dad had made reservations at a place called "The Pig and Whistle," an inn where George Washington is said to have bivouacked his troops. There I met many of my father's fellow officers and was particularly impressed by the "Rangers." They are an elite group; handsome men with beautiful wives, swirling around the dance floor, raising their glasses high and never thinking of the future that awaits them. They are truly the best-trained and best-conditioned soldiers in the world. There is no question if it comes to combat they will be asked to face the most dangerous tasks in key situations. I still think of them and wonder how they are doing.

Our visit is not long. After a few days, an alert is issued. The soldiers are no longer permitted to leave camp and civilians are not allowed inside the gates. Mom decides we may as well visit New York City for a couple of days just to see the sights. I have the opportunity to hear the Benny Goodman orchestra in person with Peggy Lee as vocalist at the Hotel New Yorker. We visit the RCA building and see ourselves on experimental television. We also watch a live broadcast of the Eddie Cantor radio show on which he features a new young singer, Dinah Shore. It would have been great fun if I hadn't been wondering whether I would ever see my father again. I knew my mother felt the same way but we never spoke about it.

Shortly after returning home, we receive news about the 34th Division. They are in Ireland. Front-page pictures show troops carrying barracks bags down the gangplank, the first American soldiers to land on foreign soil since World War One. My dad writes that with a name like "Moore" he is being treated royally on the old sod.

Our evenings at Grandma's house pass quietly. Grandma works on her knitting while Grandpa sits in his easy chair near the big radio that has a place of honor next to the fireplace. "I'll be damned," he will say to no one in particular if something catches him by surprise or tickles his fancy. Then he taps his pipe against the mantle of the fireplace, refills it, and lights it up again. Once, when I walked into the living room, he was mumbling that all the American Japanese should be put on a raft, which would be towed out to sea and sunk. I told him I just couldn't agree with that.

"Gee Whiz, Gramp," I said. "A lot of those guys went to Yale and Harvard. They're just as American as you and I!"

"Well", he said. "Is that the way of it? If a cat has kittens in the oven, does that make 'em biscuits?"

When the set is not tuned to news, Grandpa usually sits back and listens to fiddle music from Yankton, South Dakota. He has a fine Irish tenor voice and I like to hear him sing old Irish ballads but what he sees in that fiddle music I never can figure out.

Sometimes we hear Edward R. Murrow reporting live from London during the blitz. It's hard to see how England can hang on much longer. The Germans are pounding them night after night. We all wonder whether Hitler plans to destroy England or invade it. The signal is never very good and we often have trouble understanding what Murrow is saying because there's so much static. He doesn't really have to tell us too much because the sirens and explosions in the background speak for themselves. It brings the war closer to home.

Sometimes we listen to H. V. Kaltenborn reporting the latest activities and positioning of allied forces. It is reassuring to hear his usual opening line, "Ah, there's good news tonight." We read the papers and wait for mail. It is a surprise to hear that American troops are fighting in Africa. Everyone is certain the 34th Division is involved but we all expected they would be fighting in Germany or Italy. I hope there's a method to General Eisenhower's plan of starting at the top by going right after Rommel, the Nazis most famous soldier.

One by one, my friends are enlisting and drifting off. I applied to the Army Air Corps, signed the enlistment papers and waited for something to happen. Eventually, a letter arrived directing me to report to Fort Snelling to undergo a physical examination.

Fort Snelling, dating back to the early 1800s, is certainly one of the oldest outposts along the upper Mississippi. As we strip for our examination in a huge drafty room, we also find it to be one of the coldest. The doctor comes along and listens to our hearts, takes our blood pressure and does the one where he asks you to cough. It's about the same physical they give for playing football or going to a YMCA camp. The one thing they seem to be particular about is blood pressure. A few applicants got tossed out on that one. The examination is far from conclusive. One of my buddies, George Blackey, a friend from high school and a good athlete, was turned down for high blood pressure. When I saw him again a couple of weeks later, he told me he went down to the Navy Air Corps recruiting office the next day and passed with flying colors.

Having passed the physical, I am officially a member of the Army Air Corps, an organization that seems to be doing just fine without me. As weeks go by and healthy young men in civilian clothes are a rare sight on the streets and in places of amusement, it is more and more difficult to bear that questioning look. Who can blame them when so many people find their loved ones being hustled away to fight and die on land, at sea, and in the air.

Finally, in desperation, I look up the address on my enlistment papers and write to the Air Corps. I explain that they have put my life on hold and I would like to get moving. I ask if they would search to see if they might have lost me somewhere under the massive pile of paperwork heaped on their desks. I say it would be a great favor if they would just take a look. Several weeks later they reply that they are doing their very best to find places for all of the impatient gentlemen who profess to have a burning desire to fly. They promise to let me know as soon as a space opens up at the head of the line.

Toward the end of 1942, I receive a letter "ordering" me to report to the Federal Building in downtown Minneapolis on Sunday, January 31, 1943. The appointed time is 800 hours. The letter is postmarked from Washington D. C. where it is probably not common knowledge that Minnesota is still dark at 8:00 a.m. in January. It also can often be very cold and sometimes slippery.

At any rate, the time has come and the condemned man is about to eat a hearty meal after which he will take a short cab ride to a world he can only imagine. My grandma approaches the table. It is warm and cozy in the kitchen and it will be a long time before I enjoy another breakfast like the one she has just placed before me. The radio tells us the temperature is fifteen below zero. Nothing makes a hot breakfast taste better than having just come in from the cold.

Why am I losing my appetite? Leaving is not going to be as easy as I had pictured it. I notice that I am the only one eating. Mom says she is not hungry; Grandma, with the approximate capacity of a hummingbird, never eats more than a spoonful here and there except when she makes baloney sandwiches for Grandpa's poker playing friends on Thursday evenings.

Mom is biting her lower lip and I know tears will soon be falling. "I'll drive you downtown," she says.

I had hoped there would be no discussion until breakfast is finished but I swallow quickly, wash down some bacon with a swig of milk and wade into a battle I do not want to fight. "No, Mom, I'll be OK. I'll just call a cab. I don't have much to carry. They said to just take the clothes we wear and toothpaste and stuff."

Grandma sits quietly. It is not her nature to referee a contest between Mom and I, nor anybody and anybody. She quietly clears the table, putting my dishes into the sink.

"I want to go down there with you. I'm your mother; I want to be with you as long as I can. When will I see you again? Tell me that; tell me when I'll see your father again. Tell me that."

She doesn't want to cry. She is dabbing her eyes with a handkerchief, trying to stay strong. I don't want to hurt her, but I don't want any long drawn out good-byes either. Now that I'm leaving, I really wish I could stay but there is no chance of that. Even if I could stay, I would go. I don't know why. Maybe just because everyone else is gone.

"O.K. Mom," I say. "You can drive me down there, but Grandma goes too."

I look at Grandma who nods in agreement. She says, "I'll get my things."

Mom dries her eyes again, leaves the table and walks into the vestibule. When she returns, she is wearing her coat. "All right, let's go," she says softly. We hunch against the wind and blowing snow to reach the car. "I'll drive, Mom" I say, putting my small suitcase into the trunk. I help Grandma into the back seat, hold the door for my mother and climb in behind the wheel of Grandpa's 1938 Plymouth.

Mom is determined not to break down. She is in pain and my leaving is the cause. It is one of those times when there is nothing to say.

As we cross the Mississippi into downtown Minneapolis, the Federal Building becomes visible a few blocks away. "It's not fair," she says between sobs. "Your father's fighting over there; why do you have to go too? I don't want you to go."

Mom is not making things any easier. I fumble in my mind for something to say. Anything. I don't have to worry. The answer comes from the rear seat. It is in a very small but very firm voice and the message is clear. I am about to hear a declaration of reality in an unreal world. Grandma has heard enough.

"You stop that right now, Paree. He wants to go. He's a man and he's got a job to do and that's all there is to it. He's going to do what he has to do and you should be proud of it."

My mother stops crying and puts her hand on my shoulder. I turn to glance into the back seat. Grandma is sitting ramrod straight. She looks me in the eye, smiles, and gives me a wink that goes right to my heart and is still there. God, how I love that woman.

CHAPTER 2

JEFFERSON BARRACKS

My mother, Grandma and I say goodbye quickly because there is nothing more to say. We are in a "No Parking" zone at the curb in front of the Federal Building. I extend my arm to Grandma who is huddled in her coat, holding the fur collar up to protect her throat. My mother takes my hand and gives it a squeeze. She has stopped sobbing and seems, for the first time, to sense what my obligations are and to realize neither she nor I are in a position to flush them into the Hennepin County sewer system.

She puts her arm around my shoulders and kisses me on the cheek. I climb out of the car and she slides across to the driver's seat saying, "Promise me you'll be careful."

I say I will, while wondering how much latitude there is for caution in the Army Air Corps. I reply, "Don't worry, Mom," which strikes me later as equally hollow. It's only a short dash up the stone steps of the Federal Building and I push through its double doors without looking back. A hand lettered sign displays the word "INDUCTEES" with an arrow pointing toward a large, unfurnished room at the end of the hall next to Internal Revenue.

The room is crowded, filled to capacity, standing room only. I see no chairs for anyone anywhere, not even to toss our coats and hats on. We sway nervously from foot to foot. The thermostat must be set for a temperature about ten degrees above normal in hope of compensating for the deep freeze outside. Hot air pours from ducts around the base of the room. Soon it melts frost and snow carried inside on our clothes and very quickly, our leather jackets, wool topcoats, knit caps, gloves and other winter fighting paraphernalia become hot and damp causing nostrils to quiver as each item contributes a unique aroma to the barnyard stench suffocating the room. The atmosphere is less than sublime.

It seems strange to be only a few miles from home and yet be totally lost and alone, desperate to discover a friendly face. I am unaware of where we are going, and totally ignorant as to what will happen when we arrive. It is comforting to notice that others feel the same. Heads turn frequently and search the crowd hoping to come upon anything familiar. We are packed together as tightly as soda straws in a new box but we are strangers and there is little conversation.

We are relieved when the heavy silence is shattered without warning by a piercing shout from a tall, slim, mustached soldier standing on a table near the only door. "ALL RIGHT, MEN. TEN-HUT!" There is a quick reaction in the crowd with a few inductees, probably college students showing their ROTC experience, straightening up like wooden soldiers and pressing arms tightly against their sides with chins pulled back like Thanksgiving gobblers. The voice rises again. "AT EASE, MEN. AT EASE."

Those who understood the first command take a deep breath

and relax. The majority did not understand the first order and are completely befuddled by the second without any idea they have been standing at ease for the past hour and a half.

All eyes focus on the speaker. We cannot miss the three chevrons on his sleeves and even the least informed of us realize that this is a real live Sergeant of the United States Army and don't you forget it. He waves a clipboard with his left hand while clutching several sheets of paper in his right. The Sergeant pauses and studies the class. When he finds the atmosphere suitable, he tells us, slowly, emphasizing each word, that he will now start calling names; last name first, first name, middle name last. When we recognize our own names, we are to shout, "HERE!" It is our first assignment in the service and promises not to be too difficult. However, after the first five or six men answer as directed, a voice from the back row replies by shouting "YOH-HO!" The Sergeant turns slowly in the direction of the respondent.

"Who said that?" his voice is soft, shocked and bewildered. There is utter silence. We hear the tick-tick of the wall clock above the Sergeant's head. He raises his arms and waves the clipboard. "Now, you listen up. I got your name right here on this here roster. You got exactly fifteen seconds to get your sorry ass up here and five of them seconds is gone already."

Whatever his crime, the guilty party has no avenue of escape. The crowd parts allowing a short well-fed recruit to shuffle, head bowed, to the front. The sergeant examines him slowly, and then steps down from the table to put himself nose to nose with the crestfallen recruit. "Look here soldier. How the hell did you ever get in the Army Air Corps with all that ear trouble?" The Yo-Ho man studies the floor. You better answer me Mister Wise Guy. "What's the matter with your ears?"

"Nothing, sir," says Yo-Ho.

"You just called me Sir? You makin' fun of me? These here stripes don't make me no officer but I'm tellin' ya right now, soldier, I damn well earned 'em. They was earned by doin' what the U.S. Army told me to do and gettin' it right. Now you tell me you got good ears. That don't make no sense, soldier. If you got such good ears how come you can't hear what I say?" He doesn't wait for an answer. "You listen to me, son. I'm gonna pass along some free advice. Now you hear me out because I'm gonna save you more trouble than that wolf had goin' after them three little pigs. You ready to hear me out?"

"Yes-"

"Yes, what? You see these stripes. I just told you they are on my arm to tell people like you that I am to be treated with the proper respect for my rank which is that of Sergeant. You see that?"

"Yes, Sergeant."

"All right. That's better. Now I want everybody in this room to listen because there's one thing can save you more trouble than a thirsty elephant in a sandbox. It ain't complicated and this is what it is: you gotta learn that this here is the Army, men. You are now official members of the United States Army Air Corps and they got something they would like for you to do. You hear me? What they would like you to do is everything they tell you to do and get it done just like they told you how to do it. I mean, every time! If you don't agree, just tell them about it. Just don't be surprised when you find your ass in an igloo where the sun don't come up but every six months and the nearest female is 500 miles away by dog sled.

"I'm talkin' to all of you. This boy here's gonna be just fine." The sergeant reaches down and pats the Yo-Ho recruit on the shoulder. This ain't the last time he's gonna get his ass chewed in this man's Air

Force and the rest of you gonna get your turn, too. Now, I hope you got it straight! When you're told to answer HERE, you better holler HERE, nothin' else. Some of you boys will maybe be officers someday but that day ain't Sunday the thirty-first of January nineteen-hundred forty-three." He pauses for effect, softens his voice.

"Looks to me like some of you boys is bothered with a little boredom, maybe worried 'bout chow time. Well, pretty soon you'll understand the Army wants to help out by making some of these tough decisions for you. Don't sweat it! When the Army has things ready for chow, you'll eat; same as when it's lights out you get to go to bed without havin' to worry what time it is. My advice is it ain't too bad a life. Get used to it, men. You're in the Army now and you ain't about to change it."

"What I got in my hand here is a couple things the Army Air Force already got planned for you. I fully intend to tell it to y'all if we ever get through with this here roll call. It'll go quicker if y'all just sound off, HERE, when your name comes up."

He begins calling names alphabetically and it takes an hour because a few of the people are not present and the process has to stop while the Sergeant goes into another office to fill out a possible AWOL report. He finally reaches the last name on the list, someone name Zooner, who answers, "Here!"

"O.K. now, listen up!" shouts the Sergeant. "Give me your attention. Here is our schedule for the remainder of the rest of the day." There are a few muffled snickers from the rank and file, which is composed mostly of people who have just been yanked out of college. They know "redundant" when they hear it. I hold my breath.

The Sergeant glances around the room wondering if he has just missed something. He assesses his audience, observes the total quiet, and continues. "At twelve-hundred hours we will fall out and form up on the sidewalk on the South side of the building. You will line up alphabetically according to the alphabet and march to chow. Don't ask me where it will be. I don't know; how am I supposed to know? It will be someplace not bad; maybe not great but not bad. We will then march back here and await final word concerning our transportation to a designated destination, which I am not at liberty to reveal. I can tell you it will be by train. It is now eleven hundred fifty hours so put on your overcoats and meet me outside the south entrance.

We meet on the sidewalk as planned, are formed into columns of two and march three blocks to a restaurant on Washington Avenue, which is usually referred to by natives as "Skid Row." The café hosting our visit is clean and the food is decent. However, having grown up in the area I follow tradition and drink my coffee holding the cup in my left hand because people tend to and hold cups in the right hand. Holding your cup in the left hand turns the handle around and allows a person to sip from the side of the cup less used by the regular clientele, washed or not.

As we plod back to the Federal Building, a few people stop to stare and then walk on. We are young men in civilian clothes and don't look like soldiers. The folks can see that we are out of step and slouching in the typical attitude of chain gangs in the movies. Some of the folks probably suspect we are convicts being herded to the city jail which is visible just up the street. Well, we may not be prisoners but it is very clear that we are captives. Things could be worse; they might have hobbled us with a ball and chain.

By now the wheels are moving and, immediately upon returning to the Federal Building, we are told to fall into formation again. This time it is a short march just across Third Avenue to the Milwaukee

Depot. Our leader is a different Sergeant who says he will accompany us until we reach our unknown destination. He guides us in boarding the train by shouting our names in what he calls, "alphabetic order according to the alphabet." I notice that the train has no sleeping cars which leads me to guess we will arrive somewhere late tonight or early tomorrow morning but who knows? This is the Army. We may just go around the corner and stay six months.

Although it seems we are all strangers most of the men seem to be about my age. Many are probably from the Twin Cities and may have competed against my school, Edison High, and shot hockey pucks at my head, but I can't pick out any familiar faces in the crowd. George is almost bald although I would guess he is under twenty-five. His eyes are filled with wonder at visiting a new world and he seems to be looking forward to see what wonder may happen next. He smiles and laughs easily, the type of person who might become a good friend. I hope so. Right now I could use one.

George says he has read quite a bit about airplanes but has never been up in one. I tell him, "Me, either." It seems strange that throughout the entire process of being taken into the Army Air Corps nobody, so far, has asked whether we have ever been off the ground or even how we feel about the whole idea.

Our family would sometimes drive out to Wold-Chamberlain Field to take in an air show now and then or dad would take us out go there on a Sunday afternoon just to see and hear the big, noisy Ford Tri-Motor planes taking off for distant places like Chicago. All I know about flying comes from stories about barnstorming daredevils told by my Uncle Greg who worked in the refectory at the airport. He became a good friend of the pilots, who took passengers on joyrides for a small fee and became stunt pilots who made a huge crowd gasp on week ends. I never met them in person but it was easy to feel I knew some of them as we listened, week after week, to Uncle Greg's stories of their lives and sometimes deaths as they risked their lives week after week for a few dollars and the fun that went with it. It was exciting but did nothing to kindle a desire in me to imitate their lives. The war changed everything.

When I began to see friends, relatives, and neighbor boys come home on furlough after winning their Silver Wings it was easy wanting to be like them. Movies these days glamorize the Army Air Corps and radio stations play the Air Corps song over and over. Now here I am on a train guided by people who won't say where we're going. Is this smart? I could have stayed at the "U" by saying I wanted to be a dentist. The train has only covered a few short miles and we are now going through St. Paul. People are getting to know each other and can be heard chattering about where the train is taking us and some are just talking about airplanes in general. George says he would bet the house and car that none of them have ever been on an airplane although we are all enlisted in the Army Air Force. George and I agree that the only thing going for us so far has been passing a physical but no doubt we will have to undergo tougher, more important ones in the future. That future is clicking along the tracks and wherever it dumps us off, that's where everything will begin. So far we have no idea where that will be or when it will take place.

A high-pitched voice behind us is saying we will graduate as pilots, navigators or bombardiers and is describing the wonderful high life we will all be living as Officers. As people have said all through the depression, "It's nice work if you can get it." I have to wonder where he gets his information. What I have heard is that about 35 to 40 percent of the people who try for their wings will be washed out and who knows what happens to the rest. My Dad is a Captain in the field artillery fighting the Germans in Africa. Rank is very important and getting to be an officer takes some kind of doing. What's more, any of us who get through every thing and become officers are going straight into combat. Any way you look at it, we have a long road to follow and anyone who takes it for granted is liable to wind on the KP roster peeling potatoes in Nome Alaska. The way I try to look at it is to take one thing at a time and not expect any help. If I flunk everything they'll find a place for me and I'll do the best I can. When the bell rings, enlisted men will find plenty to do. Just because they wear khaki uniforms and are not be allowed in the Officer's Club doesn't mean, when the stakes are high, they aren't as important as anybody. It isn't the way I plan to go but in the worst possible case, it still seems like a better deal than being drafted and slogging through the mud with the infantry or signing up to study dentistry in order to fight the war at the University.

The war has been going on for over a year and my friends are scattered around the world in various branches of service. I think of them now as the click-clack of iron wheels mesmerizes my tired mind. Some of my friends had minor physical defects that could have kept them out of the draft; they could have stayed home safe and warm having fun with the lonesome ladies. They refused to accept their good fortune and figured out, sometimes with a little help, a loophole to get them into one branch of service or another.

In high school, twelve of us had a close knit group. We wore blue jackets with the word 'Wolves' printed on the back. With my entry, all twelve are now in the service. I am the last to go because the Air Corps had a long waiting list that held me up for six months after enlistment.

Frank Sinatra has a punctured eardrum that kept him out of the military. My buddy George Kubera has a punctured eardrum.

Somehow, George covered it up, joined the Navy Air Corps and has already earned his wings.

One of my best friends, Chuck Wallick, was bedeviled by high blood pressure and was turned down by the Army, Navy, Marines, and Coast Guard. However, being half-Irish and half-Polish, he absolutely would not give up an opportunity to get into this fight. Somewhere he heard that the Merchant Marine was looking for recruits and might have slightly softer physical requirements than the regular outfits. I borrowed my grandpa's car and drove him to the Merchant Marine recruiting office where they took his blood pressure. It was the same old story but they suggested he lie down on a cot for an hour and take another crack at it. Chuck took a little nap, got up feeling calm and rested but failed again. This time it was close; not close enough but almost.

I suggested that we visit a doctor friend of mine on Franklin Avenue. He was actually my grandma's doctor who treated her for chronic asthma that had harassed her through the years. I drove her to appointments and sometimes chatted with the doctor before we left. His office was a second floor walkup and not very large. Fortunately, when I called on a pay phone from the Merchant Marine building, he said he would be able to give us a few minutes.

It was a short drive to his office. The waiting room was empty. He heard us and shouted, "Come in." We found him leaning back in the big chair behind his desk. Norman Rockwell could have painted him there. It was all in place; the shock of gray hair, the tired eyes, rumpled white shirt covering a slightly protruding midsection, suspenders. He listens without interrupting as Chuck and I describe the situation. When we finish, he asks, "Is that all?" We nod.

Doc is far from spry but he pushes out of the chair. The effort has him breathing a bit harder but he gets around his desk and shuffles to a wooden cabinet where he fumbles with the bottles until he finds the one he wants. "Here," he says, handing some pills across the desk to Chuck. "Take these and then wait an hour before you go back for another try."

Doc asks me if I need anything and I tell him that I am already set with the Army Air Corps. "Well," he says, "God bless you, you young kids who don't know what the hell you're getting into, fighting to get into it. God bless you boys. God bless you." He runs a chubby hand through his thick gray hair. It is strange to see him that way with a tear in the corner of each eye.

We retrace our path to the Merchant Marine Office. They shake their heads in wonder when Chuck's large frame pushes its way into their waiting room for the third time that day. No question about it, they are skeptical but it must be that recruits are harder and harder to find. The headman himself dutifully trots out a cot for Chuck's relaxation and comfort. By this time we are all on a first name basis. They wait patiently as Chuck slumbers. After an hour they watch as he arises from his cot like Phoenix from the ashes and bravely submits to another blood pressure test. The nurse attaches the cuff to his arm, squeezes and listens carefully. She reads the meter, looks at our anxious faces, leaps from her stool, shoots her right fist into the air and yells, "Yeah!"

Everybody in the place whoops and hollers. The recruiter waves the enlistment paper at Chuck as if he's closing a real estate deal on the Taj Mahal. Chuck signs and we start for the door. I shake hands with the head man and thank him for his consideration. I tell him it's nice to see how happy everybody is for Chuck.

"Well," he says, "Chuck seems like a pretty nice guy but to be perfectly honest a lot of that cheering was for ourselves. He's the first recruit we've signed in three weeks. Headquarters was talking about putting us back on a boat."

Well, they got a good man. Chuck has already been on a couple of convoys to Russia with the Merchant Marine while I'm just finally getting going.

I took my Air Corps physical at the same time as another friend, George Blackey, a very good athlete. He, like Chuck, was turned down for high blood pressure. On the way home that day we stopped downtown and watched a Bing Crosby movie at the State Theater. George, not the kind to complain, was very upset. However, when I saw him again a few weeks later he was smiling. Not to be denied, George had taken the Navy Air Corps physical and passed with no problem.

The train clatters along. It is quickly noticed that we are headed south which brings smiles to the faces of all these Minnesota boys escaping the bitter winds and slippery sidewalks of their native state. Many of the enlistees are apparently from small towns and like George, and mention that they have never visited Minneapolis or St. Paul, the "Cities" as they call it.

The next afternoon the train pulls into a siding where busses are waiting to take us to our new home. We are in St. Louis, Missouri and, although the temperature is in the middle teens, it is an entirely different cold than has ever frosted my nose and ears in Minnesota. The air has an evil, nasty bite that seeks the marrow of a person's bones. Once established there, it cannot be dislodged.

We are still wearing civilian clothes and carrying small overnight bags. They tell us that GI clothing will be issued tomorrow and arrangements will be made to send our civilian clothes back home. I am wearing a sweater, topcoat and no hat; protection good enough for zero degrees in Minneapolis but no defense at all for fifteen above in St. Louis.

Busses carry us to a place called Jefferson Barracks which, we are told, was constructed for use during the Civil War. Upon arriving we wonder which Civil War they have in mind, American or Pelopenisian. The place has the eerie dilapidated aura of a ghost town. The effect is heightened by distant voices of unseen marching men shouting cadence and singing in the dusky twilight from somewhere beyond the sprawling hills. We stare at ancient huts jutting out and peeking from behind twisted trees in a leafless forest. Even in the half-light we can make out spaces between boards on the siding of our new homes.

We descend from the busses and are taken to the mess hall. After eating we are quickly assigned to our cabins that are revealed to be the air-conditioned huts we saw from the bus. We are divided into groups of eight according, as usual, to the alphabet. Each group then is led to its cabin containing four double deck bunks. Wide-open chinks between boards on the sides of the cabin invite a cold wind, which whistles in one side and out the other. In the center of the tent is a pot bellied, wood burning stove with a chimney extending straight up through the roof. Each cot is furnished with a pillow and army blanket. A woodpile is stacked outside each cabin and we are told to start a fire and feed it until the stove is glowing red hot, too hot to touch. Having lived in Minnesota all of our lives, cold is not something new to the members of our group. However, by the time we have started the fire in our stove we are all visibly shaking,

The fire glows, the stove is a brilliant crimson, but it cannot turn back the stream of frozen air pushing through holes in the walls. Each person is required to serve a two-hour shift as "Fireguard" during the night. He must also make certain the stove is well supplied with wood.

Sleep is impossible; my body is racked with pain. The single army blanket offers no protection. We get up and climb back into bed fully dressed including coats and sweaters. I pull myself into a fetal position but it feels as if every part of my body aches. It is the coldest, most miserable night of my life. Early in the morning, as the sun is beginning to rise, someone raps on our door with a walking stick. "Drop yuh cocks and grab yuh socks in theah. Tahm to get youh asses out heah."

We join the people from other cabins gathering around the corporal who has routed us out. When we are all outside, he lines us up and tells us that two of the men who came down with us on the train died in their beds last night of exposure. We are saddened but not shocked. If he had said five or ten, we would not have been surprised. We do not know their names but I know it is not I. I tell myself that if I ever get to combat it must be kept this way. I must feel that it can't happen to me. I see clearly that sooner or later a soldier must make a deal with his mortality by ignoring it.

I am starting my second day in service and have had the first lesson in defying death. I was subjected to the same conditions as the men who died. I am sorry they died but I am alive. I know now that each of us is alone out here, that there is no time to grieve. It didn't happen to me. I thank God for that and begin to believe it will be possible to handle whatever comes my way.

The corporal promenades along the line looking us over. He appears to be in deep thought. Then he stops pacing and says, matter of factly, "Whah don't one of y'all dah so ah can go home with the body?" I can't believe he means it but the fact he would say it reaffirms my new awareness; we are on our own, no one can afford to worry with us or about us.

The corporal lines us up, more or less, in a column of fours and marches us stumbling and out of step to a huge building that reeks of mothballs. We go through a long line and are given khaki uniforms, socks, shoes, underwear, shirts, belts, caps, hats, even insignia to show the world we are privates and should be treated with contempt. Everyone wants extra blankets and is supplied with two or three. No one believes that any number of blankets can defend us against the type of cold we are experiencing. People are coughing and spitting until the entire area sounds like a Greek chorus suffering from laryngitis. At the end of the first few days we hear of people going to the hospital with pneumonia. Then, just as it seems things cannot become any worse, Wham! We are stunned with real trouble. The camp is hit with an epidemic of spinal meningitis.

Soon the hospital is completely filled. Measures are taken to isolate people living in huts where someone has contracted this contagious disease. We are issued a directive that occupants of cabins in which a Meningitis patient has lived must tie a white handkerchief around their upper right arm to serve notice they have been exposed. They are also ordered to walk ten paces behind unexposed people when walking to the mess hall.

We follow these instructions but question their value because, when we arrive at the mess hall, we march in together, sit at the same tables, pass the food to each other, and serve ourselves off the same plates.

It has all the elements of a plague except disease carrying rodents. All eight of us in our hut are experiencing some form of fever and rattling cough. Dirt paths are speckled with bloody sputum but there is no room in the hospital so we feel we have to tough it through. People who go on sick call come back with a handful of pills and are told to return to duty. My throat is raw and I have chills, fever and a hacking cough. If I were still at home my grandma would slap a mustard plaster on my chest that could make a statue scream. My mother would tie me to a bedpost and station a guard outside the door. More and more I feel that going on sick call may be a good idea. If rumors are true, it won't help but I'm up against it and, for sure, there is nowhere else to go. Tomorrow is Sunday. If I don't feel better by then, I might as well go and get looked at.

Sunday dawns cold and windy as it always does in this dreary American Siberia. I go to church but skip breakfast and lunch and spend the rest of the day in bed. My nose is dry and my lips are parched. A small fire is burning just behind my forehead and eyes. It's almost dark when I find myself stumbling out the door, leaning into the wind, tramping down an uneven path to the emergency facilities, still wondering if they can be any help. I really don't feel very good.

There is no room to hold sick call at the hospital so it takes place in a large room that normally functions as a theater, church, meeting room or whatever is needed in an emergency. There is no doctor in sight. On duty is a medic taking temperatures, conducting traffic and selecting patients in a form of triage.

The soldier in line just ahead of me is flushed and burning with fever. The medic takes his temperature, looks at the thermometer, frowns, takes a fresh thermometer, puts that in the soldier's mouth, waits a short time, then checks it again. He places the thermometer in a glass full of some kind of fluid and points to a row of wooden folding chairs on the other side of the room. "Wait over there," he says, taking a fresh thermometer out of a glass and sliding it into my mouth. The patient moves away slowly.

"That poor guy's not gonna make it," the medic says, "Temperature's one-oh-five. Don't think they'll even get him to the hospital." He turns to a Corporal standing nearby. "Joey, go get that guy who was just here. He's over there on that chair. Get his ass up to the hospital."

Joey does not move. "What for? No way he gets in. I just come back. They got people layin' in the aisles up there." The medic takes the thermometer out of my mouth, glances at it, puts it down and turns on Joey.

"Listen, you little bastard, get your ass in the jeep and get that guy up the hill! You hear me? You get him up there and you get him in! This guy is sick, very goddam sick. You get him in a bed or don't come back here, Joey. You don't get him in, you better go over the fence. I'll see to it they have you washin' pans and scrubbin' toilets 'til your fingers look like prunes."

Joey stands up and starts walking toward the patient who is leaning forward, his head buried in his arms. "Geez," Joey mumbles "It ain't no matter of life and death."

The corpsman and I exchange glances. He turns his attention back to me. "Sorry soldier, I hated to make you listen to that. I been standing right here on this spot since eight a.m. this morning and Joey got me pissed." He fishes some sulfa tablets out of a big bowl and hands me a couple. "You got a hundred-two," he says. "Take these here things and see if they help. I got orders to tell guys like you to return to duty but if I was you I'd goof off and hang in the sack a few days. You ain't gonna be missed; believe me."

I go back to the hut and crawl up on my bunk. The wind has slowed down and the hut seems warmer. The stove is red hot and the bunk feels more comfortable. However, I don't feel good and decide I am not going back on duty until my cough goes away. Our duty is 100% marching and drilling. We learn commands like, "Dress right," which has nothing to do with uniforms, but helps to space out the rows when assembling. We learn that the word 'march" is pronounced as if the first letter is an 'H" just as the word 'attention', is pronounced "Ten-Hut." Along the way we learn some dirty words to rhyme in cadence as we march. It is boring beyond belief, but somebody important must feel that we will never become soldiers until we can perform these exercises as well as the Civil War fighters who first inhabited this God forsaken place.

One day as we get into formation, the corporal asks if there is anyone who can type and is willing to volunteer for work in the headquarters building. Although legend says, "Never volunteer for anything in the Armed Services!" I put my arm in the air and get the job. It is even more dreary than marching around, but is inside work which I hope will make it easier to get rid of my cough. I am learning how to be a survivor.

While conditions at the base are terrible, the food is good and varied. Even the most disillusioned of us take solace in three good meals a day. For that reason, the *Raisin Pie* incident takes us by surprise and, for a short time, dashes our confidence in the head chef who has been pleasing our palates for almost three weeks. It wasn't Christmas, but it was the middle of the night and "outside the door there arose such a clatter."

Scantily clad soldiers are running from all directions cursing, stumbling, and holding up their trousers in a mad pursuit to reach a latrine that has not been designed for such a midnight crisis. The scurrying tide has only the pale light of a cold moon to show the way. Once at the door, desperate men push and shove frantically, battling for stools with fists and elbows flying.

The late comers, the slow of foot, and the lame realize the hopelessness of seeking the civil formality of a comfortable seat and flee toward the darkness surrounding the building. Total number of afflicted GIs is estimated at 100%. Investigation the next day reveals that a small amount of soap somehow sneaked into the mixings for the raisin pie we eagerly consumed at chow a few hours earlier.

Because it is one of those unexpected occurrences which brighten the monotony of army life, and in response to the undignified nature of the entire experience, the event is sprinkled with star quality. It is a week or two before all the puns, misadventures, and home-made inaccuracies are drained from the event. Given the *Wuthering Heights* atmosphere of everyday life and death at Jefferson Barracks, the nefarious raisin pie incident will probably have blessed us with the happiest memory of our time there. We are not surprised when we hear that famous columnist Walter Winchell has called our happy home an American concentration camp.

At the end of a month, we are ordered, on a Saturday morning, to report to the sick call building at 9 a.m.. The wailing of those holding weekend passes, the first and only passes in our entire stay at J.B., can be heard in St. Louis and the outlying areas of Kansas City. However, we are now veterans of almost a month in the armed services and well schooled in the basics of left face, right face and shut your face.

When we arrive at the designated spot at the designated time, the news is not all bad. In fact, it is the best news we have had since joining the ranks. We are shipping out. We don't know where and we don't care. We are shipping out.

The procedure is neither long nor complicated. We line up and drop our trousers for a visual examination to rule out signs of venereal disease. Then the most worrisome part, the taking of temperatures. The room is populated with sneezers and hackers and some with deep rasping coughs. We are informed that only those with normal temperatures will be permitted to leave for our next base. Rumors are that our next stop will be one of several College Training Detachments at various colleges and universities in the Midwest. One of the schools is rumored to be the University of Minnesota a few blocks from my house.

Although my cough has almost disappeared and my forehead feels cool enough, the thermometer in my mouth could be a ticket to freedom or a sentence to another thirty days in hell. My belief is that no one in the room is absolutely certain they can handle another month in this place. If I show them 98.6, they will send me to the wall where people are lining up beneath the clock. Otherwise it will be a seat on the row of chairs along the opposite wall. Some of the men sitting there are crying openly. The medic takes the thermometer from my mouth, squints at it and points at the clock. It's difficult to resist the temptation to let out a cheer but there's no holding back a smile of joy and relief as I hoist my barracks bag and head for the spot occupied by the men from our hut. All eight of us will be going to the same place because our last names all begin with the letter *M*. If it weren't for the alphabet, the Army wouldn't be able to get four people together for a hand of bridge.

This could mean a trip back home; it would be like a furlough after only a month in uniform. It seems almost too much to ask. I join the guys from the hut and we all shake hands. They tell me the word is out and we're going to Coe College in Cedar Rapids, Iowa. My heart sinks for a few seconds then bounces back powered by the old cliché, "You can't win 'em all." I got all I prayed for, and that's plenty for today.

CHAPTER 3

The Invasion of Cedar Rapids

We leave Jefferson Barracks on a chilly Saturday morning in early March without the formality of waving good-bye. Although the trip from St. Louis is only an overnight train ride it seems to last forever. We arrive at Cedar Rapids just before noon on Sunday and are driven by bus through the city along the banks of the Cedar River. The moment we turn off First Avenue and enter the Coe College campus we realize this will be different.

One sweeping glance at the landscape conveys a sense that this place will be everything JB was not. The bus weaves under the branches of tall trees on each side of the winding road that takes us through rows of brick buildings toward the center of the campus. Finally the bus slows and creeps to a stop before one of the buildings that appears to be a chapel. Although it is Sunday, we see no sign of worshipers coming or going in the area.

When the door of the bus swings open, we jostle and shove our way down the steps and jump to the ground, enlivened by the scent of crisp, fresh air. We examine our surroundings and begin, slowly, to recover from the sleepy indifference induced by twenty-four hours in a musty railroad coach. There is chatter and backslapping. We are more than excited, we are truly hopeful of seeing a different side of the Army, of finding that Jefferson Barracks was only a bad dream. However, the barking cough that we now refer to as "JB Hack" assaults our hearing from all sides. We understand its message and realize a complete adjustment to finer things will take some time.

For now it is enough to squint into the glare of a brilliant sun riding between tiny white clouds in the noonday sky. It showers us with warmth and rays of hope. We greet it like a long lost friend. The smell and promise of early spring surrounds us. It is a wonderful day to be anywhere except in the bad dream from which we are awakening.

Since it is Sunday, the surroundings are quiet, almost deserted, although a few gawkers pause on their way across campus. We guess that most students must be at lunch or away for the weekend.

The watchers keep their distance in observing the invasion of their pristine and innocent world by a hundred or more khaki clad young men, the soldiers about whom the coeds have most certainly been warned. The spectators watch to satisfy their curiosity but do not run forward to embrace us as saviors of their way of life. We are raw recruits with less than a month in uniform; to them we are soldiers. I wonder if they understand how strange and insecure we feel.

The sergeant in charge of ordering us around shouts, "Fall in men!" We line up and at his command and pose ourselves at parade rest with feet spread the width of our shoulders and hands clasped behind our backs. An officer wearing captain's bars emerges from inside the chapel. "Ten-hut!" calls our leader. We snap to attention; hands at our sides, shoulders straight, chest out, chin up. The sergeant executes a heel-clicking about-face and salutes the captain. The captain returns the gesture after which the sergeant turns to face us and barks, "Left face!"

We complete the maneuver as perfectly as usual which means only one or two people turn the wrong way. The sergeant is not pleased but calls out, "Forward (pause) Harch!" We march obediently forward and up the steps of the chapel. We are soldiers, we are proud, and we are demonstrating the total amount of everything we learned in our thirty-day visit to purgatory. The students on the sidewalks do not applaud, the bands are not playing but, by God, we are marching and we are trying to forget JB for once and for all.

Inside the chapel, we fill the rows as we stand at parade rest. We remain standing until the captain emerges from a door on the side of the altar requiring another shout of, "Ten-hut!" We pop up in the pews like khaki clad jumping jacks only to plop down quickly as the captain immediately orders, "At ease, be seated."

The captain begins his prepared welcome but soon stops in the realization that he is being overpowered by the snuffling and hacking of his audience. He tries twice more and fails to overcome the involuntary bacterial barrage that does not seem ready to cease any time soon.

Finally, in a desperate shout that strains his voice, the captain submits to reality. "Men! Listen men! I have directed Sergeant Waller to march you to Greene Hall, the dormitory in which you will stay during your time with us. I have further informed him that you are all restricted to your rooms until a physician has fully examined each of you. I repeat: you are all restricted to your rooms until the doctors check you out. We trust you will find our facilities suitable and we will make every effort to get this health thing straightened out immediately. In the meantime, welcome to Coe College."

Once again we are called to attention. The captain says, "As you were!" and disappears from the stage. Outside, the bus driver has dumped our B-4 bags in a huge pile. The cargo from a second bus has been thrown into the mix. The bags have our names clearly stenciled on the side but the great trouble is that all the bags are identical. We reach, clutch, push and throw in the hunt for what contains the sum total of our worldly belongings at this particular time. As might be expected, the joy of the hunt takes over as the gentlemen, bored beyond belief, find pleasure in grasping the handle of a bag, spinning around with the ferocity of an Olympic discus thrower and letting it fly upward and onward just for the hell of it. At that point, our leader with three stripes on his sleeve and an angry red face, calls for attention, picks five men from the ranks and orders them to pass out the suitcases in an orderly fashion. The remainder of us stand at attention until the job is finished. The sergeant circles behind the formation to prop up, with colorful prose, any slackers who begin to sag slightly from the rigidity of the required posture.

Eventually all B-4 bags are in the proper hands, we reform our units and parade to a large "L" shaped building. We step out proudly singing the Army Air Corps song which is the only one we learned at JB that is fit for performance on the grounds of a coeducational institution. We feel very good and the little workout with B-4 bags has vented some of the steam that was looking for a place to blow up. Our bodies are tired, our throats are sore, and, although it is only noon, our single desire is to climb into a warm bed and sleep for several days. An uncomfortable overnight ride on a bumpy train with no sleeping car could lay a three-day fatigue on a healthy man. Most of us are not healthy.

We stand at parade rest in front of the building as our leader reads the names and room assignments, which are, as always, determined by the alphabet. When our names are called, we pick up our baggage and proceed to the rooms to which we have been assigned. Our troops are billeted on the second and third floors. The entire building is immaculate. We cannot believe the mirror image shine on the hallway floors. The military Ouija board has determined that I should inhabit a large room on the second floor with seven other soldiers whose names begin with the letter "M". Their names are Joe Murphy, Bob Myers, Bill Meiers, Bob Miller, Hugh McDonald, and Erwin Makowsky from Chicago, Illinois. The eighth man is not with us. His name is McGinty and he is apparently one of the pneumonia victims who were carted off to the hospital.

We wait quietly until footsteps in the hall and a polite rap on the door announce the arrival of visitors. We greet a doctor, followed by a nurse. The doctor identifies himself, and shakes hands with each of us. Captain Kaplan has lost no time in carrying out his promised mass evaluation concerning the medical condition of his new troops.

The doctor says he has made a quick tour of the rooms on the first floor and sent six of our people to the infirmary with advanced pneumonia. He says he has never seen such a carload of aches and pains in a group of young people like us. We greet this announcement with sorrow but a polite level of indifference. Nothing at this place will ever be worse than what we have already endured at JB. However ill our comrades may be, they will enjoy the luxury of warm beds and real doctors. Our new hosts have already earned our trust and we are confident they will take excellent care of our friends.

The doctor looks into our throats and ears and listens to our chests. The nurse takes our temperatures. After the doctor fills out his papers, he says we are in good shape and ready for duty. He is curious about Jefferson Barracks and, as he is about to leave, he says, "What's going on down there?"

We resist the impulse to regale him with the all too true horror stories we have actually lived through. The truth would probably give the doctor a shiver he hasn't experienced since taking the cover off his first cadaver at medical school. We also control ourselves in deference to the nurse, who would undoubtedly be offended by the barracks room vocabulary necessary to reveal our true feelings. On top of all that, I think we just don't care to talk about that place anymore. We want a chance to forget the place forever. The doctor tells us the captain will probably lift the room restrictions tomorrow, Monday. We ask about chow-time and he says they will let us know about it over the public address speaker. When he and the nurse leave we flop on our bunks and, in the fashion of real soldiers, we wait, lie on our backs and think about anything that comes into our heads. I find myself in circle of new friends who are of all shapes and sizes.

Joe Murphy is a big guy who played on the University of Wisconsin football team. He says he has trouble with his feet. They smell. Joe sounds somewhat apologetic. I imagine he's revealing the problem because there's no way to hide it and he doesn't want it to come as a surprise. Joe says there's nothing he can do about it and asks us to be tolerant if we sense an odd odor here or there. He is a big man and seeing him stretched out with his huge stocking feet dangling freely over the end of the bunk and his size thirteen GI issue shoes shoved under the bed, it is evident that his problem, if it exists, will be momentous.

Bill Meiers is a roly-poly country boy from Joplin, Missouri, who has an easy going, anxious to please look common to people whose comfort zone is anyplace they can pull up a chair and sit down. He is smoking a pipe and puffing quietly. It is impossible to know whether he is thinking of something or just at peace with the world. Bill is married and is perhaps the oldest man in the room. He looks to be about twenty-five which would give him five or six years on the rest of us.

The other Myers, Bob, is single, a wavy haired, thin-faced guy who smiles often and laughs at other people's jokes whether they are funny or not. More and more it seems that most of us just want to fit in. We don't know each other very well but we know now that this is how life is going to be and we want to be liked and respected.

Bob Miller is very soft spoken. He has told us that his brother, a Navy pilot, was shot down over the Pacific. He says he wants to see if he can get a choir started to sing at the services on Easter morning. It is interesting that we've only been at Coe College for two days and everybody is talking about getting involved in one thing or another. Maybe we're just adapting or perhaps it keeps us from remembering how far we are from home.

Hugh McDonald says he plays piano and likes boogie woogie. Since I play some guitar, it is comforting to find someone with the same interest. However, my favorite piano men are people like Art Tatum, Teddy Wilson and Bob Zurke who swing the standards. No question boogie woogie is popular but it all sounds the same to me.

I'm propped up on my bunk thinking of Basie, Miller, the Dorseys, Artie Shaw, and some of the big band sounds when Mackowski who has been listening to the conversation between McDonald and myself, comes over and plants himself on my footlocker. Mack says he graduated with a music degree from Loyola College in Chicago. He says he played trombone with some name bands for short periods. Our conversation is interrupted by the P.A. system which growls that chow is ready in the dining room on the first floor.

We go down the stairs together and are welcomed to a large room where everything glistens and the air is filled with a warm bakery smell drifting from the kitchen. The bill of fare, a skillfully prepared smorgasbord, offers a number of inviting choices. We fill our plates happily from shiny bowls placed on tables near the window. The variety is not overwhelming but the food is tasty and obviously designed for meat and potato people like us. As a grand finale, we swarm around the dessert table until nothing chocolate or baked, including the last crumbs of apple pie a la mode remains.

The apple pie covered with vanilla ice cream takes me home for a short spell. It was the favorite dish of Thomas Edison, the great inventor and was emphasized in the movie about his life. It was also a favorite dessert of my mother's and was served often. Our family had seen the movie together so, ever after, anyone putting a spoon into the ancient delicacy was asked, "What are you going to invent?" I wish I could mutter the phrase right now but I don't know these people well enough to try to explain anything so silly.

On the way back to our room, we stop to read some notices on the bulletin board. Of particular interest is an invitation to the women's dorm next Sunday for tea and cookies. It looks promising although there is a general lack of enthusiasm for the advertised menu. We are beginning to feel human again, which means we are anxious to see the young ladies and can't wait to learn what the Army Air Corps has in store for us.

We get the word later in the evening that our restrictions are lifted and we will fall out at 800 hours (8 a.m.) to march to the chapel for our medically delayed welcome.

At the chapel the next morning, the captain, whose name is Kaplan, greets us pleasantly and gives us a broad idea of what we will do during our duty at Coe College. Basically, we will each be given ten hours of dual training in Piper Cub airplanes but will not be allowed to solo. We will be attending classes in various subjects ranging from meteorology to economic geography and will also participate in a big parade through the middle of town on Easter Sunday.

The captain seems sincere but we are even more impressed with the surroundings. We understand we will be free on weekends unless duty calls and our persons are required to participate in actions vital to our military role. We note, without surprise, our role will include such important military maneuvers as scrubbing down the halls in the dormitory. In fact, the notice lists names and times of such duty far into the future. Our room is posted for six to eight p.m. Tuesdays and Saturdays. It seems a small price to pay for the kind of hospitality Coe College is extending to us.

The army has made arrangements for those desiring to attend religious services on Sunday. Each denomination marches to its place of worship. Murphy, Makowsky and I fall out with the group that goes, in a body, to St. Christopher's Catholic Church where the pastor keeps the first three rows reserved for "the boys" at nine o'clock mass.

As all men must from time to time, we experience major and minor disappointments. One, of the major variety, is the "Tea and Cookies" Sunday afternoon party at the girls dorm. Not having said so much as "hello" to a girl in more than a month, we happily accept the invitation and approach the afternoon with expectations that the young ladies will be similar to the girls we left behind. On that basis, we are willing to put up with cookies and tea for the pleasure of their company.

At first glance and introductions, the girls do not disappoint us. They seem slightly indifferent and distant but I realize we are not only strangers but outsiders who come packaged in uniforms that stand for everything good or bad in the history of warfare. I expect, as the afternoon progresses and we all know each other better, the stiffness will wear away.

The young ladies are shapely, colorfully attired and talkative. However, the only subject they seem inclined to speak of is their boy friends. We begin to realize that these gals are not nervous, they're aloof, even antagonistic and defensive. We are confused. We are here at their invitation. They must have thought it would be a nice thing to do. Maybe the sorority is looking for publicity, something for the paper on Monday. GIRLS AT COE ENTERTAIN FUTURE FLYERS.

Whatever the reason, it doesn't take long to realize they did not plan the party out of any burning desire to enjoy our company. The girls huddle together on one side of the room discussing future dates and campus events in low tones while we twiddle our thumbs and wonder how it might be possible to start a conversation.

They could be frightened of us. No doubt they have been warned. It's only normal that a college in good standing that suddenly opens its doors to a hundred or more sex crazed soldiers must warn its innocents to be kind and compassionate while keeping a safe distance. Just be friendly, but not too friendly. On this sunny Sunday afternoon in the year of 1943, they are obeying that advice magnificently.

They are keeping us at a safe distance and they are not friendly at all. We would like to know them better. Not having enjoyed a conversation with a living female in quite some time, we are in the position of starving men peering into a bakery window. How sad that they are not interested in learning to know us even a tiny bit better. After all, they invited us and we agreed to spend a pleasant Sunday afternoon in their company.

I munch a few chocolate chip cookies and wait for something to happen. What happens is an event that makes certain the entire afternoon will not only get off the tracks but will be a train wreck, a crash to rival the legend of Casey Jones.

It begins when a young lady named Lucille responds to the urging of a tall, thin girl to tell us about "Big George" and shatters a long, dreary silence on both sides of the room. I am encouraged. Nothing will break the ice faster than a good story and Lucille moves to the center of the room with the hungry confidence of a robin on the lawn after a good, soaking rain. Tiny but vivacious, Lucille dramatizes for us, in blow by blow detail, the grim tale of an unfortunate soldier in the group who preceded us at the school.

Apparently, in a carefree moment, the unwary recruit chided one of the civilian male students, "Big George," for putting his passion for college life ahead of his patriotic duty and deciding he can best serve his country as a pre-dental student. Lucille, cheered on by nodding sorority sisters, treats us to a live, full-scale reenactment of the physical fashion in which Big George exacts revenge for this obvious slur. At the finish, she rises from her chair, arms flailing, and describes in gruesome detail the manner in which her hero bloodies the mouth of the unlucky GI.

It is an enthusiastic keynote speech setting the tempo for the afternoon. Hearing about some poor private getting his smile rearranged by a massive draft dodger, is something we might have been willing to forego but it defines precisely the attitude of our hostesses.

They have several bones to pick concerning the little scuffle going on around the world. It has inconvenienced them greatly. Consciously or unconsciously, they resent the war because it has changed everything. Worst of all, it is draining all the fun out of college life. Why can't things be like they were before? Everything is different with soldiers all over the campus and so many of the real college kids going away. In their eyes, we are the symbols of their unhappiness. We are soldiers and all soldiers are the same.

I don't feel these girls are mean or nasty. If we told them our uniforms represent all the dark clouds and stormy days that have changed their lives, they would never believe it. I wonder if they are uneasy because their parents don't want us here. Who knows what those soldiers might do? Probably they have been told to watch their step because soldiers are promiscuous.

How then can these girls lower their guard and welcome us as if we are regular people from homes like theirs, towns like theirs, schools like theirs, families like theirs, and girl friends and wives like them. It is difficult to imagine two groups of people being more polarized than we are on this afternoon. I wonder if these people have any idea why we are in Cedar Rapids or where we will be going when we leave.

Would they believe me if I tried to explain that most of us have just been pulled out of college? Who knows? If given the opportunity, many of us might have surprised our hostesses with snippets of gossip and stories from campuses coast to coast. Who can say what witty and pun filled repartee we are all missing? On this sorry Sunday, we will never know and never care.

It results in a short afternoon as we, the khaki clad interlopers, sit and twiddle our thumbs while the girls discuss future plans for exams, dates and campus high jinx. That's what war does; it makes people slog along day after day wondering if Humpty-Dumpty can ever be put together again. From here it looks like it will be a long time if ever. It is not in the foreseeable future.

Whatever optimistic wishes we brought to the party, the sorry fact is that we are not welcome. We drift out the door before the cookies are half finished. We probably learned something today. We'll have to figure it out for ourselves but I'm willing to bet that none of us who were there will ever talk about it again.

I go back to the dorm and hit the sack. The afternoon was a big disappointment but it fits the lesson we learned our first day at Jefferson Barracks. That's the day a corporal wished someone would die so he could go home with the body. It's like the marching cadence: *Left, Left, you had a good home and you left.* There's a lot of patriotism in the air but people have their own problems and do not like to be seriously inconvenienced, war or no war.

I turn on the radio but can't find any decent music on the local station. I wish I could pick up a baseball game of some kind but the major league teams aren't allowed to broadcast into minor league towns and I'm not much interested in Cedar Rapids baseball or even whether they have a team.

My team is the Minneapolis Millers in the American Association and they don't broadcast their games on Sundays. Cedar Rapids is too far from Minneapolis to hear it anyway. I get to thinking that it is now the first of March and realize that the Millers are probably in spring training so at least I'm not missing anything there. I decide to take a little nap and hope to wake up at six o'clock to hear Jack Benny.

We have been told that Cedar Rapids is not particularly happy to have troops in town; at least not in this war. Our presence must be good for business but they don't seem happy about it. They are very polite and friendly as individuals but there are many that do not know what to make of the entire situation. It is a dry town with no alcoholic beverages for sale unless the buyer has a book of tickets. However, most of us are under the legal age (twenty-one) anyway. There are some dances in town and the music is pretty good.

A week before Easter I receive a letter from my mother stating that she and my sister will be coming to town on Easter Saturday to celebrate the occasion. I have been gone less than two months but it sounds like good news. They have never seen me in uniform and who knows when they will see me again.

In class we are studying economic geography relating to Russia. It is becoming more and more obvious that we are merely in a holding pattern waiting for places to open up in the actual aviation cadet program. The classes are meaningless and I spend more time day dreaming than listening. One afternoon a strange thing happens. I suddenly have a vision of myself standing under the wing of a large bomber talking with three other officers while other men in leather flight jackets stand by. We are all wearing parachute harnesses. The picture is vivid and lasts less than a minute but it is not a daydream, I am wide-awake. I do not recognize any of the crew. I attribute the experience to wishful thinking.

The day arrives when we are taken by bus to a very small airfield just outside of town. We see Piper Cubs lining the field in every direction and wait nervously for our first time ever in the sky. I meet my instructor, strap myself into the rear seat in the little plane and wonder where the parachute is. I ask the instructor who says you can't get hurt in this airplane unless you fall out of it. He gives me an idea of what to expect and we bounce down the runway and rise smoothly into the air.

It is surprising that being in the air for the first time does not seem strange. The view is about the same as that from the Foshay Tower, the tallest building in Minneapolis. I listen to the instructor and am allowed to fly the plane for a few minutes. The trick seems to be to coordinate the stick with the feet while keeping an eye on the horizon. The instructor emphasizes that the important thing is to keep turning your head at all times to avoid other aircraft. He lands the plane himself while describing the procedure.

I am one of the fortunate ones who are spared airsickness. As I climb out of the plane there are soldiers everywhere rushing toward the latrine carrying little red pails. So now I have been baptized in the Air Force. I have been up in the air. No one would say it was into the wild blue yonder but I feel comfortable about the ride.

Surprisingly, although it is the first time up for most of us, there is not much conversation about the occasion. Flight does not seem to be the glorious extra-terrestrial event we expected. There might be other days and mightier planes but today, for the first time, we feel ourselves to be a part of the Army Air Corps.

My mother and sister Pat arrive by bus on Easter Saturday and I get permission to meet them at the station. It is great to see them for even a short time. My mother presents me with a gold, engraved watch, which I ask her to take back home and save for me. We talk about my dad who is still in combat in Africa and my brothers, Bob and Bill, who are still in high school. Easter dawns bright and sunny and we parade through town for all we're worth. After that, the three of us have dinner and they start back to the Twin Cities.

It was a short visit but I don't feel deserted or lonely when they leave. I'm doing the right thing and feel good about it. It seems natural that those of us in service gradually see the importance of what we are doing and develop a silent contempt for those around us who have opted for "the smart thing" by obtaining a college training deferment. It must please them to stay safe and warm at home. Anyone with half a brain would prefer that kind of life. I know I would; but I couldn't feel good about it.

We are thoroughly bored with the make-work class schedule that keeps us at our desks for a few hours each day. We wonder what significance the economic geography of Russia can have in the futures of pilots, navigators, and bombardiers. Meteorology is just slightly more relevant but we would much prefer to be outside on these beautiful spring days tossing a baseball around or watching the coeds sunning on the mall in skimpy bathing suits.

Eventually, we finish our ten easy lessons in flying a piper cub and get a little break in the monotony. Bob Miller gets a musical unit going for our own entertainment. I borrow a guitar, Mac Donald plays piano, and Miller teaches three or four of the other dorm members a couple of songs which we perform over and over for no reason at all.

Then, one day Miller tells us he met somebody from the Lions Club in town and we are invited to perform at their next meeting about a week away. We rehearse *Mood Indigo* and *Stardust* at every opportunity until there are serious complaints from people in the rooms near the dining room. We rehearse in the dining room because that's where the piano is and the piano, as Mac plays it, is the difference between the men only pleading for us to try some new material instead of threatening physical violence.

Our performance takes place in the meeting room at the back of a small café in downtown Cedar Rapids. The crowd is estimated at fifteen or twenty gentlemen with the slightly bulging appearance of well fed World I veterans who understand how to enjoy a fine cigar and a sip of aged brandy. We give them our entire routine of both songs and they are with us from the word go. They like Mac's choruses on piano and are politely attentive to our singing although a wayward chord here and there elicits a puzzled look. Most importantly, they love our uniforms and what we stand for. They give us a nice hand and send us home feeling good.

Back at the dormitory we sit and talk about how well we worked together. We all felt it was worth the trouble and Bob said he might be able to arrange a few more performances.

Miller is a very observing and clever person. We are all sitting on our bunks lighting up our last cigarettes of the day when he puts on a little show imitating the procedure each of us goes through in getting a cigarette out of the pack and light it up. He rolls out a little patter to fit the demonstration. None of us realized how repetitious we were in our habits. For instance, when he got to me, he held the pack in front of his face and said, "Jack I. always takes the pack out, holds it up, looks at it shakes a cigarette loose which he taps twice on the box, lights up, takes a big puff, holds the cigarette up for another look, takes another puff and is ready for conversation on any damn subject you can think of."

We go to sleep smiling, looking ahead to our next triumph. Things are good, Coe College was a nice place to be, and it would be a wonderful place to stay until the end of the war.

The next day we learn we will be moving out, destination unknown. Now, just two days later, our bus is moving through downtown Cedar Rapids, taking us to the train. We go by the small café where we started and ended our musical careers just three evenings earlier but there is no tendency to reminisce. Wherever we are being sent, our future in the Army Air Corps will be determined in just a few weeks. It means genuine progress, we are on our way.

The rumors are that we are headed for pre-flight training at either San Antonio, Texas, referred to as SAC, a part of the eastern training command or Santa Ana, California in the western area. If a vote were taken it would be heavily in favor of Santa Ana which is just outside LA. The San Antonio Base is reputed to be the hottest spot in the entire air command.

We leave the bus and mount the train at the depot in Cedar Rapids on a glorious April afternoon. It has been a nice stay but we will not miss them and do not expect any of them to run after the train urging us not to leave. We feel great. All signs of JB Hack disappeared long ago and, in the words of a famous cigarette ad, "There's not a cough in a carload."

Once we settle into our section of the train, I whip out my guitar and strum the chords to *California, Here I Come*. We don't know all the words and we sing the title as "California, here WE come" but it is belted out with plenty of gusto until darkness falls and we climb into our bunks to have the rhythm of the train lull us to sleep. If, in the morning they tell us we are on the tracks to San Antonio we'll handle it. Either way, those who pass about three weeks of tests and physical examinations will finally be official aviation cadets. The rumor mill predicts that twenty-five to fifty percent will wash out and be sent to Aerial Gunnery School. Tonight none of us are worrying about it. We're thinking about those cadet uniforms, about hats with the propeller insignia on the front, and a step up the ladder to enter the U.S. Army Air Corp's special version of limbo. We will be regarded as neither enlisted men nor officers until we fail the program or graduate to receive silver wings and a commission.

California, here we come.

CHAPTER 4

Trip to California

The train huffs and puffs and seems to slow down or stop for any place with a depot or water tower. We have not been told officially that our destination is California but our "little train that could" is straining and hooting due west into the setting sun. Where else could we be going? For lack of any other subject, the numberless alternatives dominate our conversation. Uninformed guesses soon become "latrine rumors" which are quickly seasoned with questionable logic. Once cast out they grow faster and taller than Jack's famous bean stock. The usual reaction is an incredulous, "What stool did that come off of?"

We hope that we are, indeed, on the way to Santa Ana Air Base in southern California. Someone says he thinks it's near Los Angeles but we are gradually adapting to the military mindset that leans to skepticism in all things not tangible.

Wherever we are going is far beyond our control and a matter of no real importance. However, we are looking into a void and the view is bothersome. There are officers on the train who have the information we crave but they are sworn to silence in the interest of national security. Can it be they fear one among us might leap from a speeding train to wave hand signals to a treacherous German or Japanese spy crouched high in the Rockies, one eye on his powerful telescope? Imagine the sly smirk on that treacherous face as Benawara Arnoldasoni notifies Tokyo that another trainload of possible pilots, bombardiers and navigators is on the way to training camp. What a furor it would cause in the Japanese capitol.

There is the possibility that someone with no fear of rejection might approach the captain in command of the trip and boldly ask him about the situation straight out. That, however, will not be me nor anyone I know. To do so would be to invite a long silent stare; as if the good Captain has spotted lice in your hair. At best, being in a cheerful mood, he might reply, a bit sarcastically, "What's your hurry?" However, if the dining car has just served him burned toast or if he was unfortunate in last night's poker game as performed in the privacy of the officers' quarters, he will probably growl, "What the hell do you care?" Generally speaking, the Army is not interested in sentences that end with question marks. It is not in the nature of the military to explain why it does what it does. An honest man and good soldier might suspect, from time to time, his superiors don't have the least idea themselves.

Time has become an unsettling factor and we have more of it available than can be used. The passing hours are muggy and heavy. Conversation has dulled and we are increasingly anxious about the glacial pace of our train, which slows or stops at every tiny village with a water tower or a sign above the door of its ramshackle wooden depot. Sometimes the name of the place has been proudly painted on the roof. Often the engineer merely coasts into and out of the town. In such cases, an arm folds out from the train and grabs a bag hanging on a post. We wonder if it may be sandwiches and beverages for the crew.

The most trying times of all are when we rumble off onto a siding and stop dead for no apparent reason. At one station we sat all night and didn't get going again until after daylight. Some of us entertain the possibility that the train may be lost and is trying frantically to get back on the right heading. There is probably some more reasonable answer but three months of life as a soldier have convinced us that anything is possible. George Hendrickson tells me that the big guy across the aisle, two seats ahead of us, knows something about trains. George says he was told the guy had been working his way through college throwing switches at night for the Great Northern Railroad. I notice there is an empty seat next to him. Urged by sheer curiosity, I amble over and make myself comfortable. I don't introduce myself or even ask his name. It is neither customary nor necessary. I just say, "I heard you used to work for the Great Northern."

He replies, "Yeah, anything wrong with that?"

I say, "Not that I know of but this damn train bugs me."

"Well," he says. "What else is new?"

"Nothing," I tell him. "But nobody can figure out why this train is so slow it could run all day in a cigar box. We stop for every little burg we go through. Half the time we're out on the side track watching the other engines go by so fast the caboose is bouncing up and down."

He looks thoughtful. "I guess you know this here's a troop train. After all, we ain't high ballin' the Empire Builder Limited nor close to it. We got to allow for that. Then we got the Army, which likes to do things their own way even if it ain't the best way. I guess they got their reasons. I thought we made pretty good time with them clean stops at Des Moines and Omaha. I don't think we're doin' too bad seein' what we're up against."

"Yeah, but how come we get shunted off and have to watch those taillights disappear in the dark while we just sit there and wish we were somewhere else?"

"Them's what you call priorities. There's some reason those other trains got a special right of way 'n our job is to get the hell outa their path. There's a war on ya know."

Here is a guy who has found a home in the Army; I can see that. I sit down thinking he'll join me in a little gripe session to kill time and he comes out defending the system like a court appointed lawyer. I decide to give it one more try. "What about all these little hick towns we stop at? And how about those bags full of whatever it is that they scoop up on the run?"

"Well, my friend, you just have to know how it works, you gotta understand, in a war EVERY train's a mail train. That stuff they pull offa them hooks when we pass through are stuffed clear to the top with letters and who knows what else for people all over God's creation. Them priority trains got to get someplace in a hurry. They don't stop for nobody or nothin' and by God if we don't get outa the way they're goin' right over the top of our caboose. Me, I don't much mind sittin' while they get on with doin' whatever it is they got to do."

"Well," I tell him. "I hadn't looked at it that way."

"We don't know why they're high tailin' it. Hell, maybe they're haulin' troops that got to be someplace to catch a boat or somethin'. Maybe they're full of gyrenes from the East Coast headed out to the Pacific where the action is. We don't know! They might be in a hurry with guns and ammo or some other damn thing that ain't special to you and me. Anyway, me, I ain't in no big rush. I think I'm gonna like

California and that's where we're goin'."

"I hope so." I tell him. "You sound pretty sure of yourself."

"I'm three times double sure, buddy. If you meet somebody who don't believe it, bet your ass on it."

"Maybe the Army changes its mind and sends us to Texas or someplace."

"Not on this train, buddy. I used to work for Great Northern. This rambler started out from the Great Northern depot in Minneapolis and it don't go nowhere but west. It don't know how to go nowhere else and neither does the engineer."

I had heard enough. "Nice talking with you," I said. He turned to the window and studied the eerie emptiness of the southern Wyoming border.

"Bet your ass," he said confidently. "This is my railroad. I come out here from it and I'm goin' back to it first chance I get. Bet your ass on that, too."

I go back to my seat and scrunch down. George has his balding head buried in a farm magazine. "Well, skipper?" I say, "Get out those sunglasses and swimming suit. It's L.A. all the way!"

George puts the magazine aside but leaves it open in case he wants to make a quick return. It is a sure sign of skepticism. "What stool did it come off of this time?"

"No stool this time, Georgie, I am utterly convinced."

"You sound pretty sure. Utterly convinced is very drastic. When I think about it I may believe you."

"George," I say. "Bet your ass on it."

We fall silent. George closes his magazine and stares out the window at a deserted and barren stretch of southern Wyoming.

"I hope we get to see the Tetons," he says wistfully, as if talking to himself.

"What the hell is a Teton," I ask.

"Big rocks," George answers. "Huge rocks standing up like trees and scattered all over the place. I've never seen them but I got interested in a guy called 'The Tarzan of the Tetons' a few years back. I always hoped I might get to see the Tetons sometime. Wyoming is where they are and here we are going through Wyoming. You know, like something you never thought might happen and then it might."

"I thought Tarzan ran around in Africa and lived in a tree with some babe." I tell him. "You telling me they got apes out there in Wyoming?" I see some heads popping up in surrounding seats. It must have been the word 'babe' that caught their interest.

"I think you got your Tarzans mixed up. This one probably never heard of Africa, but he knew how to swing around in those rocks. They chased him all over hell for weeks and months."

"Who was after him? What for?"

"Well, they said he murdered somebody; in fact, quite a few people. He was some kind of maniac, strong as a gorilla and strong as a horse."

George was drawing a small crowd. They were pushing in the aisle and kneeling on the seats muttering about Tetons. "You think we might be seeing those things sometime soon?" asked Bob Miller.

"Well, there's Wyoming right outside the windows and that's where the Tetons are." George seemed hopeful. For the rest of us, our boredom had reached a point where looking for a pile of rocks took on all the fascination of an honest to goodness treasure hunt. Anything was better than staring at the back of the seat just ahead.

Peering at the gloomy, uninhabited land we are going through, it is difficult to imagine any human making a home out there. However, the thought of such a maniac as George described is enough to make us grateful for the protection of our musty parlor car.

Like it or not, George and his Tetons, along with the inimitable Tarzan, has gone front and center. We feel the red-eyed, drooling presence of our mythical rider and are grateful to nestle, snug and warm, in our click-clumping railroad car. As for George, if the big show fails to come off, he will be forever reminded of his invisible field of stones.

Darkness falls; George is crestfallen. We leave the bewildering emptiness that is Wyoming and move into Utah. George is disappointed not only for himself but also for all of us that we were unable to see his famous rocks. He sits staring at his reflection in the window. "Great story about that maniac," I tell him. "Tell me something. You never finished the story. Did they ever catch that guy?"

George rubs his hand over the bald spot on the top of his head, "Tell you the truth, Jack I., I don't know. They chased him around for a longtime, but it all happened some years ago. Who knows?"

The people begin to drift back from chow and Big Joe Murphy comes down the aisle on his stinking feet carrying a map of Wyoming which he tells us was loaned to him by Bill Myers.

"George," he says, "I found out where your Tetons went." We look at the map together. It shows Teton National Park big as life way up in the northern part of the state. Our train had moved along the southern border.

"That's the way it goes," says George. "At least we know where they are." It's a big disappointment for him because it was part of a small dream. No question, however, he feels worse about apparently misleading his audience. The Tetons take up a big share of the state; they should have been right out there for everybody to see.

Just as George is settling back, Bob Miller comes waltzing toward us whistling a classical song. "George," he says, "That story you told us about, did they catch that guy?"

"Geez, Bob. I don't know. It was a long time ago."

"Well, it's your story," Bob throws his arms up in frustration. "For God's sake, George! It's your story. Make something up. How'm I supposed to get to sleep wondering if that murderous bastard is still running around out there in the dark."

George pauses and looks into the anxious faces on every side. "O.K." he says. "O.K., I heard he outran the sheriff and the whole damn posse. The lawmen gave up the chase but his draft board never quit. They came out and got him and, to avoid the draft, he tried joining the Navy, Marines, and Infantry. They all turned him down so he joined the Air Corps and is probably on this train right here tonight."

"Well, that's a relief," sighs Bob. "A guy like that shouldn't be allowed out in public. Good night, gentlemen."

Although the pace seems like running in a pot of glue, we have crossed most of the western half of the United States according to Bill Myers. Bill, from our Coe College group, has a map and updates it every day. The thick red line indicating our route now stretches from Cedar Rapids, Iowa through Des Moines to Omaha, Nebraska and on into Colorado. We have crossed the southern part of Wyoming. Bill figures we will go through Utah from north to south and just nip a corner of Arizona. After that, it's Las Vegas and then to Los Angeles. Unfortunately, we will miss Reno, which is the big gambling and fun place in the world. It is a town being compared with Sodom and Gomorrah, famous for easy divorces and available women. Since there is no chance we will be permitted to leave the train, we won't be missing anything we would have missed anyway.

George is smiling; the disappointment of a little dream gone sour has evaporated. It is smiles all around as we head for our bunks. I stretch out and wonder if they ever did catch that "Tarzan of the Tetons." I tell myself that someday I will have to look it up. I wonder if Joe realizes what a nice thing he did for George by borrowing that map or if George realizes the Tetons will be forgotten by chow time tomorrow morning.

Personally, I am thinking that tomorrow afternoon we will be in Los Angeles, only thirty miles from Santa Ana pre-flight school where we will sleep tomorrow night. I fall asleep still wondering whether Tarzan might still be running around in those rocks.

The next afternoon we climb down from our train at a station resembling an adobe house. We are in Los Angeles and the sun is brilliant. We are at sea level and the air is fresh and clean. Trucks take us to a commuter train to cover the remaining thirty miles to Santa Ana. We are seated with the civilian population on the train and people seem friendly.

We complete our ride to Santa Ana and are loaded on trucks for our ride to the base. There are no bands playing or crowds cheering and there is very little chatter among us. Without doubt, the next two weeks will determine the course of our lives for months and years.

CHAPTER 5

California, Here We Are

Our train puffs into the station and this can only be California. We flatten our faces and push our noses against the train widows for a first glimpse of the wonderland we have been promoted to expect. We are not disappointed. The depot has an adobe exterior that reflects perfectly the publicity pictures we have ogled while checking out pinup girls in movie magazines.

Although most of us have never visited California, we have been exposed to its glamour from every possible angle. We have wondered if anything could really duplicate what we have read, heard, or seen in newspapers, books, magazines, radio, and movies. The usual attitude by most GIs is to be ready for a disappointment. Sometimes, when an expected disappointment does not occur he may feel deprived of his right to complain.

This time we are stopped in our tracks by the unreal brilliance of the surrounding area. Rows of tall, multicolored flowers pick up the rhythm of a soft breeze and sway peacefully. The sun, a huge orange ball, rides high in a blue, cloudless sky sending yellow rays splashing against the alabaster walls of the railroad station. In our topsy-turvy world of dreams versus low expectations, we have, for once, found the world as promised. We are excited that somewhere, not very far away, awaits the impossible reality of Hollywood.

For a few pleasant moments, we are out of our monkey suits and become people again. The nagging challenges that lie before us, even the possibilities of failure, cannot compete with the bevy of sweater girls dancing in our active imaginations. Are we headed for careers as intrepid airmen with all the sparkling benefits befitting an officer or are we doomed to spend our days and nights as sergeants squeezed into the tail gunner's turret of a B-17 Flying Fortress? Who cares! Bring on the starlets!

We are basically pleased with what we see. While we wait for further orders, we share a few laughs and some small talk to stifle the lull that typically follows the end of a long trip. It usually seems that none of the brass has the slightest idea of what comes next, as if nobody handed them a mimeographed sheet with all the details four days ago in the station at Cedar Rapids. We wait, we fidget. We are well aware that nobody will descend from this train until the United States Army Air Corps gives permission. It could mean anytime between now and whenever the captain and his cadre get hungry. There is always a reason for delays and always delays demanding reasons. Sooner or later we will be ordered to do whatever they have known for some time we would have to do; probably something related to getting off this train or getting on another. In time, they reappear, as we knew they must.

We were correct, the issue was trains. They order us to fall out, form into columns and march to another part of the station. We pick up our barracks bags, file out one door of the station, come back through another, and move along to a commuter train. Our captain comes down the line with orders for us to get aboard and take seats where we can find one empty. As I drag my barracks bag up the steps of the car, it suddenly comes to mind we will be sitting among civilians; an experience that has not been ours in several months.

It is strange and unfamiliar to be thrown without warning into a forgotten world of Stetson hats and three-piece sits. I ease into a seat next to someone, possibly a draft dodger. Since putting on a uniform I feel subconsciously that anyone under forty years of age, capable of walking down the sidewalk on two feet and still not spoken for by Uncle Sam must be a slacker, an out and out draft dodger. As soon as I find an empty seat and slip into it, I realize that the gentleman sitting next to me, just inches from my elbow, is not in my world, although I used to be there.

The civilians do not seem to notice us. Perhaps they are only being polite. Our dull khaki uniforms, embarrassingly naked of shiny medals, gold insignia or stripes on the sleeves, quickly identify us as beginners. Anyone with the slightest knowledge of military attire can see that immediately. The picture we present is not one to be seen on recruiting posters but we are what we are and we're going to go out and win the war for these 4-F bastards whether they like it or not. It seems, for a moment, that our uninspiring uniforms have thrust us an infinite distance from the world we once knew, the one these well meaning people still enjoy. I wonder what comes next.

A glance around the car reveals the soldiers sitting quietly, occasionally gazing at the countryside. I notice that none of them seem to be making conversation with the civilians. The gentleman seated next to me makes no attempt to undertake a conversation. He is in his late forties or early fifties, fashionably attired and working diligently, squinting through bifocals at his crossword puzzle. I peek at his puzzle without turning my head. I see several squares where I can help him solve his damn puzzle but I do not even consider it. I'm not talking to him if he doesn't care to talk to me. I am tempted to lean over and say, "I'm an American. I was born in this country. This funny costume you are ignoring is now very much in vogue. Do you recognize it? I can recommend where you might find one similar if you choose."

Our fellow passengers do not seem curious about who we are, where we came from, or where we are going. Perhaps they feel it is none of their business. Signs everywhere proclaim, "Loose lips will sink ships." Maybe it's pure patriotism that compels them to continue reading their newspapers. Many, it seems, are studying stock market reports. A few are not much older than I. Why aren't they in service? Do they feel relieved that they are not the ones being shipped like cattle to places they don't care to go? Do they see us as sad eyed livestock plodding blindly toward whatever fate is out there waiting? Have they the least idea of what we would give for permission to leave this train and go home, even for one day, to the smells of our own kitchens, the softness of our favorite chairs, the arms of our wives or girl friends? The sun is just beginning to set. It's painful to imagine such a thing on a beautiful evening such as this one promises to be.

Most of the seats on the train appear to be occupied by older men; not old, but older. They have the look of men young enough to dream but old enough to escape duty in the service. It seems to me they may be innocent misfits during these remarkable days and nights. They could find themselves right side up in an upside down world. Bald or graying heads and paunchy stomachs preserve them from being uprooted and losing the comforts of home for the duration. The time may come when we would happily trade places with them but, for whatever reason, most of us would not do so right now.

What a strange kind of hell they must inhabit. In a dazzling, dizzying, dancing world, they find themselves staring through a chain-link fence covered with signs at regular intervals saying, "KEEP OUT!" The bars and restaurants are overflowing with women and girls looking for companionship to soothe the lonely hours that become more agonizing as separation from loved ones grows longer. They are not interested in civilian gentlemen just too old or classified 4-F (too sick). One of the most often played songs on the millions of juke boxes that seem never to stop playing is entitled *They're Either Too Old or Too Young*. The second lines goes: "They're either too old or too grassy green." I guess that's why I don't think we would exchange what we're doing for the freedom these commuters enjoy. Something truly big is going on in the world and my friends and I are part of it. Nobody can say how things will turn out but we'll be able to say, "Yeah. We were there." I want to be able to say that. In many ways, our position is not much better than that of the homebodies. It strikes me that we are just the right age and disposition to enjoy the big party, the unbridled war fever on the home front, but we still may be in a "no win" position for a long time. We have been informed in no uncertain way to expect that the physical and mental demands of our training will have us confined to the base on all but a few weekends. Eventually, however, we can expect that nearby LA will provide at least a taste of the unfettered joys of the acceptable hedonism which so obviously grips the nation. The swinging bands and jitterbugging girls can whoop it up "for the boys" as much as they want but will have to celebrate without the aid of aviation cadets except on rare weekends.

There are moments when I wonder why I'm doing this. Most of us were in college and eligible for a deferment of one kind or another, at least for a year or so. Jerry Milnar, a close friend who played shortstop on the freshman baseball team switched his major to dentistry. My mother writes that he came over to say hello and was wearing his Navy uniform. He is going right ahead with his studies back in the old hometown. There are athletes at colleges all around the country being held over for football. I know that what I decided to do is what some people could say is not very smart, but I don't want to be like those people. I want to qualify for cadet training and be with the people all around me now. I don't know why; I just feel that way, as if what we are doing is the right thing to do.

A year or so ago, when I was a senior in high school, I was a very unskilled substitute on the football team. I was really too small to count for anything on a team that won the conference championship. However, I stuck it out. One cold afternoon after school we were scrimmaging and I was blind-sided by a lineman about twice my size who sent me flying against a fence that surrounded the field. When I looked up, there on the sidewalk outside the fence stood my French teacher, Miss Jacobson, her arms full of books. She looked down at me, shook her head sadly, and said, "Jack, why are you doing this?" I had no answer so I shrugged my shoulders and went back to the huddle. Miss Jacobson walked on. I guess I just wanted to belong.

It will take a maximum effort to keep up with these guys who are called "the cream of the crop." Sometime the privates and corporals call us that with a sarcastic snarl, but those of us who can pass the physicals and handle a tough class schedule will know we are put together in a special way. Maybe I'll be lucky and make up the years of college that will be missed. Right now the future is a blur, a shadow on the wall, something not worth worrying about that haunts us day and night.

One thing is certain: we want to be officers--pilots,

bombardiers, or navigators with silver wings on our chests and gold bars on our shoulders. Right now things are a bit out of focus like an old-time movie. We haven't even taken our physicals yet. We haven't even arrived at Santa Ana but we soon will. I think briefly of home realizing that my home now is wherever the Air Force puts me. I feel like a leaf riding the wind down a deserted street. Wherever it stops is exactly where it was meant to be.

The commuter train has soft comfortable seats and hums quickly over the 30 miles or so to Santa Ana where we are put on trucks and taken to a large wooden building to be welcomed. Probably, this is where the important decisions about our futures will be decided. The chips are on the table; officer's bars or ariel gunnery school. Most of us will not sleep soundly tonight.

Our welcome is not flashy and doesn't last long. A Major takes the mike and says a few things in a hurried style that gives me the impression he is starving and can smell turkey and mashed potatoes being served at the officers mess. We can sympathize because it is past the dinner hour and our stomachs are rolling like muffled tom-toms. He says he is glad to see us and warns about the sinful, venereal disease conditions in Los Angeles.

While we are turning those facts around in our minds, he orders us to fall out in front, form a column of squadrons, and march to our barracks assignments. We do so and march down a wide road fronted by barracks that are already occupied by old timers. An old timer is anyone who has been at the base for three or four weeks. Their faces appear at the windows of their barracks as we march by and we cannot escape their sorry chant of warnings and advice.

We are subjected to a repetitive and painful liturgy lacking hope or consolation. "Don't hit me again, I'll be a bombardier."

"Tell them you got a burning desire to fly!"

"Please, not Ariel Gunnery School. Don't send me there. I'm sorry I said I wouldn't be a navigator. I'll be a navigator, Please!"

The chorus continues until we reach and pass the last dark building that will be our next and probably very temporary home.

Since nothing important has happened so far, speculation time starts as soon as we are in the barracks. Rumors and semi-coordinated guesses bounce off walls and ceilings, and echo from the latrines. Conversations are completely controlled by axiom number one which provides that, in the armed forces, when no one knows anything about a subject, everybody knows something.

The barracks are long, two story, wooden buildings with identical first and second floors. Each has a latrine at one end. On either side, double decked bunk beds pointed away from the wall leaving an aisle down the center. We push our barracks under the bunks and when our footlockers arrive they will be placed along the aisle.

The setup is simple but we know what to expect in the way of inspections. We were never bothered with them at Jefferson Barracks but some very finicky 2nd Lieutenants made things difficult at Coe College. A "gig" happy inspecting officer can and will find fault with any one of several things including a spot of dust revealed as he drags his white glove across the underside of an upper bunk. A loosely made bed is a cardinal sin. A bed is considered to be loosely made if a nickel fails to bounce when dropped on it gently by the inspector. It is not unusual that a cadet finds himself gigged for a rule that appears to have been invented on the spot. There is no appeal. Gigs can pile up if a cadet is not careful. Punishment ranges from loss of a weekend pass, to marching up and down carrying a backpack and rifle for a few hours on Saturday evening. We discovered, at Coe College, that it was not wise to make a date with a girl who might also be seeing one of the junior officers.

We haven't even taken the first of several qualifying physical and mental exams but the clubhouse lawyers in the barracks are offering various estimates of the number of us who will wash out and be sent out to gunnery school in Kingman. The figures, all of which are offered by people claiming inside information, vary from ten to fifty per cent of the group. My good friend, Modesto Olivo, shakes his head in disgust and stares out the window. Mo is a realist and is revving up for the first chance to compare L.A. with his hometown of Omaha. Johnny Hudspeth says an old girlfriend from Altoona, Pennsylvania lives in L.A. and he's jumping around hunting for a phone. He won't find one in the barracks. All in all, it is quite a circus. In the center ring, people are arguing about who gets the bottom bunks. I see an empty one, throw myself on it and make myself at home. Some of the debaters hear me bounce and stop to stare. Then, in unison, they turn back and restart the dispute. I wonder why they don't just do what I did; there are plenty of extra lower bunks. Just find one and flop down. Probably it's a matter of pride. If we turn out to be one bunk short, the proudest guy in the barracks will be sleeping on the floor.

After things settle down and it's *lights out*, I lie awake thinking about what I've accomplished in the months since leaving home; coughing my way through Jefferson Barracks, marching around at Coe College, bouncing around on trains, and wondering what happens next. For no real reason, I find myself revisiting the basic requirements for being an aviation cadet. I know them well and would not be here if they had not all been met at the time of my original enlistment. Still, a person is what he knows and, so far, these are truly the only things I know about the Army Air Corps: a cadet must be at least eighteen years old and younger than twenty-seven. He needs at least a high school education. I've got that and some college to boot.

To be eligible, a man can be married or unmarried. Since every man in the world must be one or the other, it seems fair to wonder what they were thinking when they threw that in the mix.

The Army Air Corps has several limitations on size and shape of prospective aviation cadets. All my present companions are at least five feet four inches tall and not more than six-feet-four. The rule states that weight must be well balanced in proportion to stature. So far, there haven't been any really fat guys around and I'm skinny so I guess I'm safe there. They say the average cadet is five-feet ten-inches tall and weighs one hundred sixty pounds so, take away about ten pounds and there I am, a very average cadet if I ever become one.

The main thing I notice about these people is that none of them are stupid. They laugh and joke around sometimes, but their sense of humor is the kind I used to enjoy with the people who hung out in the union at the U of M. I hope I'm good enough to hang in there. So far I'm doing O.K...but how good is it safe to feel?

Tomorrow, or in a few days at most, various flight surgeons will start pulling and poking and giving each of us a physical twice as tough as we would have to pass to get a million dollar life insurance policy. The eye exam alone is expected to take two or three days. Then they have all the psychology monkey business. We hear they ask some very goofy questions. None of these tests should scare me but I don't want to feel too sure and jinx myself.

There is one big decision that must be made. We understand we can request the specialty we would prefer; pilot, bombardier, or navigator. It doesn't mean the one you ask for is what you'll get but after looking at it from every angle I think I'll request to be a navigator.

Almost everybody seems to want pilot training. However, I had to decide what my long-range goal really is. I think, more than any other consideration, I want to get my wings and be an officer no matter which of the three available alternatives it turns out to be.

I see no reason why I can't be a good pilot but the percentage of pilots washing out during training is several times higher than that for bombardiers and navigators. Why take a chance? I have a good math background from college and think the training will be a snap. I think I'm making a good decision that should just about make sure I will someday be wearing the gold bars and wings. The pay and perks will be the same for any of the three.

It's not a bad deal. Even as a cadet you earn $75.00 per month and a dollar a day ration allowance. Just in case something happens, you are given a ten thousand-dollar life insurance policy and, if you graduate and become a 2nd Lieutenant, they pay $150.00 for regular Air Corps officers uniforms. Basic salary for a 2nd Lieutenant is $205 a month if you live in a barracks or $245 if you pay for your own quarters. The problem is that washing out means the next stop is at Aerial Gunnery School as a Tech Sergeant.

They don't waste any time around here. After an on again, off again semi-sleepless night, we roll out at 0700 hours and march to the mess hall for breakfast. We have been warned, and it is heavily emphasized, that this place is very fussy about the military aspect of our lives. We never walk anywhere. We march. The only exception seems to be when visiting the PX during special times. Otherwise, we are in a column and that means heads up and on the beat with a cadet officer counting cadence. There are rules for everything and they are enforced.

We arrive at the mess hall and stand at attention until the cadet captain orders, "Parade rest!" At that point we can move our feet apart and join our hands behind our backs. Our cadet officer turns and faces the door until receiving an order than we can proceed inside. Once inside, we stand at attention behind the benches of the picnic type tables until given the command, "At ease!"

The food is already on the table. The cadet at the end of the table is the "gunner." He fills the plates and passes them on. Cadets may ask for seconds, but must eat all they are served. The gunner will not allow anyone to take more of an item if there is not enough left for everyone at the table. It's a great breakfast: bacon and eggs, fried potatoes and orange juice. When the meal is ended, we wait quietly to be called to attention. The empty plates have been passed to the gunner and stacked at the end of the table. In leaving the table we follow the same routine as we did when entering. It is a formality that we follow on all occasions where we proceed as a unit. When we leave the mess hall, we form two columns and immediately begin a short march to the large meeting hall in which we received our brief welcome last evening.

Today, the assembly is about the things we can look forward to in the coming days and weeks. The major who welcomed us yesterday takes the microphone and gives us an idea of what the program will be like. It takes him more than a half hour just to name the class courses we will be expected to master when we are not out running obstacle courses, doing physical training, marching in close order drill on the parade ground or attending other duties which he assures us are too numerous mention. It's impossible to catch the names of all the classes he outlines, but he says there will be 190 hours of them. It doesn't cheer me up any when he mentions eighteen hours of physics and twenty hours of math.

Now I hear him explaining that there may be changes in the entire focus between bombardiers and navigators. He says it is probable that bombardiers will be required to study some navigation and navigators will be made familiar with the essentials of dropping bombs. If the plans go through, they will be called bombardier-navigators. He makes it clear that they will be trained at different advanced training centers and will concentrate on their specialties.

My mind is firmly made up to ask for navigation and there's nothing here that makes me feel like changing.

The major drones on and before long we are aware it is once again venereal disease time in magnificent living color. It will be a few weeks before we are released to the sinful and debilitating horrors of dribbling sex fiends in the city of angels but the Army is taking no chances. Up comes the screen, on goes the projector and down go a couple of faint-hearted cadets who gambled a peek at the multi-colored, twisted and maimed private parts of an unidentified but memorable group of careless cadets. Most of us have learned by now to glue our eyes to the floor as we did at the age of ten when Dracula was about to sink his canines into the throat of an unwary socialite. Fainting is not something a person wants to do if he's coveting a job on a combat airplane. A betting man would say that a couple of our former companions will be on the high road to Kingman before we finish our dinner.

The less violent part of the meeting is interesting. Various officers explain all the technicalities and rules of conduct which are sharp and clear. Today, for the first time, we are referred to as "The cream of the crop." It's nice to be appreciated but it doesn't strike me as something anyone would want to say in the presence of a tough master sergeant or Marine. One thing that was made clear is that their rules, even the tiniest, are more than suggestions. In the end we have a good idea of what it will all be like. I feel included for some reason and think it will be worth all the marching and saluting.

We have been told with unforgettable emphasis that we are to be referred to as "Mister" and must put that prefix before our names. We will have no time to ourselves other than what we have while standing around waiting for them to make up their minds. The speaker closes the meeting with the happy news that after the first month we will be allowed passes into L.A. and surrounding areas which he has blasted at least ten times as being a slimy sinkhole. He remains stoic and unabashed as the crowd greets the news with a standing ovation.

In the afternoon, we are separated by our various religions and sent to separate rooms where someone from our faith; priest, minister, rabbi, or other man of faith. We meet privately. Being Catholic, I meet with a priest name Father Clasby. Father Clasby used as his role model Tom Harmon, the great all-American football player from Michigan. Harmon had been a cadet at Santa Ana and he and Father Clasby became good friends. Father fills the air with praises of Harmon and his achievements while I restrain myself from reminding him that Harmon played against the Minnesota Gophers three times in his career and was defeated every time. I could have softened the news by telling Father that the Gopher's All American during the Harmon years at Michigan was Bruce Smith who was also a good Catholic.

On the serious side, Father Clasby asks how I would feel if it were necessary for me to be responsible for the death of another person; or even many people. I can only reply that I am in a war and will do whatever I am called upon to do.

He says I will be asked many questions and may find some of them difficult. He says that sometimes, even though the answer might be 'yes,' a person has the right to say 'no' to you. It is an interesting little dispensation. Who knows when it may come in handy? In parting he tells me about a group he has started called "Our Lady's Knights of the Skies." He gives me a prayer card and medal that I put into my billfold and determine to carry wherever I go. We had a nice conversation and I liked the man. I put my head on the pillow tonight feeling a little bit more like I belong to something. This is really the Army Air Corps and they are serious. I haven't done anything yet but I know, in their eyes, I'm not a kid anymore.

When we fall out in the morning, we march straight from show to the medical area. Our physicals start in earnest today. Most of our time is spent waiting in hallways. There isn't much conversation but from time to time a bit of nervous laughter. Eventually they begin call us in, one at a time.

My turn comes and I see right away that this will certainly be different than the physical we were given at Fort Snelling during my original enlistment. These doctors know what they're looking for and today it is my mouth, nose, pharynx, larynx, trachea, and esophagus. They have three doctors in there and one of them does the examining and yells the result to one of the others who writes the result on my chart. The third doctor set up and ready for the next examination. According to my chart, they will be checking my neck, spine, belly, pelvis and genito-urinary system tomorrow. It doesn't seem possible they won't find something wrong before all this is over.

I slept well last night and it's a good thing because today they're working on the rest of me. They don't tell you what they're doing as they go along but, when the doc is squeezing my belly, I ask him what this is for. He says he is palpitating my liver. After that they pound on my back and palpitate some other stuff. Whatever it is, it must be fine because they just write on the chart but don't ask questions about anything. The word around the barracks is that somebody heard from somebody else that if the doctors get serious and ask a lot of questions about something it is not a good sign at all. So far they just keep whacking me around and palpitating stuff with no questions so it looks good.

Today, my third day of exams, went O.K. but right now everybody seems so tightly wound up. For most of us, our futures are riding on what happens in the next couple of days and there's nothing we can do about it. Our barracks has not gone through the eye exams yet and that's the toughest part. We all tested 20/20 when we enlisted but we have been warned this will be like no other eye exam a person could get anywhere else. I think my eyes are pretty good. At the University of Minnesota, on the freshman team, I swear I could usually pick up the stitches rotating on a curve ball. The coaches said that was very rare. I'll know more tomorrow or at least have a good idea.

Well, it's tomorrow and I have to admit to being plenty nervous waiting in the hallway. There are so many eye examinations that it seems a new one pops up every time you think you're out of the woods. I probably shouldn't worry. I certainly shouldn't have lost any sleep about today. So far everything has been better than good and even though there will be more coming up tomorrow I still can't believe what happened this morning. All I got to say is bring on Whitey Ford and Virgil Trucks. The test shows I have twenty-fifteen in both eyes. That's the same as Ted Williams. It means I can read little fifteen-point print at twenty feet away. I'm telling you, the doctors just shook their heads and gave me the test over again and it showed the same thing.

Maybe my eyes are too good. This could mean they'd make me a bombardier for sure. Oh, well, hell! Don't hit me again, I'll be a bombardier. Maybe I shouldn't be crowing. Tomorrow they're taking some more and different looks at our eyes.

I had trouble getting to sleep last night. Things are going well but eye tests just go on and on. A person has to wonder where they find them. Yesterday I showed them I can practically see over the curve of the earth in all directions. Now they come up with something called the heterophoria test. I'm also on tap for a red lens test and testing for peripheral vision for form. If I get past those there will still be the power of accommodation test, the power of convergence test, and the central color vision test remaining on the list.

I overheard a couple of the doctors talking while waiting for my turn this morning and it sounds like two of the guys are going to get some bad news. It sounded as if they missed more than 25% on the colorblind test. They certainly don't fool around much on these examinations. I think we all realize there is no room for easing up on any of the rules. We understand that any air crew can only be as strong as its weakest member. It doesn't seem fair that a single weakness might wash out an otherwise perfect candidate who has been passing test after test. However, it makes sense when you realize that a single flaw in the makeup of a crew member can cost the lives of the other nine men on the team. When you can't make the grade in one of the critical tests, you're gone. No muss, no fuss, just....outta here! We must be getting close to the last eye examinations. It will be a relief but to tell the truth I can't remember being out of my skin as much as I am this morning. I look at my chart and wonder, "What is unimpaired ocular muscle balance?" I get through an exam for unimpaired optical organism, anatomically and mechanically. After that they lead me to a box about ten feet down the line on a long table. There are two sticks down there attached to two strings I am holding. The doctor tells me to line up the sticks by pulling on the strings. It isn't easy. I ask what we are testing.

"Depth perception," he says. "Try it again, Mister." My blood goes cold. Depth perception has to be very important and I don't think I'm doing well. What kind of pilot, navigator, or bombardier can be of any use at all if he has no depth perception? I am slowly dying. The flight surgeon standing behind me puts a hand on my shoulder. I think, 'Oh, oh. Here it comes. Why was I crowing last night?' The personal eulogy of my career is interrupted by the voice of the doctor.

"OK, Mister," he says as I hand him the strings. "I see you want to be a navigator. With your eyes you should be a fighter pilot." He pauses and looks closely at my face. "You feeling all right, Mister? You look a little pale."

"Feeling fine, Sir," I reply. "Never felt better, Sir."

I feel great marching back to the barracks but have no desire to crow. In fact, it would be nice to get rid of the little cloud that hangs over our heads. No doubt about it; the eye exams are the "Sixty-four dollar questions." One bad answer and goodbye. Until we finish them there is always the possibility a single optical weakness can finish one or more of us. I felt the chill of it today and the experience has put a small dent in my confidence. There's a rumor that tomorrow will see the last of these optical challenges and I hope they prove to be true. In fact, they may have ended already because I notice on the bulletin board that tomorrow, we are scheduled to undergo the famous Schneider Test. It's the one that often figures in the plot of airplane movies and usually results in a tear jerking scene where the flight surgeon shakes his head, bites his lip, puts the stethoscope to the pocket of his white jacket and sadly informs "Pops," a lovable, gray haired old aviation pioneer that he is now grounded forever. In real life the man being tested puts a foot on an overturned box and then steps up with the other one. He keeps stepping up and down until they order him to stop. The examiner then listens to his heart and performs some other tests. If his score is not quite what they want, they test him for high blood pressure and a few other things until they reach a conclusion. It's really more a heart test than anything else and doesn't worry me at all.

I've been lucky so far but a person has to wonder when the Air Force will run out of things to test. Maybe it's all for the best. I have gotten this far and don't see any particular reason for not making it.

Today, they plan to check for respiratory ventilation and vital capacity as well as a stable equilibrium, a sound cardio-vascular system, nervous and organic, and a stable nervous system. While I'm lying on the table being checked over, one of the doctors says, "Why do you want to be a navigator? Your system would be perfect for a fighter pilot." Coming from him it makes me feel good but the big day is approaching and I'm not going to change anything now. Tomorrow, we visit the psychiatrists and, unless I am judged to be a complete lunatic, the path should be paved for me and my friends proceed to the next scene in this unpredictable epic. We are standing in line outside the door of the psychiatrist's office when I see Joe Murphy coming down the hallway. Although it is considered a serious matter to let anyone crash a line, I figure that if what they are lined up for is to answer questions from a psychiatrist, no one will be in a hurry. I feel confident enough and feel that Joe looks big and rough enough that we can violate the normal order of things. There are few things in army life more certain to provoke wrath and indignation than letting a friend or relative slip in front of you near the head of the line. In this case we got by with no more than a couple of scowls. I note Joe is wearing his shoes and the odor is bearable. I am glad Joe will be going in for his interview before me. It won't hurt to have an idea of what kind of questions the doctor is asking before I go in.

Joe says he thinks he will be qualified for pilot training and

I congratulate him. Eventually, the psychiatrist shows up, enters his office and, after a short time comes back out and asks that we remember to remove our shoes before entering his office. One by one, the line moves up. The interviews don't seem long and Joe and I chat about such things as what has happened to our friends from Coe College and what, if anything, he has done about his foot problem. Before he has a chance to fill me in, it's his turn to go in.

I watch Joe remove his size fourteen shoes and carry them gingerly into the office. After a minute or two, the doctor comes out, looks up and down the hall, goes to the water fountain, takes a long drink of water and goes back into the office. In a minute or less, Joe comes out, slides into his size fourteen and comes over to say good-bye in case we don't see each other in the near future. I ask him to tell me about the interview; what kind of questions did the guy ask? Joe says the doctor didn't ask him anything. "He just sat there," says Joe. "Then he got up and went some place. When he got back he said he had to leave because of an emergency. He said he hadn't seen anything that looked troubling in my folio so I could just leave."

That's the only information I got out of Joe so I go in to see the doctor with no idea what to expect. He seems distracted and looks about the room and sniffs two or three times. He leaves through my folio very quickly. He says it looks good, closes the book and says I can leave. There can be little doubt that Joe's feet had struck again, and unwillingly driven the good doctor to distraction. I gave the matter some thought as we marched to our barracks. Looking back, I think the poor psychiatrist was trying to understand what kind of syndrome could cause human feet to produce such an odor. I've often wondered about it myself.

I return to our barracks feeling that I have surely qualified for aviation cadet training. However, looking into the handbook that reveals the day by day requirements of the program, it doesn't seem like a bargain. They have told us our assignments will be posted in the headquarters on Saturday. Good! It means by Monday, those who have qualified as cadets will be moved to separate squadron areas according to their particular specialty.

There are several thousand cadets on the base but, at the next stage, pilots will be with pilots, bombardiers with bombardiers, and navigators with navigators. If they make me a navigator, I won't see any pilots or bombardiers until far into the future when actual crews are put together. I'll miss some of my friends but army life is not based on permanence. We will be sent where they think we are needed. That's the way it is and probably the way it should be. I've taken a big step, but I feel a little dull. Things could be better but they could be worse. I should feel good. If it turns out the way I think it will, I know my dad will be proud.

CHAPTER 6

ASSIGNMENTS

Our assignments as pilot, bombardier, or navigator are posted on the wall of the Operations Center on Saturday morning. Air in the room is stagnant, the silence smothering. No chatter, no friendly greetings; facial expressions betray uncertainty. Not having failed any part of the physical, odds are in my favor. What possible reason could they have to wash me out now? Such a thing couldn't happen; but it might. This is the Army. It can decide whatever it wants for reasons it is not required to explain. It is their custom to tell, not ask. Whatever decision comes my way, there will be no appeal, no second chance.

This morning the answer is right there, a few feet away on the bulletin board. This is the day we have all been waiting for but my feeling is that only a favorable decision will do. How could I call home to tell them I've failed? My heart pounds, my stomach churns, my feet feel heavy, nailed to the floor. I finally settle down, take a deep breath and shuffle toward the wall. I remember a story from a high school English class. A man has a choice to choose either of two doors. If he opens the right door, he will find a beautiful princess standing with open arms. If he guesses wrong and opens the other door, a huge tiger will leap out and devour him. It was called *The Lady or The Tiger* and I have no idea why I thought about it right now. There must be a reason.

The line moves quickly. The news, good or bad, is not complicated. Each man stops in front of a roster pinned on the bulletin board, checks for his name on the alphabetical list and moves on without comment. Some are smiling. Without question they've received exactly what they wanted; probably pilot training. Some others appear confused, take a second glance at the board and move away with a shrug of the shoulders and eyebrows raised in wonderment. My guess is they have been accepted, but were not given their first choice. Their response is not joyous, reflects the silent resignation of a heartbroken child who has been double-crossed by Santa Claus on Christmas morning. Since anyone asking for bombardier or navigator is almost certain to get one or the other, this solemn and bewildered group must represent pilot applicants with a "burning desire to fly" who have just been informed that any flying they do will be with someone else at the controls.

They are on the team and will be trained as bombardiers and navigators, but will they be able to scuttle their dream, the one about roaring into the wild blue yonder at the throttle of a sleek, silver, twin engine P-38 fighter. For months they have pictured themselves diving out of the sun to scatter a marauding pack of German fighters about to prey on a formation of B-17s. They are well prepared and climb on top wearing a boyish Van Johnson smile, making ninety degree turns, and frightening the Luftwaffe fighters break off the attack and flee for cloud cover at the sight of such artistic maneuvers. The bombers are saved. Suddenly, surprisingly, their fast track to pilot wings has come upon a fork in the road and they are ordered to take the one less traveled. To paraphrase the immortal words of poet Robert Frost, that can make all the difference. No denying, pilots are glamour boys, the swashbuckling stars of an endless stream of "B" movies, propaganda films dramatizing the air war featuring the deeds of heroic young flyers as portrayed by actors ten or fifteen years beyond the twenty-seven year age maximum for flight training.

However, there can be no argument that in the mind of citizens at large, it is the pilot who actually drives the plane and since most people in our forty-eight states have never been up in an airplane and regard one with apprehension, the pilot is idolized for his skill and courage. Very few people including wives, mothers, sisters, and casual acquaintances have a clear idea of what navigators and bombardiers actually do. According to the word from bombardier and navigator cadets who frequent the PX and have been on the base for several weeks, the pilot cadets feel themselves to be just a cut above the rest. Having been assigned to the mundane world of bombardiers and navigators, these pilot candidates must feel demoted even before being commissioned. They have no reason to be ashamed.

The fact that some people who wanted to be pilots have been sentenced to bombardier or navigator training does not mean they are unqualified. They passed every test and are cleared for flying duty. It may be they are innocent victims of a numbers game that found the Army Air Corps needing navigators and bombardiers more than pilots at this particular time.

In spite of their disappointment, these people have lost only their vanity. For some it will not be easy but when they think it over they will realize that all cadets who go on and graduate will receive the same status and benefits. They will be commissioned 2nd Lieutenants, earn the same pay and wear identical uniforms. Their hard-earned wings will be made of the same silver, shine in the same moonlight and be equally coveted by their lady friends. Unless so informed, the girls will never notice the difference in the imprint on the center of the wings: a bomb for bombardiers, a globe of the world for navigators and a shield for pilots.

Although their immediate deep disappointment is obvious, only the most passionate will be foolish enough to complain or demand an explanation. They know the rules and are already familiar with the six word vocabulary available to cadet's for use in dialogue with his superiors: "Yes, sir;" "No, sir," and "No excuse, sir!"

In the same fashion, a cadet expressing dissatisfaction with his classification can certainly expect to be dismissed by six famous words comprising a standard reply to the plea of any unhappy cadet: "Don't you like it here, Mister?" Anyone unwilling to accept the choice offered by the Air Corps is asking for a ticket to Aerial Gunnery School at Kingman, Arizona on the first train headed east.

The man ahead of me in line scans the list carefully, turns away momentarily, and then reads it a second time, running his finger down the alphabetical list. He then notices the large black notice at the top of the board. It's meaning clear: IF YOUR NAME IS NOT ON THIS LIST, REPORT TO OPERATIONS AT 1400 HOURS THIS AFTERNOON. He walks away silently, as we pretend not notice. We know that we will not see him again, unless he becomes a gunner on one of our crews.

Now it's my turn and it takes only a quick glance at the bulletin board tells me all I want to know. Life. Its message jumps at me like the headline of a daily newspaper announcing a declaration of war. There it is for all the see: Jack I Moore, serial #17142699, Bombardier. Bombardier? I move closer to read it again. No mistake, the message says, BOMBARDIER, not NAVIGATOR. This is a surprise but not a shock. From the time they learned my vision is 20/15 the chance they might want me to be a bombardier has popped into my mind at odd moments.

So the verdict is in. My future is as a bombardier. Although it is obvious my main function will be to learn to aim bombs, my knowledge of the idea is zero. There is very little information in the papers or movies concerning what other duties a bombardier might have. The news from Europe is not the kind that would lead great numbers of people to rush down to the enlistment office pushing and shoving to sign up. Information from the 8th Air Force, which is bombing Germany, seldom mentions bombardiers at all. When they show us one, they usually picture him wearing a leather helmet with ear flaps in the style of Charles Lindbergh. We never see his face because his head is pressed against the bombsight. An important thing we note is that he works in a glass enclosed space at the very front of the aircraft. In newsreels at the movies we have seen B-17 Flying Fortresses returning from missions over Germany with parts of wings and rudders missing and sometimes lacking the entire nose.

It's something to think about, but not for long. Whatever happens will happen and there will be no stopping it. Voices drift back from the day we arrived "Please don't hit me again. I'll be a bombardier." Well, I will. Why not? If that's what they want, I'll be a bombardier, a damn good one, too. They must think I'm good enough and that's good enough for me. At least I finally know where I stand. Somewhere, maybe in *Readers' Digest,* I read an article describing the bombardier as the most important man on a bomber crew. They may be right. When you think about it, the government builds thousands of planes designed for ten man crews. It looks like they actually train the nine other guys just to get the bombardier to the target. It's all in the way you look at it, but it has to be a very important job. I'll give it my best. The last thing in the world to do is complain. Hey, I signed up to be a navigator and they made me a bombardier. Now they tell us bombardiers will be learning navigation, too. Sounds like I got a little bonus.

It's good to feel both lucky and relieved. The process they put us through was no tea party. We knew many of the people who went through the whole gauntlet and are ending up with a trip to Kingman. The rest of us realize but for the grace of God any of us could be on that train. How many times have I wondered how it would be to call the folks at home and tell them I was not good enough? In this outfit, 'not good enough' can still be pretty darn good. No one can be expected to understand that fact unless they sample the mental and physical goals these people have set for us.

The people I've talked with so far seem satisfied. I saw Joe Murphy and Bob Myers from our little gang at Coe College. They will go into pilot training. It's surprising how many of us are going to be bombardiers. Mack Makowski will be one, so will George Hendrickson, Johnny Hudspeth, and Mo Olivo. Mack is a music graduate from Loyola College in Chicago and has played in a few name bands. We talk music by the hour.

It's Sunday and the PX is crowded, inside and out. PX is short for Post Exchange, a small building where service men can congregate, buy a Coke, cigarettes, candy, a tube of toothpaste or a small array of personal items. It would be a good place to kill time, but so far we haven't had many empty hours to waste. When we have some we honor a long-standing tradition common to all branches of military service. We dive for our bunks and put in as much sack time as possible at any hour of day or night. However, today the time has arrived to call home.

The telephones are on the outside wall of the PX. Making a phone call involves having a telephone and having a telephone involves standing in a long line until one is available. When one becomes available, it becomes necessary to talk to the operator. Talking to the operator results in giving her the number to be reached and listening to her saying, "Thank you. All our lines to Minneapolis are tied up at this time. When one clears up we will call you back. It will be about two hours." I thank her and step out of the way handing my phone to the next in line. This would be a good time to head back to the barracks for some sack time but there's no way. She said it would be two hours, but sometimes they call back sooner and if you miss the call back you miss the call.

I look around for a familiar face and see Olaf Arneson. We graduated together from Edison High School. Ole is big and strong, a tackle on the championship football team. He is one of the cadet officers who march us around wherever we go and has already earned the nicknames "Big Olaf" and "Olaf the Great." Soldiers normally do not enjoy being marched around by their peers and are nimble at finding subtle sarcasm to express their displeasure. Ole is a nice guy and on the quiet side, but the meaningless chevrons on his sleeves makes him fair game. "Well?" I ask, "How did you come out?"

"Bombardier," he said. "I wanted pilot but I'm pretty tall. I think that might have counted against me." He takes a swig of Coke. "How about you?"

"Bombardier! Put in for navigator but they gave me bombardier. Probably because I've got 20/15 in both eyes. I can't figure out why I went for navigator in the first place."

Ole gets called to the phone, finishes his Coke in one gulp and pushes his way out the door. Ole doesn't seem put down by being picked for bombardier. Why should I?

I think to myself, "They didn't pick me for anything. Hell, I could have made pilot easy, even the doctors told me that. So what if some of these clowns who got pilot are strutting around like they invented the loop-de-loop. Most of 'em have never been off the ground outside of one hour at CTD."

I hate it though. I hate that look, that look that says, "Bombardier? Geez, I wonder what was wrong with this guy." As far as I'm concerned the United States Government is willing to pay nine people just to chauffeur me to the target and back and that's good enough for me.

Time crawls waiting for the operator to call me back but I don't dare leave the spot where the phone is located. There are about fifteen or twenty of us waiting. Whenever the phone rings, whoever picks up the receiver calls out the name of the lucky guy who's on next. Everybody realizes that a mob is waiting so the conversations are short and to the point. However, they are anything but private.

Actually the operators place the calls for us so when my turn comes up, my mother is already on the phone. I tell her that I am going to be a bombardier and she wants to know what that means. I am reluctant to explain with about fifteen future pilot cadets listening. I tell her I will write and explain the whole thing and she asks me if it will be something dangerous. I say I think it will be all right. She says dad's last letter indicated he might come back to the States to attend the War College. My brother Bill will be graduating from St. Thomas Academy in June and she is afraid he will have to go into the service immediately. I tell her I don't think they will want anybody that young. He will be only seventeen. She says everybody at home is fine and I am not to worry. I say I don't think I'll have time to worry but that I have to get off the phone because several people are waiting. She says it was wonderful to hear from me. I say things are going to be fine and she says, "Now, you be careful."

I say "I'll call again next week" and hang up.

It was good to hear her voice, but I wonder whether she would be surprised to see me now. I think I am already a different person than the one she dropped off in front of the Federal Office Building in Minneapolis a few months ago.

We still have a long way to go. The next thirteen weeks will be a grind with a solid schedule of obstacle courses to run, classes to attend, parades to march in, and tests to take. I think of my dad having battled through North Africa and hope he does get to come back to the War College. I wish he could see me, I wish I could talk to him. I think he'd feel I'm doing O.K. so far.

We are really, officially cadets now and the use of the word no longer seems like a far away wish. However, I won't really feel like one until Monday when we get our new uniforms. They won't be too flashy, but will distinguish us from every other kind of soldier. No other branch of the US Army wears the same uniform as an aviation cadet. It is not quite that of an officer and somewhat classier than an enlisted man. The trousers are regular GI, but the blouse has gold buttons up the center and winged propellers on the collar. The hat has a large propeller on the front. We will receive our uniforms in just two days and it will make a difference. We can feel it.

CHAPTER 7

UNIFORMS

It's Monday, a day we have hoped for and pictured in our heads. Today we get our official aviation cadet uniforms. We haven't felt like we belonged to this outfit while watching the other ten or twenty thousand properly dressed cadets who live here. It's a silly thing to say but it feels like we are putting down the first little corner piece in a gigantic jigsaw puzzle. Nobody felt secure sweating out three tense weeks of testing. Because we hadn't been officially designated as cadets, we were outsiders. Then, although we had cleared that hurdle, we couldn't even participate in ceremonies or parades because we didn't have the right uniforms. It will be different tomorrow when we march to ground school in our new outfits.

The uniforms will finally identify us as true members of an exclusive, strictly administered world of tears and cheers known as Air Force Cadet Training. The sole purpose will be to make us competent in the art of dropping bombs and reading maps. Our understanding is that the road will be long and rocky. We have been given a small idea of what it will take and Makowski says it would have been easier to stay in college and try to get through medical school. Modesto ("Mo") Olivo, who is near the minimum height for aircrew training, dislikes the obstacle courses says, "At least, in medical school they don't have to jump those over those goddam fences every day."

The reference is to obstacle courses. Uniforms or no uniforms, the hurdles, ropes, ponds and profanity of the obstacle courses are already a part of our daily schedule and on the hate list of those who are short of stature or large of stomach. Since I am not one or the other, obstacle courses are not a big menace. However, the majority sentiment is that life would be better if those fences and rope climbs would disappear over night and never be found. When the subject arises, I opt out and keep my secrets to myself. Lesson number two in army life is that the last thing any GI or cadet or general needs is information that his pet nightmare doesn't bother everybody else.

Last night a captain visited the barracks and left some material that will explain more about what we are actually facing. I scanned over it but will be anxious to read it more carefully after we get back to the barracks. What I managed to decipher so far is that it will be as consuming as rumors predict.

This morning, as we marched here to the quartermasters building to get our new uniforms, we moved along with extra zing in our step. We even belted out "The Air Force Song" with a vigor usually reserved for ballads with less sanitary lyrics. We are going to be more comfortable doing things that have a meaning. We will be part of the action. The change is tangible; I feel it already.

So here we are, right on time and mentally prepared to line up and wait. The quartermaster's building is huge, one of the largest on the base. A pale sunrise is peeking through the trees and beginning to mellow the chill that often puts a sharp edge on late evening and early morning activities at Santa Ana. We are far from the first arrivals and the entire area outside the huge building is filled with cadets standing at ease, wishing for a cigarette. They can have all they want; coffin nails sell for five cents a pack at the PX. Unfortunately, they won't be puffing on any this morning. Smoking is limited to the barracks and a few other designated locations.

This is going to be a long session. Apparently all the new cadets; pilots, bombardiers and navigators who were approved at the same time as us will also get their uniforms today. The number could run up into the thousands. We may have to mill around most of the morning. Waiting is something we do better than most thanks to hours of practice. So we are waiting, letting our brains idle and wishing for a cigarette. Just standing around affects different people in different ways. As individuals, at least in the Army, people seem to develop personal capabilities for managing unused time. In my case it's a tendency to look inside my head. Whenever time becomes unbearable, I create a defense by thinking too much, day dreaming about abstract things and putting myself in a different world. It may be an automatic response, something the brain does to keep the body alive when people are forced to stand around doing nothing.

However, everyone learns in a short time that *Rule Number One: It is useless to consider how long the wait will last* helps to control unnecessary tension. Nothing in the world lasts forever so it is helpful to remember that, eventually, someone will invite us to step inside. When that might happen is not worth the worry.

We remain at parade rest, hands behind our backs waiting for Blankenship, our cadet captain, to give us permission to stand at "ease." He takes his time as usual, walking by the ranks and looking at the crowd. Suddenly he remembers we are still at parade rest and shouts

"At ease!" with a volume that causes two nearby squadrons to leap to attention. They are shocked and very embarrassed. We get the wide open, round eyed look that asks, "who the hell is this guy?" We shrug and they shrug back as if to say, "We understand. We got one of those bastards too."

Blankenship appears unaware of any consternation. There have been discussions in the barracks concerning Blankenship's leisurely showmanship and indifference about giving simple commands like "At ease." He leans heavily on his ROTC background. It is matter of indisputable fact that cadet officers are almost always former ROTC students. Whenever the situation demands, the officer in charge will ask, "Any ROTC people here?" A hand or two will go up and they'll pick their man right then and there. Makowski says he's happy that Blankenship is also a bombardier because it means they can never wind up on a crew together. For some reason, cadet officers are not often very popular. They wear decorative armbands and are referred to as "brown noses" when out of earshot.

Officially at ease, we are now free to gripe in subtle tones and shift freely from foot to foot. We can also look around, if it does not take us from our place in the formation. I hold my hand high to block the rising sun and peer around the crowd in hope of seeing any of my friends from Cedar Rapids. As bombardiers, we are now completely separated from the living quarters and classes of navigators or pilot groups.

Nobody guesses how lengthy our wait might be. It will take as long as it takes, and that's how long it will take. At least, this morning, we know why we are here and what is going on inside. We know the delay is not the result of our superiors sitting inside dunking donuts and making plans for a big party at the officers' club. We also know they are not in there planning to give us each a ten-day furlough or even a weekend pass in which case it wouldn't matter how long we stand out in the noonday sun.

All we want is to get into the building and get our new look if it takes all day. The cadet uniform is not fancy, but it has more class than strict GI issue. Meanwhile, I go again into my "waiting" defense. I look over the silent mob of young men like myself who are willing, even anxious, to put their futures in the hands of people to whom they are only serial numbers. I'm sure we all wonder sometimes if we are doing the smart thing. We know the safest play would have been to get a uniform and deferment at the same time by staying in college. We probably are not being smart yet our biggest worry is that we might not be allowed to stay. That's clearly the way it is and there's no sense trying to figure out why.

At this point there are many things we would rather be doing. Our average age is probably between nineteen and twenty-three. It doesn't seem fair that gentlemen at that stage of life should lose the companionship and comfort which might be furnished by young ladies of approximate ages. We could settle for a little action at either end of that spectrum. Young ladies here and there may be missing us, too. After all, the Army Air Corps flight surgeons have determined we are as healthy as it is possible to be. The result is a sad situation where everybody loses; at least until we are reprieved. For the foreseeable future we will remain caged within the limits of Santa Ana preflight training base.

What happens tonight? We have permission to shower, shave, proudly don our new uniforms and be all dressed up with no place to go. No girls! No movies. No dancing. No sports. No fun at all. We should be pounding on walls and demanding our freedom. It's interesting that there are few complaints regarding the situation. In many respects the armed service is a great teacher and lesson number one is the undeniable realization that you are not the only person on earth. Those who accept that premise are probably the soundest sleepers.

A GI wearing corporal's stripes pushes his head out the door and waves for us to enter. Blankenship looks us over, gives us the commands and we go inside. Unfortunately, "inside" only means out of the sun. Many forms of the verbal noun used to represent defecation are muttered to highlight our disappointment. The huge room is packed from wall to wall and the atmosphere reeks with a pungent and consuming odor of mothballs. Their aura floats upon a moldy cloud of perspiration manufactured by the bodies in the overcrowded room, but clearly the mothballs are in command. The smell reminds me of opening the cedar chest in my bedroom back home. I wonder if my room is the same after all these months. Probably one of my young brothers has taken the place over. It really doesn't matter unless he changed the pictures on the wall. Memories of home are gradually fading. Although thoughts of home are distant and unreal they pop up now and then. Occasionally, a face, or sound, or song or one of a hundred other things can trigger an unexpected nostalgic flashback. Usually the spark is not so cruelly unbearable as the odor of mothballs. Whenever it happens, the scene creates a moment of sadness, a quick snapshot of what used to be.

Home is not in my immediate plans and there are other things to think about. I come out of my trance momentarily. In the real world, Makowski is sniffing the foul air. He says maybe the Army is testing a new weapon on us.

Cadets are squeezed in everywhere, gazing into empty space

while swarms of non-coms hustle behind a long counter. The line moves forward very slowly. With each plunge ahead, the heels of GI shoes clack against the cement floor with a staccato sharpness. Mack says it sounds like we're being attacked by flamenco dancers.

I decide to try killing time thinking about what comes next. Technically we will still be enlisted men but different from GIs. We are aviation cadets, a unique group. It will be that way until we graduate from training. At that time they will usher us out of the Army with an honorable discharge only to swear us in immediately as commissioned officers. Our return to civilian life will last about five minutes, just long enough to sign here and sign there.

Most of us will be 2nd Lieutenants and a few who just slide under the tent will not get the gold bars on their shoulders. They will be called *flight officers* and wear strange blue and white insignia denoting to one and all that they screwed up someplace. It tells the world they are good enough to complete the program but not quite as good as everybody else. It has a semblance of the way unfaithful wives were punished years ago in old New England. We frequently see flight officers around the base. I always wonder what their problem was.

Anyway, why speculate? We haven't been up in the wild blue yonder; we haven't even started ground school. Anything can happen. Yet, it doesn't hurt to take the long view. If a man can hang in there and finish the job, some good things will happen. Tradition has it that a graduate will get more than wings and a commission. For instance it's almost certain that the first place he will be ordered to go is home. Graduates usually receive a ten-day furlough. It is something of a tradition. No cadet in his right mind would take this as a promise or guarantee but it's well worth thinking about. It could happen.

The reason there isn't more griping is that most of us regard our condition of temporary internment as a short-term inconvenience. The true sword of Damocles, the monster worry, is fear of washing out. Having qualified to be cadets and notified family and friends to spread the news, our price of failure has become unthinkable. We have won a couple of hands and are ahead of the game, but we aren't home yet.

We want to be officers. Tomorrow we start ground school and the rumors of what they have planned for us is menacing to say the least. We haven't been officially notified what to expect but Johnny Hudsmith from Altoona, PA has hinted at possessing some important information from an anonymous source. Johnny is a free spirit and it wouldn't be surprising if he picked some general's pocket.

He says we can expect about 180 hours of classes. He also says the training has been expanded from thirteen to eighteen weeks. We will soon know the facts because ground school starts in less than 24 hours. Johnny's news about extending our training for five extra weeks has made us somewhat thoughtful. It means five weeks extra before we make the next step, the move to Aerial Gunnery School. Johnny also says there will be many hours devoted to examinations on tough subjects like math and physics and those kinds of things. Testing is something we have all had enough of by now.

Tests mean passing grades and flunks. Flunks could mean washing out. If that's the way they're looking at things it means we are all on trial again. The rumor of what is in store for us has expanded, as all rumors must. A sharp drop in overall confidence and comfort level is obvious. There is a distinct change of attitude in the barracks. It's much quieter since we have heard rumors of what will be expected of us. There could well be something ominous in the fact they have lengthened the training from thirteen to eighteen weeks. Why would they do that? Gone is the carefree banter. Having been appointed cadets; we all felt we were "in." Now, even the squawkers and talkers are somber and thoughtful. Our hearts are heavy with the realization that what we thought was the finish tape may have been only the first hurdle.

No doubt about it, mentally and physically they are going to challenge us in every way possible. At least we will have our uniforms, and we've passed all their tests so far. Well, if someone has a weakness it's better to find out sooner than later. We have never been led to expect they would ever send anyone out of here to the next step who was not 100% fit for the job. Just the same, how tough do they want to make it? We hear stories. Nobody's perfect. None of us have been tested for anoxia in the pressure chamber yet. Cadets who pass out in there or even those who faint on the parade ground in the 110 degree heat are rumored to be taken directly to the infirmary, given a six-four physical and washed out. It could be possible. The Sunday parades at Santa Ana are big deals. The grandstands are brimming with important people like movie stars and Air Force generals. It's not watching bicycle riding clowns and potentates from the shrine marching up and down the street. These are parades where several thousand cadets; pilot, navigator, and bombardier trainees; march in squadrons onto the parade grounds and stand at 'parade rest' with feet spread and hands clasped behind their backs for two or three hours with a California afternoon sun blazing down on their heads. We haven't had to stand a parade yet; we didn't have the right uniforms.

All of us are very healthy or we would not have survived beyond the physicals and psycho exam and been declared competent for further training. None of us would expect a calamity on the parade ground. The trouble is, if the rumor is true, it reveals that we are being tested every time we step out the door. We still have things like the pressure chamber to go through. Who knows what might happen there? What about tests on radio code or physics or meteorology? Nobody's perfect. Sometime later today we expect to receive a complete list of the ways our time will be spent from today on.

I've never passed out in my life even during August football practice. I remember one day on the freshman baseball team at the University of Minnesota. The varsity needed a catcher and our coach sent me over to where they were practicing. When we got the third out of the first inning, I took off the mask and started for the dugout. The coach, Dave McMillan, asked where I was going. I said, "That's three away coach."

He said, "Get back in there, Moore." That was it. I caught for both sides and never got to the dugout in the entire nine inning game. It was hot, and humid, well up in the nineties and my legs were like two sticks of rubber but the thought of a collapse never entered my mind. Now, I'm not so sure. There are all kinds of things that could happen.

We keep moving slowly and finally reach the front rail. It's something to see. These GIs are racing back into the racks and rushing out with enough clothes, shoes and other stuff to keep a soldier comfortable through a rough winter in Antarctica. We wait our turn. A PFC (Private First Class) behind the counter asks us our sizes ranging from shoes to caps including GI underwear socks, shirts, pants, coats, a tie, and insignia. They give us two sets of shirts and pants, brown OD's and *suntans*, as well as fatigues. The dress-uniform coat is similar to that of an officer but is strictly GI and far from the sleek green uniform blouse of the officers.

It is the dress uniform hat, the "hot pilot" headpiece that gives my heart a little jerk. It has a large golden propeller above the visor

112

giving us a clear distinction as cadets. Unfortunately, unlike those of smiling, devil-may-care pilots in the movies, the grommets are still in the hats. It keeps them stiff, round and flat without the raunchy, crushed look, which is the glamorous trademark of "flyboys." We have been assured that grommets will stay in the hats and hats will stay round until after graduation. It will be many weeks before any of us are treated to a special reflection from the mirror in the latrine.

In addition, our uniform of the day will be crowned with the standard barracks cap, a favorite with American Legion old timers hitting the streets on national holidays. We are forced to wear it everywhere because cadets are not allowed outside the barracks with heads uncovered. The rule is not new to us and applies to everyone including officers. A bareheaded soldier is considered to be out of uniform.

The uniforms we are being supplied today will be what we wear until the day we become officers. It will furnish us an appearance that is unique and easy to distinguish. We will be easy to spot by those who want to catch us at something or simply are not fond of our position in military limbo. No one will mistake us for either officers or GIs.

Traditionally, we have heard it said that nobody loves a cadet. Well, why should they? It could be that *paddle feet* (non flying people) and GIs both resent being told Air Corps trainees are somehow elite. None of us really believe it. Much is made of our position as future airmen, but we still have not even seen the inside of an Army plane. Most of us have never even been off the ground in an airplane of any kind. There is absolutely no assurance that any of us will clear all the hurdles and become 2nd Lieutenants and get to combat. However, whenever a high ranking officer addresses us as a group, his theme is that we are very special people from whom great things are expected.

The unvarnished truth is we haven't done anything except pass a tough physical and called home to tell the folks about it.

How we will fare with the officers assigned to be our mentors is slightly cloudy. The younger officers, mostly 2nd lieutenants, will run us ragged on the obstacle courses, curse us on the drill field, and give us gigs for every little thing on Saturday inspections. We know this is true because they have told us so. Those gentlemen are, in fact, frank and, at times, insulting in comparing us to dumb animals and body parts. Right now they have us where they want us. Eyes shining, voices booming , they deal discipline from all corners of the base. All that and we haven't even started ground school.

Like it or not, we really envy those people. They have a nice life; dining at the officers' club, dancing on Friday evening when the bus from L.A. rolls in with a bevy of beauties from the USO, permission to leave the base whenever duty permits. I'm determined to make it, but it seems a long way off. When we finish here in eighteen weeks, we will head for aerial gunnery training at some lonely coyote infested desert in Arizona or someplace equally barren. That will be followed by months of training at advanced bombardier-navigator school before we ever wear wings and bars and are accepted at any officers' club.

Most of the men in our barracks seem ready to accept whatever comes along but, for the first time, the process seems to be getting to a few unhappy cadets. The symptoms of their displeasure are bothersome to everybody. Who could enjoy watching them shuffle around finding fault with everything, bitching and griping, trying to capture a willing listener? They seldom succeed. Mackowski says they're disillusioned and probably didn't read the fine print on the enlistment application.

I feel sorry for them. Maybe being an aviation cadet isn't exactly what those guys anticipated. My opinion is that they just don't understand the game. The key is to be patient and wait to see what comes next; the answer is to accept whatever that happens to be. People who go around singing sad songs all the time risk being called front and center. Once in the limelight, a cadet can expect to be blamed for everything from scuffed shoes to the rise of Hitler.

We have only been on the base a few weeks, but many things have become evident. It's important to remember what we're doing here. The war is real and we are in it. As time passes, things will become more difficult and the pressure will mount. Cadets who can't handle the system and let it be known become very ripe for a trip to aerial gunnery school followed quickly by a place at the waist window of a B-17 over Berlin. Well, it may not be *all* bad. They'll have their aerial gunners' wings and sergeant's stripes plus a high time in jolly old England.

Hopes and ambitions in the armed service are always subject to change, but without doubt, most of us would rather be sweating it out here. I have my own vision, the picture of being able to walk into any officers' club anywhere on earth with wings on my chest, bars on my shoulders and a lovely lady on my arm. I also anticipate a smile on my face.

I wonder about the older officers who will actually be giving us classes in everything from *Morse Code* to *Identification of Enemy Ships and Aircraft*. They seem to be an older and kinder breed but there is a gulf between them and us. It is probably that they seem as old as our fathers and remind us of the college professors we left at home. Without a doubt, their job is to fill our heads with basic military information considered valuable to our future performance. We don't have much of an idea what that might be, but we are anxious to get started.

One thing about our officer friends, old or young; they love to hop on a bus and head into L.A. for the weekend. How we envy those lucky bastards. The convicts in Reading Gaol had more freedom than we enjoy. Being confined to the base for an indefinite time wouldn't seem so bad if we didn't know what is going on out there. The frustration is doubled when we see "ground pounders" heading out the gate smacking their lips in anticipation. There are many things to do and see in L.A. including pretty girls, bars, great music, and fine restaurants. It is a cornucopia of pleasures to excite the imagination of any young gentleman capable of passing a GI physical. Should we be resentful that it can also jiggle the interest of our pot-bellied instructors? We watch with envy as they run for freedom. Nobody holding a two-day pass should be expected to waste extra minutes walking.

We also note cadets from advanced classes in the happy throng. We envy them also but see, in their eagerness, a promise that our day will come.

I watch our future instructors pounding each other on the back and demonstrating obvious joy at the prospect of a visit to the sink hole of venereal disease that they keep warning us about. Most of them are in their thirties, even forties. To us that seems old. Chances are they would never be drafted so they must be volunteers giving what they can. Looking at it that way, it seems fair enough that they have a chance to feel young and get a seat at the party that's going on big time around the edges of the war.

But nothing is permanent in the Army. How do those guys sleep? Tomorrow they could get a message from operations that puts them in the mailroom at Tonapah, Nevada for the rest of the war. They must certainly be aware of the possibility. Perhaps it makes them jittery and a bit jealous. We have a different set of dreams, which do not include worry about losing something we never had.

The truth is they have nothing to cry about. As permanent party on the post they don't have a bad deal. L.A. is right outside the door and we hear there are very many girls in that town. Chances are good these officers will never be sent overseas as long as Santa Ana is hosting pre-flight school. Personally, so far as myself, most of them have been decent. On the surface they appear distant, sometimes rough and mean. They don't seem to like us much but how could they? The line between officers and enlisted men is carefully drawn. They have their world, we have ours. Their job is not to make friends but rather to kick the last vestiges of a civilian attitude out of a soldier's mind. The rules are few but specific. Even the least of them is vigorously enforced. Any cadet who neglects a quick and proper salute to a 2nd Lieutenant can expect to be wracked up, chewed out, and put on report. Those few who still feel some of the rules are simply suggestions are playing "Catch me if you can!" The problem is, they can. When they do, the punishment can take many different forms, but is never nice.

Those who have gone before us left word, via graffiti, that "Nobody loves a cadet." Now, qualified, suitably attired, and easily identifiable, we will be aviation cadets for the entire world to see and a few iron ass 2nd lieutenants to push around. They control our immediate futures and are well aware of their power.

We know they will be rough, they already are. Sometimes it feels as if the Air Corps is always testing, trying to find a weakness, trying to weed out the people who might break down at the wrong time. It isn't easy to stand nose to nose, seeing the drivel run off his lips as some former grocery delivery boy shouts, "Get your head out of your ass, mister!" A man has to be a realist. There's going to be more of that stuff before there is less, and probably some forever.

We have already been caressed by the taunting sarcasm of the enlisted men. Usually they disguise their feelings with comments just within earshot such as, "Look at all da Bing Crosbys!" when we are standing at parade rest outside the mess hall. They have to wait until we are seated before they can go inside. They see no reason for such a distinction. Neither do we, but fairness is not an operable word in this man's army. If, as in this case, we have no rank but find that higher authority has offered us a privilege, we accept it without complaint.

The game is to grab little privileges as fast as you can before somebody changes the rules. When fate rolls the dice and comes up snake eyes, there's no alternative but to forget about it. If you run up and down every street and through every barracks on the base crying "Foul!"--you'll never, not ever, hear a single word of sympathy in any language from anybody, including your best friend. The common response is "Tell it to the chaplain!" In the case of someone less tactful it could be, "Blow it our your barracks bag!" or something even less spontaneous and more profane.

My stream of consciousness is broken as a PFC (Private First Class) behind the counter says, "Next." He takes my sizes and disappears behind a wall returning quickly with his arms full of clothes. I slip into the uniform coat and put on the visor hat. They fit! The hat still has the grommet inside making it smooth, round, and flat. At some future time, the grommet will be removed and the hat will be scrunched and crunched to give it the classic "Hot Pilot" look. "The Look" will not be seen on any aviation cadet's head until the day he graduates and is commissioned if such a time ever arrives. The front of the hat shows a large, gold propeller rather than the eagle worn by an officer. In addition to our regular, khaki OD (Order of the Day) shirt and pants, we receive summer-type suntans. Either of the uniforms is worn with a beige color tie tucked into the front of the shirt.

The blouse, to be worn for parades and formal occasions, is similar to an officer with propeller ornaments on the lower part of the collar and a U.S. insignia on the upper part. Officers wear an insignia denoting their group or specific Air Force assignment. Cadets, not having been assigned to a regular combat airforce, wear an "Air Force" patch on the left shoulder of shirts or dress coats. The formal visor cap is worn on special occasions such as parades.

There is no question about it now; I'm an aviation cadet. Soon, I'll even look like one and it's music to my ears when we are given permission to walk back to our barracks rather than wait until the last man is equipped and ready for a formation. The bulletin board at the barracks carries the information that the "order of the day" for uniform is *suntans*. It is a typical summer morning in southern California with a temperature of about eighty and climbing fast. *Suntans* looks like the proper call for a uniform today and possibly far into the future.

For now though, it's dress up time. "Hey, Mack," I yell at Makowski. "Where do these propellers go?"

Mack already has his dress coat on. I hardly recognize him. "On the coat," he says. "Put one on that American Legion cap, too. Hey, you guys, Jack I. wants to know where the insignia goes."

That's about as funny as Mack ever gets.

"Well," I say, "I can see where you put yours which probably means if I put 'em opposite they might be right." We try everything on; posing and posturing before the huge glass wall in the latrine: *Our glassy essence portrays such tricks before high heaven as make the angels laugh.*

We are happy, overjoyed. It would be a fine day for a celebration if the United States Army Air Corps could see it that way. Unfortunately, they do not. As usually happens when one or more of us is too happy, the interlude must be rudely and officially terminated immediately.

There is no specific rule that forbids an aviation cadet to smile. That's just the way it is. The only use for a smile is to give some corporal a chance to say, "You laughing at me, Mister? Wipe that candy ass smile off you face, Mister! You hear me, Mister?"

Today heavy footsteps pound on the stairway leading to the barracks front door. A huge shadow blocks the entrance, a shrill voice shouts, "Tenhut!" The shadow pushes itself into the room, reveals itself as Captain Melby and fades away. We jump to attention and freeze. The captain looks us over, shakes his head, shrugs his shoulders and purses his lips. After a pause, he says, "At ease, men."

We relax but are not at ease. His aide, a skinny little sergeant with a shrill voice steps forward and says, "Listen up, men."

The captain waves his arm and says, "Get yourself a place to park. I got a few things to say y'all want to know. Now, men, I see you musta got your new uniforms today and I see you got em on. Well, now, allow me to suggest that you take 'em off right now and get back into your good old fatigues where you'll be more comfortable and I'll make a bit of a suggestion to y'all. That suggestion is you fold them dress clothes real neat and put 'm nice and gentle into your foot locker because it's gonna be a bit of time before you'll have need of 'em. Maybe more than a bit. Meantime, it's my duty and pleasure to explain just what's gonna claim your time in the next few months. Believe me, it won't be no wine, women and song. I can tell you that right now." He turns to his aide, "Shorty, pass out them copies of the curriculum so the misters can get an idea of what we got planned for 'em."

120

The captain notices we are still standing, waves his hand and says, "At ease, gentlemen. Corporal Peterman will do a nice job of seein' everybody gets one of these lists of what's to come durin' your time here at the base. When you look 'em over just remember we're not askin' you to do anything the men who come before you didn't have to do. Now, you may want to ask some questions once you read what's gonna be expected during your stay. Well, don't ask 'em. Just do what your superiors order you to do and the time is gonna fly right by."

The corporal has finished distributing. The captain stands up and Shorty shouts, "Tenhut!" We all jump to attention and watch as they go out the door and up stairs; the captain waddling, the sergeant bouncing. Destination, the cadets on the second floor. On our floor, all the tenants read furiously, looking up occasionally, stopping for breath and shaking their heads. I quickly understand what Johnny Hudspeth is worried about.

The paper is headed "BOMBARDIER-NAVIGATOR PREFFLIGHT PROGRAM OF INSTRUCTION, JULY 1943" and runs for nine pages. Immediately I start looking for the rough spots. I see 48 hours given to code, listening to dots and dits. It sounds like something anybody should be able to learn. Nothing to worry about there I flip to the next page and see, among other things eighteen hours of Physics. Physics was the closest I ever came to flunking a subject in high school. I slacked off on the homework and was plenty scared. It should be easier the second time through. The Physics classes will be combined with Meteorology, about which I know nothing. They also will have 20 hours of math. It's another one I can handle because of high school and college. It says we will have 18 hours of *Maps, Charts, and Aerial Photography*. We will study 18 hours on *Identification and Tactical Functions of Aircraft*, 12 hours of *Chemical Warfare Defense*.

There are several more items on the list but my eye suddenly catches an item that underlies the entire regimen. It includes 40 hours each of *Physical Training, Drill*, something-called *Squadron*; plus twenty hours of *Military*, 15 hours of *Small Arms*, 5 hours of *Military Courtesies*, and *Customs of the Service*. There will also be 18 hours of conditioning exercises, 25 hours of running exercises, eleven hours of competitive games plus one hour of test evaluation.

I think one of our toughest problems will be trying to get into a classroom routine. We can expect they'll fire things at us bang, bang, bang and then spring a test. Going back to school and hanging on to our concentration will not be easy. There will be those days when boredom hangs over the classroom and the clock on the wall drags along at half speed. Makowski has a degree in music and has put in his time. He says claustrophobia has caused more dropouts than lack of intelligence.

As far as close order drill, PT and inspections, things like that, all anyone will need is common sense. I notice they have a category called *Ceremonies* which reminds me we have not yet faced the California noonday sun. Even if they consider it to be a test where failure is fatal to our careers, it should be the easiest challenge in the world. If a cadet does not fall on his butt, he passes. We will get the answer on this one on Sunday. I hope it rains.

CHAPTER 8

THE BIG PARADE

Here it is Sunday and we are marching to take part in our first big weekly parade. Every cadet on the base except those on fire guard duty is required to take part. The sky is pure blue, cloudless. The sun is high and the air warm. We are not in the habit of checking the exact temperature, but today it could be called "typical" providing typical means a hundred degrees and rising. Uniform of the day, as posted on the bulletin board, is suntans. Suntans consist of a shirt and slacks of a light tan material, probably poplin. The Army undoubtedly feels we will be more comfortable fighting sunstroke in suntans than heavier woolen full dress uniforms.

I silently congratulate the decision-makers at command for considering our comfort. However, they have been less than merciful in requiring neckties and it doesn't seem probable that skimpy barracks caps, true relics from World War I, offer any possible protection from the sun. We have been advised to flex our knees and wiggle our toes occasionally to stimulate circulation. The idea is to prevent cutting off the blood supply flowing through our legs. For some reason, such a thing sometimes happens when a cadet stands at attention or parade-rest for two or three hours. It has been rumored that fainting can cause a cadet to be washed out. We don't know if that's true, but we have orders to remain in ranks if someone nearby runs into trouble. We have been assured special medical details will patrol the area and take charge of the situation.

Nearing the parade grounds, we can see the back of the grandstand. All seats are filled and people are standing three or four deep around the perimeters. The Army Air Force band is playing "The Stars And Stripes Forever" and it makes me feel three feet taller. In the right situation, a good marching band can pick up a crowd, lead 'em to the river and make'm jump over the falls. I love it. I feel great. I can't help smiling. This is different than anything we have done before; as different as comparing a ukulele solo to the big bands of Glen Miller or Tommy Dorsey. Flags fold and unfold lazily in the soft breeze.

Just as we reach the entrance to the parade grounds, the band goes silent and we pick up the shouting of squadron leaders as they steer their troupes toward designated spots in the formation. "Form a column of squadrons! Left column! Left turn! Harch!"

A shiver runs up my spine. It reminds me of pre-season football practice where a team runs up and down the field with the quarterback shouting signals as they run plays at a phantom opponent.

We reach the parade ground just as the band strikes up the Army Air Corps Song. It causes a few moments of strangeness, of unreality. This is really me, a cadet in the Army Air Corps. I'm here; it's really me. Listen to the band, look at the flags of the United States of America. I'm a soldier serving my country; those flags floating up there are my flags. A few months in the Army haven't brought me any closer to the real war than radio and newspapers can take me.

I am beginning to realize that we have some importance. The Army didn't ship us to Santa Ana to mop floors and peel potatoes in the mess hall. We appreciate the cheering and applause given each squadron as it passes by.

It is reasonable to believe that the spectators who cheer and applaud us so generously share our uncertainty. Probably they have loved ones scattered all around the world. That's the way it is for most people these days. I think of my mother working in a defense factory praying novenas for my dad who has been fighting with the 34th Division in Africa. He made it through that campaign but who knows where he might be right now.

The fighting has been going on for over two years and the end is not in sight. Perhaps these people who came out to see us today are silently praying for their husbands and brothers to return safely and that we can make it possible by being their replacements. I wish it were possible. The B-24's and B-17's in Europe are hitting tough targets and taking huge losses. Those men and planes will need to be replaced but it won't be by us. Someday we will be replacements, but not yet. We're only starting to get ready. All of us: pilots, bombardiers and navigators are due for long stretches of advanced training before we can even think about carrying our own weight. Our situations require intense and precise training and there are no shortcuts allowed.

Although Santa Ana is an air base where nobody learns to fly, it is a place where future flyers have to start. No doubt some of their families have chosen to wait here for their return.

It seems that everyone is waiting for someone or something. I try to focus on the future, but can't see beyond the remainder of this afternoon. I look forward to the end of the parade, to getting the burning sun off my back, to going to the air-conditioned mess hall and to drinking a quart of water with my next meal. Tonight I'll be tired and will sleep well. There is no reason to toss and turn worrying about what happens next. In the morning, the Army will knock on the barracks door at 7 a.m. and tell us what to do. Anything beyond tomorrow is only a guess. I have dedicated my future to the United States of America, which will return it one day at a time. That's how it will be until the war ends and I am wherever it has taken me. I submit to another inescapable lesson of life in the Army: "Don't worry, it only gives you something more to worry about."

As our squadron makes its entrance, I notice the American flags flying all around the perimeter of the parade ground. The grounds are surrounded by a huge crowd, which must number in the thousands. We proceed to our position and stand at attention until given the command for parade rest. We must remain in that position, feet spread shoulder wide and hands clasped being our backs, until the end of activities, at least two or possibly three hours.

Time passes slowly as a continuous flow of squadrons enter the field. The navigators, being the first to arrive, are already in place. Our turn this week is second; second to arrive and second to leave. The pilots, who are third this week, will come in last and be the last to march out. They are certain to be at parade-rest for at least three hours. Positions are rotated each week. We have not been on the asphalt very long and it could be imagination, but I could swear something is burning the bottoms of my shoes. I begin to feel the sun. It's time to start flexing knees and wiggling toes. I do so although I'm feeling fine. It doesn't appear anyone around us is having trouble.

This may be a long afternoon and there is absolutely nothing to do but think and sweat. As usually happens in such situations, my mind digs around for random thoughts just to keep the motor running. It seems to me, for whatever reason, this afternoon has an aura of importance, a feeling that it will not soon be forgotten. Things are coming together. I realize why I'm here and why my fellow cadets are here and why, in many ways, we are so much alike. We are a group of young guys with physical and mental qualifications to perform a very specialized service. We have been tested and found healthy. We also score well on IQ tests. Hot stuff! We are the cream of the crop, the men who will dive out of the "Wild Blue Yonder" and have the Japs and Nazis screaming for mercy. Sounds exciting. The trouble is we have less time in the air than Donald Duck.

I know that from this day on, whenever I see the Stars and Stripes I'll remember what I saw looking up at the flags and marching to the band as we entered the parade grounds. I'll remember how, at that moment, I was seized by the realization that I am in the middle of history. The whole world has done a Humpty Dumpty and I'm one of the King's men trying to put things together again. Maybe we can, maybe we can't...but the future looks dim if things go the wrong way.

Suddenly I hear a slight commotion in the ranks several rows ahead of us. Two medics come from nowhere and rush past us. We are not supposed to turn our heads and none of us do. We know the rules and we don't know who may be watching from behind. I didn't see medics but the tempo of their GI shoes beating on the asphalt had all the characteristics of a Gene Krupa drum solo. I can imagine what happened, but it's not something I want to worry about. Physically, I feel more bored than tired. However, there's no harm remembering to flex those knees and wiggle those toes. I notice the cadets standing at parade rest in front of me share those sentiments.

The afternoon is dragging along relentlessly. One of the generals in attendance is giving a speech, but the public address system reverberates repeating every word he speaks again and again. I couldn't understand anything he said, but the message must have ended. The folks in the grandstand just gave him a nice hand. It shouldn't be too long before we have the retreat ceremony. It will not be lengthy but, after that, the squadrons will begin to pass in review and that will take a very long, agonizing time. We will have to wait for all of the navigator cadets to pass in review before we, the bombardiers, can have our turn. They will take a half-hour to forty-five minutes and the sun shows no promise of setting early.

It is a relief when we are called to attention and the familiar soaring sound of the bugler fills the air. Every Army base retires the flag at sundown. The retreat ceremony is not long but it is respectful and solemn and it makes me feel good. The bugler owns the air. The only sounds are the notes from his horn, the only movement is that of the flag descending slowly in response to the music. We hold our salute; the flag flying above the grandstand comes down gently and proudly. When it nears the ground it is quickly retrieved, carefully folded and carried away.

In standing retreat at Jefferson Barracks, Coe College pre-pre flight and here at Santa Ana, I notice an interesting similarity. An eerie silence always follows the ceremony; as if the flag has disappeared before they could finish their thoughts.

The time has come to pass in review and the navigators, on our right, are the first to get going. Since there are more than a thousand navigators, it seems to take forever for them to parade to the front, make a left turn, and march by the reviewing stand. Over and over we hear the shout of the cadet captains calling "Eyes, right!" as they pass immediately in front of the reviewing stand. That's the critical moment, crucial seconds when each squadron is expected to be perfectly aligned and make a crisp turn of heads at the command, "Eyes, right!" They actually keep score and grade each squadron as it passes in front of the reviewing stand.

We wait another half-hour or more before the space formerly occupied by the navigators is completely empty. When our turn comes we have to tell Blankenship it's time to go. He finally gets the idea, calls us to attention and marches us to the front, then left toward the reviewing stand. Makowski mumbles "I hope he remembers to give us 'Eyes right'!" My blood runs cold. The top brass always demands a high standard on execution of close order drill; especially when they are on the reviewing stand. If Blankenship screws up, we are going to be subjected a very creative tirade from the ground pounding 2nd Lieutenant responsible for our squadron. He could hand out enough gigs to keep us walking tours every Saturday night for the duration.

Tours are a punishment consisting entirely of putting a rifle on your shoulder and walking back and forth in front of the barracks. *Gigs* are marks against your conduct, which result in various penalties. We start moving, make our turn and are about to pass directly in front of the reviewing stand. Now, right now, is the time for Blankenship to give the command. He must have forgotten. Then suddenly we hear the command! Blankenship didn't forget! His primordial shout of "Eyes right!" could have been intended to shake the grandstand as well as many of the reviewing officers and their guests. We snap our heads to the right and I'm looking directly into the faces of two startled generals wearing quizzical expressions. One turns and says something to the other. I can't hear what he says but if I read his lips correctly, he was asking, "What the hell was that?' We keep right on marching in the direction of the mess hall.

It's amazing how tired a person can become merely standing under a hot sun. I wonder about the cadet, whoever he was, who was carried away by the medics. At least he passed out in the navigators section, so he wasn't one of our people. All in all, it was an exciting day, but I want to get something to eat and go to bed. It's ground school again tomorrow morning and they say we may be going to the pressure chamber.

CHAPTER 9

THE PRESSURE CHAMBER

We find ourselves, this afternoon, midway through what must be considered a full but typical day. After dividing the morning between running and climbing on the toughest of three different obstacle courses, we spent the remainder of the morning having our ears clobbered by dit-dahs and dah-dits listening to Morse code and trying to make sense out of it. Learning Morse code isn't that difficult, but being confined to a little cubbyhole wearing earphones and trying to interpret the language of crickets creates a weird illusion, the sensation that a person could raise his eyes and see Buck Rogers zooming around the room. At the present time I can take twelve words a minute. We will be expected to take something over twenty before we finish.

Following our code class we had some chow. There have been rumors that we would soon be tested in the pressure chamber. This time, the rumors were true. We are now marching and singing on our way to that very place. I spot the "chamber" as we go over a hill and into a small forest. It doesn't look like a fun place under any circumstances but the real nervousness is caused by the fact it is probably the last test that can wash someone out in a big hurry. We have no idea what to expect. It could be scary.

The chamber is a one story, windowless, block of concrete with a single outside entrance. The place has an aura, the same foreboding presence that gives an audience shivers in a horror movie. I am quickly convinced that nothing good is going to come out of this place.

We have been briefed and informed as to what will happen. We are about to experience an anoxia run. Anoxia is the medical term for a situation in which the body fails to get enough oxygen. I've taken the trouble to do some reading about it. When such a situation takes over, the lips and fingernails turn blue. In all probability, this will be the only signal to warn that something is terribly wrong. There are no other visible indications. You will feel no pain. Anoxia is a phantom, an untouchable, invisible enemy. If detected in time it can be corrected by restoring its source. If not discovered and restored it will lead to collapse and possible death.

We go inside, pass through one door, walk a few feet and go through another. The doors are large and thick, reminiscent of those on bank vaults. When the two doors slam shut and the big wheels on each door have been turned to assure an airtight position, they create an airlock. The airlock is necessary because it is not possible, in an emergency, to rush directly out of the chamber and immediately begin breathing at an entirely different pressure level. In the airlock, pressure will be conformed to meet conditions outside the room. It will then be safe to leave the airlock and enter a normal environment.

A staff sergeant who will apparently be in charge of today's operation orders us to take seats on wooden benches lining each side of the chamber. A GI watches us through a large window at the end of the chamber closest to the door. The door to the chamber slams shut.

132

The staff sergeant goes over and spins the wheel a few times until he's satisfied everything is air-tight.

If the Army has a plan to rid itself of a few cadets on the basis of claustrophobia, the set up is perfect. However, my concern is something different. I was once booted in the nose during football practice and have a deviated septum, a curve inside the nose that sometimes clogs things up. Never having been up to high altitude, there's no way to know what effect the change in pressure might have on that condition.

We have all been given small, green oxygen masks and sit quietly studying the surroundings and waiting for whatever happens next. Soon, the sergeant stands up and introduces himself. He then loses no time in getting things started. He tells us that our first exercise will be an anoxia run. Seeing the questioning look in the eyes of most of the cadets, he explains what such a thing is all about.

"Gentlemen, this will be a very short and simple test to learn how you can handle a shortage of oxygen. We are now reducing air pressure and will proceed to a simulated altitude of 17,000 feet. At that altitude, you will sit quietly for ten minutes without benefit of an oxygen mask. At the end of that time, I will notify you to put on your masks and we will proceed to the next phase. There's no need to worry. If, for any reason a problem arises, we can get you out of here and on full oxygen so fast it will make your eyes bulge. In the meantime, let me cover some things you can expect. You are going to grow larger around the waist. As air pressure falls the gases in your body will expand. Don't worry if your belly seems to swell. My advice is, just loosen your belt. As we get up to thirty or forty thousand your body gas may be seven to twelve times what it is now. Another thing, check your fingernails once in a while. If your fingernails or lips look blue, anoxia is setting in. One of the strangest things about anoxia is that you won't feel it coming. If we have to revive you, you'll deny you ever passed out. You just won't believe what happened."

This a big test because I'm sure it's the last one where they can find something that can get a cadet washed out in a hurry. I feel like I'm doing fine. The ten minutes must be more than half over and I don't notice anything different, my fingernails seem about the usual color. I feel a little thirsty but that's all. Suddenly, the tall redheaded cadet seated beside me falls asleep and collapses in my lap. The sergeant yells "Mayday!" The door flies open, another GI appears and in no more than a few seconds the cadet has been carried out and put in the airlock. The airlock door is slammed shut and a few minutes later our Sergeant is back in the chamber and saying, "Ten minutes are up. Put your masks on."

The mask slides over my mouth and nose, I take a couple of deep breaths and am treated to a huge surprise. The world comes back to life. I can't believe it. It seems that all the lights in the chamber are suddenly turned on. It takes a minute or two to realize that all the lights in the chamber were *not* suddenly turned on. In just ten minutes I had lost part of my vision without the slightest idea of what was happening. The sergeant takes the floor again and says we will now gradually climb to an altitude of 32,000 feet where we will sit for an hour. He explains that 32,000 feet is the base altitude. Planes climbing beyond this altitude at full oxygen are subject to the same pressure restrictions as planes leaving the earth without a supply of oxygen.

We sit at 32,000 for a long time until he announces we are going up to 42,000, the maximum for people using the little, green, constant-flow masks we are wearing. My stomach is swelling, as are those of the people around me. It is not painful, but the atmosphere is almost as bad as the mothballs we suffered through at the quartermaster's building. Finally, the sergeant announces that we will descend slowly to an altitude of 18,000 feet. At that point, we will be dropped at the average speed of a parachute jump. The bottom drops out of my world. So far, so good; but a speedy jump from 18,000 feet could play tricks with my ears.

I swallow hard and work my jaws as if I'm chewing gum although I have no gum. How can I keep my ears open? There's no way to clear my nose while wearing an oxygen mask. The left ear feels all right but the right one is starting to ache. We finally get down to 18,000 feet and the pace of our fall picks up. The fire in my right ear is turning into a conflagration, but it's absolutely necessary to keep a straight face. We finally hit the ground and I keep hoping my eyes won't start to water. I am feeling pain in my right ear that matches the worst toothache imaginable. As we file out my problem seems to be a matter of covering up until we all file out. Once outside it will be possible to put some distance between the damn chamber and myself. I figure my best move will be to hide in the crowd, try to get pushed through the door and run like hell before I start to scream. I might be saved yet.

My last shred of hope dies when we get to the door and the line stops. A flight surgeon is checking each cadet as he exits. It's a quick exam, a look in each ear and a pat on the back. I'm sure it won't be that short with me. It isn't. The doctor puts his little flashlight in my left ear and says, "Fine." He moves around to my right and puts the light up to his eye. He says, "hmm" and takes another look. "Well," he says, "It's a little red in there but I think it'll be all right." I get out of there as fast as I can. I wish now I had thanked him. My fate was in his hands.

When we get back to the barracks, I notice the big redhead's bed is made up but his footlocker is gone and so, I guess, is he. That anoxia is strange stuff. I make it a point to remember what we learned in there today. I hope my ear is better by the weekend. It will be our first two-day pass; it's like getting out of jail. I hear Stan Kenton's orchestra is playing at Balboa. My friend Bernie Parsons from Vancouver, Washington said he is probably going down there on the bus. Maybe I'll decide to go along. Kenton's band has some wild arrangements, but they cut their own groove. It's said there is a dance pavilion down there that's as big as dirigible hanger.

CHAPTER 10

OFF THE BASE

This will be our first time to step off the base in more than three weeks. Even the air we breathe tastes different. Bernie Parsons and I sign out and catch a bus that is going to Balboa, which is reputed to be a fantastic place. I have no idea of what it will be like except that it has a large ballroom and Stan Kenton's Orchestra will be there this weekend. Another advantage is that it is not far from the base and we won't spend much time traveling. We had the usual Saturday inspection of our quarters this morning so we really didn't get started until after chow. The bus moves along smoothly. The countryside is tinged with a pastel quality that mimics a spectacular work of art.

In a short time, we begin to smell the ocean, the bus makes a left turn on Balboa Boulevard and there we are. We stare. We blink. The scene that meets our gaze is classic Norman Rockwell as seen through the eyes of F. Scott Fitzgerald. Nothing in our homes towns (Minneapolis for me, Vancouver for Bernie) has prepared us for the spectacle of attractive young ladies crossing the road sipping cocktails and wearing expensive furs on a warm summer afternoon. Many of their escorts simmer in the sunshine fashionably garbed in tuxedos and top hats. Sailboats and yachts bobbing in the bay provide a perfect backdrop for the beach that is packed and looks like standing room only. Without further conversation, Bernie and I leave the bus and push our way in the direction of the nearest bar.

We order a couple of beers and I suggest we walk down to the beach and look at the ocean. Bernie, coming from Vancouver, cannot see why I am so excited about looking at all that water. I explain to him that Minnesota has 10,000 lakes but no ocean that I know of. I've never seen a real live ocean before. I ask Bernie if he has ever seen a lake. He suggests we go back to the bar. We do.

The bar has no front door and I get a chair where I can see out to the ocean. It's a big thing for me and is something I'll be sure to put in my next letter home when I get time to write. All of a sudden the doorway is blocked by the large figure of Joe Murphy, former member of the University of Wisconsin football team; an old friend with smelly feet. It has only been a month or so since we left pre-preflight in Cedar Rapids, Iowa. Joe says some of the other people from Cedar Rapids are with him over in the pilots' section. He mentions Bill and Bob Myers, Magginty, and Lemon Head. Joe got down here last evening and tells us about his adventures on the beach with a beautiful woman he met. It's the kind of song and dance you hear often in the Army. It's the kind that always involves a beautiful girl, never an ugly one. In Joe's case I probably believe it. Joe's not the kind to brag; he doesn't have to. We have another beer and are chatting a bit when a very pretty girl approaches the table and says, "Hi, Joe."

Joe consults his watch and says, "Right on time." He then arises to his considerable height and says, "See ya!" We watch them go out through the open door and disappear into the crowd. Bernie says, "I hope he didn't take off his shoes!" I reply I'm sure he didn't or she wouldn't be back here today. Bernie says, "Let's get something to eat."

We leave the bar and roam up and down the boulevard trying to decide where to chow up. We finally settle for hamburgers at a sidewalk place and sit around people-watching until it's time to go over to the ballroom where the action will be. It's still very early, but when the band is great like Stan Kenton's, it usually features several famous sidemen. Watching and listening to them warm up can sometimes be more fun than the concert itself. I think the greatest tenor sax solo I ever heard was at the Prom Ballroom in St.Paul. We got there early. The stage was empty except for a few musicians warming up and chatting with each other. Suddenly, the mellow tone of Ben Webster's tenor ran the scale softly a few times. Then, he began quietly to work over the haunting chords of "Body and Soul." He played several choruses; no two were the same. For me, it was once in a lifetime. Even the other players in the band who were tuning up put down their horns and stopped to listen.

It won't be quite that way with Kenton. His music offers sounds from sweet pop to screeching dissonance but they do it all well. We head for the ballroom and find it as large as expected. The place is crowded. As expected, the band is wandering around the bandstand tuning up and shuffling music around. Unfortunately, it is already too crowded for us to approach anywhere near the bandstand. We find a couple of chairs, gawk at any of the girls who appear to be unaccompanied and wait for the band to start. Eventually, Kenton, who is as tall as his voice is deep, takes the microphone, greets the crowd, raises his right arm the band strikes up his theme.

Kenton then announces the next tune will be dedicated to the men from Santa Ana air base; the song is, appropriately enough, *Eager Beaver*. It's one of my very favorite jump tunes and the floor quickly fills with jitterbugs. Bernie and I sit on the sidelines wondering how to ask someone to dance. It has been a long time.

The band plays song after song and takes a break. Bernie and I go up to the bar and have a drink. The band comes back and plays a nice dance tune. I notice a girl who I think has been looking at me, but I don't know what to say. There are so many cadets and officers around; why would she want to dance with me? How long has it been since I've danced? It's been months. I hate to be rejected; what if she says, "No thanks." Bernie seems to be in the same frame of mind. Here I am in my shiny aviation cadet outfit and I've forgotten how to ask a girl to dance. No, I haven't forgotten, I just don't know what to say. There are plenty of women here tonight, maybe one for every fifty service men including GI's, cadets, sailors, Marines, and officers of all kinds. Bernie and I sit on the sidelines and slowly watch our first and long sought, greatly anticipated escape from captivity die on the vine. The competition is overwhelming.

"Bernie," I say, "go ask that girl in the blue dress to dance."

Bernie says, "You go ask her. You're the one she's been looking at." I realize the situation is hopeless. I have nothing to lose but, at the moment, loneliness seems preferable to rejection. Bernie has an excuse that sounds pretty lame but given the facts gets my sympathy. He says he doesn't like the band. "It's too loud, too wild," says Bernie. "Give me Guy Lombardo anytime."

I resist telling him that the musicians I played with referred to his favorite bandleader as "Stinko" Lombardo. He decides to go over to the beach and see what's happening down there. I say I'll hang around and listen to the band.

Later on, when the band begins packing up, I search around

the beach looking for Bernie. There are thousands of people lying around and I stumble over some of them, but no Bernie. Finally, I decide to fold up my blouse for a pillow and flop down on the sand to grab some sack time.

Sometime after sunrise, I am awakened by someone kicking sand in my face and yelling, "Come on, Jack I. Time to get going!"

I pick up my blouse, brush away the sand and put it on. My new cadet hat with the propeller on the front also needs brushing. We start for the boulevard to get some breakfast. I ask him how much time we have until the bus leaves.

He says, " We got enough time to eat. Besides, I have to tell you what happened right after I left. Up comes this beautiful babe..."

"Hold it' I yell. "Hold it right there. Don't even start. In your case, if it is true, she has to be ugly." We found a place, had pancakes and sausage and laughed all the way to the bus.

Tomorrow is Monday and it's back to the real world of trying to recognize the profiles of enemy planes in 1/100 of a second and take 20 words a minute in Morse code. It felt good to get off the base for a short time but, strangely, it was nice to get back. Home is where you know what to expect and, at the moment, Santa Ana is home to us.

ı

WHERE IN THE WORLD IS DEMING?

Today, Sunday, the Aerial Gunnery School at Kingman, Arizona is holding a commencement exercise to declare us all bona fide gunners meticulously trained to fire many kinds of lethal weapons in various directions with unpredictable results. We have filed into the building where our commanding officer first greeted us seven weeks ago. In observing the usual tradition observed by ranking officers everywhere, he has seldom passed our way and then only at a distance. However, in my mind, he visits me often. The picture of the Colonel, in full, parade dress, sitting in judgment during my trial will probably never disappear completely. The recollection is distinct and inescapable as it revives that occasion in bits and pieces and at odd times.

My greatest fear at the time was that the army would not be fair. Having already witnessed the icy impersonal indifference with which the brass were willing to dash a cadet's hopes and expectations, it was natural to enter the hearing room convinced they would have my ass for breakfast and never bat an eye. Three sleepless nights had warned me to be braced for growling officers with decorated chests, vicious expressions and red faces. By nature and by training they would be pumped up and drooling, eager to make an example of a hapless cadet who was wriggling in the net. It would be a good lesson and the military way of preventing future careless cadets from being so stupid as to shoot the wings off their own airplanes.

The reality was completely different. Being the accused, I was motioned to a chair just a few feet from the Colonel. It was close enough for me to smell his after-shave lotion, which must have been splashed on lavishly. He ran the hearing in crisp and formal military style without personal comments for or against. When he glanced at me, his expression was somber, perhaps sad. It was as if he was asking himself, "What the hell is this kid doing here?" He never gave me the idea he would take personal delight in washing out a cadet just to make a point.

Now, on the edge of another milestone in a long, lonely journey we will meet again. The journey may end in any one of several ways and only a few weeks ago the Colonel could have swung the ax and ended it without further delay. We were face to face during a very important half hour at a very crucial time. Now, in a few minutes he will put a diploma in my hands and gunner's wings on my chest. The army being such a now you see it, now you don't dog and pony show, it will be interesting to see if he even recognizes me. Cadets come and go every seven weeks around here. They dress alike and all are about the same age. When gathered in bunches they have no more individual presence than khaki clad grasshoppers. Why should he remember me anyway?

The Colonel's talk is short and to the point. Like most of the squadron, I haven't been paying that much attention but basically it sounds like a speech he wrote once and now delivers every seven weeks. He's telling us we're a good bunch of guys and thanking us for being "on the ball." There isn't anything he can add about our future as gunners because none of us intend to keep that title one-minute longer than required. Our next step is to finish the dream and become commissioned officers with the title of bombardier. Perching in front of an open window at twenty-five thousand feet and battling frost bite in temperatures of thirty-five below is not the carrot in front of our noses.

The Colonel is now, however, feeding us a small helping of crow by recalling our skepticism about learning to field strip and reassemble two kinds of machine guns blindfolded. At that time he guaranteed we could do the job easily. Our reaction had been to groan and stare in disbelief. We have to admit he had it right so there's no denying he earned the right to work us over a little bit and remind us of the occasion. He tells us to believe in ourselves, to take what we get and whistle while we work. He says, in his opinion, our success proves we have twice the potential we imagine. That, he adds, is ten times more than we will ever use. At least he doesn't call us the "cream of the crop." We are tired of being tagged with that phrase and might have booed the Colonel in spite of the medals on his chest.

We accept his kind comments and try to look interested even though his speech is starting to remind us of the sleep inducing high school graduation speeches most of us squirmed through a couple of years ago. On his main point, we can see the wisdom of at least giving a tough job a try before bailing out. Being a person totally unfamiliar with hammers and screwdrivers, proud to possess complete ignorance and hatred for tools of any kind, this cadet still doesn't understand how the feat was accomplished. Strangely, looking back, after four full days of audiovisual study and the repetitious hammering of unsympathetic instructors, the task was simple. As the Colonel predicted, we took those guns apart, put them back together and finished the task with time for a smoke before mess call. Everybody passed, nobody even struggled. The Colonel saw things in us that boggle the imagination.

At last we have arrived at the part of the program it seemed we would never reach. A 1st Lieutenant is calling names and cadets are marching up front, in alphabetical order, one by one, to receive their credentials and shiny Aerial Gunners wings. To the casual observer, there is very little difference in appearance between Aerial Gunners wings and those worn by a bombardier or pilot. If we ever get a furlough, Gunner's wings will be enough to crown us 'Knights of the Sky' and dazzle lonesome young ladies in the old hometown.

In some ways it's a big achievement but as much as we may pride ourselves on winning our silver wings, everyone knows that we may have won a scrimmage but the game is still on the line. Gunners are non-coms with a top rank of Sergeant. Bombardiers become 2nd lieutenants at graduation. We want that commission with all its privileges and pleasures. Winning it will be the big prize; a ticket to the officers' club along with higher pay, fancier duds and more places to go and things to do on our free time. We believe everything will be nicer, sometimes even pleasant. It'll be more fun than winning at bingo, lotto, or being drawn to win the set of dishes on bank night at the University Theater. We seem to be closing in.

They finally call my name; I slide out the end of the row and stroll up the aisle wondering if the Colonel will recognize me. Probably not. I salute him; he returns it and hands me my wings. He pauses and gives me a second quizzical look. I finish the salute. I'm smiling as I leave the stage knowing the Colonel is wondering where in the hell he's seen that cadet's face before. It's nice to feel you made an impression on somebody even if they don't realize it.

This afternoon we caught a train for Deming, New Mexico. Nobody's heart will be broken to leave Kingman but at least, when we came here, we had some idea of where it was. The same cannot be said for Deming. It is somewhere down near the Mexican border and we trust that the engineer will know where he's going and will stop his train to let us climb off when we get there. Our ride will carry us from life at sea level up to more than seventy-five hundred feet when the train peaks out at Flagstaff, Arizona. As we move along and continue to climb, the engine clearly begins to huff and puff. Through the window we begin to see pine trees. When the train stops at Flagstaff, the civilians are seen going about their chores wearing sweaters and jackets. Obviously they are tuned to a different thermometer than the folks in Kingman. In seven weeks we adapted to an overheated, blistering climate that made life difficult on earth and in the sky. We may arrive in New Mexico to step off the train into five feet of snow. It won't make any difference. We all know it's time to run the last lap and no one is focusing on anything else.

The train struggles along picking up speed as it starts downhill. My friends, my only friends, are daydreaming, heads bobbing in cadence with the train as it clicks and clacks toward our new home. They are silent, too silent; eyes empty, lips drawn into upside down smiles. Watching them down the length of the car is like seeing row after row of unemployed dead pan comedians sitting motionless, elbows braced on arm rests, chins supported in their palms. It's another of those times for analyzing private dreams.

Pain in the ass or great guy, the men on this train will be my immediate family for some time to come. Nobody likes everybody. In the weeks and months from Jefferson Barracks to Kingman, friendships have been formed and tiny hatreds have been put in place. Mostly, we just try to get along by minding our own business and holding our tongues. For instance, most cadet officers are less than popular but some manage very well. Olaf Arneson from my high school class is well liked but Ollie is about six feet three with the build of a football lineman and a ready smile. He enjoys being called "Olaf The Great." People built like Ollie tend to be given a bit of slack.

There are several cadets on the train who I knew back home. Shadow Eide lived up on Johnson Street just a couple of blocks from our house in Northeast Minneapolis. His real name is Robert but no one ever called him that. The first time I heard his real name was at mail call when the corporal sang out, "Robert Eide" and tossed him a couple of envelopes. Shadow sometimes played in our pickup baseball games up in Columbia Park. Al Greenstein is on the train. He went to a different high school but I used to see him around the Student Union at he U of M. George Hendrickson is from Ely, Minnesota. We met on the train leaving Minneapolis on our first day in the service. You have to like George and we have been friends ever since.

Another Edison High grad is Gehard Jacobs. It's nice to meet people you know, but the truth seems to be that the Army is a new life. You make new friends. What was happening before enlistment is a memory from a world that no longer exists. There doesn't seem to be any tendency for people to hang out together just because they came from the same old hometown.

It is not wise to let a friendship become important because the army sends people wherever they want them to be whenever it suits their plans. Each time we move we lose some friends. The people I met at Jefferson Barracks have been forgotten. There were eight of us living in a ramshackle shelter together. For a month we marched to three meals every day and coughed together every night battling our way through a murderous epidemic that took the lives of people around us. Now I don't remember any of their names. I picture them only as players in a bad dream.

Coe College was not a bad place at all but Joe Murphy and his smelly feet, Lemon Head, Bob Myers and the rest of my roommates are now in pilot training at air fields spread around the western part of the United States. Coincidence may bring some of us together later on but the odds are against it. Now, some of us have been ordered to Deming and others will take their advanced training at Albuquerque. Looking around the train it is easy to note that a few friendly faces have vanished. The best way to keep the same group of friends is to spend time with people whose last names have the same first letter as yours. The alphabet effect stretches a little in each direction. It's probable that people whose last names start with "H" through "R" are on this train and are my oldest friends. Mo Olivo is with us and George Hendrickson is a few seats down the aisle talking with Mackowski. The sword cuts two ways, I am happy to note that a few of the absentees were well known for big mouths and bigger egos.

Johnny Hudspeth is on our train. He's hard to understand sometimes but is fun to be around. One of the weekends at Kingman he just plain disappeared and everybody wondered where he could have gone. Kingman is a place where there is just no place to go and no way to get there anyway. We kept wondering until late Sunday evening when John came strolling into the barracks carrying a brand new set of hand tooled leather luggage. Since the Army furnishes all the luggage they want anyone to have and John needed a new collection about as much as a venereal disease, we circled around him and waited with raised eyebrows muttering, "What the Hell?" John slid the luggage under his bunk and gave us the facts.

One of the AT-6 pilots came from somewhere in Pennsylvania and knew a cousin of Johns and one way or another Hudspeth talked the Lieutenant into taking him along on a Saturday hop up to Reno. John said he had a little luck gambling and wound up with a couple of hundred bucks. "I'm tired of winning a few bucks and then losing it all back," said John. "I decided this time to spend the dough before it went back where it came from. It would be nice to have something to show for my winning. So I leave the table to go shopping and everything is closed. The goddam sidewalks are rolled up at midnight. So I go to the saddle store because that's the only place open. It's really not open but there's a light on and the guy inside is waiting for his girl friend to get off work at the club where she dances. The guy is happy to make a sale so he gives me a sweet deal on this luggage. What do you think of it? Nice?"

Two hundred bucks is a lot of money even when there's no place to spend it. We shook our heads and went back to our bunks. Nobody felt like answering Johnny's question. There was absolutely no chance the army would let him keep his prize so there was no desire to start a conversation about it. What we really wanted to know was about the women in Reno. Johnny said, "A gentleman never tattles," and went to sleep. The next day the luggage disappeared. It is a fair guess that Johnny found someone he could talk into taking it into town and putting it on a train to Pennsylvania.

G.I. Morris is on the train and going to Deming. Right now he is sound asleep with his feet stretched out in the aisle. G.I. doesn't like the army, but he hates it in a way that can be tolerated. G.I. seldom squawks or bitches, but he is a one hundred percent cynic about anything the Army says or does. He comes from Seattle, and formerly worked in a factory that manufactures B-24 Liberator Bombers. G.I. was an inspector who checked over the aircraft before they were sent out to the army. He says he has no confidence at all about the condition of the Liberators that they put together. His dialogue about the Liberators tends to be repetitive but he sounds sincere and a bit shaken when he says, "Listen, Jack I., I'm telling you how they make those goddam things. They got these women who don't have any idea what they're doing. The foreman gives them different colored wires and says to connect the red with red and green with green. Like that. Geez, I don't see how in hell those things fly. It scares the crap out of me. I used to thank God I'd never have to go up in those flying shit houses. You wouldn't believe some of the stuff the inspectors sign off on. If the Air Force ever tries to put me on B-24s I'll quit, no shit. I mean it!"

It's hard to figure out what he wants me to do about it. I say, "Well, G.I., better tell it to the chaplain. Up to now the Air Corps hasn't asked me to comment on the quality of their aircraft. When they do, I'll tell them I know a guy who should be called to testify."

He gives me his usual and final salvo, "Bullshit, Jack I., you don't even care, do you? You got a smoke?"

I pull out a pack of Phillip Morris filters and toss it to him. He puts one between his lips and says, "Got a light?" as he puts my pack of cigarettes in his pocket.

I say, "Yeah. When you toss me back the pack!"

Typically he will throw me the pack, I toss him a folder of matches. He lights up and wanders out the door with my matches. That's my buddy, Gerard Ignatius Morris. The Army Air Corps is not for everyone, but sometimes it seems the misfits are the most interesting people around. G.I. will probably sleep all the way to Deming.

I drop off myself and am awakened by squealing brakes as our train coasts to a stop. It is daylight and trucks are waiting to take us to the Deming air base. Our first look is the sight of small barracks which will undoubtedly be our living quarters. We also see one larger building that could be an airplane hanger. We are immediately marched to the squadron area and assigned to our new homes, two cadets to a room. My roommate will be Karl K. Nielsen from Payson, Utah. I know him as K.K..

CHAPTER 11

HELLO KINGMAN

We go back to the barracks and carry our footlockers outside where they will be picked up by trucks and carried to the train along with our barracks bags. It is almost sundown as we climb aboard our train and begin a ride to learn about aerial gunnery and sample social life as practiced in the Mohave Desert. Our destination: beautiful Kingman, Arizona and its noted aerial gunnery school. We have faced the red hot Santa Ana sunshine for more than four months. Now, the lieutenant commanding our trip to Kingman is telling us slowly but emphatically in a genuine Arkansas drawl, "Getchu selfs PREpared fo' a wum' welcome Mr. Kaydets. Ah am talkin' bout some fahr in the wood stove straight outa hell." His warning surprises no one.

We all know Kingman will be our next home and have a good idea of its location as computed by Rand McNally. We have noticed, in fact, that Kingman is not far from Needles, the desert training center where temperatures are said to blow the head off thermometers and shoot mercury a hundred feet into the air. Well, there is no possibility we can change the climate and this is the month of July. The farmers almanac says it will be followed by August whether we like it or not.

Everyone knows Kingman is located on Route 66 but who knows where that is? Nat King Cole's hit tune, *Get Your Kicks On Route 66,* is being played to death on jukeboxes everywhere. Take a seat in any restaurant, ice cream parlor or bar, if the tune is not already playing, put a nickel in the slot and hear Nat sing the names of every town on a highway that runs coast to coast. That's the sum of what we know about our next home.

We click along the rails thinking our own thoughts, gazing at the barren landscape and find nothing to lighten our hearts. As we approach sundown, the white-hot sun is losing its punch. In the lengthening shadows we see only sand and cactus. Mack, who has the seat next to me, says it looks like hell will look when the fire begins to die. We are experiencing an unusual lack of conversation as if everyone is thinking about home. Some of my friends established semi-serious relations with girls they met during our stay at Santa Ana. Such romances are more 'star crossed' than any pairings conceived by Shakespeare or shared by lovers on the Titanic. There is little chance the lovers will meet again, which usually is perfectly fine with the dashing cadet who is leaving town. However, we are a long way from home and need the comfort of a human voice that is not barking orders or telling us to get our head out of our ass. Even men who have enjoyed only the most casual relationships admit to a slight sense of loss. Perhaps a touch of sadness has them feeling thoughtful and silent. If their funk has about the same duration as when we left Cedar Rapids, it can be expected to remain at least until the smell of her perfume fades away.

The atmosphere is very unusual. Somewhere on a troop train there are always a few people who claim inside knowledge about where we're going and what will be happening. So far, on this trip, anyone who has interesting information is keeping it secret. The number of times Kingman has been mentioned stands at zero. Who wants to hear about Kingman anyway? We only know it as a sandy inferno where washed out bombardiers and navigators go to become tail-gunners.

Conversation picks up a pace or two when Hudspeth breaks silence to inform us that Kingman is an authentic cowboy town, a shoot 'em up board sidewalk muddy road relic from the real Wild West. John, who reads fan magazines, says Hollywood often shoots movies about gun duels right there on the street in front of the swinging doors on the old saloon. George recalls his folks once took him to Duluth to see a horse opera. He says Tom Mix was firing twenty shots at a time out of a six-shooter and never stopped to reload. Mack comments the Army should try to learn how he did it.

Nobody cares. It's almost midnight and everyone is thankful this will be a very short train ride. Lieutenant Everetts, the 1st Lieutenant in charge of the train, says we should probably reach Kingman about three a.m.. The Lieutenant is from Arkansas and expresses his opinion in a slow drawl that chews up about five minutes of empty riding time.

We visit the dining car and eat some chow. Later, when darkness falls, it converts my train window into a mirror. I stare at the glass and evaluate my new "butch" haircut. There isn't much left on top; it isn't pretty. My consolation is that no one who matters is going to see it, so why worry? It's time to lean back and let the rhythm of the train's wheels lull me to sleep. Later, the familiar tune of jabbering cadets ends a very brief slumber. The men are picking up barracks bags, pushing their way through the exits and jumping, sometimes tumbling, to the ground.

When we are all off the train, Lieutenant Everetts calls us to attention and orders us to form a column. We shrug our shoulders pick up our barracks bags and step off into the darkness trying to follow a rocky path that we can feel with our shoes but not quite see. The sky must be cloudy because there is no moon. The only available light flows from the caboose of our former train that is already bumping down the tracks and will soon vanish to leave our world in total darkness. However, as we stumble forward, we grow nearer to a blinking neon sign mounted on something somewhere in the distance. It acts as a beacon leading us to our destination. My guess is that it will not have been worth the trip when we actually see it.

Military precision has deserted us. Normal speed of troops on the march is four miles per hour. Our shuffling cadence is dragging along less than half that fast and becoming informal. We are a wobbly imitation of the crisp, close order discipline that has been practiced for many weeks. We brace ourselves and wait for the Lieutenant to rack us back and threaten anything nasty that enters his mind. That's what Lieutenants do when they're frustrated. Raggedy close order drill tends to frustrate them worst of all.

Lieutenant Everetts doesn't say a word. He must be as sleep happy as the rest of us. We shuffle along and are finally called to halt before a small building that is not quite totally dilapidated. Eventually, aided by information on the blinking sign, we recognize a barbershop. None of us believe what is happening. It's three in the morning and they are ordering us to line up for haircuts. I look at the big clock hanging in the back of the shop. The little hand is on three and the big hand points to six. Three-thirty; I must be dreaming.

Once inside, a makeshift hand-printed cardboard sign reveals that the cost of a haircut is seventy-five cents. Three barbers are busily swinging away with clippers, ignoring time wasting finesse that might be required by use of scissors. The order of the day seems to be, "get 'em in , get 'em out. If they holler, let 'em pout." A tall sergeant is supervising the operation, dutifully pushing cadets into chairs and whisking them out as quickly as they can be shorn. My turn comes and I shrink back. Site of the empty seat chills me. It brings back the gloomy finality of a vacant electric chair I once saw in a newsreel. The sergeant says, "Next."

I tell myself, "Oh, no!" and start to explain that I am very satisfied with my hair in its present condition. I run a hand over my nearly bald skull to demonstrate the thoroughness with which it was cropped earlier this same afternoon. I attempt, as politely as possible, to make clear there is no more hair on my head and that I must therefore unfortunately decline their services. The room becomes silent. The Sergeant stares in disbelief. I humbly offer to pay the obligatory six-bits and excuse the barber from further responsibility. It's not a matter of money; I am more than willing to banish my pride and pay their boldfaced "highway robbery" price of seventy-five cents for a two-minute clip. The problem is that I am Irish and am driven by nature to argue with all my eloquence against having my hair any shorter than it is when there is none on my skull to begin with. The Sergeant grits his teeth and turns to the Lieutenant, who drawls, "Don't you like it here, Mister?"

I get into the chair. The barber runs his clipper over my bare head a couple of times and is paid seventy-five cents for the pleasure. As soon as we are outside, Makowski says, "Hey, Jack I., you forgot to leave a tip."

All I want to do is get some sleep. We march toward the barracks area when the gloom is suddenly pierced by the howling of an honest-to-God coyote. It sounds like the animal is a long way off and I'm happy about that. K.K. Nielson, who comes from Provo, Utah, tells us to listen for an answering howl that will come from a different direction. We wait and the second coyote soon sends its reply. I ask K.K. how often those animals talk to each other like that. He says, "Every night."

I ask how long they keep it up. K.K. says, "All night long!"

I notice the weather is not as suffocating as we were led to expect. The air is calm but cool, good for sleeping. I decide not to ask K.K. any more questions because the hour is late and I am not getting any answers that cheer me up.

Thankfully, when we reach the barracks, the bunks are all prepared. I flop into the first one available. The last thing I remember is the distant wail of a coyote; the next thing is waking up and getting ready to march to chow and then to an orientation meeting where we will hear what comes next. It's 7:30 a.m. and the air is still fresh and cool. I am ready to believe that stories about Kingman being Mother Nature's frying pan are only latrine rumors and not to be taken seriously. Time will tell.

We cannot be far from the flight line. The crackle of engines turning over, coughing, catching on and starting up drifts in from somewhere close by. We listen as the engines find a rhythm that purrs, grows to a steady roar and then, finally, swells to a piercing scream as crews rev engines up to full power. The sound is totally new to us, as is the view of Quonset huts sprouting from a sea of sand. The rising sun outlines them and sketches a colorless, misshapen skyline. We don't know what kind of aircraft are making all that noise but they are loud enough to be huge.

Marching to chow, we watch cadets running to catch and climb into a row of trucks. I notice that almost everyone is carrying a towel on one shoulder. Mac says, "Skeet."

I ask him, "Why the towels?"

Mac says, "You'll find out the first time you fire one of those shotguns. If you want to shoot skeet you have to have a shotgun and if you need a shotgun, believe me, you better have a towel."

George says, "You're telling us those guns kick!"

Mac says, "Like a cancan dancer."

Before we get to the mess hall, we see a line of trucks full of men wearing GI uniforms. The trucks move at a steady pace while men standing in the back are firing at targets posted along their course. It looks like fun. After breakfast, we march to a very large Quonset where we will be addressed by a Lieutenant Colonel who will reveal what we can expect in the next six weeks.

We have learned to pay attention to these welcoming advisories. They are usually delivered by ranking officers at each new stop and it gives us a chance to think about what comes next. Colonels and majors are capable of giving us the real story in no uncertain terms. They have authority and are therefore able to provide dependable information, the kind not likely to change or end up as a latrine rumor. Knowing what to expect cuts down on "worry time." Most of us have learned our own strength and weaknesses. It's important to know what's coming and plan for it.

When the Colonel steps up to the microphone to welcome us, we are sincerely interested in hearing his message. The majority of us have never fired any kind of gun. There could be a few exceptions like George Hendrickson who comes from a town named Ely in northern Minnesota. Most people are hunters and fishermen in that territory. So here we are after about six months in the Army Air Force preparing for war. At this point, most of us know nothing about guns and none of us have ever been up in the sky in any kind of Army airplane.

The Colonel doesn't waste time. He tells us that the course

has been changed from five to seven weeks. Headquarters has been securing information from gunners on actual combat crews. What they learned has forced changes in the curriculum and made it necessary to add another two weeks to the training period. He describes, in general, what will be emphasized. One thing for sure, we are going to know more about machine guns than anyone in the old trigger-happy Al Capone gang. Before we leave this place, the colonel says we will put in forty hours on fifty caliber and six hours on thirty caliber models.

The Colonel explains that one of the most import lessons learned from the combat crews is that aerial gunners absolutely must be qualified to repair their weapons during the heat of battle. To do that, we must be able to determine what went wrong. For that reason we will spend twenty hours working on malfunctions and how to repair them. The course has us firing various turrets on the ground and in the air for fifty hours. We will also spend 44 hours learning how to manage gun sites and focus on targets.

The Colonel does not get a standing ovation when he announces we will be put through another twenty hours of aircraft recognition. Santa Ana pounded us mercilessly on that subject. Enough is enough. He finally gets to the subject most of us have been anticipating. Up to now we have been as flightless as turkeys. It will be nice to feel we deserve the word "aviation" that is proudly attached to our classification. He assures us we will spend several hours in the sky firing at air borne targets and makes the point by informing us that there will be familiarization flights on B-17 Flying Fortresses starting tomorrow morning. Flight lists including the time for trucks to the flight line and names of cadets in each group will be posted in all barracks at 1700 hours today.

Because most of us have so little experience with any kind of firearm, the Colonel makes it clear we will start at the bottom learning to handle shotguns and .22-caliber rifles. He says our air-to-air firing will be from four engine B-17 Flying Fortresses and twin engine B-19 bombers. Targets will be pulled through the air by AT-6 single seat advanced trainers.

I've never been up in the air in a B-19, but I do know something about them. They were actually passenger planes called the "Lockheed Orion" before the war. They were the flagship passenger planes for Northwest Airlines that is based in Minneapolis. My Uncle Greg worked at Wold Chamberlain airport and often talked about the Orion as the class of the fleet and a very dependable aircraft. I remember reading somewhere that several of them were refitted to carry bombs and sent to England for use against the Nazis. For whatever reason, the British gave the planes a trial and sent them back where they came from. Now, the Army Air Corps has apparently found a use for them in aerial gunnery training.

The Colonel stresses a few things that will be mandatory before any cadet can be eligible to graduate and win his aerial gunner's wings. Basically, each cadet will be tested and must demonstrate, without coaching, his knowledge of the nomenclature and malfunctions of machine guns including the ability to take 30 and 50 caliber machine guns completely apart down to the smallest screws. The process is called 'field stripping.' The cadet will then be given one hour to reassemble each gun. In addition, every cadet must demonstrate an ability to recognize and correct the most common malfunctions.

As a person who has never been a hunter or handyman, it is probable I would have a better chance of hitting a home run off Bob Feller's 105 mile an hour fast ball than succeeding at what the colonel has just proposed. Magazines and newspapers have carried stories written about the great success the military is having in the field of audio-visual instruction but, up to now, they haven't claimed any miracles. Not even my own mother would back me on this one.

I decide to follow a strategy that sometimes eases the tension when a person finds himself absolutely backed into a corner. My first move is to thrash around for a ray of hope. Often such a thing is difficult to find, but in this case there seems to be a tiny one poking through a cloud.

Experience tells me the Army is not in the habit of proposing things that will be a total waste of time. They don't put something into a program without being very certain most of us are capable of handling it. There is reason to believe I'm at least average. The argument makes sense and convinces me, at least temporarily, that given time and instruction, resourcefulness and inspiration will save the day. It is then that the good Colonel drops his final bomb.

"You will accomplish this feat in a single five day week," he says with finality. "Classes will begin on a Monday morning and you will be tested on the following Friday afternoon." He pauses, reads the disbelief in our eyes and says confidently, "I understand your uneasiness regarding this test but, believe me gentlemen, you will be amazed at your own capabilities. You will put those guns back together within one hour and have time left for a smoke!" He pauses and sweeps some lint from the shoulder of his uniform.

"The fact is, gentlemen, we have such great confidence in your abilities that we must insist that you do the job blindfolded. I repeat, blindfolded. This is war, men. There can be no exceptions. Gunners sent to combat from this school will be the best. Every cadet who graduates will possess the invaluable ability to keep his guns chattering through the dead of night or in a smoke filled fuselage."

The Colonel smiles, lets his words bore into our consciousness and casts a nod to the Tech Sergeant who immediately calls, "Tenhut!" We rise to attention, shaken but determined.

The Colonel says, "At ease," turns and walks away. He didn't say what week that test would be given. I remind myself that these hurdles are often not as bad as expected. I'm learning that smart soldiers save their worrying until a crisis is knocking on the door. There is some consolation in the Colonel's absolute, one hundred percent confidence that we can do the seemingly impossible.

I don't want to think about it. It's much healthier to speculate about our first plane ride. It would be nice to be in one of the groups scheduled for tomorrow morning. Who knows what it will be like? There's no use guessing. If it's enjoyable, the future should be fun. If flying bothers me, it will be necessary to hang in there and learn to love it.

We exit the meeting hall and wander into an atmosphere designed for fire breathing dragons. The old timers laugh and tell us this is nothing. They invite us to wait until afternoon.

How this can be? Last night the air was smooth and cool, great for sleeping. This morning, at reveille, it was sticky but not too uncomfortable. Now the place is already unbearable although the morning sun is hardly above the horizon. It isn't even noon! All we know about deserts is what we saw in books and movies. What we are looking at and trying to live with in this dreary hideout is well beyond anything we saw there. Rudolph Valentino couldn't last long enough to kiss the sheik's daughter in a place like this. We weren't expecting camels, but where are the sand dunes? If this is the desert why doesn't the ground feel like sand? It's like cement. We see cactus everywhere but nothing else growing. I've had a feeling that my throat is full of dust ever since reveille this morning.

A person has to wonder if pioneers in covered wagons ever passed this way and how many left their bones to parch. Maybe the cool nights will save us. The place is livable, even a little chilly after dark. We stop in front of the PX and go inside to get a Coke. We didn't expect air-conditioning and there is none. The Coke is ice cold and like everybody else, I chugalug a bottle and head for our hut to get some sack time. The idea is to strip down to shorts and spend the rest of the afternoon watching sweat run off your chest and arms.

When I wake up, the groups and flight times are posted. There's my name. Tomorrow will provide my first ride in the sky, preferably in a B-17 and not a BT 19. If an aircraft isn't good enough for Winston Churchill, it's not good enough for me. As twilight falls the air cools, the coyotes start singing and I drift to sleep wondering what the world will look like from up there.

This morning, after chow, the trucks are waiting and take us up to the flight line. We are treated to the sight and sound of a B-17 that is being warmed up to carry us above and around the great states of Arizona and Nevada. The pilots are walking around pre-flighting the plane, looking things over, and chatting about their adventures in Reno last weekend.

Reno is the place to go in this part of the country according to the AT-6 pilots who are allowed to sign out a plane and fly down there on weekends. It must be a semi-official privilege they get for putting in a dangerous week of dragging a long piece of cloth around the sky for totally inexperienced and wild ass gunners to shoot at. The word is that their planes get hit by mistake occasionally but as of now, none have actually been shot down.

As for Reno, the town has everything a growing boy could

desire if a person believes the tales in the PX and mess hall. Many of the stories are second hand since the pilots are 2nd Lieutenants and spend much of their spare time in the little cabin that suits them for an officers club. In any case, they describe some very high caliber weekends.

Reno is neither Sodom nor Gomorrah, but is famous worldwide as a place where divorces are quick and legal. As a result, the town is full of anxious divorcees looking for things to do. There is a legend that the ladies' first act of matrimonial freedom is to cast their golden rings into a pond not far from the courthouse. Their second act is to seek comfort and companionship while beginning a new and unfettered life. Even allowing for the normal poetic license permitted in relating off base experiences, Reno comes over as a place that a person might enjoy visiting. Realistically, it is not a dream fashioned for gunnery school cadets. A little voice says, "Forget about it." It's good advice but now and then a person has to think about crazy things that sometimes happen and wonder, "What if?" It makes time move faster. Someday I may become an officer and be able to go wherever I want to go on weekends.

There will be ten cadets plus our instructor, a staff sergeant, on the flight this morning. Soon he calls us together and says this will just be a short trip to familiarize us with the inside of an airplane and give us a look at the countryside. The Sergeant warns that the ride may be a bit bumpy because of thermal waves caused by high temperatures on the ground. Warm air rises and as it rises it cools. Desert temperatures react to the process and produce thermal currents and drafts that can toss an aircraft around. He says thermals are sometimes uncomfortable and can range from mild to violent, but are usually harmless. He says he will be showing us the different turrets and explaining how they work and will also talk to us about various parts of the plane.

When he finishes his briefing, we clamber up into the belly of the big bomber. I have to pinch myself. Books and magazines, movies and newspapers are filled with pictures of this famous aircraft. B-17 Flying Fortresses are making history over Europe. The plane is big, bigger than I expected, much larger than anything we used to see out at Wold Chamberlain. Everyone has read about the 8th Air Force and its missions into the heart of the German Reich destroying targets like Berlin and Stuttgart. Now, here we are trying to talk above the roar of its four engines running up, getting ready to take off. When it does, we'll be on board.

The instructor leads us through the bomb bay to the waist area where gunners spend their time. He tells us to sit on the floor and make ourselves comfortable for takeoff. The big ship bounces and squeals a bit as the pilot taxis out to the end of the runway and waits for the tower to give permission for takeoff. The four engines roar again as the pilot turns up the power and holds the brakes. When he turns it loose, the plane makes a quick jump and begins rolling slowly down the runway gradually gaining speed. Soon we feel the plane lift and ease itself into the air. The end of the runway quickly passes beneath us. It's hard to believe. After all this time, we are actually off the ground staring out the waist window of a huge Flying Fortress, looking down at the world. The instructor swings the waist windows open to give us a better view. We examine the gun mounts where the gunners would stand behind their 50 caliber machine guns.

For all we know, at this moment in a faraway sky, Army Air Corps gunners are opening waist windows and scanning the clouds for German fighter planes as a formation of B-17s fights its way home under attack by the Luftwafe. It is probable some of those gunners received training right here at Kingman. It is also possible some crews will not make it over the channel and return to their bases. The world has become a wild and crazy place, but everyone has to be somewhere and more and more the feeling solidifies that this is where I belong. These are not times to duck under the covers. It's good to feel right about what I'm being called on to do. At least for now.

The plane is very large, but was certainly not built for comfort. We are not invited to go forward to the bombardier's compartment, but here in the waist the walls are bare and the only place to sit is on the floor an the plane offers a variety of spells with which we are not familiar. To get through the bomb bay we had to follow a narrow catwalk with bomb racks on each side. Our instructor warned us not to step off the catwalk because it would not hold our weight. The bomb bay doors are designed to give way if any bombs should be accidentally released.

The Sergeant goes up to the flight deck to talk with the pilot and co-pilot. He returns and says the pilots want to get in some flying time and will take us over some historic scenery down below. We get word on the intercom that we will soon be passing over the Grand Canyon. The sergeant opens windows on both sides of the waist, we look down below and there it is, the Big Ditch. What a view! We fly over some other famous sites like the Petrified Forest and Hoover Dam. It's our first view of these places from the air. Everyone agrees that the pictures we have seen, even in the movies, do not do these places justice.

The Sergeant pulls open the trap door of the ball turret and cranks it into position below the belly of the Flying Fortress. Looking into it from our angle offers a wonderful but distant view of the scene below. We have a picture similar to looking through the wrong end of a telescope. When the trap door is open the guns point straight down toward Mother Earth. With the trapdoor closed and the gunner in position he is locked inside an iron ball that rotates to cover three hundred eighty degrees of the sky below the plane. It must be a lonesome job. The gunner cannot see any part of his own aircraft and has no unassisted way to escape from the turret during an emergency. He must hang in space until the turret is retracted and the trap door opened.

We wonder where the Air Force finds people willing to be locked in, lowered below the belly of the plane, and expected to spend hours waiting for something to happen. It is certainly not a place for anyone with claustrophobia. George Hendrickson is on the flight. We exchange quick glances.

Reality dawns slowly but inescapably. We, the future bombardiers, are the 'willing people' by default. It will not be necessary to volunteer. "The bombardier, as chief armorer on the crew, must be proficient in firing all turrets and all types of guns and ammunition. He must be ready for any emergency." That's what it says about bombardiers in the fine print and, if that's' what they want, that's what we'll do. No problem. We follow the instructor to the tail end of the ship and examine the rear turret where tail gunners must lie on their stomachs scanning the sky for enemy planes.

We are only up in the air for a couple of hours but it feels like a big step forward. After the Fortress drifts down and settles into a smooth landing, we scramble out onto the tarmac smiling and chattering in a very good mood. More than ever is there a feeling of certainty that this is the right outfit. Up in the air the temperature was comfortable. Now, as we jump down to the runway, we are hit with an effect similar to looking into a vat of molten steel in a busy foundry on a hot summer afternoon.

There can be no relief from it and riding on the truck taking us back to the barracks conversation is about the rhythm of this climate. Actually it could be worse. The mornings are not bad, but in the afternoon the temperature soars above a hundred degrees; sometimes way above like a hundred thirty. The feeling of sand in the mouth is just something that can't be helped according to the old timers. As long as the nights stay cool and dark the place is probably capable of sustaining human life if anyone ever wants to live here. That's not to say the wild swing of thermometers is the whole story. As with every place we've been from Jefferson Barracks to Coe College to Santa Ana, there's always something. Here at Kingman, we are getting comfortable with the taste of sand in the mouth every morning. We're learning to stay out of the bright sun at bad times of day. We've even learned to close our eyes and let the coyote love songs lull us to sleep. Now they've put a notice on the bulletin board warning about rattlesnakes.

Talk at the PX after chow centers around several cadets, perhaps as many as four or five who have decided after their first flight that flying is for the birds. One of them was in our barracks at Santa Ana. He was one of a few who were simply unhappy with army life. He talked about how much he missed his wife, how they had met in grade school and never gone out with anyone else.

She was, in his eyes, the greatest little gal in the world and what the hell was he doing out here wasting his time doing kid stuff, marching around, going to stupid classes. I remember telling him that kind of stuff didn't bother me. I shouldn't have said that. His eyes were red and bulging before the words were out of my mouth.

"That's your trouble, Jack I., nothing bothers you. You can take that shit. You go right along with those bastards. They tell you to jump, you jump. You think they care about you? Hell, no! I wish I'd never heard of this Army. I don't need it. I had a good life and a good wife. I want to go home!"

I knew better than to prolong the conversation. Maybe he was just having a spell of the blues and would get over it. I guess he didn't.

I asked one of the staff sergeants what would become of people who just quit. He said they would probably be made 'permanent party' at some God forsaken place where they can work in the mail room as buck privates for the duration.

It's difficult to understand why anyone would come this far, go through all the pressure at preflight school and then just quit. The sergeant says the infantry is on the lookout for warm bodies with no place to go. According to him, it might take an act of congress but in the end we're all in the same Army. He says if it was up to him, that's where the quitters would go, right in with the "dog face." Let's see how they like that.

Well, at least for now, I like flying and am anxious for my next flight. The class schedule is moving along and we are working on nomenclature and malfunctions right now. The most important malfunctions are things that make a machine gun stop firing; things like failure of the shell to go into the feedway, failure to extract the shell from the ammunition belt, failure of the shell to feed into the chamber, failure to fire, failure to control fire, failure to extract the shell from the chamber, and failure to eject the shell. At present we are working on symptoms and learning how to recognize the various failures. It's much less complicated than I thought it would be. Our training is concentrated and strictly 'hands on.' No one in my family will ever believe it, but when we go out to the range later this week for our test, we will be upbeat about recognizing and fixing those malfunctions. It will be 'duck soup.'

Right now, however, our excitement is focused on the B-19 aircraft running up its engines out here on the blacktop. It's still possible things will get going before we melt. Not that we have anything against the cloudless azure afternoon sky, but it is very warm here on the black top. We never ask what the temperature is anymore. Our only concern is survival. However, there is every reason to expect an environment more incompatible with human life when we reach a higher altitude. In ground school at Santa Ana we learned about the 'adiabatic lapse rate.' It states that warm air rises and as it goes up it cools at the rate of two degrees per thousand feet.

My choice would be to climb straight up to about twenty thousand feet and lose forty degrees in the snap of a finger. We know such a thing is not about to happen. The B-19 revving up a few steps away was not created for fancy trips into the stratosphere. I doubt it is even fitted for oxygen.

There are six cadets plus two instructors in our group. One of the instructors signals for us to get moving and we climb aboard the plane. We find it is very small compared to the B-17 we were passengers in the other day. The purpose of our mission is to learn how to lead a target when firing at a moving object. We will aim at a long strip of cloth being dragged by an AT-6. The AT-6 is a single seat low winged fighter that is usually used by cadets in advanced fighter training. I mention to one of the instructors that for some reason it looks familiar. He asks if I've seen any movies that showed Jap Zeros attacking all over the place. I say, "Yes."

He says those were AT-6s painted up with big red 'meatballs' on the wings and fuselage. He predicts the Jap air force will not run out of Zekes until Hollywood runs out of red paint. Just then, our little British reject jumps forward as the pilot releases the brakes. We roll down the runway and in no time at all I'm on my way for a second trip to the wild blue yonder. By the time we have reached a couple of thousand feet we are looking at each other and wondering what is going on.

The plane drops suddenly as if it has fallen down an elevator shaft. Then, "BAM!" A huge, invisible hand smashes against the underside of the ship and bounces it up in the direction of the clouds. Up, up, up and, then, DOWN! like a child batting a balloon around the living room.

One of the instructors notices our concern and stands up, grabbing the first possible handhold. "Don't worry," he advises. "We're just getting a little action from thermal currents but you'll get used to it."

Since there are no seats in this aircraft, everyone except the instructors are seated on the floor and bouncing on our backsides. I have only been in an airplane once before. On that occasion, in a B-17, nobody experienced or even thought about being airsick. Quietly, a queasy discomfort is sneaking into my stomach. A glance at my companions reveals some various and unusual shades of pallor. I thank God that if I begin to heave I will not be the only one. In a few moments I receive some comfort for my misery. One of the instructors, a tall thin GI with a raggedy mustache rushes toward the back of the plane leaping over our outstretched legs. We watch him bend over a red tin can and make full use of it. I hope there are more red tins somewhere and that they will be readily available. I am not officially sick but my stomach is rolling and quietly warning, "Just wait." One by one my fellow cadets parade to the rear of the plane making offensive sounds and filling their red tins. The odors coming from that area are now overwhelming, but the battering of the hull of the BT-19 goes on and it is clear that air sickness is contagious. It is also true that no cure is possible other than returning to solid land.

When the co-pilot rushes out of the flight deck door and charges past us, I become concerned and pray the pilot, at least, will be immune to this disconcerting malady. When the co-pilot goes back to the flight deck, he pauses to inform us that the force of the thermals is too heavy and we will be descending immediately.

As the plane drops nearer the earth, thermals ease up but there is no denying an appearance that the plane is delivering a load of cadavers. It was not a pleasant outing and nothing was accomplished but we have learned about the impact of thermal currents more powerfully than could be expected from any classroom. What's more, we set a record that can never be broken, only tied. It was a rarity, a flight where 100% of the people on board, including the flight crew, became airsick.

Going back to the hut for a shower and some sack time the bad taste and queasiness slowly fades into the merely unbearable phase. By the time the truck pulls into the squadron area, I know I'll be ready for a solid meal when its time for chow. A half-hour ago it wouldn't have mattered if the mess hall burned to the ground. That was a half-hour ago. I'm a healthy boy and the food is good here. I'll eat. We are looking forword to our next attempt at air-to-air firing. They say it will be on a B-17. It won't be right away however because we won't be around to enjoy it. This is the Monday morning that we climb into trucks for a ride to Yucca Flats. The trip will take us about thirty miles from our home base. We will spend a week, which is called on bivouac, although we will really not be roughing. There will be small barracks and other facilities such as a mess hall and regular bunks. Rumors are that they want to give us a week of physical activities and forced marches. It will be fun in the sun where temperature seldom rises above one hundred thirty degrees.

So far we have been attending classes, spending most of our time indoors. It may be a good idea to get out in the fresh air although the common feeling in our ranks is that close order drills and long hikes on the Mohave Desert in the summertime are very close to cruel and unusual punishments made illegal by our forefathers in the Constitution.

When the trucks pull up and drop us off at Yucca. It is eleven-hundred thirty hours, almost noon. As usual, when arriving at any unfamiliar location, we are assigned to barracks, throw our B-4 bags under our bunks and look for the bulletin board. We find it wired to a post, dangling at a peculiar angle surrounded by huts that will be our homes for a week. At least it will be our address for mail call, assuming the Armed Services Postal Service can find the place. The program for the rest of the day is scribbled in chalk and orders us to fall out for a ten-mile hike at thirteen hundred hours. While we are still shaking our heads and digesting the bad news, one of the sergeants accompanying us blows a whistle, which silences all conversation. He sees a few cadets who are barracks bound, heading for the sack. "Hey, you Misters, get your asses back here!" Most of us stop. The sergeant blasts three more times on his whistle and the escapees, heads down, shuffle back to the pack huddled around the board.

"Seems to me the Lieutenant offered you all the pleasure of policing up the squadron area," says the Sergeant. "Now if that don't appeal to you men, maybe the Lieutenant can think up something else. He tells me they might need help down at the bakery cooking up bread for you all." He stops and becomes confidential. "Now I heard some people on the truck bitchin' about the heat. Well, to tell the truth, it ain't much above a hundred–five right now and probably won't go up no more than another twenty during the entire afternoon. If any of you gentlemen ain't satisfied with that, wait till you slide between that old wood stove and the oven down at that bakery. If you ain't satisfied with that, wait till you pull open that big, heavy iron door to slide out them trays of sweet smellin' manna from Heaven and get yourself a blast of white hot heat on your face. Any volunteers?" Silence. His eyes travel around the group which has assumed the 'look down at the desk' position assumed by unprepared students.

"Well," says the Sergeant putting unusual emphasis on each word. "Let's just do as Lieutenant Everetts says. This here area is full of trash and it's in the Lieutenant's mind that we should clean it up the most fast as possible. Seems to me if we get right at it, we can get to chow and back and still put in a little sack time before we got to fall out for that hike." He puts the whistle back in his pocket and walks away. I watch him strut down the path that puts distance between him and our lousy job of policing up. There is no limit to the number of times the Army says 'WE' when they mean 'YOU.'

The policing doesn't last very long. At first, there were several of us picking up litter around the area. The heat is getting worse and worse. We are really on a big league desert without trees to provide the least little bit of shade. I am so busy cursing my situation that I don't notice I'm out there by myself. I hear a voice from inside the hut. It's Mack. "Hey, Jack I, what the hell you doing out there?"

"Policing up! What the hell you doing in there? They'll send your ass to the bakery?"

"It's a hundred-twenty-eight above out there. Everybody

174

decided we'd rather die in here. You better get in here. They're pushing for a revolution in here! Nobody wants to go on that little ten mile walk the Lieutenant thinks we might enjoy."

I have to believe they're setting somebody up for something. I hate the hike idea, but what can we say? The Army owns our bodies and if they decide to burn us up like some ancient Greek sacrifice to please the gods in Washington, all we can do is go quietly. It's up to them.

I am surprised to find out how serious these cadets really are. Maybe they have a point. Even in the hut, shaded from the sun, there's no relief. The men are lying on their bunks, motionless, as petrified logs. They aren't moving a muscle, no exertion whatsoever. Sweat runs down their bare bodies, forming tiny rivers running along arms, and legs. Perspiration drips from my hair to forehead and into my eyes. It stings and when I rub them, it stings worse.

The heat is brutal, much worse than anything we have experienced. Who could blame us if we decide not to go for a little hike? We're supposed to be training to fly around the sky and drop bombs, not open up new frontiers in the Wild West.

Well, actually, who could blame us? Realistically, it could be a very long roll call. Start with the top brass of the United States Army Air Corps and run down to Lieutenant Everetts and several noncoms who would give up a date with Betty Grable for a chance to see a cadet hammered in a court martial.

The top brass would be the worst. They don't concern themselves with blame or innocence. A lifetime of training has instilled in them the glory of strictly interpreting rules and regulations. Refusal by a body of cadets to accept an order would strike them as wonderfully unimaginable and worthy of the full force of the law. They'll be on it with savage eagerness of starving wolves and leave no meat on our bones. Joe Perfetti, a lanky guy from New York with a smartly trimmed mustache says he has an answer. He is granted the silence that says, "Let's hear it." Joe's message is simple, but perfectly attuned to an audience going crazy with the heat.

Perfetti says, "We don't do nothing to get in trouble. We don't refuse no orders or nothing like that. I mean they could have our ass for that. I'm saying we just disappear."

Somebody from a top bunk says in a choked voice, "You a magician Perfetti? I tell you one thing, Joe. Don't throw no blanket over me before you chant the magic word. I don't need any more heat!"

"Nothing to it," says Perfetti. "We just leave. Right now. Who can stop us? We find some places to hide. What about the freezer outside the mess hall? What I'm saying is, when they blow the whistle we won't be around, our watches were wrong so we started early and got lost. We stick together. No way they throw us all out. You think those GI instructors want a sunstroke? The Brass will be in their sacks snoring. The only thing could drag them bastards out in this heat is if they got promised a promotion.

Unbelievable, Joe is getting through, selling his nutty idea and these guys are buying it. Everybody goes dashing out the door, leaving the hut in a hurry, taking off for anyplace to hide, anything that looks like shelter from sunstroke and officers. The scene is amazing. One minute there are half-clad cadets heading in all directions. Suddenly there are none in sight.

Moe and Mack and I run for the mess hall and find it empty except for the cooks and some GIs who are washing dishes and mopping up. Mac explains to them what's going on. The GIs who are doing K.P. think it's the greatest thing since Haley's comet and help us find hiding places.

176

We have a good thing going. The mess hall is a much larger place than our barracks which are nothing more than small huts. The air is actually breathable. We've been hiding about an hour when Moe peeks out the window and sees one of the GI's leading a small group of crestfallen cadets from our barracks, including Joe Perfetti, back to the squadron area. The game is up. We brace for whatever punishment will eventually be leveled. No one bothers us when we crawl out of our hiding places. Mac and Moe go back to the hut. I decide to join the group surrounding the bulletin board. No one seems terrified. Cadets are standing in small groups laughing and talking about the usual rumors and off base experiences.

Something is out of kilter. Officers should be taking names and kicking butts. Where are they? No way will we be allowed to get away with our brief AWOL this afternoon. I spot Bernie Parsons in the crowd. He doesn't seem disturbed so I ask him, "Where's all the brass? I hope they take it easy on us."

Bernie asks what I'm talking about. I tell him I think Lieutenant Everetts is a pretty good guy, but somebody is going to chew our asses out bit by bit. I think we made him look bad and 1st Lieutenants don't like that.

Bernie asks again what I'm talking about. I tell him I'm talking about us all sneaking away so we wouldn't have to take a ten-mile hike in this damn heat. He says, "You kidding me? Who took off?"

I say, "Everybody in our hut."

When he stops laughing, he says. "Don't you guys ever read the bulletin board. Whose stupid idea was that?"

I tell him, "Perfetti."

He says, "That figures." He's one of my best friends but he's laughing like an idiot and can hardly wait to take off and entertain the crowd with our stupidity. He's over there now making a big thing of the story by waving his arms and pointing around. I follow his finger and it points toward the bulletin board where I read:

TODAY'S HIKE POSTPONED
WILL BE RESCHEDULED.
MOVIE TONIGHT - MESS HALL 1500 HOURS

For the first time I realize how stupid we really look. Maybe it's not so bad. The hike was called off, how can they we penalize us for missing an event that never happened. Perfetti is one of those people who are as lucky as they are foolish. Maybe we'll come out all right and not get too bad a penalty. Even so, it isn't something to feel good about. No question we will be laughed at and pointed out as idiots. There's more to it than that. We did a stupid thing and, in this man's army when you do something where your head is really up your ass, such stupidity becomes a classic, a recurring fable to be enlarged until those who were involved won't even recognize it.

There's my good friend Bernie over there telling the story to anyone who will listen. He has a very large, attentive audience laughing it up right now over by the mess hall. They can yak as much as they want, my worries are about something different.

The problem could concern Lieutenant Everetts. What if the brass thinks he lost control of us and calls him on the carpet? If that happens, will they put some kind of penalty on the people in our hut? During chow and marching to the mess hall, I watch the Lieutenant eating with the other brass. Nothing about their conversation seems unusual. No one is pointing at us. Although we haven't heard anything to the contrary, no one can be sure we've heard the last of our little snafu.

We sweat it out all during our week at Yucca. It appears bygones are bygones, everything has been forgotten. The week at Yucca goes fairly fast. We do a lot of physical training, even got to throw a football around and play some softball. It really feels nice to have a bat in my hands again. It's interesting how people gradually adapt to the heat. I'm beginning to believe the human body can adjust to any situation if given the chance. The weather hasn't turned cooler but now toward the end of the week we are able to ignore it and carry on with our business. This morning we finally took the postponed long hike that terrified us last Monday. It was a long walk but not nearly as bad as advertised. We returned to Yucca about noon and stopped just long enough to get some chow and climb on the GI trucks for a bouncy half-hour ride back to Kingman.

Thinking about it this morning as we boarded trucks to return to Kingman, I realized what a welcome relief it was to forget about marching to classes and spending the days looking at the guts of machine guns. It has been only a week but the general atmosphere is like going home from a vacation. Few things in life can be more satisfying that sliding into your own bed after being away and here we are, back in our own sacks after a week in the sun and a bumpy pounding by the rear seats on the back of a GI truck.

Hudspeth was really right in his description of Kingman. Any fans of hootin', tootin' ridin', shootin' movies must feel a vague delusion of having been there many, many times. Downtown Kingman looks and feels exactly like a shoot 'em up town from the old west. It wouldn't be surprising to see Gene Autry come clomping through those swinging doors riding a horse and crooning about sagebrush.

Our trucks stopped there and Lieutenant Everetts gave us fifteen minutes to jump down and run into the saloon for Cokes. The board sidewalks get a man thinking one of the bad guys in a black hat will jump out of a dark corner with guns blazing. It's good to be back in our own beds. Everything about Yucca was tough. The heat sapped everybody's strength and there was no social life, which put it on a par with Kingman. Just the same, it's good to be home.

Nights in Kingman are always cool and made for sleeping. Everyone is tired tonight. The hut is very quiet. People have hit the sack early and fallen asleep very quickly. No card games or rolling dice tonight. Our peace and quiet lasts for a couple of hours before a tremendous racket starts. It seems that I have barely closed my eyes when there is a pounding on the door amid shouts of "Everybody up, everybody out. Five minutes to get into fatigues and fall in."

We roll out of the sack, throw on our fatigues and plunge outside. It's cold and dark out there. We fall into ranks and the cadet captain calls, "Ten-hut." Lieutenant Everetts walks up and down our ranks as we stand at attention. He does not appear happy. I note the parade ground is full. It is not only the cadets from our hut out here. If this is some kind of punishment, it includes everybody, not just us. This could be good news. Finally, the Lieutenant stops and says, "Parade rest!" It's not warm at all out here. Some of us are shivering.

After a pause and another look up and down the line, the Lieutenant begins his little speech, which we don't really care to hear. "Good evening, Gentlemen. As you may recall, the intense heat at Yucca Flats forced us to cancel our scheduled hike on last Monday afternoon. It has come to my attention that some of our cadets broke ranks and decided their private plans would not permit them to join our full squadron on that occasion. Apparently they were sensitive to the unbearably high temperature and felt justified in making a decision to avoid whatever discomforts the sun might impose. The matter was called to the attention of Colonel Schnell who prefers to make such decisions himself. He considers them to be his own responsibility. Therefore, this evening being pleasantly cool, he has suggested the entire squadron take advantage of the climate and spend an hour or two in moderate temperatures perfecting its close order marching techniques." He turns to the cadet captain and nods. The cadet captain shouts "Ten-hut." We snap to attention, the Lieutenant walks away and is soon swallowed up by the darkness.

The cadet captain orders, "Form a column of squadrons, Forward, harch." Off we go: hut, hut, hut, hut, into the night. The later it gets the colder it becomes. We are suffering the punishment known as a 'moonlight drill.' It could have been worse. They could have ordered us to attend five hours of venereal disease movies. Someone must have told them we hate close order drill even more than venereal disease movies. Any way you look at it we are marching to nowhere and hating Joe Perfetti more and more with every step. It is no comfort to know that the rest of the squadron who did nothing wrong feel the same about us as we feel about Joe.

Every now and then a glance up at the sky reveals that it is almost entirely covered with stars. It's hard to believe there could be so many stars in the sky at one time. In Minnesota we like to look at stars as much as anybody, but never have I seen so many in one place. The air over the desert must be very clear. There are so many stars that it's a wonder the sky can hold them all. The magic and wonder of the blinking stars has a hypnotic effect. It has me stomping along without thinking about time or the monotony of close order drill.

Obviously we are being punished, but I remain star struck until our marching finally ends and we are back in the sack. It was a chilly experience but one well worthwhile. We paid our dues to the

Lieutenant and should be free of any other disciplining for the time being. Probably, someday, there may be an opportunity to look through a large telescope at stars that have yet to be discovered but never, never will I forget the millions that shimmered over Kingman on this cool evening.

Well, we got back from Yucca on Sunday and Monday. We had some fun shooting skeet and firing at moving targets from the back of a truck but today is the day we get to pull the trigger. We are ready to climb into a B-17 and are scheduled to do our first air-to-air firing from a B-17 this morning. An AT-6 will drag a long target along behind him and we will take turns firing. Each cadet will fire shells with a different colored tip making it possible to tell who puts a hole in the target.

For the first time we will be up in the air experiencing the true feel of firing at a target moving through the air. Our group is standing on the runway waiting for the GIs on the gas truck to top off gas tanks on our B-17. We don't expect to have any thermal wave trouble on this trip. The Flying Fortress is more than twice the size of the B-19 in which we got bumped all over the sky the other day.

Finally we get a signal from the pilot and our instructor says, "Let's load up." We climb in, go back to the waist and sit on the floor as the four props lift us off the ground and pull us up to our altitude.

In the waist, the gun ports are already open and the 50 caliber machine guns are mounted for us to fire over the left wing. Our instructor very carefully explains to us what the procedure will be. When it is a cadet's turn on the gun, he will watch for the AT-6 pulling the target and aim the gun. When the instructor makes certain the burst will clear the huge wing of the Fortress, he will say, "Fire!" At that point, the cadet will fire a burst at the target.

Although the B-17 is much larger and more stable than the plane we were in last week, it is still subject to thermal currents, although to a lesser degree. I watch the first cadets take their shots and notice that at times a wing will come up just as the instructor calls 'Fire!' I can see that it will be wise to give the wing plenty of clearance.

When my turn arrives, I track the target, get it in the sights and when the instructor calls 'Fire!' I shoot. The burst clears the wing, but a single shell makes a small arc and falls into the wing creating a small hole. The shell was obviously a *short round*, a shell that does not fire correctly. It was moving so slowly that we could see it fall. The instructor does not mention anything about it and I don't take it seriously. Having seen pictures of Flying Fortresses limping home from their targets looking like flying sieves, I can't imagine that a single hole in the wing poses any danger. Obviously, neither do the instructor and other cadets on the plane. We continue our practice without any conversation about the short round.

We finish our mission and ride a truck back to the barracks. A few minutes later, a GI comes into the barracks and asks for me. He says he has orders to drive me back to the flight line. We get into the jeep and he tells me the pilot is roaring that he will have my ass and is spitting nails. We get to the flight line and I see a 2nd Lieutenant standing under the wing of the B-17. I'm hardly out of the jeep before he starts. I salute and say, "Aviation cadet Jack I. Moore reports as ordered, sir."

He doesn't return the salute and calls me a son of a bitch. He shouts, "You could have killed us all, you stupid bastard. I'm about to personally see they kick you out with your ass in a sling. You're through as a goddam cadet. I'm bringing you up for a court martial. Your ass is numbered. Now get the hell back to your barracks." He pauses. "One question; why the hell didn't somebody come up and tell me what happened?"

I answer, "No excuse, sir."

He says, "Get your ass outa here!"

I salute. He walks away.

The jeep takes me back to the barracks. The driver asks, "What the hell did you do to that guy?" I don't have an answer because as far as I know there isn't one. When the jeep drops me off I don't know what to do. I find myself in a terrible position and whether or not I did anything wrong isn't important. It all comes down to how they look at it. In three days my world can fall apart and its out of my control. I decide to look for the only help that seems to be available. I'm not officially restricted to the barracks yet, so I head for the church.

It's a small building lighted by a few rows of colored candles and the red light next to the alter. Somehow it seems cool and comfortable. I pass up the pews, walk to the front and kneel at the communion rail. I say one Hail Mary after another and ask her to help me. No one else is there. I am desperate. I think about how far I have come and what it will mean to fail.

When I feel absolutely hopeless, I begin to pray again. I pray and pray because I have no other hope. Finally, I make the sign of the cross and leave the church. I feel better. I feel that it might turn out all right. When I get to the barracks, Moe Oliva says a GI was here and left an envelope. I open it and learn I am confined to the barracks until further notice. I am ordered to report to headquarters at 930 hours on Friday morning.

There is too much silence in the barracks. It is as if I don't exist because no one wants to picture himself in my situation. Even my best friends like Moe and Mack keep to themselves although I know they share some of my anxiety. They know there is nothing they can say to change things or make me feel better.

I think of the matter 100% of my waking hours, which means most of the time. Sleep does not come easily. Two things are certain; I will have to appear at the hearing and I will be given a chance to plead my case. What is my case?

(1) The tech sergeant who was in charge of our group is responsible for no one notifying the pilot. He told me when to fire; all the other cadets heard that. Since he was in charge, it was up to him to notify the pilot.

(2) I do not think it would be wise to blame the instructor. In the first place, I don't believe he did anything wrong. Secondly, the Army does not like excuses and shifting blame to him would sour my best witness. In a real sense, he and I are in it together.

(3) The round that entered the wing was definitely a 'short round' and he can confirm it. It is clear that the burst was not carelessly fired into the wing. All of the bullets except one, the short round, cleared the wing. It was clearly a defective shell.

Now it's Friday morning and I'm sitting outside the huge double doors behind which the brass are holding their meeting. I was met when I came in by a captain who advised me about the military aspect of presenting myself upon entering. He was pleasant but there was nothing new in his advice. Actually, all he did was disturb one more, last interview I was having with Holy Mary, whom I was praying would be my real advocate.

Finally the doors are open and the captain signals for me to enter. I walk down the center aisle, hold a salute and say, "Aviation cadet Jack I. Moore reports as ordered, Sir."

The Colonel at the head table says, "Be seated." I take the chair that is open for me. I am stunned momentarily by the size of the room and the number of people in it. At least twenty high ranking officers are seated at the head table and the balance of the room is filled with officers ranked from lieutenants to majors.

The chief officer describes the charge and asks me to tell my side of the story. I explain that the instructor gave me the order to shoot and quickly add that I am not blaming him because I know that he, like myself, felt the area was clear. I also point out that the bullet that caused the hole in the wing had to be a short round because it was the only one in the entire burst to fall short. I try to emphasize that I did not fire an entire burst into wing. It was damaged by only one bad cartridge that misfired.

When I finish, the Colonel asks if anyone else has any questions. Nobody does. He then asks if anyone has any comments to make. First Lieutenant Everetts our commanding officer stands up and there is no question in my mind that what he says next will determine my fate as an aviation cadet. I don't know what he will say. He has not been popular with the squadron and the little revolt out at Yucca Flats gave him a black eye for losing control of the group. He got a little revenge by calling that 'moonlight drill' but if he wants some more, he has a chance right now to plunge a dagger through my heart. He owes me nothing, but he is my commanding officer and without question his opinion carries heavy weight. My heart pounds and thoughts of my dad flash through my mind. I see him in his field artillery uniform battling in Africa. He salutes me and smiles. The smile fades, he turns and walks away. There is nothing I can say. Lieutenant Everetts rises from his chair and identifies himself to the Colonel. The Colonel gives him permission to speak. I hear his Arkansas drawl, as he proclaims very slowly but firmly, "Ah don't b'leve the kaydet was at fault and ah thenk he should be restored to duty as soon as possible."

No one else in the room has anything to add which gives me a flicker of hope. The Colonel tells me to go back to my barracks and wait for their verdict. I salute, make my way down the aisle to the door and leave the building. I think I'll be O.K. thanks to Mother Mary and Lieutenant Everetts. I say Hail Marys in gratitude as I head back to the barracks with hope in my heart. I wonder why the pilot didn't testify against me. I didn't even see him in the room. It's no use worrying about him any more. What's done is done; I can only wait.

Early in the afternoon, a runner comes into the barracks and hands me an envelope. I open it and read that I am cleared to return to duty immediately. I say a few Hail Marys for the Lieutenant and myself before heading for the mess hall to join the rest of our squadron, which is already at chow. I find a chair at our squadron's table. Bernie is the gunner and passes me a plate and silverware. No one says hello. They know if the decision had gone the other way I would not be here. The food is great and my appetite has returned. We march from the mess hall to the trucks that will take us to the range for our test on malfunctions, a test that must be passed for graduation. This one and then, starting Monday, the first session on thirty and fifty caliber machine guns. We have five days to develop the ability to detail strip and reassemble the guns blind folded in one hour each.

Today, the range is setup for our test on malfunctions and repair. There are seven little open sheds in a row. Each shed has a gun with a different malfunction. The challenge is to 'hand charge' the gun and pull the trigger. The cadet must then determine what the malfunction is and explain how to repair it. We had good instructors and most of us go through the line very quickly.

On the truck returning to our base, it is still difficult to believe how quickly and completely they taught us to handle weapons we never dreamed of firing. We all hope they will do the same kind of job getting us through the blindfold tests. We really have only four days to get ready. If we do, we'll be aerial gunners entitled to wear silver wings, but still aviation cadets on the way to advanced training as bombardier-navigators.

Nobody seems to care about my little trip through hell. It was never mentioned at its worst and causes no conversation now that it has ended.

This is not a surprise. The United States Army Air Force is neither a boys club nor Greek fraternity. You are your own man. When everything goes SNAFU, you give it your best shot and either beat the system or try to smile as they put the blindfold over your eyes. This is an anything-can-happen outfit where we are already acquainted with a "There but for the grace of God go I" philosophy. The phrase steadies us when a friend is struggling and keeps us realistic when everything is downhill and shady. My trouble was my own business. The crisis is over and that's that. The outcome is not a topic for killing time in the latrine. We seldom hear gossip in conversations at the PX or in the barracks. Rumors, humor, and hyperbolic bitching? Yes, by the hour. Pure, over the back fence, tongue wagging about someone else? Never! Who could they get to listen?

The week is slipping by. We are spending long days working on the project that demands us to detail strip and reassemble 30 caliber and 50 caliber machine guns in one hour each with our eyes covered. We are warned that as soon as a gun is fully detail stripped, an instructor will mix the parts around on the table before allowing us to the begin to reassemble The idea is that we must succeed by knowing the "feel" of each part rather than attempting to remember where we put the part on the table. They want us to show the ability to perform this task under conditions that might be encountered in a smoke filled fuselage. When the machine is reassembled, we will hand charge the gun and pull the trigger. It will not be loaded, but must function. Cadets who hear the trigger click tomorrow will be awarded wings on Sunday and be on their way to advanced bombardier-navigator school somewhere in the Air Force Western Command area.

Knowing the quality of the cadets in our group, there should be no reason that any of us will not pass this last test. After four and a half days of lectures, films, and close, hands-on, supervision, the prophecy made by the Colonel our first day on the base is about to ring true. Tomorrow is the Friday he promised we would complete the blindfold test in less than the allotted four hours and have time for a smoke. He's going to be proved correct and, on Monday, we are going to get our gunner's wings and leave the burning sands of Kingman for our next, so far unidentified, home base.

Everyone is wondering where we will be sent for advanced training. The rumor mill is grinding but the mirror in the latrine shows that my hair is beginning to grow out. I don't care where we go as long as we get there in the daytime and there isn't a barbershop.

CHAPTER 13

DEMING ON THE GROUND

New Mexico calls itself the "Land of Enchantment" but, other than a weird climate, Deming Air Base offers the usual odors and facilities encountered at other short stops on our way to glory. A barracks is still a barracks, a bunk is still a bunk, and a mess hall is a place to eat. Weather is always a factor and, in that category, Deming is a real humdinger. It seems preordained that whenever we go into a new area we find ourselves adapting to unfamiliar combinations of wind, rain and average temperature. However, we did find one surprising similarity between Deming and Kingman.

They say rain is as rare in Deming as we found it in the Mohave Desert and Yucca Flats. According to the captain who delivered our prescribed welcoming speech the place is practically bone dry with an average rainfall of only nine inches per year. He says we are in a zone called "arid continental." The news provokes Mack to whisper, "My God, they've sent us to another desert."

A second unexpected revelation is that we can look forward to fighting for breath while stomping around the drill field or running half mile laps in physical training. We are now residing at an altitude of 4,331 feet above sea level. Since we have just lately pulled in from Kingman, definitely a sea level community, our lungs will need some reconditioning. Fortunately, having been tested in the pressure chamber at Santa Ana, we will all be able to recognize early signs of anoxia and be ready to call for help if our lips or fingernails turn blue. It will be a tribute to the general good health forced on us by the Army if we are able to do anything but sleep for the next couple of weeks.

Apparently, we will also be meeting other atmospheric effects in our new home. The captain created a minor shock wave by warning that the altitude will cause unstable temperatures that sometimes drop as low as 30.5 degrees in winter. Even in Minnesota, anything below thirty-two degrees is freezing. We are now moving into October and wondering what comes next. Will bad weather force the powers in command to ground all aircraft and toss us into the infantry? Probably not, but as long as we are here, it would be fun to anticipate the possibility of a White Christmas. We don't even have time to think about it. The captain quickly informs us that any snow will melt as soon as it hits the ground. He then adds that when those powerful winter winds howl they will also be filling the air with blowing dust. There may be some compensation in falling snow and howling winds. At least we won't feel pain in proportion to that of our fellow cadets from California and the deep South. It will be a nice payback to them for being so amused by the spectacle of our semi-cremation in the perennial heat wave that cooked us in Kingman. Mack says as soon as the first cold wave hits we should slide over to their barracks and invite those bastards to a snowball fight. G.I. says he'll be satisfied to see a couple of frozen ears and maybe a nose or two turning blue. One thing for sure, those guys are going to be crowding close to the fire and cussing Mother Nature.

Leaving a desert where the red hot earth sizzled right through heavy GI shoes and finding ourselves shipped to another sand pile that may freeze our toes should surprise us more than it does. Actually, the move is being calmly accepted as just another cruel turn of events. A person could probably dig around and find an element of disappointment in there someplace but in our untypical world, what else is new?

The environment here at Deming is new to us and possibly threatening. We come from all around the USA but no one seems to have heard of an 'arid continental climate.' Adjusting to conditions that lack any familiar pattern is difficult. Watching mercury run merrily up and down the thermometer provides a fascination similar to watching colored fish in an aquarium. The atmosphere changes from hot to cold without rhyme or reason. Mellow, bright and sunny afternoons suddenly turn gloomy with a threatening overcast. We have been told that heavy turbulence in the afternoons makes accurate bombing difficult while night bombing is usually treated to starry skies and smooth sailing. There must be a reason for such a phenomenon but no one seems to know what it is. In our short time here we have spent some hours in ground school trying to absorb lectures and theories about factors that affect flight including meteorology. We have wondered if there is an explanation for the unusual atmospheric situation in Deming that makes dropping bombs difficult at a certain time of day. There probably is not.

Old timers tell us we can throw our books out the window on this one. They say only God can change the weather and He never passes through Deming. Our meteorology instructors don't seem to care one way or another. They are mostly paddle feet who fly only when they can catch a hop to El Paso for a weekend in Jaurez. A little turbulence clubbing an AT-11 Beechcraft Airplane around the sky interests them about as much as the chance for a blind date with Madam Ouspenskya.

For us it will be important, a hurdle to be faced sometime in the future. Anything that can short circuit graduation at this late date is definitely food for thought. The stories about night bombing present an entirely different picture. According to legend, at dusk, just about the time werewolves are pushing up the lids of their coffins, everything changes. The air calms down, clouds break up and the sky becomes a moonlit path to the target. The world is soft and cozy, targets are easy to see and the shack down below seems to welcome a bomb with open arms. If true, it offers an excellent reason for saying *"Get your hits at night!"* the local slogan. We're tired of hearing it repeated over and over, but are ready to believe it must have some basis in fact. We won't know for sure until we get up in the air.

Because there are no unmarried young ladies in the cadet lounge, the subject of bombing, sometimes referred to as "pickle aiming," underlines most conversations. In the fashion of regular humans, cadets talk about what they think and what they think about, other than pinup girls, is posting a circular error of 230 feet or less and putting four "hits" right on target.

In the final analysis everything will depend on proficiency. Proficiency is the Army Air Corps word for "Show us what you can do. It has to be our way and it better be right." Proficiency, as they see it on their records, will be the golden egg that can put a cadet where he wants to be, but by now we have enough experience to know the United States Army Air Corps will not make it easy for anybody. They know what they want and they want it demonstrated, on the ground and in the air, before qualifying a cadet for all those good things like a commission, gold bars, and a ten-day furlough. Some of their hurdles are very specific. We have been told that in the judgment and on the records of the United States Army Air Corps a bombardier cadet must prove himself proficient by dropping at least 150 bombs with an average circular error of 230 feet or less. At least four of the bombs must be direct 'hits' that impact inside the target circle. Direct hits are sometimes called "shacks." Last night I wrote a letter to my mother trying to explain, as simply as possible, what will be necessary in order to graduate in a few months. After several aborted attempts that ended in the latrine garbage can, it seemed wise to throttle back and tell her the usual things that I know make her feel better. Holding the message to things she needs to hear, Mom will be pleased that I am feeling fine, working hard, and obeying her orders to be careful.

If I had been writing to my dad, who is in the field artillery somewhere over seas, he would have understood the process although nomenclature is different from one branch of the Army to another. Once a person can identify a few abbreviated terms, the procedure becomes as simple as understanding the difference between a CE (Circular Error) and a hit. Each cadet will drop approximately 160 bombs that count and every one of them will be photographed, measured, and entered in his record. The CE is a continuing average of the distance by which a cadet's bombs have missed the target circle. The target is small and we bomb from an altitude of eleven-thousand feet so a direct hit is comparable to a long home run or a blind date with a pretty girl. They say there is no smile big enough to express the joy of a cadet who has just watched one of his one hundred pound sand-filled bombs send up a puff of dust as it hits inside the target circle. It helps his CE because the bomb counts zero error and lowers his CE average. If it hits anywhere inside the circle addition, he gets credit for one of the four shacks he needs to qualify in tactical bombing. Nothing could be better.

At the other end of the scale, no error can ever be listed as worse than 700 feet. That's the limit. For whatever reason, possibly in an effort to avoid further embarrassment to anyone who might launch such a wild ass missile, the Army has decreed that errors of more than 700 feet will be considered to have a score of 700 feet, and will be scored as such. People were wondering in the barracks last night what an error of 700 feet would be. Not having dropped any bombs that were measured we can only guess, but all that changes today. McQuitty says it's two football fields and one end zone. I'll take his word for it but it seems to me, if anyone pitches it out there seven hundred feet off target more than a couple of times, he will need to be an 'HB' ("Hot Bombardier") to have any chance of getting his average down.

Mack brought the subject up at chow and we spent some time guessing what kind of wanton destruction a hundred-pound bomb might be capable of when dropped from an altitude of five thousand feet or more from any likely release point around the base. G.I. named a few locations that he wouldn't mind seeing victimized by such a wild pitch but, in the end, it was concluded that a 700 foot error would only be likely if the pilot got lost and flew some poor cadet to the wrong target. From everything we've heard about the unfriendly turbulence that sneaks in and starts thumping airplanes on most afternoons, if some cadet does throw one out there a country mile, it will probably be in the daytime when the 'arid continent' wind is howling. Some of the cadets who are already bombing for score seem very frustrated. They rant on and on, seemingly unable to stop. Personally, my feeling is that conditions couldn't be that bad but as long as we haven't started flying, it's not my problem. Someone should tell them to shut up and go get another milk shake but, since I've never been in their position, common sense whispers, "Keep your mouth shut." To be fair about it, there could be more to their crying than bad sportsmanship. Somewhere along the line, most of us learn to respect the old adage that tells us "Where there's smoke there's fire." Many cadets who are currently dropping bombs apparently feel the same way. The slogan around here, repeated ad nausea, is "Get your hits at night!" Another gripe common among some cadets reflects their disappointment upon learning that Deming is not one of the Seven Wonders of the World. Certainly we would rather be in Hawaii, but we have already visited a few places that promise less than what we find here. For my money, Deming is not even close to matching the dreary corner of fiery hell that we found in Kingman. We have checked Deming out on the area map that is used in our classes for pilotage navigation. Pilotage is navigating with your head and eyes. From what we have been able to gather so far, it is a method of following railroad tracks, rivers, mountains, highways, water towers and various checkpoints along the way. It sounds very similar to techniques used by the fearless and often unfortunate pilots who gave their lives in establishing a nation-wide airmail service back in the twenties and thirties.

The town of Deming is a one day ride on a good horse from several small towns scattered within thirty or forty miles from here. Closest are Las Cruces, Silver City, Lordsburg and nationally famous "Truth or Consequences" which took its name from a very popular radio game show.

In relation to size, it can be said that a cadet on open post, on foot and in no particular hurry, could probably manage a complete circle of downtown Deming in less than half an hour. It might take a bit longer if he stops at the Indian Shop to look at souvenirs. The Indian shop offers the possibility of examining, or even buying, gifts from a large supply of baskets, pottery, rugs and jewelry. If so inclined, he will be welcome to slake his thirst at the Central Bar or, if he prefers, dine and drink at the popular Mission Café. As a backup, if nothing of interest appears on the horizon, he may decide to pause and rest his feet inside the trendy Greyhound bus terminal. In the event he feels tempted to leap on one of the busses and leave town, he will find free ice water to swig while he regains his senses in the spiffy, air-conditioned passengers lounge. If he feels so inclined, he can sit in lonesome comfort until the cows come home or even longer, depending on what he's waiting for. If he enjoys watching people coming inside to get free ice water on a hot day, he will be well entertained. If he's hoping against hope for female companionship, odds against meeting a pretty girl out for a good time would offer about the same chance for success as riding down into the Grand Canyon on a three-legged mule. Actually, in it's own area, Deming is not far from mountains and other tourist attractions. In the late eighteen hundreds, people came here for their health. Mack says it might be interesting to find out why.

The best-informed sources, those to be relied upon for information about social opportunities and amusement outside the fence, are 'Permanent Party' (soldiers who are full time residents). Here at Deming those folks are bitterly pessimistic and offer no hope for happy sessions in the moonlight involving tasty beverages and pin up girls. Basically, they blame El Paso and explain tearfully how different life would be if the Alamo had been built in Deming. Unfortunately, El Paso was settled about seventy five miles east, just too distant to make weekend visits accessible unless some cadet kept a car on the post, which is not allowed, or has a friend with enough connections to rate the use of an airplane. It would mean busy weekends and exciting experiences but permanent party people say "Go ahead and dream if you want, Mister, but you're not going to see El Paso, Jaurez, or the

Alamo this time around." All we can do is envy pilots and instructors who manage to capture an AT-ll now and then. I tell myself, "You're still a cadet, Mister; as far as your dreams of El Paso? Forget about it!"

Now that we know this is an 'arid continental' climate, we can stop wondering why we never see grass. The ground is strewn with little stones. When a high wind whistles through the barracks area it picks up a bunch of pebbles and fires them at our faces and legs. The tiny rocks sting as sharply as darts. We often find ourselves leaning forward, marching with heads lowered to protect our eyes. From a distance we could be mistaken for a line of struggling camels crossing the Sahara.

Because the weather can be cold or hot at any given time, our uniform of the day varies from suntans to GI overcoats in accord with the temperature. Usually we wear khakis but the last few days have been cold and the command to get out heavy GI overcoats was on the bulletin board this morning. G.I. Morris, always on the alert for a bone to pick, is grumbling because the coats are heavy and cumbersome. I explain to him that the coats do keep us nice and warm which is the reason we wear them. He points out that once inside the classroom, everyone tosses his coat into the first available empty space and because the rooms are small, hot and overcrowded we are treated to an unhealthy variety of odors. His point is that our classrooms are only a few steps from the barracks and we can easily manage to make the trip in good health and, to use his terms, "Not have to smell all that shit."

However, the command is on the board and anyone who ignores it is asking for enough gigs to keep him walking tours on the base every weekend until he graduates. I tell G. I. to let it ride. We have to worry about the guy because he keeps talking about going over the fence for a trip to Jaurez. He's smarter than that, but is not pleased with the way they're running the Army.

Our eighteen weeks here are turning into a marathon. Everything except flying time is being crammed into our schedule. The training program is a grind and no one expects it to ease up. Right now we are in a high intensity mode requiring consecutive sessions, day and evening, in ground school. Between classes we break for an hour or so of PT (physical training) or, just in case we might forget that the Air Corps is still the Army and forget to bear ourselves in a military posture we have a stultifying hut, hut, forty-five minutes of close order drill. Sentiment among the troops is that it offers nothing to enlighten a young soldier and could be harmful to his feet. Maybe it's the Army's way of taking our minds off the books. Sack time is at a minimum. Our schedule has acquired the relentless momentum of an eager beaver trying to cram a year of college into one semester.

Our days and nights are split into three sections. We hit the ground running at 700 hours and every minute is programmed until the last class folds up at 1900 or later. When we start flying in a few weeks, our schedule will change but at present it contains some extra sessions of PT. Days and nights are split between two sessions of ground school and one of PT each day.

Today, and every day this week, we are marching directly from breakfast to calisthenics on the barren, grassless parade ground. The officer in charge is 2nd Lieutenant William T. Boyle from Brooklyn, New York. His chiseled features and athletic build are typical of those guys who always walk out with the prettiest girl in the bar at closing time. Lieutenant Boyle talks with a Brooklyn accent and likes to open his PT sessions with a few words of welcome. They are always the same. "Take off yuh shoits yuh bums and lowah ya heads slowly into duh doit!"

The Lieutenant realizes that most people, including cadets, don't look forward to calisthenics so he depends on the loyalty of three assistants, all of them corporals, who refer to cadets as "gadgets." Their purpose is to keep order on the drill field; to prod slackers and prevent half hearted effort on the part of weary participants. Yes, there will be order on the drill field! The "Terrible Trio" as they have come to be known, roam up and down through the prostrate ranks, handing out "gigs" and threatening selected hours of misery for cadets goofing off during pushups and burpees.

The Lieutenant also makes it difficult to cheat by standing on a platform right up in front looking down at us. He personally leads every exercise from beginning to end, bouncing, leaping and shouting cadence. There can be no doubt Lieutenant Boyle takes his duty seriously and wants each of us to be in top shape when we meet the enemy. Most of us, not including G.I., admire Lieutenant Boyle's determination to make everyone an Apollo. It would be difficult not to respect the way he pours his own energy into an unappreciated crusade to put us into the best possible physical condition. Nobody seems to be fond of "The Terrible Trio." Mo Lund describes them as sub-human enforcers lacking any redeeming trait to justify participation in a civilized society. All in all, the Lieutenant and his henchmen are only doing their nasty job, driving us to the outer levels of endurance. I think they see it as survival of the fittest and if some do not survive, so be it. The Lieutenant is dedicated to doing the best for the deserving and the devil take the hindmost. During a short rest period, Mack says, "I think they're trying to kill us for our own good."

I say, "The system works. My first physical fitness test (PFT) at preflight I only did eighteen sit-ups. Our last PFT before leaving Santa Ana I made over 200. Something must be doing me some good." G.I.

Morris says, "Jack I., you don't give a shit do you? How come nothing bothers you?"

Mack looks at G.I. and says, "G.I. how come everything bothers you?"

One of the three enforcers looks over and growls, "Hey, you gadgets, knock it off!" Lieutenant Boyle climbs up on an overturned box, and blows his whistle. He doesn't pretend we're practicing for the Olympics gymnastic team. He wants to improve our legs and lungs so he saves further real punishment until the end. In the meantime he gives us a chance for some lighthearted fun by tossing a football into the crowd and shouting, "Let's do some football heah!" I smile when he throws us that pigskin. Minnesota is a football state, and it makes me feel at home to smell the leather and feel a football in my hands.

I'm surprised so many cadets don't care much about throwing a football. Of course, with some of these guys, anything except sack time, lying around doing nothing is considered boring and interferes with their favorite pastime, which is sleeping. Those of us from Minnesota, which has been fielding great teams year after year, feel good about competing, even if it's only in a game of touch football.

Anybody who cares about sports knows the Gophers have been National Champions almost every year in the 30's and that Bruce Smith, the Gopher's "All-American" boy, won the Heisman trophy in 1940. There are, however, a few players like Joe Miller from L. A. who are also enthusiastic. Joe played some halfback at USC last year. Except for him, I can automatically grab the ball from anybody and be the quarterback, which means I get to run and throw passes and have some fun. Although it might be expected that someone would complain about Joe and me hogging the ball, nobody does. As for us, the ball belongs to the one who gets there first. I wish we could choose up teams and play all day.

When Lieutenant Boyle figures we are sufficiently worn out, he blows the whistle and waves his arms. We follow as he takes off on a brisk run around the perimeters of our squadron area. The Lieutenant is serious about running and has refined the art of knowing exactly how far a healthy American youth can run before reaching the very edge of collapsing in a heap. Slackers are watched closely by his merciless assistants who cajole, threaten, and insult weary stragglers stumbling and gasping toward the finish line. The first few times we ran my chest burned and my side ached. After several sessions, the grind has become less and less painful. However, nobody complains when the Lieutenant dismisses us.

We go back to the barracks, change into our uniforms and wait to be called out, lined up and marched to chow. K.K. and I are slouched on our cots puffing Lucky Strikes and trying to catch our breath after a long run. The door opens and G.I. pushes his way into the room. He notices we're smoking and a grim shadow falls across his face. Suddenly he turns fatherly. "What's the matter with you guys? You trying to get cancer? Think about your lungs you dumb bastards. You go out and get 'em all fired up and then suck in a pile of shit. God, you must be crazy."

We can't believe what we're hearing. Is this the real G.I. Morris, a genuine yellow-fingered chain smoker, playing the role of our family doctor? Our first thought is that this is a new pitch. G.I. has decided to take a medical approach to mooching a cigarette. We have to believe his lust for nicotine exceeds any consideration for our breathing mechanisms. We wait for a move one way or the other but his sincerity is being substantiated by the fact he has neither lighted up nor asked for a light. The chance that he may be serious causes a short, thoughtful silence as KK and I exchange glances. It must be admitted that sincere or not G.I. is making sense. People like K.K. and I should know better.

202

My lungs were on fire after PT and if you think about it, inhaling a lot of crap under those conditions could do some harm in there.

K.K. remains very thoughtful. He's regarded at ground school as a brain, one of the disgusting cadets who catch on to everything the first time around. Probably he agrees that what we were doing is stupid. However, the one thing I'm sure of is that neither of us is going to stop smoking. We savor it as being the only recreation a cadet can really count on. However, quitting would definitely offer some advantages. It could prevent me from doing such dumb things as Saturday when I snuffed out a cigarette and left it in the ashtray on K.K.'s desk a couple of minutes before inspection. It earned us a few gigs and inspired a few harsh words from K.K. who seldom stoops to the use of profanity. However, the situation calls for some positive action and I decide silently not to light up anymore when my lungs are already burning. What K.K. decides to do is his own business. We don't have a chance to discuss the matter because the master's whistle summons us to stop whatever seems important to us at the time. Our lives are subject to whistles. Their shrill commands push and pull us through long days and sleepless nights. They must be obeyed and, in our Pavlovian world, only 'mail call' moves a cadet faster than a bid to the mess hall.

Outside, we fall into formation and begin a silent, empty eyed march toward the mess hall where we expect to be rewarded, as are trained seals, with a bit of something for our stomachs. We are not looking for pheasant under glass, but we know whatever it is will be tasty. The food here is well prepared. The standard menu often includes steak and potatoes. Servings are large and a huge sign on the wall reads, "TAKE all you want but EAT all you TAKE!" Not many men our age who have just run a couple of miles will leave this kind of food on the plate.

However, there is more than good food happening here to make us homesick but happy through the noon hour. For a touch of the past we are dining to the sounds of a live twelve piece swing band which is, at the moment, working its way through Glenn Miller's *Little Brown Jug*. Now, that fades away and the band swings into Tommy Dorsey's version of *The Song of India*, an arrangement pulling nickels into jukeboxes everywhere. It's a great arrangement so there's no reason to complain although it would be nice to hear some Count Basie now and then. Just last year the Count played at the Minneapolis Armory and all of us in Red Melgren's band stood pressed against the bandstand from start to finish. The Count had Jimmy Rushing and Billie Holiday for vocalists plus the best rhythm section in the world. It was a real thrill to see and hear one of my idols, guitarist Freddie Greene, in person. We hung around by the bandstand until they turned out the lights and started locking the doors while the band swung on *One O'clock Jump*.

I keep thinking about that experience while we eat and during the short march to the hanger that houses the bomb trainers. We can expect to spend the rest of the afternoon riding on trainers and attempting to make direct hits on paper targets. It's not as simple as a person might think and more often than not we will be scalded by metaphors from the lips of our instructors that cause us to blush. We have about ten minutes free time between sessions; just long enough for a cigarette and fast trip to the latrine. The schedule calls for two or three hours per day in the large hanger riding a bomb trainer.

The trainer is a rolling version of the Eiffel tower. Unlike that world famous erector set in France, it is capable of scooting across the hanger floor and simulating a bomb run. The cadet and instructor perch at the very top, about twenty feet in the air. At a nod from his instructor the cadet unclutches the bombsight and the trainer crawls slowly across the hanger floor, hopefully in the direction of the target. Tension increases as the bombardier twists knobs, peers into the eyepiece of the bombsight and attempts to line up cross hairs with the target. To have any success at all, the cadet must learn to keep his concentration while being treated to a colorful, often sarcastic, play by play mumbled by the 2nd Lieutenant at his side. However, success or failure in lining up and staying on the target will be determined by the bombardier's ability to twist two knobs on the bomb sight while moving down the bomb run. Can that be difficult? Well, try it sometime. All it actually involves is working both hands simultaneously with each performing a separate function. Picture Beethoven trying to play a fugue on the organ with arms crossed, one above the other, one palm up and one palm down.

For a cadet, the most embarrassing thing about the trainer is that it always manufactures a result. Every practice run results in a verdict. At the end of a run it's "Bombs Away" and a metal plunger smacks down on the paper target making a loud clack and recording a hit or miss. As they say, "Close only counts in horse shoes." The trainer performs a valuable service in providing functional simulation and making it possible for fledgling bombardiers to practice without blowing up the building.

None of us would have guessed dropping a bomb could have so many complications. At times it is very frustrating. We spend most of the day and night up to our hips in maps, cardboard E-2 and E-6 computers, bombing tables, protractors, and a briefcase overflowing with notebooks and scratch paper. Our training calls for eighteen hours of physics, a subject I passed but never grasped in high school. They say it's important for us to become familiar with basic principles and terminology of meteorology. Last night we studied about weather and atmosphere including a subject called "Composition of Forces." Today we focused our attention on lectures about resolution of forces, atmospheric pressure, accelerated motion, energy and friction.

The situation is complicated by our need to acquire two specialties, bombing and navigation, at the same time. Unfortunately, the subjects don't overlap. Studying every kind of map ever invented is probably vital to prospective navigators, but much less critical to those of us who are destined to be bombardiers. After all, when everything is said and done, every crew will have a full time navigator on their aircraft. Maybe the Army Air Corps feels we will be able to step right in and start navigating in case the regular navigator runs into trouble. At this point, most of us would say, "Don't count on it."

We will not take a full course in celestial navigation so we won't be of much help at night. Flying pilotage in the daytime over a country with which we will be totally unfamiliar doesn't sound promising either. Maybe they know what they're doing; they usually do. Nevertheless, it seems like a waste of time to have everyone spending the same number of hours studying identical subjects in each session. At present, the emphasis is on maps. Maps, maps, maps. Take your choice of charts: polyconic, or gnomonic. Try to understand them and get ready for a two-hour session dealing with problems of interpreting the damn things.

It seems like we've been hitting the books forever and everyone is anxious to start flying, dropping bombs and doing actual pilotage navigation missions. We wonder if the brass have forgotten why we were brought here. Now they tell us we will be starting a new subject called, "Identification and Tactical Functions of Aircraft." It's a lofty sounding title but the class is actually a replay of time past. In preflight school at Santa Ana we spent hour after hour sitting in dark rooms, straining to memorize silhouettes of battleships and aircraft being flashed on the screen in something called the Renshaw System.

Fortified by solid hours of repetition, we actually learned to identify and call out the names of ships and planes as they flash on the screen at one-one hundredth of a second. You should have heard the groan when our instructor announced that we have been sentenced to plowing through the same routine again. When a G.I. asked why we had to prove ourselves one more time, our instructor said it doesn't do any good to identify the enemy if you don't know what to do next. We suppose that's where the tactical function part comes in. In the manner of most of his fellow 2nd Lieutenants, he ignores the icy reception, smiles and explains that when we get to combat, intelligence officers will hold critiques after each mission. He emphasizes that any information given to them must be entirely accurate and reminded us that our study in pre-flight had included only British and American aircraft.

Whose fault was that? It's a wonder some incredibly brave cadet didn't mention that the Japanese and Nazis were both very much in the war during the time we were at Santa Ana. Someone might have asked why ships and planes of the Japs and Huns weren't included in our training at that time. It would have been a loaded question, one that would paint the instructor into a corner. For that very reason, no one was stupid enough to ask it. Even G. I. Morris passed on this one. Embarrassing a 2nd lieutenant in front of twenty-five aviation cadets could easily create a lifetime enemy armed with many opportunities for revenge.

We have now been here for several weeks but haven't started to fly. For no good reason it makes a person feel inferior. We have been working hard and learning some important facts but until we get up in the air we can never feel that we count for anything around here. It is no fun listening to people reviewing successes and problems when you haven't shared their experiences. Most of us settle for keeping our mouths shut and our ears open in the hope we may get some early insight into what to expect later on. On rare evenings when we don't have classes, we can hang out at the cadet's lounge, gulp down a milk shake and listen to other people's problems. There is always the chance of hearing something that might hold a clue about our next step up.

In my experience, the one thing that hasn't changed from Jefferson Barracks to the arid continental plains of Deming, New Mexico is that soldiers of all ranks have an unquenchable desire to know what's going to happen, who it will happen to, and when it will take place. The rumor mill turns constantly, usually in the latrine, and almost never produces anything worth hearing. The usual reply to a rumor is, "What stool did that come off of?" Nevertheless, a rumor is a rumor and will always draw a crowd. The wonder of it is, why? Even if they had all the facts, they couldn't change anything. When the Army wants us to know something they put it on the bulletin board and they mean it. Sometimes it even happens.

We are the Class of 44-2 and no longer the newest cadets around. The class title of 44-2 identifies us as the second class expected to graduate from Deming in A.D. 1944. Surprisingly a day seldom goes by without rumors that we will be held back, pushed forward, or transferred to the horse cavalry. It appears we will be spending Thanksgiving, Christmas, and New Years in good old New Mexico. The other evening we had a bull session in the barracks debating whether Santa Claus would come this far South? No one, not even Charlie McQuitty, has any idea what that will encompass.

McQuitty, from Saint Joseph, Missouri is one of those all around experts who exist in every barrack. In ours, they say, "If you want to know something about the world, ask McQuitty." There are people around who seem to feel Charlie is too happy, as if he has found a home in the Army. Personally, I like the guy but, on the other hand, who cares? His opinions won't get me through the next four or five months.

It's probably human nature but each time we arrive at a new place, I wonder if someone from home might turn up. There are several cadets with us from Minnesota, but they don't have any more recent local information than me. It would be nice to meet someone to chat with who could pass along the latest poop about little things at home. Who wouldn't like to hear the scuttlebutt about the girls we left behind even if the news isn't that good? As far as the guys, most of our friends are somewhere around the world serving in all parts of the globe in various branches of the service. It would be nice to hear about what's happening to them.

I thought I might have run into someone like that just after we arrived here in Deming. The first time we went into the hanger to check out the bomb trainer we were shown around by a smiling little 2nd Lieutenant who introduced himself as Marty Zinn. While we walked around the hanger and looked at the trainer, he asked us each where we came from. When I replied "Minneapolis," he said, "Bingo!" It is also his hometown. I told him we have several other Minnesotans in our group and mentioned a few names. He didn't recognize any; in fact, he didn't even know my high school buddy, Rex Werring, who is an instructor right here on the base. None the less, Lieutenant Zin impressed me as an easy going kind of officer who is not too proud to be seen talking with a cadet from his home town. I looked forward to meeting him again. Deming isn't really that big a place, but cadets don't go into the officers' club and officers stay out of the cadets' lounge so our chances of meeting again are very slim. Sometimes it seems our biggest disappointments are about little things.

Tonight we are enjoying a rare evening of comparative freedom. Classes have been canceled because our instructors are attending a meeting so Mo Lund and I have ambled over to the cadet lounge for rest and recuperation. Mo Elmo J. Lund of Salt Lake City, Utah, is one of a kind. Among other things, he has a curious habit of replying to questions with an unexpected observation from out in left field. This evening, when I called out, "Hey, Mo! Why don't we walk over to the lounge and get a shake?" His reply was "What's this 'We' stuff? You writing a book or something?" *We* is the title of an autobiography and best seller written by Ann Morrow, the wife of Charles Lindbergh, the famous aviator who flew across the Atlantic Ocean in an out dated contraption. No reply is expected. We proceed down a path to the lounge.

Mo reads in his spare time. People who do that are exasperating to argue or debate with. Quoting facts and figures doesn't work with Mo and using outside sources curls his upper lip. His usual defense is "Hey, Jack I., where the hell do you find this hypothetical legion you always dig up?" He has a natural knack for dead pan humor and the mindset of a Ph.D. Before entering the Air Corps, Mo drove a bakery truck in Salt Lake City.

The lounge is full and, characteristically, Mo has wandered off into the crowd. I stand around until a chair is available. The table is occupied by a pair of cadets who say they are from the class of forty-three-seventeen, four classes ahead of us. Their class is bombing in the daytime this week and, as usual, the conversation gets around to turbulence. I listen while they discuss events of the day between themselves. They really aren't paying any attention to me. It's as if I am watching them and listening from far, far away. I think briefly that I should get up and find another table. If there is another empty one, I can't see it and, anyway, this is a free country and I have a right to be here. I gather from their conversation that Homer has already earned his qualifying hits and feels good about his CE. His buddy, Barney, seems to be a couple of hits short and sounds concerned about the rough ride he had up there this afternoon. Homer seems worried. "You got to get with it, Barney. You're gonna miss the goddam boat." Barney continues tapping the table with his fingertips, takes a deep sigh and says softly, "I only need two more. That ain't many but what is somebody supposed to do. Them clouds was three miles deep. I got good eyes, Homer, but nobody can see through that much shit. I got to get lucky. That's what I got to do."

Homer says, "Well, you should have gotten lucky at night when there weren't any clouds up there at all."

Barney takes another deep breath. "Well, Homer. It's too late for that now. I got to do what has to be done. Daytime or no daytime, by God, I'm gonna do it."

"It isn't that easy in the daytime, Barney. This afternoon was no bargain. Not when a man can hardly keep his head down long enough to look into the sight and twist the damn knobs, not when your ass is bouncing off the floor and the nose of the plane goes up and down like a yo-yo. The goddam instructor said it was the worst he's seen since he's been on the base."

"Well, I can't afford to think about that stuff. Tomorrow is due to be a nice day. I can feel it. I'm getting those last two tomorrow. That's all it's going to take, Homer. A nice day, a little break in the weather and it won't be no problem knocking down two if the wind don't blow and the goddam turbulence ain't too bad. I can do it, Homer.

Once again, I get the unwelcome feeling of having barged in on a private conversation. Maybe it was a wake. I pick up my glass and leave the table doubting that they know I'm gone. Barney has used up the best ninety of his 160 projected bomb drops. Chances are his CE isn't in good shape and if he gets his other two hits it will have to be in the afternoon, which is not so easy. Everybody around here knows that turbulence can convert a bomb run into a miserable experience. The popular opinion is that, here at Deming, turbulence and cloud cover make things much more difficult in the afternoon than at night.

He is struggling because he put himself crosswise with the system, which means he made things difficult for himself. Being crosswise is never a good thing and often leads to a condition known as FUBAR which is serious. As things stand now, he's coming in on a wing and a prayer although he acts confident. Maybe everything will go just right and he can make it the hard way. I hope he does.

The slogan, "Get Your Hits at Night," is heard almost as often as "Tough shit" or "Oh, my aching back." The warning is even featured on a large sign suspended in back of the counter here in the lounge. Here's hoping Barney comes through. Their class expects to get their wings and commissions in mid-December. What a gift from heaven that will be; graduating, getting wings, bars, a ten-day furlough and going back home for Christmas. What a shame it will be if Barney screws up. I don't expect ever to know the ending of that little drama because there are hundreds of cadets on the base and not much time to wander around meeting people. Any free time is spent with people in our own barracks who make up the closest thing we have to a family in these trying times. Our lives these days consist of chow, class, PT, chow, school, chow, school and hit the sack. The big moment is mail call, which can also be the most disappointing.

Barring any change in the Army's projected schedule, we will probably finish up sometime in February but who knows? To ask any of our instructors when we might graduate would invite a blistering "Don't you like it here, Mister?"

It seems only human nature to envy those guys from 43-17 but sooner or later a person must learn not to waste time on impossible desires. I can't put together any dream sequence that finds me unwrapping presents at Grandma and Grampa Flavin's house on Christmas day nor can I imagine birthday gifts the next day, December 26th. My brother Bill and I were both born on that day three years apart. Bill and I won't lose anything as far as birthday presents go because we never have received any before. People always say, "This is for both" and let it go at that. Bill is sixteen, a cadet at St. Thomas Academy in St. Paul.

We are finally getting closer to flying and everyone is feeling more interested in what goes on around here concerning bombing in the afternoon. Cadets with grim faces gripe angrily about turbulence. They say it plays handball with the Twin Engine AT-11s and often converts an average flight into an adventure. They also complain about bomb runs being aborted because cloud cover forces the bombardier to play hide and seek with the target. Their tone reminds me of fat guys at Santa Ana calling the world unfair because they couldn't haul their stomachs over high walls on the obstacle course.

Night bombing seems to be an entirely different matter. Instructors tell us that on a bomb run, pilot and bombardier must coordinate as smoothly as Siamese twins joined at the brain. In some situations the bombardier may actually take control of the aircraft using the PDI (Pilot Directional Indicator) to guide the plane over the target. Any bomb run is vulnerable to forces that sometimes cannot be defended and we've had enough experience on the practice trainer to respect the bombsight as a temperamental piece of machinery which sometimes is as delicate as it is effective.

Obviously, the purpose of a bomb run is to provide a smooth and stable path to the target. For that purpose, the bombsight contains a gyroscope spinning at high speed to keep the bombsight level in relation to the earth in spite of changes in the attitude of the aircraft which often occur. Sad but true, a bombardier may accurately calculate the factors that will affect the flight of his bombs and correctly install that information in the bombsight, only to learn that Mother Nature is in a mood to play little games. The best conditions sometimes turn sour if turbulence rocks the plane or cloud cover suddenly obstructs the bombardier's view. The duties of a bombardier become very complex when he finds himself at the mercy of the elements. Turbulence can force the aircraft to launch into an aerobatics gymnastic exhibition or clouds may drift over the target making it invisible. He can only press his eye against the eyepiece and keep twisting the knobs. Usually, such problems complicate the situation, but won't ruin all chance of a successful bomb run. However, they definitely introduce luck as an influence on the final result. The situation could be worse.

In the worst case, the gyro 'tumbles' and puts the bombsight out of commission. To say such a thing rarely happens is small consolation. When it takes place, the party is over. The bomb run is aborted and a whimpering bombardier finds himself peering into a world gone dark. The problem won't cause danger to the aircraft but if it is a problem with the gyro that is not something that can be repaired in the air. Is there anything a pilot can do to help a bombardier when an aircraft decides to act like a P-38 Lockheed Lightning and begins dancing all around the sky? Well, he can pray.

The Norden Bombsight is a product of Honeywell Heat Regulator Company in my hometown of Minneapolis, Minnesota. It is one of the most valuable and often used weapons in our country's arsenal and early in the war was a closely guarded secret. The sight was stored in a vault under lock and key. Bombardiers checked it out of the vault for each flight and carried it to the aircraft while brandishing a 45-caliber pistol. The routine was repeated upon landing. The secrecy of the bombsight was so important that bombardiers were required to take an oath. It was called *The Bombardier's Oath* and reading it gave me goose bumps. It says: "Mindful of the secret trust about to be placed in me by my Commander in Chief, the President of the United States, by whose direction I have been chosen for bombardier training and mindful of the fact that I am to become guardian of one of my country's most priceless military assets, the American bombsight, I do here, in the presence of Almighty God, swear by the Bombardier's Code of Honor to keep inviolate the secrecy of any and all confidential information revealed to me, and further to uphold the honor and integrity of the Army Air Forces, if need be, with my life itself."

Fortunately for us, it is no longer necessary to worry about keeping this secret or lugging the sight back and forth. The Nazis have now recovered specimens from Flying Fortresses shot down in enemy territory. Probably the secret our government kept as long as possible was related to the use of the gyroscope, heart of the bombsight.

Turbulence during flight is not a rare condition and not a major problem unless it occurs in the wrong place at the wrong time or is unusually fierce. Seemingly it just happens that at Deming, rough air is much worse during the afternoon than after sunset. It won't be long before we will be meeting the problem face to face. Each of us will drop 160 bombs and 50% of them will be dropped before sunset. Because of weird and persistently difficult bombing conditions during daytime, the word has been passed down from class to class to get as many hits as possible during the evening bombing phase. Therefore, the slogan, "GET YOUR HITS AT NIGHT!"

On any given evening at the cadet lounge, it is no trick at all to check the crowd and identify cadets with low CEs and their quota of necessary hits. They chat aimiably, enjoy ice cream sodas or Cokes, and talk about graduation.

Those who are not making decent progress are not so jolly. A few have invented streams of colorful adjectives for the occasion; cursing low clouds, and reviling merciless winds. There is true urgency in the large sign hanging behind the counter in the lounge. The sign has probably been there since the class of 43-4 the first group of Deming cadets to graduate were commissioned and sent on their way March 6th, 1943. It will no doubt be here long after we leave. Just five words of warning: GET YOUR HITS AT NIGHT!

I wonder where those graduates from the class of 43-4 are now. They left here almost a year ago.   There have been hundreds of missions since that time. We understand that the war is really hot in Europe including huge groups of B-17s and B-24s on raids deep into Germany. There have also been a number of big battles at sea in the Pacific. I wonder what those former cadets who were sweating out graduation a year ago are going through now. Strange as it may seem we don't really pay much attention to anything outside our base here in Deming. I don't picture myself in combat and there is no conversation in the barracks about the war. I trust we're winning, but they keep us so damn busy here there isn't time to worry about anything else. The

216

fact is, we haven't even met a soldier who has ever been in combat. However, there is a general feeling of unity among the cadets. We're all running the same gauntlet. Things happening to our struggling friends can happen to any of us. It's not a huge worry but does put something unpleasant on a person's mind. I find it haunting and remember one time my mother wrote the date of a dental appointment on our kitchen wall calendar. I flinched every time I looked at it and couldn't let myself see beyond that fatal day. The anticipation was much worse than the ordeal itself. It's a situation any cadet should avoid.

Sometimes it's difficult to get to sleep even if a person is dog-tired. I can't help thinking about Barney, the cadet from 43-17 who I listened to, but never met. I must be some kind of dodo bird to worry about what happens to some guy who completely ignored me in the cadet lounge. Who has seen the wind? I think it's really that I can't help being curious. Tomorrow afternoon he will make another try for the elusive last two hits. I wonder if he is losing any sleep? What has to be going through his mind? He may be in the sack, but I bet he's not sleeping.

What will he be thinking tomorrow afternoon as he stares through the plexiglass of the bombardier's window looking for a break in the clouds? Will the sky be like velvet or will a vicious wind be tossing that AT-11 around the sky like a cat playing with a ball of twine? Maybe it won't be that bad. All we know is what we hear. Maybe today the sky will be calm. They tell us turbulence is not a threat every day. The law of averages says some afternoons will be better than others. We also hear that some afternoons the clouds are nowhere to be found. If that happens, staying on the target will be easier. If a cadet can find the target and the plane only bounces a little bit, no problem. With decent conditions anyone has a chance to shine. Who knows? Maybe his luck will change. He only needs two hits. How will he feel as his first bomb release falls toward a sure shack? Will he be excited, waving his arms, pressing his face against the glass nose of the AT-11, following the path of the bomb as it drops toward the shack? Does he tell himself it can't miss? Now, all he needs is for the cadet running the camera to get a picture and confirm the hit. Suddenly a cluster of clouds slip over the target making any kind of photograph impossible. No picture, no hit. His heart sinks. Maybe the instructor will vouch for the hit? No one actually saw it smash into the shack. He raises his eyes toward the instructor who says, "Hell of a run, Mister," gives him a thumbs up and makes a notation on his clipboard.

The instructor tells the pilot to go around again and turns to the cadet, "Well, Mister, you had two, now you got three. We have to be out here for two hours so let's find out if those blue skies are gonna let us get number four so you can sleep tonight." It's my old habit of putting myself where I've never been, but I couldn't help thinking about it. Maybe I was testing myself as much as Barney from 43-17. Something like that could happen. I'm beginning to get an idea of the tremendous pressure waiting for us when we start dropping bombs for keeps and know they are photographing every single one.

Old timers tell us most cadets facing a crisis come through. I hope Barney will. I said a couple of Hail Mary's for him tonight. I wonder why I can't get to sleep. Usually, I'm so wrung out at night that it's one last coffin nail and into the arms of Morpheus. I intend asking God to help that guy from 43-17. I wonder if anyone did that for me when I was going through my trouble in Kingman. The way it turned out makes me think somebody did. It was probably Mom. She really likes to make novenas and it's surprising how often they seem to help.

It won't be long now. Tomorrow we are going down to the

flightline to look things over and, next week, we go up in the air for practice bombing. It will start us on a schedule where everybody wants to be lucky. There can be no question that lucky is better than unlucky and good fortune can be very helpful, but wise men warn that it is never smart to depend on it. Bad luck does not exist in the Army. It cannot exist there because it is considered to be an excuse. An excuse is an explanation for an unfortunate event. The only acceptable explanation for an unfortunate event is "No excuse, Sir."

Here I am, gazing up at the big sign over the door of the cadet lounge one more time. It hasn't changed. "Get Your Hits At Night!" I'm going to try and remember that.

One anxiety that seems to hang around full time is the knowledge that anything can happen to anyone at any time. For one thing, our eyes tell us that the Beechcraft AT-11 is not a B-17 Flying Fortress or B-24 Liberator. We put in flight time on B-17s at Kingman and know what a long-range bomber is like, how it cruises along up there as if it owns the sky. Turbulence is no problem for those babies. We haven't been up in a twin engine Beechcraft but have heard all we want to hear about the plane and its disturbing habit of bouncing around the sky like a volleyball on windy afternoons.

How bad could they be? We see AT-11s taking off and landing day and night around here and most cadets who make it this far graduate. A good case can be made that AT-11s are doing the job. We certainly hope so because very soon we'll be depending on them to carry us out and back on various adventures including navigation as well as bombing. They say we're here to learn to be bombardier-navigators but it's becoming clear from the attitude of ground school training instructors that we will be about 90% bombardiers and 10% navigators. We expect to learn very little about celestial navigation, a very complex subject, but we have been working on pilotage navigation and will fly some missions using that.

Although we haven't been dropping bombs from the sky, we have been working on the trainer and attending ground school. We know a bombsight is a very finicky piece of machinery with more than a few limitations. We know what a bombsight will and won't do and, above all, we know how much will be riding on our performance in the next few weeks. All of us will sweat and suffer; some may not make the grade. They won't get much sympathy because all of us are faced with trying to get past the same gargoyles.

When we start bombing for score, every bomb will be photographed. It will also be measured and every foot of every bomb that misses the target will be added to our total and figured into our average circular error (CE) . A bombardier will be considered proficient who achieves an average CE of 230 feet or less and hits four shacks; close doesn't qualify. The word is, cadets who fail this hurdle are usually held over to the next class and some may be washed out completely. I have read the signs and hope to get my hits by the light of the moon.

The camera doesn't lie. However, it is rumored that sometimes cadets battling to get their last few hits will be given a break here and there. One source of aid might be from camera malfunctions. As they say, "Cooperation leads to graduation." The cadet taking pictures of a falling bomb through a hole in the floor of the plane is in position to be a lifesaver for a struggling fellow cadet. A miss is not a miss if there's no picture. Instructors are said to expect a significant rise in the number of camera malfunctions as a class moves toward the end of training. Anyone playing that game is on thin ice. Instructors threaten cruel and unusual punishment, for anyone guilty of breaking the rules to help a friend. We have all been notified that any cadet with a photography proficiency below 75% will be called to the attention of the faculty board. Yet, we hear stories that instructors themselves have been known to offer a little first aid. Mercy is the last thing any cadet can anticipate, but it's a matter of fact that once upon a time every instructor has gone through the same routine. Rumors warn that asses will be chewed and gigs will be handed out but, when it's a close call, who knows? *The Cadets Pledge* states that "Cooperation leads to graduation." Personally, my advice would be, "Don't depend on it!"

Those of us who have come this far have learned to adapt. On the other hand, starting next week the true meaning of circular errors and shacks will be first and foremost in our lives. Right now we have our hands full trying to become bombardiers and navigators at the same time. It doesn't help that the climate in Deming at this time of year is unpredictable. If we complete our training according to plan, we will be here in Deming until the first part of February, which will include most of the winter. We have already been told that winter temperatures at our altitude can drop down to freezing levels.

Starting Monday, we will be flying every day so our schedule will be revised. When we fly mornings, we will have ground school in the afternoon, and drill or PT at night. Next week we will be at the flight line in the morning and drop practice bombs. The following week we will fly in the afternoon and the week after that it will be flying at night. Ground school will continue at times fitting around the flying schedule which will rotate each week as we move through afternoon and night bombing.

We are now at the end of October and evenings here are much like Indian Summer back home. Minnesota is beautiful in autumn. The leaves turn to bright red and gold and by now the football Gophers are already into their schedule. I wonder how those athletes, using their talents to stay out of the war, can sleep at night. Maybe the armed services have created a new classification of 4F relating to people who are too healthy to fight.

I think the things I miss most this time of the year are the smoke of bon fires, the smell of wieners roasting, and the tiny edge on the breeze that we call sweater weather. Thinking about it brings a touch of sadness, but I wouldn't change a thing. I feel good about myself. I think I'm going to be all right. I know I can handle whatever comes up. Maybe next year we can all be home for Indian Summer to taste the apples and feel the little bite that makes the air smell sweet. I can't lie to myself, I miss it, but right now my mind is on leaving the confining boundaries of life as a cadet and entering the more permissive world of a commissioned officer. The unanimous voices of wisdom from the cadet lounge go round and around in my head. They keep repeating. "Get your hits at night."

We leave the building shaking our heads, wondering what comes next. The trainer is fun, a giant toy that has already given us a good idea of how a bombsight works, but the machine has been pre-programmed in order to operate for training purposes. Conditions are always the same and variables that must be considered on combat bomb runs are lacking. When we begin bombing in the air, each bomb run will be unique and based on information from many sources. Our main tool in learning to set up a bombsight is the cardboard E-6-B computer. We are busy in ground school working on "theory of bombing" studying gyroscopes, bombs and fuses, operation of bomb racks and controls and C-2 computers. These are just a few of the tools and factors a bombardier must determine and have the skill to apply. He must also have the knowledge to change them, if necessary, before and during a bomb run. Often the most important details of setting up the bombsight occur when the aircraft is in the area of the target. He must possess the knowledge and ability necessary to compute such factors as air speed, ground speed, prevailing winds, temperature, altitude, time lag and other forces affecting the trajectory of falling objects and be able to perform all these requirements while under the pressure of combat. We leave the building shaking our heads and wondering if all this practice will really help us when we start bombing for keeps. It will be interesting to see what happens when it's time to apply the many factors we have been studying in ground school. It's a lot to learn but they pack it in and somehow we seem to catch on.

Yesterday was a bad day at the hanger and included being chewed out for about a half-hour by a 2nd lieutenant because my OD shirt was all wrinkled. The guy spit and chewed as if I was giving secrets to the Japs. The reason I was wearing the wrinkled shirt was because it had been in the bottom of my barracks bag for a couple of months. At Santa Ana and Kingman we wore suntans because of the heat. Never once did my ODs come out of the bag. Now, yesterday, they post a notice that the uniform of the day will be ODs. Where am I supposed to run to have my shirt pressed? I wasn't the only one with the problem, but maybe I was the worst. Some of the second lieutenants seem to enjoy finding a warm body to pound on. One thing for sure, I just stood and took it. No question he was lying in the woods waiting for me to give him an excuse. If I were stupid enough to do that, it would have brought the cadet code into the picture. It hurts just thinking about how he would have exploded if I gave him that chance. I repeated, "No excuse, Sir," about twenty times. It's interesting that none of the other cadets who witnessed the ass chewing even mentioned the episode. There but for the grace of God go them.

We are the class of 44-2 at Deming, which means we may graduate sometime after Christmas or New Years. The alphabet has determined that we are in Section II. Our flight leaders are First Lieutenants Faulhaber and Turzan. I'm really happy with the people in our group. Mo Olivo from Omaha, Nebraska is in our wing. Elmo J. (Mo) Lund from Salt Lake City, Utah is there as well as Mack Makowski from Chicago; Willie Mayer from Seattle, Washington; Bill Norman from Pocatello, Idaho; Jack Nichols from Ely, Nevada to name a few. George Hendrickson is here too but is in a different wing. Of course G.I. Morris is here and not particularly happy about it.

Ground school is intense because we are studying both bombing and navigating at the same time. We have two sessions, one during the day, the other at night. The proficiency requirements look tough just because there are so many different subjects being covered. I always thought they had one kind of bombsight and that was it. Now we learn we must be proficient on three different ones. Being proficient is not a classroom test. When we finally get up in the air and begin to bomb for keeps, our bomb drops will be photographed and analyzed. They've thought of everything. One of our courses is titled, "The ability to calculate rapidly the time interval between successive releases necessary to get a desired spacing of your bombs." Maybe it sounds simple but try it some time. The night sessions sometimes feel a little fuzzy. The other night, one of the instructors was showing us how to operate with a defective bombsight. I still don't know how you can do that. It might just be a misunderstanding of the word 'defective.' They have been teaching us how to preflight a bombsight to determine if it may be defective. It seems to me if it's defective they ought to send it back to Honeywell Heat Regulator Company, the people who make the damn things.

I try to absorb everything in every class but sometimes during night classes it's difficult to stay awake let alone remain sharp. Going from 0700 hours to 2000 every day eats up a lot of energy. Other times I get crabby, making a fuss in my own mind about the word "defective." Maybe I'm just misinterpreting the word but to me it still means 'useless.' Thank God there are always several of us working the same problems. It would be nice to find out I can learn to fix a defective bombsight. I'll get the answer sooner or later. As far as that goes, I could fix one right now, if it was broken.

Yesterday we began working on navigation. It has now been determined that as bombardiers, we will spend our time on dead reckoning navigation and will not be specified as celestial navigators although we have been spending class time learning about the stars and such complicated subjects as sidereal hour angles and weird looking maps. We are also working on meteorology and have been told that before we finish we will have as many or more class hours than would be required for a degree in that subject. Mack says, "At least we'll know when to come in out of the rain."

I hadn't given the matter much thought but many cadets in our group already have degrees, some have more than one. Others, like myself, left college to enlist. Our intention is to complete college after the war. In as much as we have completed enough work on the subject, for a degree, wouldn't it be decent on the part of the AAF to hand us a degree in meteorology that can someday be included in our manuscripts. Isn't that a silly thought? However, it would be a very nice gesture.

On the subject of degrees, last evening after class we sat on the floor in front of Charles Hash's bunk listening to his stories about scandals in history. Hash is from Delta, Pennsylvania and has a Ph.D.

degree in history. It was really something. Our forefathers got around more than any of us would think. Charles told us he did his final paper about the carousing and questionable activities of people like Washington, Jefferson, and Lincoln including their wives and girl friends. Some of his revelations were hard to believe, but Nash backed up his yarns with plenty of facts. We were fascinated and the session lasted until lights out. I dropped off to sleep wondering what a person can believe anymore, wondering how it will be when we start flying next week. I still wonder how a bombardier can hit a target with a defective bombsight unless you get it fixed and it becomes no longer defective. I also wondered if Alexander Hamilton was really the son of George Washington.

In the morning, after chow, we marched to the flight line just to look things over. The main building is really about the size of two double garages. Inside we see wooden benches, tables, folding chairs, old wooden chairs, one-legged chairs, counter tops holding stacks of parachutes. At the back of the room stands a large blackboard. At the present time it carries the names of twenty or more cadets from one of the classes just ahead of us. At the top is written the figure 1300 (1pm) which must be the time they took off this afternoon. There is also a message for the pilots ordering them to "log two hours." I'm watching the board, seeing if I recognize any names when somebody shouts, "Ten Hut" and we all jump to our proper straight-backed position. A second lieutenant has taken the floor wearing the professional scowl that people in his position adopt when they really mean business.

He says, loudly, "My name is Woodrow W. Weed and for the next few weeks I'll be your flight lieutenant. At this time it's my duty to tell you men you got yourself into a dangerous business unless you prepare for every situation and pay attention every second. Our experience is you can expect a close call on an average of one for every hundred hours you spend in the air. I mean a tight situation. If something goes wrong, I'm the one who will have to inform your dads and mothers, your wife, or whoever is your closest kin. Men, I've had enough of writing that kind of letter. I'm gonna do what it takes to get you out of here in good shape. I'm gonna ask yah, I'm gonna plead with yah, I'm gonna beg yah, but right now I'm tellin' yah. Keep your head out of your ass, misters. Listen to your instructors and get your hits at night. Our job is to get you through here and on ahead where you can maybe do something good for your country. There ain't nothing formal around here. You just check on the chalkboard, see who your pilot will be, and what instructor will be going along to try punching some information into your head. If it ain't too much to remember, here's how it goes when you come in here to get your assignments. This is not just about what you will do; I'm telling you EXACTLY what you will do. You will observe on the chalkboard your assignment including the names of your instructor, pilot and aircraft number. You will then walk over to that table over there and pick up some parachutes. If you need them at all, you're going to need four. That's one for the pilot, one for the instructor, one for the other cadet who will be your partner and one for yourself. If you forget one, it will be yours. My suggestion is you and your partner each carry two because the pilot and instructor probably have aching backs and are trying to get in shape for Saturday night." Lieutenant Weed pauses to check for a reaction from the pilots and instructors who are sitting on wooden tables, wearing leather flight jackets with fur collars, dangling their legs, They react to Lieutenant Weed's humor with the indifference of people who have heard the same story many times.

"Right now," continues Lieutenant Weed, "it's my pleasure to introduce some gentlemen that you'll be spending many hours in the air with during your remaining time in Deming."

We feel an uneasy moment of silence. Lieutenant Weed says, "At ease." Turns and walks out a door at the back of the room.

Mack says, "I think he means it." I shrug my shoulders. Tomorrow we start dropping practice bombs from the air. Next week we will probably start bombing and keeping score. Lieutenant Weed doesn't dismiss us so we just mill around looking the place over. In a few minutes someone calls "Ten-hut" again and another officer takes the floor. He introduces himself as 1st Lieutenant R. C. Stevens and says he is commander of Section Two. His flight lieutenants are Lieutenants Pete Dobill, Donald E. Young, Gordon M. Moody and Woodrow W. Weed whom we have already met. They look bored, wave when they are introduced, and leave the room.

We get into formation and march back to the barracks hoping to have the remainder of the afternoon for sack time. No such luck. Our cadet colonel, "Olaf The Great,"marches us right past our barracks. We march to the building where instructors are waiting to continue our venture into the world of protractors, maps, plotters, computers, manuals, bombing tables, notebooks, and all the other equipment necessary to demonstrate our ineptitude and focus attention on the long and uncertain path that still lies ahead. They can do whatever they want. Monday we take the big step, the move that puts us in an airplane because we have a job to do. Our schedule will be revised. Next week we will be at the flight line in the afternoon and drop practice bombs. In the morning we will turn ourselves over to Lieutenant Boyle and his crew for PT. Our session of ground school will be at night. Yes, even though we will not be flying, ground school carries on. The schedule will rotate each week as we move through afternoon and evening bombing.

I'm not worried by the last few weeks of training although we all know it will be vital. The Air Force has tested our bodies and plumbed our minds.

We have been tested and tested and not found wanting. Clearing one hurdle after another has given all of us a feeling of confidence. We have taken their toughest shots and remained standing. We will handle whatever comes next.

Up to now I feel satisfied but I can't lie to myself. Thinking about all the pleasant things we're missing sometimes gets a person down. There is no social life, and each day we wake up to find a future that is uncertain and well beyond our control. It is now October in Deming. The Minnesota countryside is magnificent in autumn. Before gas rationing, people drove hundreds of miles to Duluth in the north or Winona in southern Minnesota to see the turning of the leaves, to stare with wonder at forests of red and gold colors defying description, spectacular beauty well beyond human portrayal. I'll miss the breeze from the north that rustles the leaves and gives the air a bite. In many ways it's the best time of the year.

The Minnesota Gopher football team will be playing and I understand most of the players are athletes recruited by the armed services and kept in college specifically to play sports on behalf of the Army, Navy, and Marines. I hope none of them get hurt. It would be a shame if they get all bruised up while so many of their contemporaries are enjoying free airplane tours over Germany in B-17s or seeing the Sahara Desert through a slit in the front our luxurious new tanks. I wonder if my dad is still in Africa battling against Rommel and his Panzers. As far as I know, he is still somewhere overseas. I haven't been writing home often enough and need to improve on that. When our training is finished there will be a furlough and some of us can get together then. Right now, I'm coming to the end of a long road. Once it stretched out of sight, but now I can almost reach out and touch the end. In the meantime, echoes from the cadet lounge keep calling, "Get your hits at night!" Starting next week, I intend to do that, and some in the daytime, too.

CHAPTER 14

DEMING IN THE AIR

This morning we marched to the flight line immediately after chow. The sun is still trying to come up, as is my breakfast because this morning, for the first time, we soar into the wild blue yonder for the purpose of dropping bombs that will count and put us on the final track to graduation. It's not as if a guy feels that the Army Air Force band should show up and honor the occasion by blasting a few bars of the *Army Air Corps Song* written by Fred Waring, whose radio program is popular in the barracks because it carries daily baseball scores. The band will not be necessary because, up to now, there is nothing to celebrate but, for sure, when we hit the clouds this morning with a load of fake bombs that will help determine the final results of this remarkable year, it moves our lives ahead and puts us on the clock to our next adventure as they always say on the radio when Jack Armstrong starts battling a new adversary.

Up to now we can only guess what our crucial final month will bring. Today is the day our planes will carry real practice bombs consisting of a hundred pounds of sand wrapped in a steel cover. By sundown we should know how much we learned in long sessions day after day riding on trainers high in the big hanger. This week we will be practicing and scores will not count on our proficiency rating so a man should be able to relax and get ready for next week when every bomb dropped will be important and count on our proficiency rating. We came here to learn to be bombardiers but today will be the first time I've had a glimpse of our foreseeable future. When and if we graduate in what we hope will be a few weeks, real warfare will be our routine for the duration. Everybody knows this war is being fought in the air and its easy to see we're going to find ourselves right in the center of it and all. I've been so busy hoping I would become a HB (Hot Bombardier), become an officer, and get a furlough that I hardly gave the war itself a second thought. It seemed far away. The canons were booming far away.

This black of night we will be up in the sky honing our skills somewhere among the clouds, perfecting our trade and rehearsing for an inevitable afternoon or dark night when we must begin to ply the trade to which we have dedicated ourselves: dropping bombs on strangers from high altitudes. Our dream will have been achieved and yet a change of atmosphere in the barracks reveals a lurking uneasiness about what it all means. A person could wake up to discover his next assignment will toss him into the whirling vortex of an inescapable nightmare. There is little or no need for chatter or discussion of what life may demand from us after graduation. We look forward to a short furlough after which we will be ordered to some remote air base where they will form our new crews; pilot, co-pilot, navigator, radio man, flight engineer, armorer and four gunners. Because we are in the Western Air Command, odds are we will find ourselves on the desert many miles from the nearest feminine companionship. Our planes will be either B-24s, also known as Liberators, or B-17 Flying Fortresses. They are the only four-engine long-range bombers used by the Air Force and consequently the only aircraft with complete ten man crews.

All we know about B-24s is what G.I. Morris has to say about the B-24s he helped put together up in Seattle, which would be to ground every one of them right away. Anything G.I. says on this subject comes off a stool with a certain amount of credibility. Unfortunately, hands on experience has him horrified at the thought he might someday end up in one of the B-24s he had been working on. "Ending up" is what bothers G.I., he says he believes the rumors that Liberators often blow up in the air for no particular reason. Since his skepticism about these aircraft which he unlovingly calls "Flying Shit Houses," has been heard over and over by anyone trapped into giving him five minutes of their time, G.I.'s anxiety is not creating any phobias around the barracks. However, during loose minutes of undisturbed mental roving, it does make a man thoughtful.

Some things are probably certain. Most of us will become commissioned officers, which means better pay, some privileges, and glittering silver wings on our stylish dress uniforms. It's what we expected and exactly what we will get. Professionally, we will have acquired a rare skill in the art of dropping explosives on people, places, and things around the world. We will be moving in from the outer edges of the battle field and thereby become active contributors to the war effort although our net value in future battles is never discussed around the barracks. The accepted attitude points to graduation, receiving a commission, pinning on the wings, receiving a furlough and not dwelling on what may happen after that. For the last year we have been further from combat than the only son of a member of congress.

Sometimes, thinking about the year of training that seemed so long and passed so quickly has a person wondering if anything in our little world is real or even worth the trouble. Although it is neither wise nor worthwhile to think about a future that may not exist, it's probably normal for an anxious thought to sneak into a person's mind during idle moments. It seems the war will never end and where will we be when and if such a thing happens? A person, even a cadet, has to be realistic from time to time. With a little luck, the world will still be here and people will still be people. I sometimes have the feeling that one afternoon in the distant future, old folks, examining musty archives, will learn that Deming air base, in the winter of 1943-44, graduated another herd of one-trick ponies and that will be that. As a group we are well qualified at one thing and one thing only; we will be good at aiming those power packed pickles but, after that, what are we good for? If the war goes on until 1950, my mother will still be writing to ask what a bombardier does and telling me to be careful.

Now, standing here, studying the long line of aircraft, all of which are AT-11s, it is easy to understand why there has been disappointment around the barracks concerning the planes that will carry us through the next few weeks. Most of us expected machines that would be sleek and much larger. No question we are somewhat spoiled by our experience flying gunnery missions on huge, famous B-17 flying Fortresses at Kingman. However, no one is making a real a fuss about it. Everyone realizes that AT-lls are what we have and exactly all we're going to get. By this time, we have become experts at Military Behavior 101, the ability to adapt.

From this day on, our principle focus is no longer theory of bombing. Now it's "Bombs away!" It's time for watching them drift toward the earth and whispering softly, "Get in that circle you little bastard." The target is a small triangular shack in the exact center of a white circle. The circle is painted on the ground with the same kind of lye used to mark sidelines on football fields. The shack, centerpiece of the target, is constructed of metal and firmly planted to take hits from hundred pound bombs. Tradition has it that the damn thing sometimes dances around when the wind is up.

It has been almost a year of days that go slowly and weeks that pass quickly since a sunny Saturday morning at Santa Ana when we were designated aviation cadets. Our names were posted on a wall bearing testimony that weeks of testing had found us healthy and of average intelligence. Therefore we were being taken into the fold and tendered the honor of studying to become bombardier-navigators. We were not asked if such a future meshed with our dreams.

Today, at last, the complete picture is forming. In a matter of moments, in this chilly, foggy dawn at a God forsaken little airfield only a short ride from the Mexican border, we are about to take the first step. We will soon change from earth bound, wingless, uniformed turkeys to soaring eagles uniquely prepared to serve our nation in the wild blue yonder.

We have marched. We have studied. We have been tested for any possible weakness at every turn. Today, although it will just be for practice, we finally go into the air with the sole purpose of dropping bombs. It's a benchmark day.

We stand quietly at parade rest moving from one foot to the other in the half-light of early morning. We watch as pilots swing up into their planes. Seen through a morning fog, the aircraft appear to tilt backward, balancing on their tails with glass noses pointing toward the sky. Their silhouettes could be those of squatting animals waiting to be fed. Suddenly we hear a monstrous throaty cough from each aircraft as engines struggle and strain to come to life and start the fans turning. We listen as pilots work their engines up to full power and check the mags. Soon the overcast is shattered by crackling pounding in the air. Back home it might have been a parade of Model "A" Fords with broken mufflers going down Central Avenue during the Fourth of July parade.

As the AT-11s reach full power, engine nacelles shudder slightly. It's a twin engine aircraft manufactured by the Beechcraft Company and is far from the most expensively assembled aircraft on the Air Corps list. However, its utility is remarkable in that it can be refitted to serve the various training requirements of bombardiers, navigators or aerial gunners. Although it does have twin engines, its fuselage, only thirty-five feet long and a wingspan of less than fifty feet from tip to tip, is not imposing. Nevertheless, the AT-11 airplane has a little something for everybody and the Air Force orders them by the thousands.

The models we will fly in have been refitted with a glass nose, bomb racks and a large hole in the floor of the rear section allowing bombs to be filmed as they drop. The model prepared for navigators has a top turret to which a cadet can ascend and 'shoot' stars at night. Although we spent many hours in the classroom studying celestial navigation, our curriculum has now been changed and bombardiers no longer have any need of an upper turret.

However, we still are concentrating on pilotage navigation. Aviators have used pilotage since the Wright brothers first lifted off and soared about forty feet. Basically, it is a system based on the belief that what you see is what you get. In the early days of aviation, old timers with ear flaps on their helmets and lacking instruments to keep them on course took what was available which, for the most part, consisted of steady nerves, a good memory and an ability to spot stationary visible objects on the ground. What they came up with, called *pilotage*, was not only the best thing available, it was the only thing. Pilots had to depend on roads, bridges, hills, rivers, church towers and other markers while hoping everything would show up where it was supposed to be. As time passed they learned to keep a log book and wherever possible kept track of temperature, wind direction and other factors that influence ground speed which is the rate at which an air plane is actually moving across the earth. With such information and a certain amount of luck, pilots had a reasonable chance of knowing where they were, could guess at a semi-accurate landing time, and usually put his aircraft on the ground somewhere near where he wanted to be. The trick then, as it is now, was to keep up with the facts. One bad step and the pilotage navigator is faced with putting Humpty Dumpty together again. With the log in decent shape, it's possible to hope for the best.

However, since it's now obvious the emphasis of our training is on being full time bombardiers and not part time navigators, there is an obvious change in attitude. The word is out that we will no longer be flying pilotage-training missions and the news caused a shift in attitude. No one, including our instructors, takes navigation training seriously anymore. Our future is in getting a low circular error rating on our bombing record. It would be difficult to find anyone in our barracks worried about pilotage navigation any more.

The same news covers *Celestial Navigation*. We are still studying stars in the classroom but won't be tested. Many of us, including me, are happy to forget about *Celestial Navigation*. We know where the North Star is. Finding it is about the only part of *Celestial Navigation* most of us will ever remember. The subject is full of new turns and crazy angles and is a tough subject to learn under pressure. Yet, it's easy to feel very stupid when we realize that Columbus, and possibly the

Phoenicians, were using the same system hundreds or thousands of years ago.

I won't miss *Pilotage* either. The basics are simple but the execution can get very hairy. My first and only pilotage navigation mission, a round trip to Silver City, took place on Sunday afternoon last week. Silver City is one of the few places where cadets can find a little action on a weekend. As we buzzed along over the desert I got to thinking how nice it would be to be down there instead of up here. The result was a catastrophic daydream. I got behind in keeping my log and had to scramble. There is no way to catch up, but I tried. The log looked like it had been written in Arabic. I offered the pilot a couple of long shot guesses as to new headings and after some surprised looks he put the plane on a new heading. Unfortunately, my corrections headed us to Lordsburgh, a mining town about 30 miles off course from Silver City. The pilot looked at the log and said, "Well, Mister. Silver City isn't the kind of place we might want to bomb even if we had any bombs. Guess we might as well turn around and go home unless you want me to swoop over Lordsburgh so you can help mine their coal for 'em."

I welcomed the sarcasm. When a 2nd Lieutenant makes a wise crack he is out of his barking dog mode for at least a little while. That was then. Right now the important thing is for Lieutenant Weed to emerge from the flight room. We wait until he comes out and signals Olaf Arneson, our cadet commander, to call us to attention and lead us inside.

We quickly break ranks and move into the flight room. The door closes, muffling engine noise. I think of a September afternoon when I was about ten years old. My Uncle Greg took me to the auto races at the Minnesota State Fair. I loved the noisy racket and the smell of smoke from the cars. Most of all, I have never forgotten September sunlight reflecting from the red, blue, yellow, and orange radiator hoods of those open cockpit race cars flashing around the dirt track. The drivers sat up straight in the cockpit while mechanics pumped at superchargers to reach speeds of eighty miles an hour. Louis Schneider, who had won at Indianapolis on Memorial Day, didn't race but did run a solo exhibition lap while the crowd stood and cheered. I have the same feeling listening to the AT-11s running up this morning. One of those planes is ours. I wonder what comes next.

A person might feel the situation could create some anxiety but the room is very quiet; no nervous laughter, no conversation. We understand that the usual flight contains three cadets, a pilot and an instructor. In addition, the plane usually carries five one hundred-pound bombs, Looking at it from the outside and making a guess, this seems to be a full boat. When we get around to dropping bombs there will be two of us at a time, cadet and instructor stuffed into the nose. Makowski says we should quit bitching because sardines have it a lot tougher than we do. The flight room itself is very crowded. All the chairs are occupied and most of us have to stand.

It doesn't take long to find our names and those of our pilot and instructor chalked on a large blackboard covering one wall. We are in wing number two and the old GI alphabet game is in full swing. There we are; AC, Jack I. Moore; AC Neil Kahler and AC Edwin.T.MacBride. The name of pilot and instructor are on the blackboard.

Thanks to the alphabet, all of the cadets in our ship are from the same barracks. No introductions are necessary. Eddie Mac Bride from Hingham, Massachusetts, like myself, likes to roll dice and play cards so we get along fine. We aren't sure what to expect but since the bombs we drop today won't count against us we really have nothing to lose. According to Lieutenant Weed that will be the case all week. He gives us some very restrictive warnings about being careful and repeats the proper procedures for our conduct at the flightline.

The Lieutenant puts particular stress on the importance of papers that must be filled out after every mission. There will be plenty of them. It seems like there are forms covering everything except our credit rating. All forms must be filed after every mission. The most important and wide ranging requirements include altitude computation sheets, target series sheets, 12 C forms, equipment forms, plane number, pilot's initials, and bombsight number. There is also space for various questions from the pilot and instructor. My guess is that those questions will be brief and invariably followed by statements of some length.

Lieutenant Weed explains again that this week our missions will be practice runs. We have not been asked to pre-flight the bombsights and will not be judged on today's results. He then advises us to pick up our chutes and be outside waiting for the pilots when it's time to go. Since the pilots are already waiting in their planes, the best we can do is pick up parachutes, hurry out to the runway, find the plane with our number on it and climb in. The whole process doesn't take long but, unfortunately, we lose some time while Eddie tries to get his parachute harness untangled. Finally, we salute the two officers, climb into the airplane and are directed to the back of the plane. They do not seem favorably impressed by our delay in getting on board. The pilot snaps an added reminder to put our seat belts on tight. Eddie and I trade glances and wonder why they are scowling and shaking their heads. We didn't hold them up that long. What do they expect? It's not our fault somebody left his chute harness all tangled up.

We were only a minute or two delayed. The incident passes quickly and is soon forgotten; a crude reminder that the Army Air Force is long on altitude but allows no latitude.

The AT-11 starts rolling down the runway and doesn't have to go far before the nose pulls up, the landing gear folds into the wings and our instructor comes back to the waist. He settles on a bucket seat, opens his bombardier bag, pulls out some papers, and says, "Moore and McBride. A couple of Irishmen. Who's Moore? Who's McBride?" We point to our nametags; he stands up, gestures toward me and says, "O.K. Mister. Let's go up front and see what you can do."

I should be nervous, at least more than I am. I feel sure I'm ready. I've only been looking forward to this for several months but even if I get nervous and drop one on the officers' club, it won't be held against me today. At least they promised it wouldn't. My heart skips a couple of beats. This is it. I'm really here.

Getting to the nose requires a crawl through the bomb bay, under the bomb racks past the flight deck and a slide into the nose. The five one hundred pound bombs in the racks, three on one side, two on the other remind me that we are actually at war. I pass the pilot and creep into the nose. The first sensation is that the nose is every bit as crowded in there as we imagined with just enough room for the instructor, the bombsight, and myself. Then I gaze through the plexiglass and get the shock of my life. Like almost every other cadet, I came into the Air Corps having never been off the ground in an airplane. In pre-pre flight at Cedar Rapids, we had one or two short rides in Piper Cubs and at Kingman we were given a few rides in B-17s to try air-to-air firing. Nothing has prepared me for the view that flashes before my eyes from the nose of our AT-11. It seems the whole world is a giant map being unrolled before my eyes. I'm hanging in space, unable to see the wings of the plane. In all my life I have never seen anything like this. Unfolding before me is a complete, unobstructed panorama stretching for more than 180 degrees.

The world down there is a carpet, a colored canvas unfolding endlessly, an ever-changing panorama. This is not the view we got from the waist window of a B-17 at Kingman. We were looking at the same world but only seeing part of it at any one time. The Foshay Tower is the tallest building in Minneapolis and looking out from the top offers a nice view in all directions but the building is stationary and we always see the same thing. Only the bombardier in his little glass house can see what I'm seeing.

Nothing in the world can match the sensation of sitting back and watching old Mother Earth spinning along right before your eyes, changing the picture from minute to minute. I'm in a glass basket up here, feeling like Babe Ruth hitting his sixtieth home run. Pilots spend their time reading dials and watching the horizon. Navigators have to sit in the middle of the plane and squint at their maps. Best of all, the crew will be doing it all for me, working their asses to the bone getting me to the target while I sit in my little office out in front watching the world go by. I think I'm going to like being a bombardier. The instructor takes the cloth covering off the bombsight and leans back before pointing to the bombsight and nodding toward me. My first real bomb run is underway.

At the Initial Point (IP), I click the pilot to let him know we are starting the bomb run. The next move is to switch on the bomb rack by setting the toggle switch to the "ON" position. As soon as we are flying straight and level, I 'uncage' the gyro. Now I have to swing the sight into position with the vertical cross hair on the target and then use the displacement knob to swing the horizontal cross hair also onto the target. The next move is to put the telescope motor toggle switch in an 'on' position. Since we are not using evasive action, and are going straight in, I level the bombsight gyro with the leveling knobs to center bubbles mounted on the gyro housing. I check the gyro again to be sure the plane is flying straight and level. The drift angle has already been preset. The release lever has to be put in firing position and locked. I watch in the telescope as the rate hair and vertical move together to release the bomb automatically and then shout, "Bombs away!" to inform the pilot that the run is over. We watch the one hundred-pound, sand-filled bomb drift toward the target until it hits the earth in a cloud of dust just off the edge of a white circle painted on the ground. It's not a 'shack' but it did hit in the target. I can live with that for a little while.

Our instructor turns to me and says, "O.K. lets try again. The air is so soft up here today I might try one myself." Everything is going better than had been expected. I'm still knocked out by the view from my position in the nose. The pilot takes us away from the target, makes a big turn and gets on course for another attempt at the target. The huge mountains looming in the distance fascinate me. The instructor waits a short time and says, "Well, Mister. Would you like to make a bomb run?"

I say, "Yes, sir."

He says, "Do you think it might be a good idea to click the pilot and let him know about it?" I come out of my trance and click the pilot. What an idiot I am! We are almost at the initial point. How stupid can I be? I'm scrambling, trying to find time for any bomb run at all. The bomb bay doors are open, my hands are twisting the knobs as fast as I can go. I keep the vertical on the target; the rate hair seems to be crawling up in a big hurry. Sooner than I would have liked. When the rate hair and vertical cross the bombs are released automatically, I tell the pilot, "Bombs away!"

The bomb drifts down and goes well beyond the target. It wasn't good, but it could have been worse. If the instructor hadn't waked me up I might have lobbed the thing into a Catholic church just outside the base. I remain silent waiting for the tongue-lashing I richly deserve. It never comes. The instructor stays quiet for a minute or two and then shakes his head. Finally he says, "You know something? I watched that first run and there's no question you know what the hell you're doing. On the second run, even after you went to sleep and got everything fucked up, you were able to complete the run but, hey, failing to click the pilot is just goddam stupid. Turning off your brain is the kind of thing can get somebody killed. I know what you're going through. I went through it myself. Just keep your head out of your ass, Mister. You'll be all right."

I go back to the tail and tell Eddie to get up front. I feel very lucky. The mistake won't count against me because this week is just for practice. In the second place, I met a 2nd Lieutenant with a heart of gold. They have large bunches of instructors on the base so I may never see this one again but I start going over the routines that must be followed. Normally, it's necessary in ending a session to close the bomb bay doors, cage the bombsight gyro, disengage the bombsight clutch, turn off the telescope motor, turn off the gyro, and turn off switches to the bomb bay. Suddenly, I realize I did not go through that procedure when I left the nose. I must be nervous. What am I worrying about? There is no reason to shut down the sight because Eddie and Neal will be using it. Eddie hears me coming, crawls by without a word and disappears down the catwalk toward the nose.

No question the tail must have been whipping around on my second run. Neal must know there was something was going on but whatever it was won't bother him. Thank God we aren't keeping score and our bombs aren't being photographed. My stupidity will be forever buried in the sand at Deming.

The AT-ll can carry five bombs in the bomb bay rack so today with three cadets on board Neal only got one turn on the site. That was O.K. with him. Neal likes everybody and everything and likes to laugh. After Eddie takes his second turn at the bombsight we come back to earth. We have to fill out the required forms which takes a little time but after that, because of time differentials in return of the various flights, we are allowed to walk, not march, back to the barracks from the flightline. I appreciate the fact that my two friends don't ask what was going in during my second bomb run.

I flop onto the sack and analyze where I'm at. Next week the bombs will count. Am I ready? Yes! It has become more and more clear that a bombardier just needs to learn a few subjective moves and follow a routine. Today we didn't have to set up the sight or make last minute corrections. No question they'll have us doing those things as time moves along but it shouldn't be too tough to handle the mental side of this damn bomb dropping Olympics. This morning I didn't hit a shack and only friendly gremlins saved me from going to sleep and dropping one on the officers' mess. It doesn't sound like a great start, but remembering how comfortable I was, how much at home I felt in the air, in my glass house on the nose of that airplane gives me something to look forward to in the morning.

Today was nothing to brag about, but tomorrow will be better. If I have to be in the Army, this is where I want to be. It will be fun to spend the rest of the week getting sharp for next week when everything counts. We hear that the Army has raised the bar. Today we received word that the Air Force has instituted a new measure of proficiency. From now on, to qualify for graduation, a cadet must have hits on 22% of bombs dropped. We will have plenty of time to worry about that next week.

CHAPTER 15

Never Say Never

Practicing how to drop bombs from an airplane would be fun for some people, but not for us. Here we are, college age scholars playing with equipment worth enough to shoot a Hollywood movie; probably one featuring fraternity boys plotting to kidnap the Homecoming Queen and rush her off to South America. Unfortunately, we're too tired to dream about Homecoming Queens or even take a second look at the sweater girls mixing shakes in the cadet lounge. For this, we are indebted to our patient, hard-working, flight leaders, First Lieutenants Faulhaber and Tarzan who control matters in our section, Section 2. Although we have only rumors and no credible proof that clearly cites them as the villains, popular opinion from loud mouths around our barracks has tried the case and finds those two responsible for our new schedule which consists of ninety percent work and ten percent sleep.

Faced with the dilemma of adding flying time to a curriculum already crammed with ground school, physical training, and the traditional sideshow they refer to as military training, it appears our cagey flight leaders conceived a plan to lop time off each end of the eight hours allocated for sleep. It is now being used for flying time averaging about two hours per mission plus critiques and paper work after each flight. Our regular schedule remains in place. The system, which Makowski calls "The Faulhaber-Tarzan Squeeze," is uncomplicated and is undoubtedly the schedule every class has been required to follow at this stage of training. Night classes now run a little later, PT starts earlier in the morning, and marching to and from the mess hall takes care of the military training obligation.

Although this strategy has us bleary eyed and gasping for air, the plan is certain to prevail. It cannot fail because the powers that be have decreed its success. We will make it work because that's the best thing for us to do. The fatigue factor is sky high and drains more than a good night's sleep is able to put back. Most of us will be very tired before the evening of our graduation party at the Mission Inn when a man can dance the night away and say for sure, "It was worth it!" In a more gentle society someone might be tempted to complain but then, in our little world, who would listen? Moe Lund wonders what kind of clocks they use up there at headquarters. There is a certain amount of bitching because "The Squeeze" adds three hours to our work schedule, day or night.

The wind is cold and darkness falls early now that we are moving into November. Deming is a long way from Minneapolis but, surprisingly, I'm reminded of home. The arrival of winter announces itself here at Deming in much the same way it huffs and puffs into Minnesota. The sun appears washed out and casts a gloomy shadow as it sets earlier each afternoon. A bite in the air signals impending frost and we accept the fact it won't be long until our first snowfall. Cadets from the South and West won't be happy about it, but anyone from up North will feel the signs. It will be fine with us if snow holds off until it's time to deliver a white Christmas. In a few weeks we will go on bivouac and spend a couple of weeks on the mesa practicing low altitude bombing. Cadets who have been there say it means toughing life out in a stove heated tent surrounded by slit trenches. Shaving will not be required which is a good thing because there will be no water available for that purpose. The word is that most cadets take advantage of this opportunity and grow a beard. It's difficult to know exactly what to expect because returning cadets telling the story have probably exaggerated wherever possible. We will be in close quarters, and I hope the good Lord puts me in I with people I know.

We will be bombing at low altitudes using a little wire outfit called the five-and-dime bombsight because it looks like a gadget that should be on sale at Kreseges or Woolworths, the well known ten-cent stores. Meantime, we'll be in the air dropping bombs every day to practice low altitude strikes. There will be no ground school classes. It almost sounds as if some of the strict regulations of our daily life at the base will be suspended during our time out on the desert. It would be nice to spend some time in a place where we are not continually tiptoeing through a minefield of commands and specific things to do at precise times. Sometimes we have to wonder what they're thinking about. For instance, flying adds three or four hours to our work schedule day or night. In all segments of the military, work is anything that prevents a soldier from hitting the sack. In the world of an aviation cadet this amounts to a twenty-eight hour day. At the flightline, getting equipment, finding and meeting with the instructor, listening to a lecture about safety by Lieutenant Weed and lugging our parachutes out to the ship can use up a half-hour or more. Projected length of flight time is chalked on the black board and almost without exception states, "Length of mission two hours." Like most of their orders, this one means exactly what it says and what it says is "Stay up there and don't come back after one hour and fifty-nine minutes." If we finish bombing early, we must remain aloft fluttering from cloud to cloud like homesick angels looking for a place to spend the night. Pilots don't care for this rule and sometimes mutter nasty words under their breath, but there is a reason for it. Last Sunday on a navigation flight our pilot got us back to the field about twenty minutes early with the result that Mo Lund and I were treated to a real dog and pony show while our pilot tried explaining to Lieutenant Weed why one of the most carefully enforced regulations had been violated. The pilot reached for an alibi knowing he would only get one shot. In no way can he lateral off the blame to his passengers.

"Couldn't help it, Woody" he said firmly. "The ship was eating up gas and we were running short. Had to get back here before we ran out." Weed's groan ricocheted against the walls and could have been heard throughout the flight building but, fortunately, crews that will soon fill the place are still up in the sky, doing their duty. Our pilot had made a serious mistake by choosing an impossible excuse. Even the most stupid cadet on the base is aware that the faster you fly the quicker you use fuel. He knew it and knew that Weed knew it but he had to say something. There was nowhere else to go. Lieutenant Weed shook his head and rolled his eyes signaling utter disbelief, then turned and walked to his office at the back of the room.

Our pilot left the building knowing he will not be punished. No first lieutenant is going to throw the book at another unless a woman is involved. Secondly and most important, Weed is very concerned about safety in the air. Almost all of his speeches stress his dislike for being forced to notify families of unfortunate cadets. He's a big man with a loud voice and his soliloquies always start; "I've asked ya', I begged ya', now I'm tellin' ya. I'm tired of sendin' these letters to somebody's folks. You men might as well get used to it; like it or not, you're gonna have a close call every 100 hours so don't get caught with your head in your ass."

We understand his attitude and know there's a good reason for pilots to observe the rule about landing time. Deming Airfield, at any hour, is a very busy place. The sky is full of AT-11 aircraft with each one carrying two lieutenants and three cadets. It works better if they don't all try to land at the same time. The goal is to control the landing pattern and have planes come down on the runway instead of each other.

From our standpoint, we didn't gain any sack time by landing early. Someone had to critique us and there was no one around except Weed who was wandering around wearing the expression of a man with a sour stomach. Any cadet knows the look. The rules have been broken, someone will have to pay and we are the only targets in sight. After a mission we normally spend as much as a half-hour being critiqued and completing required paper work. Lieutenant Weed questions us for two hours and doesn't dismiss us until the last flight has landed. Marching back to the mess hall I picture him leaning over his desk writing a letter to a family knowing it will break their hearts. I wouldn't want the job. He took his anger out on us because he couldn't kick ass on his friend. It's not tough to see his side of the picture. I like the guy.

This week we are on the afternoon shift. Most of the people in our barracks have finished the first round of night bombing and indications are that almost everyone has gotten their share of hits. It's not a matter that comes up in ordinary conversation but, when people live so close together, reading attitudes becomes automatic. At first, with bombs being measured and counted for the record, the need for concentration was intense. Now, having laid down some hits and knocked off a shack here or there, my guess is that most of us who bombed at night did well enough to relieve the pressure and pump up a new round of confidence.

As we had been led to expect, bombing at night was a pickle aimer's dream. The sky was filled with stars, and a pleasant breeze pushed us along a smooth path to a smiling target looking as big around and shiny as a harvest moon. Without interference from Mother Nature, our pilots delivered a straight, stable bomb run 100% of the time. My partner, Makowski, also enjoyed seven consecutive evenings of watching his bombs dive toward the target as smoothly as Santa Claus sliding down a chimney on Christmas Eve. Pilots were relaxed, instructors were smiling. Mack and I each dropped four bombs on the first evening of night bombing resulting in three hits and a shack for me and four hits for Mack. It was the first flight where our bombs counted and we hustled to the flight building to be critiqued by our instructors and fill out the necessary papers and charts feeling as if we had finally been initiated into an elite club. Once inside, I notice that none of the cadets crowded into the room are talking about success or failure. We were not out there swinging at golf balls and there is no trace of a clubhouse atmosphere. We don't hear those who did well asking other cadets how it went, hoping for an opening to tell their own story. Conversations at the various tables are serious and respectfully quiet.

I guess what we're doing is not a game. At least I've never looked at it that way but, when the cards are all on the table, we're doing something where the score is damn important and the prizes are things that no amount of money can buy. If the day of our graduation ever arrives, I expect to hear two speeches. The first, by Colonel Milton Murphy our commanding officer, will be to congratulate us; the second, the one that will dance in my head goes; "Step right up gentlemen and accept your commissions in the Army Air Force of the United States of America. Your new uniforms, the ones with silver wings on the chest and gold bars on the shoulders are all yours and, by the way, look for a nice raise in pay. Did I mention we look forward to enjoying your company at the officers' mess?"

In my early childhood, I learned to play several kinds of card games ranging from poker to Racehorse Smear and contract bridge. Everybody played: Grandpa and Grandma, all my uncles, my brothers and sister, and all the guys in the neighborhood played one kind of game or another. I learned them all, and have a good idea of when to bet 'em or forget 'em, and can recognize a game when I see one. In my opinion, if anyone should ask, what we are doing here has all the qualities of one heck of a game. I know this much for sure; if I can keep going and graduate, when Colonel Murphy reaches out to give me those silver wings, it will be the best hand I have ever held.

It's important to remember this is only the start. Mack and I did fine in our first crack at night bombing but everything we've heard since arriving in Deming is that your grandma could get hits at night. Experts rate night bombing as a "must do" exercise where shacks jump up and catch the bombs.

Well, we did O.K. One thing I like about night flying is that they keep the mess hall open until eleven or twelve to feed us. I don't know why but after a night mission I get ravenous. There's something about it that makes me feel I've done something important and deserve a good meal.

Tonight, Mack and I lean against the wind, pushing our way through an inky darkness, heading toward the mess hall. Winter is on the way. Even a Minnesota boy can feel the deceptive chill that burrows into the marrow of his bones here in Deming. It's the kind that calls for warm blankets and hot coffee as soon as possible. This type of weather reminds me of Jefferson Barracks and the thought makes me quiver. The clock on the wall says almost ten hundred hours and we're tired but once we get inside the mess hall the flow of warm air is liquid and wraps itself around us. We put hamburgers, fried potatoes and coffee on the tin trays and find the food is as good as it smells.

Night bombing is only a start but we feel good about it. Things could change drastically tomorrow when we start bombing in the afternoon and may be forced to face the fabled winds of Deming. It is something to anticipate but right now I am thinking only of hitting the sack. I got my hits at night and there's no reason I won't get some more tomorrow afternoon; winds or no winds. We have a long way to go and there are other hurdles than just a few winds and clouds. We are going into a stage called qualification bombing that tests standard proficiency. Each cadet is required to drop 145 bombs with a circular error of 230 feet or less.

Sometimes I seem to be riding a merry-go-round that never stops. We march from one event to another but nothing changes. When we go from night flying to afternoons we maintain a regular rotation with ground school classes in the morning and evening. That means pushing physical training back to evening so this week it will be ground school in the morning, flying in the afternoon and marching to chow. After that we are permitted to lower our faces into the dirt and digest our dinner while doing push-ups and other back breaking contortions on a grass free minefield of tiny stones.

At first, the pressure of having every bomb photographed and measured for accuracy created a palpable tension that put a shadow over everything and everybody. It could be felt even when we had a chance for valuable sack time. The barracks bristled with sharp tongues

254

and quick tempers. It's really amazing that now, when we are deep into the toughest part of our training, when the stakes are highest, that tension has been replaced by hope and confidence. I got my hits at night and really believe I'm as good a bombardier as anybody in our class or any other class for that matter. Maybe not! Sometimes it feels as if someone is watching over me. Maybe my mother's novenas are paying off. Whatever it is, leaning over a bombsight feels like the most natural thing in the world for me to do. My dad always described life as a big wheel that spins slowly and changes things from day to day. His code: remember, when you're at the top of the wheel things are not as good as you think, when you hit the bottom, remember it will soon pick you up. I guess the wheel is up for me right now. I hope it doesn't go down before graduation.

All of us who have been flying at night during our first week of competition were well aware that night bombing offered the best chance to pile up some points. It was everything they promised and I got my hits; so did almost everybody else. Labeling myself a "hot bombardier" is probably premature and this afternoon I may well be tested by the infamous "Deming Nightmare," treacherous afternoon winds capable of tossing an AT-11 around like a rag doll. The word around the cadet lounge is that accurate bombing is sometimes impossible in the afternoon. Two successful and rewarding weeks of nighttime missions have raised my confidence to a high level. I try to picture the worst conditions that might occur, but don't find anything capable of producing a situation too hot to handle. I know my trade. Flashbacks of discouraging experiences recited by veterans of these same skies cannot dent my overriding confidence. Yet, from deep in my psyche where results of similar experiences are stored, a tiny voice whispers, "Look out, fat head."

It looks like demonic skies are not prepared to challenge us today. Nothing in the near vicinity hints at severe atmospheric conditions. The sky is blue, the breeze moderate. Today I'm paired with Neil Kahler from Chicago, Illinois. Kahler is a happy go lucky kind of person who likes to laugh. I consider him one of my better friends among the whole bunch. As we climb into the aircraft we sense no high winds, and see no sign of overcast. Perhaps the feared daytime winds of Deming have taken the afternoon off. Maybe the afternoon terrors portrayed in the lounge are a fraud drummed up to frighten unwary cadets.

We have heard so much about the fearsome weather that blows into Deming during most afternoons that it looms like a foreboding experience, something to be challenged and forgotten. Now, at least for this afternoon, we may be disappointed. My hope of challenging the Deming skies may prove to be a toothless milk run. It's comfortable to know that the conditions we are observing will probably mean a few more hits when the reports are added up, but who cares? I got my hits at night. There will be no problem if I don't get another hit during the entire week. However, it would be interesting to learn whether that tiresome phrase "Get your hits at night" has any truth in it. Today, windy or calm, Kahler and I are prepared to take turns lying on our bellies in the back of the plane to photograph each other's bombing results.

Getting those pictures is difficult, important, and somewhat dangerous. The photographer must lean out and hold a large, heavy camera through a huge hole in the floor of the plane. It is possible, with a bit of carelessness, for a cadet to fall through the floor and out into space. A cadet named Willard Netzley from the class of 44-5 did so and got an eleven thousand-foot ride down in his parachute and a five-mile walk back to the base. Cadets are required to keep parachutes buckled on at all times.

Any cadet failing to get the picture of a bomb dropped by his partner is in trouble; especially if the bomb in question is on a wayward path that might count against the man who dropped it. The instructor will rave if he thinks you're cheating. The cadet motto "cooperation leads to graduation" riles instructors beyond belief. We understand the notice on the bulletin board stating that anyone with a photography proficiency of less than 75% will be brought to the attention of the faculty board.

Missing a photo, even one of a bomb headed for the target, creates unhappiness on the flight deck because the pilot must do it all over again. The cadet who dropped the bomb is either heart-broken or relieved depending where the bomb finally hits. The befuddled photographer can only listen as three people chew his ass at the same time.

Today we take off and start our climb to the specified altitude of 5,000 feet just in time for a big surprise. The AT-11 has been straining as it climbed and now, as we near bombing altitude, it begins to bounce and crab into the wind. The twin engines are working hard as they buck the wind, but we finally reach 5,000 feet. The sun is now only partially visible and angry blue-gray clouds obscure the ground. It as if someone threw a switch and changed the horizon. Kahler and I bounce around in the back as the aircraft rises and drops wondering what it would take to bounce us off the ceiling. We have become very conscious of the huge hole in the floor beside us. Kahler and I exchange glances that ask if it's possible to use a bombsight on the back of a bucking bronco. The instructor picks up his notebook, nods toward me and says, "Let's go, Mister."

The ship sways from side to side as I stagger through the bomb bay, crawl past the flight deck, and squeeze into the nose next to our instructor. A peek through the nose window reveals angry rolling clouds. I kneel down hoping my head won't be slapped against the bombsight. I would like to tell the pilot, "I am convinced; the afternoon winds at Deming are real. Let's concede and go home." I thank God for letting me get my hits on smooth and peaceful evenings and am totally certain that under present conditions no bombardier exists who can put a bomb anywhere near a target ten times bigger than the one I will aim at.

The pilot keeps the nose pointed up and I locate the target through a split second opening in the clouds. We are all over the sky and I tell myself it's just a matter of time until one of these plunges or quick turns will tumble the gyro and everything goes black. If that happens, it will be necessary to abort the mission and go home which will be just fine with me. The hairs on the site are moving toward each other and when they meet, regardless of wind, rain, tipped gyro or St. Elmo's Fire sputtering off the propellers, this bomb is going to be released and where it will hit the earth is anybody's guess. I am totally helpless. I watch an angry, boiling gray cloud slide beneath us and spread a blanket over the target. The hairs meet and I manage a very weak, "Bombs away." There is no way of making a semi-coordinated guess as to where this one will land. I privately concede to the winds of Deming and all they stand for but my right eye remains planted on the bombsight observing a stormy picture of vicious clouds. They fascinate me; I see it as the sky cover that is about to conceal the official landing place of the wildest bomb ever released by mankind. Suddenly, the site comes to life. As if by magic, clouds clear for a moment, just long enough to see my bomb and watch it settling into the center of the target. This cannot have happened, but it did.

The pilot is laughing, and pumping his fist. The instructor shakes his head in disbelief. I say a Hail Mary, and hope Kahler got a good picture of that one. Tomorrow at the cadet lounge I'll be shouting, "Get your hits at night." They better believe it. Kahler and I drop our two bombs each but neither of us comes close to another hit. I don't think I can ever forget mine:--a bomb run where nobody saw the target until the bomb landed smack in the middle of it. Not only that, Kahler must have been jumping around like a monkey in the back of the plane to get the picture but he did. I like Kahler.

Right now, as things move along, our class, 44-2, will graduate on February 5th, 1944. A few cadets are struggling to get enough hits to qualify and the instructors are working hard to pull them through. It's almost dark and I'm dog-tired. I make a quick move and grab a chair only to hear the captain in charge of our section yelling my name. At least I think he's hollering my name but, as usual after a mission, the flight room is packed with people filling out papers and instructors chewing cadets and warning them to get their heads out of their asses before it's too late. Even though I'm not certain it was my name being called, its absolutely necessary to make sure. That involves pushing my way through the hustle and bustle to an office at the rear of the building where the captain does his business. I salute and say, "Aviation cadet Jack Moore reports as ordered, sir."

He shuffles some sheets of paper and, after a pause to study them, gives me a sharp look that conveys the seriousness of our meeting. After a pause he points the information sheets toward me and growls, "You get any hits today, Mister?"

I reply "Yes, sir, I got one, Sir, but I already had enough before that."

"Wait a minute. You telling me you already got your hits. I don't see that here. Let me take another look at this goddam book. You say your name is Moore?"

"Yes, sir."

"What the hell are you doing here? I want Morse. John Morse. Go out there and get John Morse, and tell him I want his ass in here on the double." I breath a sigh of relief that he wasn't looking for G.I. Morris, who could be wanted for almost any infraction in the book. I know Johnny has been struggling to get the pickles in the jar. He's a nice guy and my heart goes out to him, but time has about run its limit. I find him, and give him the news. John's jaw twists a bit, he says nothing and starts toward the captain's office.

By the time Kahler and I get our papers filled out and leave the building it is past ten hundred hours and very dark. It's the empty, quiet time of night that poets such as Edgar Allen Poe and William Shakespeare liked fooling around in. Even by our standards back home, this is a cold night. We crouch and push against a fierce wind that moans between the barracks. It cuts and bites. I feel like I may be getting a chill but once we are inside, smelling good food and beginning to thaw out, the thought escapes me. The place is warm, the food is good. We walk back to the barracks. I hit the sack, turn out the light and go to sleep only to awaken in the middle of the night with a sore throat, shaking as if every bone in my body is on fire. The shadow of Jefferson Barracks haunts my effort to fall asleep. I hope I feel better in the morning and hope it won't be necessary to go on sick call. The rumor is that the base is suffering from a flu epidemic but no one in our barracks has been hit. This close to graduation, taking time out could really mess things up. I sweat out a long miserable night divided between trips to the water fountain and latrine. It seems the sun will never come up. At last, it shows up, but brings no joy. I had expected to be feeling better, but if anything I'm worse.

I turn myself in for sick call at 800 hours and am startled by the number of cadets lined up and waiting. It appears most of our class is hacking, coughing, and shivering with the collars of their GI overcoats pushed up over their ears. As a result, the doc gives us each a dose of sulfa and tells us we are in the middle of a flu epidemic. In addition, he grounds the whole bunch of us for the next twenty-four hours. Major Gifford, commander of students, posts a notice telling us we are excused from classes for the remainder of the day. He explains that although we are grounded, we will be required to report to the flight line this evening, after chow, and inform them of our situation. Our cadet officer is directed to explain that the flight surgeon has grounded us for twenty-four hours and we are not to fly under any circumstances.

After chow, we march to the flight line and our cadet captain explains to the officer in charge what our position is and must be. The officer in charge says, "Don't give me that bullshit. You hear those fans turning? My pilots are waiting and instructors are ready right now."

Our cadet officer, Olaf the Great, makes one more try. "Excuse me, Sir, but I was ordered to inform you that these men, including me, are grounded for the next 24 hours by the flight surgeon."

Olaf will not win the debate. The officer in charge says, "You look healthy enough to me. Nobody told me about it. Pilots are here, instructors are here, and this flight is ready to go. My advice is you men get your asses into that building over there, fill out your forms, and take advantage of this beautiful cool evening to get yourselves some hits."

Olaf does an about-face and calls us to attention. We march through the twilight, and halt at the door of the flight building where he turns us loose and we cough our way inside to prepare for the mission. My legs and back feel stiff, and I have a headache. Everyone seems to be dragging. Some have beet red faces, the color of high fevers that we learned to recognize at Jefferson Barracks.

Our mission runs the usual two hours, but I feel as if it has been a couple of days. After we land and fill out our forms, most of us head straight for the barracks instead of making the usual stop at the mess hall. Because it is difficult to talk and cough at the same time, there is very little conversation as we beat our way back to the barracks. I don't know how the rest of them feel but I know I'm sick. None of us, even the big brains, men with something to say about everything, don't know anything about sulfa and nobody knows why the Doc grounded us. He must have had a reason. We flew against his orders, what kind of price will we pay for that? It's difficult to avoid thinking about the situation because coughing and hacking make sleep impossible. A betting man would put his money on a crowd of cadets showing up at sick call again tomorrow.

As it works out, at sick call this morning, there are more than twenty of us waiting for the flight surgeon who showed up late. He wastes no time starting to take temperatures and pick out those with the highest numbers. I am waved to the larger group isolated on the far side of the room. When the Doc dismisses those in the smaller group and tells them to return to duty, it becomes clear that the rest of us will be hanging around for further treatment. Having finished picking his winners and losers, Doc asks the nurses to conduct the rest of us to the infirmary. It's O.K. with me. I don't care where they put me if the place is warm. Right now I'm wondering if I can make it as far as a bed. For the first time in months I'm completely indifferent to the war, the Army, or silver wings in the moonlight.

This is worse than Jefferson Barracks, where I thought I was as sick as any human being can be. More than anything, I want to be warm and stop shaking. One by one the nurses conduct us to infirmary and tuck us in. I stumble into the bed, pull a GI blanket up under my chin. It's incredible but when the nurse props a pillow under my head I begin feeling better immediately. The soft, clean bed reminds me of home. I lie between the sheets feeling better by the minute. It might be the warm bed and soft white pillow but by evening I feel good, and drop off to sleep. When I awaken a stern feminine voice is ordering, "O.K., Mister, time to shed a little blood for your country."

A glance at the empty bottle in her hand signals that I'm next to face the needle. I tell her I'm fine and expect to return to duty tomorrow so it won't be necessary to take another jab at my arm which has been pierced over and over for the good of my country. I have wasted my breath. She has the needle and the permission of the United States government to use it as she sees fit. I am about to learn that GI nurses don't argue they just do their duty. She caps the vial containing her latest collection, picks up an empty one, bites her bottom lip and slides the needle into my arm smooth as an Ella Fitzgerald love song. Finished, she corks the bottle, holds it up to the light, smiles sweetly and says, "Sorry, boys, but it looks like you'll be here all week."

The other patients slowly raise their heads and stare in wonder. She is already at the next bedside and explaining, "It's this flu epidemic. They aren't taking any chances of spreading it around any more than necessary. It's doctor's orders. He isn't taking any chances. The new rule is that anybody confined to the hospital must stay seven days."

The room remains silent as she finishes her rounds, strolls out the door and turns off the light. I lower my head to the pillow. Across the room G.I. Morris mumbles that she must be Dracula's daughter. Someone echoes, "Yeah, call her D. D. and hold up a cross next time she comes around with that needle."

The news is a shock but it could be worse. The food is good and the place is warm, but what about flying time we're missing? How can we ever catch up? The first day in here everybody slept and was quiet but now we all feel good and the natives are growing restless. Twenty healthy young guys with nothing to do will always find some way to pass the time. Sometimes, they can get pretty wild. Our major entertainment has been peering out the window watching it snow for two days. At first it was a new phenomenon to some cadets from warm climates, but now Mother Nature has lost her magic and been supplanted by an irresistible urge to throw things. The fun starts when G.I. Morris picks up someone's shoe and flings it at no one in particular. Since it is the only game in town, everybody wants to play. As time passes, the shoes gain momentum. Finally when Herky Helms opens the back door and fires someone's size twelves outside into the snow pile the fun becomes a GI issue footwear outdoor shot-putting contest. I determine that the day may be heading for a bad end and choose the position of innocent bystander and enjoy the action until Bernie Parsons dives under the bed and throws my shoes out the door into the snow.

The excitement comes to an abrupt end when D. D. and two other nurses burst into the room shouting, "Are you guys out of your minds?" We stop in our tracks momentarily before running toward the back door to reclaim our shoes. D. D. reaches the door first and slams it shut while ordering us to hit the sack on the double and stay there. She is a very angry nurse as are the three confederates standing at her side, red-faced and breathing fast, opening and closing their fists.

We straggle to our beds like little boys caught in the cookie jar, wondering what comes next. We don't have to wait. What comes next is neither a cyclone nor a typhoon, but hits with the power God grants to women when they declare themselves and really mean it. Mothers usually have this quality to a high degree and the only defense is to sit and listen.

D. D. takes her position at the center of the room and states with conviction born of good reason, "You men are idiots. Plain and simple. I can't believe anyone with the average IQ of men in your position can be so stupid. You come in here half dead with temperatures off the stick. We feed you, give you medicine, get you well, and now we find you running around barefoot in the snow like you're training for a relapse. Hey, guys! You got good bodies, but where are your brains? You shook off this flu bug, or whatever it is, but listen to me: a relapse will be something much worse. I know what I'm talking about. You're scheduled to be out of here in a couple of days. At least those who don't develop pneumonia because of your little romp in the snow. Please, for everybody's sake, settle down and keep your head out of your ass."

She and the other nurses leave quietly. The room remains silent when they are gone. The ladies in white have given us a few things to think about, some bad, some good. Most pleasing is D.D.'s statement that we will be leaving the hospital in a couple of days. Now, at the end of the week, there is a decided lack of coughing and throat clearing; pretty strong evidence most or all of us will not be relapsing. On the other hand we have no idea what will happen concerning the week of flying time we lost. D. D. will probably not come around this evening. Since we have been pronounced healthy, there is no reason for her to take our blood. If she doesn't come around and we leave tomorrow, I know I will never see her again. There is no reason I should miss her, she is no raving beauty, but I feel she is someone it would be nice to meet at another time, during different circumstances. Something about her seems special. Maybe it's just what she does and how she does it; remembering all our names and what towns we come from, things like that. It may not sound like much but such things become very important when a person is surrounded by indifference. Years from now, if I'm lucky and come through the years ahead, when I've forgotten most of the names of people I spent time with in the Air Force, I can see myself telling the guys about the shoe fight a bunch of cadets had at Deming. I'll tell them about the nurse we called Dracula's daughter and how she saved us from a bout with pneumonia. I don't know why, but I'll remember D. D..

This morning the doctor came in and said we can return to duty immediately. He also said we should report at once to Major Gifford, commandant of students at headquarters. I'm plenty nervous about what is going to happen to the rest of my life as a cadet. My class, 44-2, will graduate on February 2nd 1944 and I'm now a full seven days behind them in flight time. I don't know how I can catch up. I have enough hits, and my circular error is good. I guess I can only pray my bombing records are good enough for them to give me some kind of break. I really don't think they're going to wash us out because there are twenty of us all in the same position. We certainly didn't catch the flu on purpose. I won't complain no matter what. I'll pray that they'll let me finish up and get my wings and commission. Christmas is only a few days away and if they tell me I can stay around and make up my time, even if it means a week or two of KP, it will be the best Christmas present I ever received.

Like any cadet, I hate to go down to headquarters. I feel that I don't belong there and am trampling on hallowed ground. It may be that the people who rule there are in complete control of my life with the absolute power to quash my future with a few strokes of ink on a piece of paper. I don't know any of them. In several months at Deming I have never had a conversation with anyone ranking higher than a first lieutenant. I have never met Major Gifford, but now I find myself standing before his desk. I note that he is a ground officer who wears a tiny mustache and speaks softly. I have never met him until this morning, but I report as ordered and go into his office feeling he has my future in his hand. He returns my salute and tells me to take a chair. I look up and notice he is going through a large stack of papers. He doesn't waste much time once he finds the page he wants. He looks up and says, "How you feeling?"

I say, "Fine, Sir."

He says, "Well, your bombing record is very good, but we don't see how you men can catch up with the class of 44-2. I think there are about twenty of you, all good men. We decided that the best thing for everybody is for you to take yourself a furlough, then finish with 44-3."

He hands me my furlough orders and says, "Enjoy yourself, Mister. We'll see you in about ten days."

I say, "Thank you, Sir" rise from the chair and salute.

He returns the salute and says, "Have a good time. Dismissed."

I'm going home for Christmas. I want to sing and dance but I can't believe what is happening. There has been no way this could have happened but it's only for ten days. There is no time to waste. I hope I can get a hop at least as far as El Paso. It may have to be the train from there. The furlough is ten days starting today. I can't afford to miss a minute. I know one thing for sure--miracles can happen. I'll never say never again.

CHAPTER 16

SANTA CLAUS LANE

I grab my B-4 bag and stuff it with uniforms, clothes, and travel necessities before rushing down to the flightline. I don't bid anybody good-bye because no one is around to hear it. Now that I think about it, "Good-bye" seems to be a term seldom, if ever, heard around here. Who needs it? The reason could be that nobody ever goes far enough away to be missed. When people do leave, the departure tends to be permanent. They fade quietly out of the picture and are never mentioned again. If I should run into anyone I know on my way to the flightline, I'll just holler, "See yah" and leave them standing there wondering what the hell Jack I. is up to. Personally, I haven't said good-bye to anyone since leaving my mother and grandmother on the steps of the Federal Building in Minneapolis last January.

It may or may not be possible to find a plane leaving for El Paso. Today is Friday, but there should be at least a few officers starting early toward the joys waiting just across the border. A minute saved is a moment earned when dealing with rare free time. A weekend is nothing less than a two-day furlough, a chance to brush off the cobwebs, to sing and dance instead of marching to a dreary cadence. Hopefully, it won't be too long now before I will be working under the same rules and wearing the same kind of monkey suit. I can't let myself be jealous just because a couple of lieutenants will no doubt soon be hearing imaginary songs of sirens beckoning from the Rio Grande. Trumpets will blare and I hope whoever will give me a ride will have a happy time across the river tonight in Jaurez. My day will come but, if I can't catch a ride this morning, that day will not be soon. My only hope is to stumble upon an AT-ll with room for one more body even if the traveler happens to be a cadet. Being on a lucky streak makes it easier to hope.

My mind is still spinning with joy, but I'm one ride short of escaping from Deming and starting for home. I have tried to keep expectations reasonable. Any thought of getting a hop that goes all the way to Minneapolis is out of the question. Such an event would require a miracle and I've already had one of those today. The flight line is filled with AT-11s, a work horse aircraft designed to cart cadets around the sky and take officers on short junkets to places of enjoyment. It is improbable that one has ever been seen north of Texas. Any true passenger plane leaving the runway will no doubt be loaded with top brass traveling on important business.

I'll just have to take things as they come and hope, if Lady Luck stays with me, to catch a train or bus heading north. This will be my first visit home since leaving almost a year ago. No doubt the temperature will be bouncing around zero and streets could be buried under six feet of snow but I'm going home. This cadet is arriving on a trip made possible through the courtesy of a flu bug and I'm so happy I'd thank him for biting me if such a thing was possible.

Nothing is ever perfect. This first visit home was expected to feature me as a 2nd lieutenant with bombardier wings and an officer's uniform. Such a vision has carried me along for the last eleven months. However, after thinking things over, it seems entirely possible that an aviation cadet uniform complete with aerial gunners wings will give me a flying man's profile. There is no regular Air Corps detachment in the Twin Cities. The only soldiers wearing wings of any kind will be those on furlough or returning from combat. Gunner's wings will be novel enough to let people know I'm an operator from the wild blue yonder so what's the difference?

Right now, a more serious preoccupation is the necessity to go begging up and down the flight line trying to find that ride to El Paso. It seems like the best bet to get me out of town and moving north.

There is no denying that the plan has some serious drawbacks. A cadet must be very cautious and willing to take a kick in the ass even to think about asking superiors for a favor. I've never done it before and don't like to do it now, but there is no other way. It will be necessary to go from plane to plane stating my case and taking care to observe all military formalities. Using the proper deportment means approaching the plane carefully, attracting the attention of the officers inside, saluting, and saying briskly, "Aviation cadet Jack I. Moore reports to ask a question, Sir."

So far the usual response is, "Keep it short, Mister!" These guys have their minds completely focused on what lies ahead in Jaurez. For the most part they grant me the honor of an audience and listen politely to my story but, beyond that, they are obviously more curious than interested. Without exception they ask to see my orders stating permission to leave the base. The orders contain numerous abbreviations, which can be interpreted to state that this cadet is free to wander around anywhere he chooses during the next ten days providing he reports back to his base in person on the date specified. The orders don't contain information about where to go, how to get there or what to do while being there.

Trying to get and hold the attention of first and 2nd lieutenants primed for a weekend in Jaurez is not a productive way to pass the morning. Understandably, most of them are in a big hurry which results in quick, negative and final decisions. Instead of asking questions they just say, "Sorry, Mister." It saves time for everybody except me but the process is gradually taking on an air of hopelessness.

Finally, fatigue and common sense dictate that it is time to concede defeat and give up for the day. My next attempt will have to be taken at the Greyhound bus depot in downtown Deming. I am not excited at the prospect and not even sure that they have service every day. For no particular reason I wander toward flight headquarters to get a Coke and try to sort things out.

On the way I notice a pair of 2nd lieutenants who are leaving the building and walking toward the flight line. One of them is an instructor who has tutored me as a student on a couple of flights. He remembers my face, looks at my B-4 bag and asks, "Where you bound for, Mister?" I show him my furlough papers and explain the predicament. He asks if I'm ready to go right now. I want to say, "You can bet your boots!" but wisely settle for an enthusiastic "Yes, Sir!" They continue walking toward the plane and I stay right with them.

When they have seated themselves in the plane and are ready to slam the door, the instructor turns to the pilot and says; "I know this cadet, Shorty. We might as well give him a lift. What have we got to lose?" Shorty checks my papers again, writes some information on his flight manifest, and tells me to climb in back. I pick up my B-4 bag, hoist it into the rear of the plane through the camera opening and pull myself up and in. The sun is shining brightly this morning and the dice have come up seven one more time.

The flight to El Paso is short. Unfortunately, as often happens, being in a hurry summons the demons of delay. We arrive at El Paso in almost no time only to learn that a plane ahead of us has crashed on landing. The tower orders our pilot to stay in the pattern and circle until the runway can be cleared. It occurs to me that in my excitement I have neglected to phone the folks in Minnesota with the good news of my impending arrival. It's probably better that it happened this way because, at the moment, there's no way to guess how much of my furlough will be eaten up by planes and trains and delays like the one going on right now. The call can wait until I'm back on the ground with a chance to reach a telephone. That could be in Kansas City or some other place where it will be necessary to change trains. With so many events in my life taking place so quickly, concentration has focused solely on getting home. I swear a silent oath not to forget telling them I'm on the way.

As we circle over the wreckage down below again and again, it becomes clear that the accident is not serious. Shorty notes that the airplane blocking the runway was once a yellow bi-plane, purses his lips, turns to his buddy and mutters, "Goddam ground loop." My former instructor, sitting in the co-pilots seat, nods agreement. Almost every pilot in the Army, Navy, or Marine Air Corps has gone through primary training and taken his first lessons in a Stearman Trainer. Cadets in pilot training call it the "Yellow Peril" because of its tendency to drop a wing tip and ground loop while landing.

On the runway or in the air the Stearman looks like a relic from World War One. The sight has me to thinking of the Red Baron dog fighting Eddie Rickenbacker of the famous "Hat In The Ring" squadron over France and Germany in World War I. With goggles in place and white scarves trailing in the wind it was a game of winner take all. Body and wings of the planes were constructed of wood covered with cloth. The parachute had not yet been invented.

Damage in the situation below us doesn't seem severe. Firemen and the ambulance driver are milling around with hands in pockets looking unconcerned. The Stearman has some bad wing damage but doesn't look any worse than usual. It would be nice if they got that tub out of there. My time is limited and the clock is running.

We continue to circle and circle until, after a few minutes that seem like hours, they finally give Shorty clearance to land and he wastes no time putting us on the ground with a two-bounce landing. He taxies near the front of airport headquarters and rushes inside. A few seconds later he sprints out into the sunlight and is joined by his buddy. I watch as they break into a bouncing trot toward the bridge that leads to Jaurez. Like all of us, they have been warned to be wary of the ladies they may meet and told not to eat nor smoke anything that has been left on a table. If they follow instructions to the letter, they will not even drink the water. Whether they follow instructions is nobody's business except the United States Army Air Corps, but my friends are certainly in a hurry to meet their fate.

There they go, quarters, dimes, and nickels clinking in their pockets as they hustle across the bridge. American soldiers are forced to exchange paper money for gold and silver coins or two-dollar bills. Thanks to Hitler that's the only American money that merchants in Mexico accept as legal tender. Earlier in the war, the Nazis showed up in Mexico, a country that has remained neutral, and counterfeited every known type of paper money being put into circulation by the United States. The bastards then spread the worthless money all over Mexico and soon an American soldier GI or general couldn't buy a glass of beer with a thousand-dollar bill. Unfortunately for the Germans they didn't copy two-dollar bills because they knew we didn't have any. In fact, there's a nasty expression that goes, "He's phony as a two dollar bill." However, somebody in Washington figured things out and it wasn't long before our mint was printing two spots by the carload. As a result, two-dollar bills are now 'good as gold' in Mexico.

The backs of Shorty and the instructor meld into the crowd on the bridge and its time to face reality. My trip has gone as far it is going to go until another means of transportation comes along. There are only a couple of options and one of those is not worth considering. That's the one that suggests waiting around hoping for an empty plane going north. Chances of that happening do not exist. Buck Rogers will probably fly the first direct flight from El Paso to Minneapolis sometime in the twenty-first century. In the meantime, I have only ten days of freedom, which have now shrunk to nine and one-half.

The need for immediate action is obvious. I select the second and only real option, which forces me to pick up my B-4 bag again and start trying to find the local railroad station. After stumbling around and questioning several people, here I am standing in line at the ticket window of a very small and over crowded railroad station. I am silently praying that tickets will not run out before I reach the head of the line. Lady Luck smiles one more time on this wonderful morning and I'm able to purchase a ticket for a train that will go almost directly to Minneapolis-St. Paul and is scheduled to leave in about an hour. It will be necessary to change trains at Kansas City, but when we leave from there, the train will be on a track leading non-stop to Minneapolis. Once again it's time to hoist up the B-4 bag which I swing to clear a path while elbowing my way up the stairs of the coach. In the end I outrun a couple of GIs and a young lady carrying a child under each arm to establish my claim to one of the last empty seats.

Folks are standing in the aisle when the train stops puffing and jumps forward. It would seem reasonable that a few passengers must go tumbling down the aisle like bowling balls but the folks stand firm. In the best tradition of wartime railroad etiquette they hold their ground by clinging to anything handy and remaining unassailable. Wherever they are going they are prepared and determined to tough it out. It seems restful to lean back in my seat and listen to wheels clicking and grinding on the way to Kansas City, Kansas. That's where I'll transfer to the Hiawatha and be headed straight for the Milwaukee depot in Minneapolis.

After a year of riding troop trains populated exclusively by soldiers of every rank and ambition a soldier is poorly prepared to tolerate the civilian cargo on an everyday, wheel clacking, whistle blowing, overpopulated, diaper smelling, kids in the aisles, ride on a civilian train. The atmosphere is similar to the seven circles of "Dante's Inferno."

Two things are obvious: everyone is in a hurry and there are not enough places to sit. When a nice old lady two rows ahead of me leaves her seat momentarily, probably to visit the latrine, she returns to find her place occupied by a fat, middle aged civilian smoking a long cigar. She stands helplessly, swaying with the train and gripping the back of a seat and receiving no sympathy until a Marine sergeant with several medals draped on his blue dress uniform steps across the aisle and offers her his own place. The Jarhead then proceeds down the aisle and stares into the culprit's eyes until the poor man begins chewing his cigar. Finally, the wayward civilian rises, offers his place to the Marine and wobbles down the aisle toward the dining car. When the door closes and the seat-stealing civilian is out of sight, the Marine slips into the deserted seat, stretches comfortably, turns and waves with a smile to the other folks in the car. After the Marine takes her arm and leads the old lady to the open seat, she starts to applaud and in a moment the whole car is giving the Marine a big hand.

Once again the inescapable restrictions of being on the fighting side of a war become painfully clear. We lead a snapshot life and the best experiences are short-lived or missed entirely. The Marine has several combat decorations. What are they for? Where has he been? Why is that old lady traveling alone? Where is she going? I'll never know. For no particular reason it would have been nice to talk with those people, to know what was driving them. The trouble with me is curiosity that sometimes runs out of control. It's not a big deal but I wonder about so many things. My dad always said that life is nothing more than a string of experiences. I sometimes feel as if life is a big jigsaw puzzle and memories are the pieces needed to complete the picture. Put them all together and they become the history of a life. An aviation cadet finds very little time to chat about things like that even in the unlikely event he knew anyone who wanted to listen.

As the train rolls along I manage to take a short nap. When I awaken the view along the countryside is flat and brown but shows evidence of increasing population and it seems certain that Kansas City can't be far now. The sun is still up but shadows are beginning to fall across the countryside. My stomach tells me that I haven't eaten since breakfast so I decide to walk back to the dining car and get a sandwich. I don't want to lose my seat, but there seem to be a few empty places in the car now so it seems safe to leave. Perhaps some of the travelers got off the train while I was sleeping. The thought prompts me to pat my stomach and make sure the old money belt is still there. I know we were scheduled for a stop at Oklahoma City, which is a fairly good-sized city. No doubt some of our passengers could have left the train there.

I get myself a ham sandwich and, feeling well fed and convivial, stop on the way back to my seat for a friendly chat with the conductor. He tells me about his nephew, a navigator, in the Army Air Corps with the 8th Air Force in England. He isn't sure what kind of airplane the kid is on. I tell him it is probably a B-17 and he says that sounds like what it is. He says his sister, the boy's mother, worries a lot. I have no answer for that so, after a short silence, we shake hands and part company. He pats me on the shoulder and says if we don't run into any problems the train will glide into the Milwaukee Depot in Minneapolis sometime this evening. Everything will depend on whether the train I'm changing to in Kansas City is on time and ready to go.

We pull into Kansas City right on time, but all hell seems to have broken loose inside the station. No one seems to know exactly what the trouble is but the word is that somebody with a gun has been shooting inside the place. The station is a huge, concrete building and policemen are everywhere but when I ask one what's going on he says all he knows is that someone inside started shooting up the place just firing at random. The cop says when he first got there and for a short time after that, shells were ricocheting off walls inside the crowded building. He didn't think anyone had been hurt. My heart sinks at the thought that this might keep us from rolling out on time.

I can see my train from where I'm standing. It's already puffing and making noises. It has the air of a train that means business, as if the locomotive is anxious to leap ahead as soon as the engineer gets the word. While I'm waiting, an MP comes over and asks to see my furlough papers. I take them out of the money belt and hand them over. He takes one glance and hands them back saying, "What the hell does an aviation cadet do in this war?"

"I'm training to be a bombardier."

"That what them wings you got on mean?"

"No, those are Arial Gunner's wings. We had to go through that first before we could go to advanced bombardier school."

He still seems confused but has a friendly nature compared to what most of us have been led to expect from the military police. He extends his hand and we shake. He says, "Well, have a good trip. Take care now!" As he turns and walks away, I pick up the B-4 bag and walk slowly toward the train glancing at the station building and wondering what happened there just a short time before we arrived. The fresh air tastes great and I feel relaxed and in no particular hurry until, suddenly, people can be seen starting to board. My memory flashes back to the battle for seats when we left El Paso. I hoist the B-4 bag one more time hoping it will next be raised in Minneapolis at the Milwaukee Depot. I picture it being tossed it into a taxicab for the short ride marking the end of my unanticipated journey, which has been defying all odds. When the conductor shouts, "All aboard!" I push quickly into the battle to assure a place to sit. The train shudders as the line of cars bump together and I know the next time my feet hit the ground it will be in the Milwaukee Depot in Minneapolis, Minnesota.

The middle west of the United States is full of towns. From the train a traveler can watch them flashing by like a colorfully animated atlas.

Gradually the names of towns become more familiar and easier to recognize. Soon we reach towns with names that are truly familiar, places we have visited at one time or another. We pass through Des Moines, Iowa and then Rochester, which has one of the finest hospitals in the world. We are in Minnesota, almost home. Soon I will reach for my B-4 Bag one more time. A little voice whispers, "Not quite yet." I've become more than a little overanxious and completely forgotten we must stop at the St. Paul Depot before proceeding across the river to Minneapolis. I replace the B-4 bag on an empty seat beside me and gaze at my myself being reflected in the mirror created by darkness outside the window. I do so for most of the short ride across the Mississippi in the dark. At last, late in the evening, we arrive at the St. Paul Depot and stop just long enough for passengers to depart.

It has been a long day and is producing a real battle between the sandman and myself. It's imperative not to fall asleep. Imagine the unbelievable farce it will be if I drift off and forget to leave the train when we arrive in Minneapolis. Having already forgotten to notify my family that I'm on the way, the last thing I want to do is wake them from their sleep to say I'm on the way to Chicago and will take the next train from there to the Twin Cities. The ride takes less than a half-hour, which is spent trying to peer into the black night looking for snow. It is really too dark to make a reliable guess as to how deep the snow is or if there is even any out there at all. It will be nice if there is just enough for skiing, but not so much it interferes with driving and skating.

People around here expect a white Christmas. Merchants depend on it and usually have plenty of snow to provide a proper setting for the holidays and keep cash registers ringing. Hunters count on snow for tracking deer. Skiing and tobogganing are wonderful pastimes. The prospect of not having a white Christmas becomes the number one topic of discussion at bus stops and grocery store aisles when sidewalks are bare in late November.

Entering the Milwaukee Depot in Mineapolis, the lights of Washington Avenue come into view. Coasting slowly we are moving and it's just possible to see the neon sign and indoor lights of the café that served us breakfast the morning our rag tag group of volunteers marched off to war. It brings back the memory that two of that group died of exposure in their beds that first cold night in Jefferson Barracks. Will any of us who were there forget the corporal who gave us the news and asked, "Why don't one of you guys die so I can go home with the body?"

I grab my B-4 bag and stand on the 2nd step of the exit as the train slows to a stop. The bag seems heavier than before but I still have enough stamina to throw it into a cab and tell the driver the address is 1036-13th Avenue South East.

It's embarrassing that I forgot to tell them I was coming. They won't be expecting me but there's a light in the front window where they have hung two blue flags noting that Dad and I have gone to war. The sidewalk has not been shoveled, but I lug my bag up the steps and open the front door knowing it will not be locked. It never is. I go quietly through the front door and there's Grandpa Flavin in his favorite chair with one foot braced on the mantle by the fireplace. As I would have guessed, he's listening to fiddle music from Yankton, South Dakota. He turns in his chair to see who came in and shouts, "Julia, you better get in here, we have a visitor." Grandma comes out of the kitchen, through the dining room to shout "Oh, my God!" and give me a hug. Grandpa gets up from his chair, raps the bowl of his pipe against the mantle piece, shakes his head and says, "Well, I'll be dammed." I'm too happy to speak ,but I'm home, I'm home, I'm home! And nothing has changed but me.

A Christmas Tree stands by the front window trimmed with the same decorations I remember as a little boy. My Mother always says they are the same ones that were hung there when she was a little girl. This will not be a long vacation but I have already received my gift, which is Christmas itself. I thank God who can believe me when I say this was a gift I didn't expect. I'll be home for Christmas and my birthday.

I don't see my mother and the kids and ask where they are. Grandma explains that Dad has returned from the African campaign and is stationed at the War College in Louisiana. That's wonderful news about Dad who has been fighting Germans in the African campaign. I won't be seeing them on this trip but the disappointment is less than it might be because I expect to graduate and get another furlough in February.

I chat with Grandma and Grandpa for a short time, but I'm tired and they are past their usual bedtime. Grandma says I can use the front bedroom upstairs. I say I'll see them in the morning and walk slowly, dragging my B-4 Bag up the stairs. Can this be real? The bed feels great but it's difficult to get to sleep. Now that I'm home I suddenly realize I don't have any idea about what to do tomorrow which will be Saturday. That should make it a little less difficult to reach people on the phone. The problem is, whom can I call? Since I didn't expect to be here there was no time to make plans. Because there will be so little time, anyone who is going to be seen will need to be found on the double.

I should call Jackie, the girl I left behind me. At first she wrote often, almost every day. As time passed, her letters trickled off which was probably due to my indifference about answering them. What is there to say? My world is completely changed and corresponding would be trying to converse in separate languages. I should call her anyway just for old times sake. I want to call Jerry Milnar for certain. He was my closest friend all of last year. We were both on the University freshman baseball team and together almost every day and often evenings. Jerry was the shortstop and also a very good golfer. He wants to be a dentist, and has joined the Navy V-2 program, which will let him stay out of the service. As I understand it, he is actually in uniform and lives right on the campus. The Navy pays for his education and nobody shoots at his head. All they ask is that when he graduates and becomes a dentist and, if the war lasts long enough, he has promised to spend six months in the Navy after graduation.

It's a good deal and sometimes I wonder why I wasn't smart like that. In my heart I know I could never do it. I could never face the guys coming home from combat if I played chicken about this thing. I'll be seeing Jerry for sure and we'll be friends but something will be missing. To me, he will always be the guy who hid behind a book and got paid to fight the war without ever leaving home.

Although I feel tired, getting to sleep is difficult. My bed is much softer than the bunk a soldier normally adjusts to. I'm concerned about wasting my furlough. It arrived without warning and a large part of it has been used up just getting here. There is no way to be certain that any of my friends are even in the area. When morning comes, it brings with it the magic of Grandma's bacon and eggs wafting up the through the stairwell and settling in my room. It fires my appetite and covers me with a laid back sense of peace. The Army cannot touch me here, the war is far away. I can hardly wait for breakfast. When I arrive downstairs, Grandma and Grandpa are seated at the kitchen table. I know they were waiting for me. I wonder how long. Grandma has kept the food warm and we eat quietly, without conversation. I am so fortunate. There is so much love in this room.

When we finish and the dishes are in the sink, Grandpa leaves the room for a few minutes and when he returns it is to drop the car keys on the table and tell me to have a good time. I tell him to be sure and let me know when he wants to go someplace. He says he might not mind running over to Stanley's. I say, "Let's go!" and we're off in a cloud of snow. I wonder if Gramps will offer me an orange pop the way he used to do. I won't be twenty-one for about a week so I guess I can't legally have a beer in the state of Minnesota, but I needn't have wondered. Stanley glances at my uniform and puts three beers on the bar, one for Gramps, one for me and one for himself.

He says, "You don't look like the same kid, Jackie. You don't look like a strong wind might blow you away anymore."

I say, "You look pretty good yourself."

He says, "I'm not getting any younger. I can't work the hours I used to. Pretty soon I think I'll retire like your Grandpa and not stop in to see my old friends like he doesn't."

It's no surprise that Grandpa can't get around. He has never learned to drive and never had an interest in doing so. I feel a shot of guilt and promise myself to do what I can to help him while I'm here. Nothing has changed in Stanley's Bar. The pinball machine I used to play waiting for Gramps to finish his beer is still there in the same corner near the end of the bar. I pull out a couple of nickels, click them into the machine and listen to the balls rolling around. It's like old times just to pull the plunger back and let it fly, shooting the balls aimlessly and watching for Gramps to empty his glass. My glass is half-empty when Gramps pulls out his gold pocket watch and says "I think we better get back to the house." I say, " Great," although I was kind of looking forward to an orange pop.

When we get outside, I take a couple of deep breaths. This is not a cold day. The temperature must be about twenty degrees, give or take a few for the breeze and sunshine. Stanley's Bar is on Nicollet Island surrounded by the mighty Mississippi where it divides the city of Minneapolis. Not far from where we stand is the spot where Father Hennepin decided to beach his canoe and start building a church. I think God planned this for a beauty spot to challenge the imagination; a chain of spectacular islands near the birthplace of the mighty Mississippi overlooking St. Anthony Falls. It's possible the good Lord may have been disappointed. Unfortunately, the riverbanks are populated by huge grain elevators. Gramps, who held the first stationary engineer's license in the state of Minnesota, has spent most of his life right up to retirement keeping the machinery running in an elevator further down the river. With Saint Anthony Falls as a power source, Minneapolis is now known as one of the great milling centers in the world. Making flour is profitable, but not designed for pretty pictures, so Nicollet Island was never given its chance to perform in Mother Nature's beauty contest. Eventually it settled for its own skid row and red-light district as well as a highly respected Catholic high school. It has also become home for several firmly rooted businesses like Stanley's, which have developed a happy clientele through the years by serving people needing a place to go. I have no idea how long Grandpa Flavin has been a patron of Stanley's but it is as long as I can remember. We ride home in silence. Grandpa seldom asks questions but asking him one can produce an interesting answer. Once, at the dinner table, my sister, Pat, asked if he had ever had a girl friend other than Grandma. He thought about it for a minute and replied, "Well, I was engaged once."

Patricia, the curiosity champion in our neighborhood, pushed right into Grandpa's bid for a straight-line asking, "What happened? Did you break up?"

Grandpa tapped his pipe on the table, thought about it carefully and replied, "No, I guess I'm still engaged."

When we get back home, I go upstairs, unload the B-4 bag, hang up my uniforms and go downstairs to get on the phone and see who might be around to furnish some conversation. It seems logical that even if my friends are out of town, their parents can tell me where they are and how they're doing. The process is slow because I have to look up phone numbers that I used to know by heart.

My first call is to Jerry Milner and I have a chat with his mother. She says he is living at the University om Minnesota but comes home on weekends. She really seems interested in how I am doing and says they will all be happy to see me. She assures me that if I call this afternoon Jerry will be home.

A call for Joe Kozlak brings the news that he's in Hawaii, a corpsman at one of the hospitals there. Wade Cole's mother, one of the nicest people in the world, tells me that Wade is at Ohio State University and is in an ROTC program. Bob De Lane has enlisted in the paratroopers and his dad said he doesn't know where the hell the kid is. Larry Zamor is in the Marines. I know Chuck Wallick is in the merchant marine because I helped him enlist in spite of his high blood pressure. His brother, Bill, thinks he heard somewhere that Blair Berg and Roy Lawson, who were both state high school wrestling champions, are either in the Marines or Navy. Marve Saline's brother, Lindy, who graduated from high school with my sister Pat, says Marve is in the Navy somewhere on the East Coast. George Kubera is in the Naval Air Corps. The only one of the old gang whose location I know for sure is Rex Werring, who is an instructor at Deming.

It's a long unproductive, interesting afternoon but when my ear begins to throb and Grandma comes in to say supper is on the table

I decide to call it a day. Only then do I realize that the clock reads six o'clock and evening has descended on my old hometown. When we finish eating, I dial Jerry Milnar's number again and reach him as he's going out the door. He's on the way to a party at the U and has a heavy date with a girl he is now engaged to. We chat for about ten minutes after which he says he will pick me up tomorrow, Sunday, around noon. I say, "Good deal." I'm now left with the option of calling my old girl friend Jackie, playing 500 with Grandma, or listening to three hours of fiddle music from Yankton, South Dakota. I call Jackie's house.

Her mother answers the phone. She doesn't ask who's calling but passes along the information that her daughter is not home and gives me a number where she can be reached. A girl answers the phone on the fifth or sixth ring and asks me to hold on. Sounds in the background are those of a pretty good party going full speed. Jackie comes to the phone and I identify myself. She says,

"Oh, my God!"

I say, "Sounds like a real nice party. Where's it at?"

She says, "No, no, don't come over here! Call me tomorrow!"

I say, "I'll only be around a few days."

She says, "Call me tomorrow. I'll be at home."

To her I say, "O.K."

To myself I say, "Forget about it." And hang up.

Sometimes a handful of words contains a truckload of wisdom. I feel much better about not answering her letters.

My conscience is cleared but suffering two hours of fiddle music is a stiff penance for a venial sin. In addition, I lost two out of three games of 500 to Grandma. Sometimes I think that little old lady could have made a fortune playing cards on boats and trains. When the big clock in the dining room chimes eleven times, Grandpa turns off the radio and it's lights out. I crawl under the covers and wonder what tomorrow will bring. It will be Sunday so we'll be going to mass. After that, I'll meet Jerry Milnar and learn what he has in mind, if anything. The only sure thing is that two days of my ten-day furlough are gone and time flies.

In the morning, I want to take communion, so I have to skip breakfast and we take off for nine o'clock mass. My grandparents are charter members of St. Lawrence church which was built back in the eighteen-nineties. Ordinarily, nine o'clock mass is for children but the eleven o'clock solemn high mass with the choir and priest singing and the certainty of a long sermon will run for an hour and a half or more. Because we intend to receive Communion we can't eat or drink anything after the previous midnight. People sometimes become very hungry and, on rare occasions, pass out at later masses. Grandma is frail enough as she is.

Nothing has changed about the church including some of the people seated around us. Stain glass windows impose a melancholy darkness and kneelers still make a hard sound when people kick them over with their toes. I don't recognize the priest saying mass because we are seated near the rear of the church. For most of the service, I see only his back. The choir is good, especially on Panus Angelicas where our plumber George Sampson displays more than ample volume.

Going down to the rail for communion offers an opportunity to search for familiar faces. It's only a year since my last visit, but I find very few. It is also surprising that there are many soldiers and sailors but few Army Air Corps people of any rank. At the end of mass, the priest says some special prayers at the foot of the altar and the entire congregation joins in singing the *Star Spangled Banner*. As we are walking out the door, I notice a large sign bearing the names of soldiers from the parish who have given their lives. It's very probable that I would know many of them, but I have no desire to read it

As I turn away, there stands Bob Picha who was with me on the Gopher freshman baseball team. Bob was a charter member of our little group that usually attended mass from the balcony and sometimes from the hall outside of that. He's says he's still at the U but has enlisted in the Marines. Noticing my gunners wings he asks if I knew Bill Fay. I say, "Sure." I remember him from ball games we used to play over at Van Cleve Park before our family moved up northeast. Bill was a pretty good pitcher with a big roundhouse curve. I think maybe he pitched for St. Lawrence grade school, too.

Bob tells me that Bill, an aerial gunner, was killed in a big air raid against the Germans somewhere in Africa. I tell him, Bill must have been on the famous Ploesti raid against oil wells in Romania. If I remember right, the planes took off from somewhere in the desert and hundreds of B-24s were lost on that raid. Bob asks how I like being an aerial gunner and I explain that I'm in bombardier school and should be finishing pretty soon. After that, who knows? I tell him I'll be seeing Jerry Milnar this afternoon and Bob tells me to say hello for him. He says he expects the Marines to call him up soon but they have so many enlistments there's nothing to do but sweat it out until he gets the call. We wish each other good luck and I go to find Grandma and Gramps who are waiting by the door of the church. I'm starved.

We sit down to a big breakfast because that's the kind of breakfast Gram always makes. I just have time to finish my fourth slice of French toast when the front door opens and Jerry walks in. He's no stranger to this house and often slept over since we were living so close to the University and there was plenty of room. He also was on the list of favorites with my grandparents because when Grandpa's brother, Dick, needed some blood and they asked me to give some, I said fine and Jerry asked if he could contribute too. Jerry is not Irish, but after that the Flavins treated him as if he was.

I'm glad to see him and as we head for downtown it seems like old times. It's the first time we've seen each other in uniform. I tell him he looks like a doorman in his dark blue navy coat and white hat. He says if I can't shoot any better than I hit a baseball, he can't understand why they would make me an aerial gunner. I tell him the reason is a government secret.

The Sunday traffic is very light and downtown is almost deserted. Milner says there's a place on Hennepin Avenue set up for GIs to go, get free soft drinks, and sit around doing nothing. He says it's the most likely place I might run into some other guys who are in town on furlough. I say, "How about the girls?" He reminds me that he is now engaged so he doesn't get around much anymore. I know his girl-friend, Delores Williams. She's very nice and is the only girl I have ever seen Jerry go out with. I know how crazy he is about her and am not surprised they will be married. I tell him, "She's too good for you. Here you are studying to be a dentist and you want to marry a girl whose father owns an electrical company. How's her twin sister?"

Jerry says, "Forget about her. She got married last summer."

I tell him, "You're no help Milnar." He tells me the town is full of unattached women but I have to go out and find them myself. I explain to him that I haven't even talked to a girl in almost a year. He tells me that's impossible, that women are all over the place looking for company. I tell him that's not the case with Army Air Corps aviation cadets.

I say, "Jerry you wouldn't believe some of the places they send us. Ever hear of Jefferson Barracks, Missouri or Kingman, Arizona? How about Deming, New Mexico? California would have been nice but most of the time we were looking through a chain link fence. When we got loose we found out L.A. has about 300 GIs for every woman. It probably doesn't make any difference because our schedule is from 7 a.m. to 10 p.m. and when the weekend comes, all a guy wants to do is sleep."

Jerry parks the car in front of a building near the State Theater that is flying several flags in front. A large sign says "Welcome military personnel." We walk up a flight of stairs and are welcomed by some young ladies offering coffee, soft drinks, and cookies. We have our choice of easy chairs or a seat at one of the tables. We choose a table, take off our top coats, and order a couple of Cokes. This is not a fancy place and as I glance around it is obvious that there are many more GIs than officers. The place is not overcrowded but is almost full and the service is good. I think the workers must be volunteers. They certainly seem anxious to please us. The cookies are good although Jerry says they're chocolate chip and will play havoc with my teeth.

I feel flattered when a young guy about eighteen or nineteen comes over to the table and asks if he can talk to me for a few minutes. I say, "Sure," and he says he noticed my aerial gunner wings. He says he wishes he could be a gunner when he becomes eligible for the service next year and wonders what it will take to get into the Army Air Corps. I explain that all he needs to do is enlist, and pass all kinds of tests, physical and mental. After that, they will tell him where he fits in. I don't tell him that the men not qualified as pilots, navigators, or bombardiers are the ones who get to be aerial gunners and are sentenced to spend seven weeks of purgatory on the desserts of Arizona.

I tell him that qualification as an aerial gunner is required of bombardiers, and how I expect to finish bombardier training and become a 2nd lieutenant next month. When I mention that graduation will result in becoming a crewmember on a heavy bomber his eyes widen and he says, "Wow, you'll probably get to fly on B-17s."

I could tell him I've already flown on B-17s at Kingman Gunnery School but Jerry is wiggling around on his chair and looking bored. I decide to back off the hero role. The young man is seeing silver wings in the moonlight just as I did less than a year ago. Answering his questions and feeling his eagerness to sneak under the tent and become a clown in a worldwide three-ring circus does not strike me as strange. I know the urge very well, as do my friends back at Deming. It was inspired by a touch of patriotic fervor and confirmed by fear of being the only able bodied man remaining in the neighborhood. In the Air Corps we take pride that the physical and mental bars are higher than some branches of the service, but any man between eighteen and twenty-seven who can pass the physical has a chance. He must be willing to ask himself every day, "Am I good enough?" If he is, odds are good that he can follow his dream. Is it worth it? We all think so, but nobody knows why.

Jerry and I shake hands with the young man and excuse ourselves. He thanks us and we go down the stairs and out to the car. It has not escaped my notice that the kid never asked Jerry anything about the Navy. Jerry is one of the most competitive people I've ever met. I have to admit to a certain amount of satisfaction realizing that being ignored was the reason he wanted to hustle out of there leaving half his Coke on the table.

We drive around for a while and then stop at his house up in Columbia Heights so I can see his folks again. Later, he drives me home and drops me off. It is a nice visit but something in the world has changed. This is no longer the planet I used to inhabit. After almost a full year of isolation from the real world, training for a future that has no relation to real life and little value to society in general, it is not possible to avoid the sense of being needed but not necessarily wanted.

After only a couple of days of listening and walking around it seems obvious that the civilian side of life is moving along at a happy pace. The bogey man Depression is nowhere to be found. Money is no object; anyone who wants a job has one. Jerry said some of the women at the arms plant are earning up to twenty-six dollars an hour and working as many hours as they want. The arms plant runs 24 hours, three shifts per day, seven days per week. They still have plenty of jobs to offer if they can find people to fill them. My mother worked at the New Brighton arms plant until she went down to Louisiana to be with my dad.

There is no escaping the realization that a war is still a war and every Gold Star hanging in a window represents someone who will not be returning to the neighborhood. Some people are like our family. They have been affected by the war but seem willing to take things as they are and hope for the best. It's also difficult not to notice some others, people who have never had it so good but can be heard complaining about gas rationing and being overworked. The worst of the Depression having disappeared, bars and cafes are filled with willing young grass widows and every sundown brings another New Year's Eve. It's all there for the taking for those who can stay around to enjoy the song and dance.

The problem is that I'm free as the breeze and ready for fun, but don't know where to turn. I called Marylin, the girl I dated on the evening of our high school graduation. She had written to me a couple of times and I answered back. The letters were from New

York where she has become a Powers model. Since I don't know anyone else, I call her house hoping she might have come home for Christmas. Believe it or not, she answers the phone and invites me to come over sometime. I tell her I will only be around for a couple of days so she invites me to come over this evening. We talk about school and some of our mutual friends, but she keeps pushing the conversation back to New York and it becomes obvious that there must be someone back there who is very important in her life. I finish my Coke, excuse myself and head Gramps' old Plymouth in the direction of Jax Cafe, which is owned by the family of Joe Kozlak.

As usual, the place is crowded. I run into George Blackie who is wearing a Navy Air Corps uniform. This is something of a surprise because when we had our first physicals for the Army Corps out at Fort Snelling, he failed because of high blood pressure. I knew the Army had made a mistake at the time, because George is not only a nice guy, he's a very good athlete. He says that when the Army turned him down he took a Navy physical the next day and passed with no trouble. George says his brother Bud chose the Army and is about to get his pilot wings at an airfield in Texas.

I don't hang around because George is with a girl and doesn't need any help. I don't know who said it first, but Grandpa Flavin has said it often, war is just a few young men's hard luck.

For the first time since leaving the base at Deming I wonder what my friends back there are doing tonight; probably not much. This furlough means I will not graduate in the class of 44-2, which means the end of some friendships that have lasted through Santa Ana, Kingman, and Deming. A few, like George Hendrickson, go all the way back to Jefferson Barracks and Coe College. It's always difficult to predict what will happen in the Army, but I don't expect ever to see most of them again. That goes for Moe Olivo who I met way back at Cedar Rapids. I'll miss Mo Lund, and Makowski, as well as Willie Mayer, Carlton Moore, and K.K. Nielsen, current inhabitants in our barracks.

On the other hand, the men who shared my week in the hospital and are also on furlough will certainly be back to finish their training in the class of 44-3. For better or worse, G.I. Morse will be around along with Ben Squibb and about fifteen other flu bitten people.

My social life on this furlough is offering nothing to brag about but it's nice to be here this evening, Christmas Eve, when uncles, aunts, and various offspring gather at the Flavin household. I haven't taken the time to visit with most of them on this trip but they are all here now. I was the first grandchild in the family and aunts and uncles still refer to me as "Little Jackie." I had hoped seeing me in uniform might hint to them that I'm now grown up but relatives, one and all, are happy to see me and anxious to talk about friends of theirs who are also in the service. Later in the evening gifts are opened one by one and, as usual, Grandpa gets a new hat and fancy tie which he puts on immediately. All in all, it is a very nice evening, but I'm not sorry to see it end. Tomorrow we will attend church and come home to a wonderful dinner. In the evening, I will board the train for my return trip to Deming.

With only a few hours left on my furlough it's necessary to concede this has been a very quiet visit. The trip came about too quickly to make any real plans or track down a few friends. Graduation, only a month or so away, will provide a chance to look ahead and make some preparations in advance. That's what is on my mind stepping up into the Hiawatha for a return and possibly final trip to Deming in the air.

294

CHAPTER 17

WE NEVER SAID GOOD-BYE

Going to our new barracks, G.I. and I find ourselves struggling against a typical Deming winter evening, leaning into a vicious whistling wind that has us bent forward, dragging our B-4 bags and moving ahead one foot at a time. It reminds me of pushing a stalled car up hill.

When we finally arrive at the barracks we are running on empty but pleased to see that no lights are visible in windows of the building meaning the status of the inmates is "Lights out" which translates, in GI language, to "Stop whatever you're doing and go to sleep whether you like it or not!" We are tired beyond belief and the last thing we need is a bunch curious strangers looking us over and asking stupid questions.

"Lights out" is quiet time. Crap shooters have been forced to put away their dice and homesick cadets have finished composing weekly messages home and put away their pens. Cadets who enjoy literature more than gambling will have slid page markers into their present reading material. The lucky cadet who has temporary possession of

God's Little Acre will have slipped it under his pillow hoping to find it there in the morning. *"The Acre,"* as it is called, is super popular reading material but copies are scarce and sometimes disappear unexpectedly. For most of the group 'Lights out' is just one more stupid rule that must be obeyed. For them, it's a matter of sighing a long sigh, taking a last look at a Betty Grable pin-up, and wondering if the girl they left behind is still waiting. For us, at this particular moment, it will be a Godsend.

We open the door as quietly as possible, closing it slowly to avoid a possibility the wind will slam it shut with a crash loud enough to wake even the heaviest sleepers. Such a thing would be unfortunate but our luck holds, the door clicks silently into place. We are inside. Not a creature is stirring but that makes no difference. At this moment we couldn't see Santa Claus if he was driving his reindeer around inside the building and tossing presents to the troops. The room is totally dark with the exception of a feeble shaft of gray shadows dribbling from a dim green bulb above the partially open door to the latrine.

I can't see G.I. and don't want to call out, although he can be heard mumbling. Darkness magnifies my perception. When a sleeping cadet suddenly snores it shreds the darkness and mimics the roar of a hungry lion hunting for breakfast. We need to find empty bunks to sleep on. We're tired and want some beds to sleep on, but what can we do? G.I. is growling to himself that this darkness is a case of gross negligence on the part of the United States Army Air Force. He mutters that his training hasn't prepared him to swim around in a pool of ink and asks himself where the light switches are in this God forsaken place? No doubt there's a light switch somewhere on the wall but "So what!" It wouldn't occur to G.I. that turning on the lights and waking the entire population of the barracks is not what we need. The situation is gloomy and soon becomes worse.

Light from the little green bulb isn't strong enough to outline obstacles in our path so we are forced to grope around in the dark, stumbling and fumbling from one shin cracking collision to another, banging our heads and knees against bed posts. According to the rules there should be no way that we can be crashing into footlockers that have been left to stick out in the aisles. G.I. keeps muttering about being forced by the Army to receive unjust and painful punishment and soon turns his venom toward the mindless cadets who left belongings in the aisles for people to run into and beat up on themselves. It has been my habit to try cooling G.I. down when he starts pulling the trigger against the Air Force without provocation but, this time, he may have a case.

Every cadet on the base has been lectured ad nausea about order and cleanliness in the barracks. The basic rules, which have been stated and restated, clearly stipulate that the barracks have special places for everything. Each item must be properly stowed in its designated place. Trunks are to be completely pushed out of aisles and stowed beneath bunks. We have been lectured on this subject almost as often as we have squirmed in our seats listening to horror stories about the possible outcome of fancy-free sexual adventures. This rule is usually adhered to carefully because violations can be easily be discovered and are difficult to hide or explain. Of course, nobody is perfect but try telling that to a gig happy second lieutenant when he drops by for Saturday morning inspection. There's no use crying about these things but it does make a person wonder what kind of hoodlums our new friends will turn out to be. All we can do now is plunge around hoping to find empty beds by accident.

G.I. continues his shuffle cursing the Army Air Corps under his breath, keeping his recital just a shade lower than the periodic piccolo solo being provided by water plinks at regular intervals into a distant and unseen sink somewhere in a far end of the building. We know it originates from a latrine. The sound is familiar and often heard during restless nights when sleep refuses to come around and finish the day. Mack calls it "latrine music."

Fortunately for us, if we just avoid creating a huge disturbance, the odds of waking people at this hour are on our side. These people, whoever they are, have been putting in long hard days alternating between flying and classroom work seven days and nights per week. If the Army could create an eighth day in the week, no one doubts they would find something more for us to do even if it meant going on KP duty in the kitchen. When a cadet hits the sack to end a long day, which often includes part of the night, he is planted there, knocked out as cold as Max Schmelling, the Nazi prize fighter who went down in thirty seconds of the first round against Joe Louis. These guys won't be jarred awake by any disturbance less than an earthquake or the sound of a whistle ordering the group to fall out for mail call or chow. The sight of an empty bunk has a Pavlovian effect that increases a cadet's overwhelming fatigue and makes him indifferent to the outside world. Sack time is valuable and not subject to distractions that normal sleepers would find very annoying. Unless G.I. stumbles down the stairs there is room to hope we won't arouse the entire squadron. We don't know who or what we will see when the sun comes up but our reception will undoubtedly be better if we don't stomp around on their dreams.

I haven't been able to see G.I. since we entered the barracks but it's not difficult to follow his trail as he wanders around crashing into things and talking to himself. Eventually the thumping of his size 12 GI boots can be heard stomping across the floor followed by a thud indicating some first place action has taken place. No doubt G.I. has spotted something, cast his body toward an empty bunk, and landed safely. Since the deed is followed by a long silence it can now be assumed our troubles are over. We are going to be able to sneak in and will not be forced to spend the rest of the night explaining to a bunch of strangers just what the hell is going on here. All's clear. G.I. must be settled away for the night because he can no longer be heard swearing in the dark and kicking somebody's footlocker.

It's time for a sigh of relief. G.I. loves sack time better than anything except innocent young ladys, and I can hear him snoring long before I finally run into an unoccupied area near the far end of the building. In accordance with the rules my B-4 bag slides obediently under the first empty cot.

Pale gray shafts of daylight are already sneaking into the barracks and an early sunrise is fighting behind the hills for a place at the table. There is no joy in seeing it rise to shine on a day such as this that promises to be as unpredictable as it is inescapable. We are certainly not heading into the kind of situation a man wants to face after a long dismal train and bus ride followed by a sleepless night. There's no sense bitching about it or running to the chaplain. We are where we wanted to be and a year in the Army has made it clear that facing things is what soldiers are supposed to do. The best thing right now is to replace hope with reality and forget about trying to find some combination of things that could possibly make the coming day worth living. My old friends are gone, my furlough is over, the barracks are full of strangers, and I won't get any rest for another twelve hours. Where does a man turn when his ass is tired, his mind is foggy, there is no chance for a peaceful interlude and nobody cares?

We don't have enough facts about the situation to wonder what comes next. Whatever the schedule calls for it won't contain orders to go back to bed or can we expect any consolation from instructors or other cadets. To make the future even less promising, we have been dumped in with a bunch of strangers and are now in a different class: 44-3 instead of 44-2.

Friendships formed almost a year ago dating from the terror of Jefferson Barracks, the easy life at Coe College, the testing and uncertainty leading to confirmation as cadets at Santa Ana, the searing heat of Kingman, and the unrelenting grind of Deming all have ended abruptly. They cannot be replaced so we must move along. They have been my only family for a year. I got to know some of them well but it will be better if they are soon forgotten. In the fashion of the ancient Arabs, my best friends have folded their tents and quietly stolen away. They left me in the desert of Deming and never said goodbye.

Makowski, Mo Lund, Modesto Olivo, John Hudspeth, from Altoona, Pennsylvania; Ed MacBride from Hingam, Mass.; Willie Mayer from Seattle; K.K. Nielsen, former roommate from Payson, Utah; Bill Norman from Pocatella, Idaho. Where are they now? That's easy; they're about to go on furlough. They will soon be officers in the United States Army Air Corps home on leave, strutting around the neighborhood in their new uniforms featuring silver wings and gold bars. That's where they will be. Brand new officers with wings, money, a little more freedom and a lot more class. They will soon graduate and, in a week or two, they will probably be put on a crew learning how to climb in and out of a B-24 or B-17. Except for a miserable flu bug, I could be with them, but I'll make it yet. We have been told our graduation will take place near the end of February.

For the time being we will be working with an entirely new group of instructors and will know only a few of the cadets in our class. Hopefully, some of our fellow flu victims may be coming back to join us. Who knows? For some reason my thought processes are swimming around in a puddle of nothingness. Common sense is yapping, ordering me to close my tired eyes. Who or what we may see at sunrise is only a new beginning and won't have any true or serious effect on what happens next. Apparently and fortunately, although yesterday was Sunday, the cadets we will be joining must have had a tough day at the flightline. We haven't heard a single sound out of anyone; not a groan, cough or cry. They lie in total silence, privately sawing away at whatever dreams are on their hit parade. It's a good feeling to finally be stretched out in the bunk beneath warm blankets but, in no way, does it result in a magical slide, into a deep and healing visit to Never Never Land. My eyes are shut tight but fatigue and the new and strange surroundings create vague ideas that turn my mind over and over, rotating like wheels of uncertainty that turn slowly from one subject to another.

Without question this is a big world and for sure it is totally FUBAR, but whose fault is that? Life won't be quite the same without Mack and Moe and those guys. The voice of experience says, "Get used to not seeing them or any of those other guys. The faster they are forgotten the happier you'll be." Wherever they are it is far away and they are busy doing their own thing.

My mind is still going round and round when the whistle blows to route us out for chow and bring my new world slowly to life. Occupants of the barracks roll from their bunks one leg at a time;

brushing sleep from their eyes, looking around and taking a moment to make peace once again with their confusing presence in an unreal world.

It takes only one slow turn of my aching head to confirm, as expected, that most of these people are strangers. A more thorough look around the room reveals the hairless skull of George Hendrickson from Ely, Minnesota. Since there's no question that G.I. is also around here somewhere it now can be said for sure that there will be at least two guys in the bunch who know my name. I haven't seen much of George since we arrived at Deming because his last name starts with 'H' and mine with 'M' so we have been in the same class, but in different wings. It's good to see George; he smiles often and makes everybody feel good. As might be expected, Olaf Arneson is there wearing his cadet officer tags and preparing to lead us to the mess hall. Shadow Eide from North East Minneapolis is sitting on his bunk making a slow effort to struggle into his fatigues and another turn of my head reveals Al Junes from Menahga, Minnesota. He asks where I've been and listens to my explanation. Al says, "How the hell did you work that out?" and walks away shaking his head.

As we line up in front of the barracks for a march to the mess hall, it's possible to recognize a few other cadets but most of the group are total strangers. There's no way to guess where they came from but their sunburned faces raise the possibility they've been working in the sun. No talking is allowed in ranks so there's no way to pick up any accents that might offer a clue as to where they came from. It really doesn't matter. We're marching straight from chow to the flightline so I'll meet some of them there. The early morning air is chilly and promises a gray and windy day; one that will not be the best for dropping bombs. The first thing everybody does when we get inside the flight building is check in, meet our instructor, and take a look at the big chalkboard leaning against the wall at one side of the room. It tells us what our mission will be and to see how we are paired up for the day's flying. My name is up there with that of Bernie Parsons, my old buddy from Santa Ana and two other cadets from the new group, total strangers.

We take chairs circled around the 2nd lieutenant who will be our instructor during the flight. As usual, there is little time for conversation. We can already hear the crackling of the AT-11s that will carry us around as the pilots turn up their engines. After a short talk from the 2nd lieutenant who will fly with us and critique our performance we pick up parachutes and lug them out to the flight line. I'm still savoring the taste of what was once two stacks of pancakes from chow this morning. They were great, just right, perfect for a cool day like this I tell myself while patting my stomach in satisfaction. Their warmth has taken the sting out of a cool and sunless morning and helped brush the sleep from my eyes. GI pancakes dripping with butter are a great way to start the day and are almost enough to make a man think he's back in his grandma's kitchen.

CHAPTER 18

WHO THE HELL ARE THESE GUYS?

When we reach the plane we take turns hoisting the chutes and pushing them up through a large hole under the tail of our ship. The opening is large, big enough for a careless cadet to fall through and find himself swimming through the air. Not long ago one of the cadets from the class of 44-5 named Willard Netzley was sitting on the catwalk fixing his flashlight when the pilot banked suddenly and sent him sailing through the air at eleven thousand feet without an airplane. His chute opened and Netzley got down without any further trouble except that he had to wander through the cold and dark desert for five hours before finding a road where he was picked up and brought back to the base. He says he expects to hear the end of it in 1965. Cadets are forced to wear parachutes at all times in the air.

Although I've already earned the required number of hits for graduation and am not under a lot of pressure it won't hurt to finish up well. After graduation we will move on to someplace where they put crews together and no doubt they will combine the best pilots with the hot bombardiers to form high quality crews based strictly on our performance as cadets. It will be good sense to keep on churning away right up to the last practice bomb. Taking ten days off to go home has not helped my confidence but I don't think it will be too difficult to pick up where I left off. The weather isn't going to help because, as expected the wind is now firmly in charge at Deming. It causes a person to wonder how much technique has been lost because of my trip home. I feel confident that I have been around here long enough to handle anything that might develop but it does bother me to wonder how much I may have lost during a nine-day vacation from spinning the knobs and setting up the bombsight.

The problem isn't about forgetting something big. At this stage of the game, basics have been burned into our brains by practice and constant repetition. The devil's tools are little traps designed to sneak up and make a bombardier look like a complete idiot; subtle moves that must be played with the clarity and precision of a concert pianist. I feel just slightly uneasy but this is far from my first recital and I realize that a bomb run doesn't have to be perfect to be good. On the other hand, there's absolutely no limit to the number of little things that can ruin a bomb run or cause embarrassing errors.

When the wind is up, as it is today, there are times when a bomb may decide it has a mind of it's own. Even a practice bomb is not predictable. It consists of sand wrapped in a bomb shaped steel cover and weighs a hundred pounds. Releasing one into the air and hoping it will sail through several thousand feet of sky to land somewhere near the center of a small circle on the ground has the power to break a cadet's heart or shrivel the expression on an instructor's face. We are playing a game where close is not good enough! Before we graduate, each cadet will have dropped 145 bombs and his proficiency rating must show an average circular error rating of one hundred sixty feet or less if he expects to graduate.

Cameras record every run from "not so good" (outside the circle) to "good" (inside the circle) to "terrific" (hitting the shack in the center of the circle). A few weeks ago things were moving smoothly for me. It was simply a matter of following the process, of turning the proper knobs and seeing the right picture in the site while watching two lines move toward each other. After that it's "Bombs away!" and the result drifts silently into the hands of the Lord. The only possible lurking disaster would be forgetting to let the pilot know the bombs are gone. It's hard to withstand the fury a pilot and instructor can pour on a cadet who forgets to tell the pilot that the bombs are gone and he can make his turn for the next run. I don't expect to be that forgetful and there is no reason to believe anything has changed. So, right now, why am I feeling confident and uncertain at the same time. Why does a little voice keep repeating, "You have enough hits to graduate right now. Stop worrying, but don't screw up. Nothing short of a colossal calamity can hurt you now. Don't try to think one up. For God's sake, don't let one get away and take out the officers' mess." Two weeks ago such an idea would have been unthinkable, this morning it's the only thought running through my mind. It will probably take a few days to brush the furlough out of my head and get back to challenging the world of 'what's next?' According to the proficiency rules I already have enough hits to meet the required rules and graduate. That position should produce a smooth sailing, happy, state of mind without a worry in the world. Woah, not so fast so fast, cadet Moore. This is the Army and they make the rules. Where is it written that they can't change them anytime they want?

I needn't have worried about today. My partners were Bernie Parsons who I've known ever since Coe College, and one of the new guys named Jimmy Southard from St. Paul, Nebraska. He said his buddies call him Smiley and he really does seem happy with life. Jimmy says he likes to play cards; we'll see about that. He also does pretty well on a bombsight based on what he showed us today. In spite of a wind that was using the sky for a handball court and batted us all over the sky, Jimmy got a shack and put two inside the circle. It amounts to a very good day's work. I managed to get one in the circle but didn't even come close to a shack and tried to act satisfied with having landed the other two bombs safely in the state of New Mexico. Tomorrow will be another day and the old sizzle seems to becoming back.

After we finished our flight and filled out the necessary forms Bernie and I walked back to the barracks with Jimmy who explained a few things about our new friends including who they are and where they came from. It turns that they are cadets who originally qualified for pilot training but washed out along the way. Their first stop had been at San Antonio; a place they hated and still detest with fervor most people reserve for Hitler and the Japs. Fortunately for some of them, when they washed out as pilots, the Air Corps offered a second chance to fly and get a commission by becoming bombardiers. Those who accepted the invitation were sent to Kingman, Arizona for seven weeks to earn the title of Aerial Gunners, a qualification required of all bombardiers. By joining the class of 44-3 we will raise the number of cadets expected to graduate in our class to one-hundred sixty-five which will make it the largest in the history of the base.

I asked Jimmy why so many of these guys decided to take the Air Corps offer. He replied that going through bombardier training looked like a better bet than pinning on their newly won gunners' wings and taking the next plane to Europe where the 8th Airforce is taking tremendous losses battling the luftwafe in missions over targets like downtown Berlin. It's no surprise that there is an urgent need for replacements. The action is red hot and Jimmy says there was some hesitation at first. However, when the commanding officer added the words "or else" to the invitation things began to move faster than a P-39 in a power dive. I also asked him why his friends carry such a fierce hatred for San Antonio, a place his buddies seem to despise more than loaded dice. Maybe it's the climate, but what else is new? Everyone in the Western Bomber Command knows that San Antonio has a climate three degrees hotter than hell, but these guys are not going to get any sympathy around here where we all know there is no place on earth hotter than Kingman. These guys must know that. They just finished their seven-week sentence in the Deming blast furnace.

Whatever happened there at San Antonio, it hit them bad. They call it the SAAD Sack, and talk about it with a savagery most people reserve for Nazis and Japs. Maybe they're burned up because they washed out of pilot training. Whoever they are and whatever they think, we better get to know each other soon. We are all going to be around here flying and attending classes together until we either graduate or end up babbling to the shrinks who run the nut house over at Section Eight. Frankly, after only a few days, our part of the barracks is tired of listening to these guys bitch about "Klub Kanvas- hotter than blazes in the daytime, cold as hell at night." Well, they won't have any trouble with the heat in Deming at this time of year. By the time we finish up at the end of February they will probably be complaining about frozen fingers or trying to beat away the flu.

It may take some time for us to sort things out but these guys have taken the place left by our unexpected furloughs and the coming graduation of Class 44-2. If rumors coming off the third stool hold up, which cannot ever be guaranteed, we will all graduate in late February.

Today it turned out we were paired with one of the new guys named Jimmy Southard from St. Paul, Nebraska. I hadn't worried myself sick that I might have forgotten every thing I ever learned about dropping a bomb but there is a gray cloud over every move we make these days and it makes a man wary. Even though I had secured enough hits to qualify for graduation before leaving on furlough it would be wise to try finishing with the best circular error possible. The Army Air Corps seems to love adding and subtracting things so having a good proficiency rating could make a difference in the kind of crew I will work with when the time comes.

The IQ of the men around me is very high and the chance of finishing near the top on the final proficiency charts would require plenty of luck. We have realized from the beginning that luck would be the golden goose of our careers. When Lady Luck takes the day off nothing goes well. The result is usually an afternoon or evening filled with forcefully delivered suggestions from an impatient instructor. At this stage of our training we all know how to aim a bomb. The trouble is, as airplanes go, the AT-11 is not very big, in fact can be considered small. Sometimes, when the wind opens its bag of tricks the plane goes up and down like a runaway elevator and the bombardier might as well try to focus on a target while bouncing through the white water canyon on a raft. It's easy to think about becoming an HB (Hot Bombardier) when the sun is shining but, at this time of year, at the mercy of winds strong enough to grab a 100-pound bomb and send it fluttering crazily off course toward the Alamo or points North, South, East and West, all bets are off.

For any cadets who haven't achieved enough hits to meet proficiency rules required for graduation the situation is critical. One possible solution might be a streak of good bombing weather, a couple of weeks where the plane drifts through the sky pushed along by soft breezes, and the pilot can give the bombardier a stable ride toward a target that looks as big as a harvest moon. Such a thing is possible but, as Makowski used to say, "The only defense against bad luck is good luck but don't count on it." In such situations, a silent prayer is probably a better bet.

Our class has more than 150 cadets and each of us believes he knows everything there is to know about dropping bombs. Unfortunately, this is the time of the year Mother Nature gets into the game and she seldom plays fair. We have no defense to tame this nasty old bag of wind but I hope she finds it in her heart to be gentle with some of these guys who must be praying for balmy weather.

Another cadet and I were waiting for our plane to land to take us on our afternoon bomb runs. Our plane was late and all the other cadets had departed on their rides. After a seemingly long delay, an officer came out of the flight building and said, "you can go back to your barracks, you won't be flying this afternoon."

We decided to skip the barracks and went straight to the PX. We had just finished our Cokes when another cadet came in and told us that two planes had collided attempting to land and several people had been killed. My cadet buddy and I said nothing. We had found out why our flight was canceled the hard way. We had many, many friends up in the sky that afternoon. As it turned out, the cadets involved in the collision were from class 44-5.

CHAPTER 19

AN OFFICER

It is a sunny Sunday morning, the morning after we have completed our training, received our wings, and celebrated the occasion as thoroughly as the limited social parameters of Deming, New Mexico would allow. We are now commissioned officers and I am now a 2nd Lieutenant. We had a party and the next morning I got on a train that took me all the way across Texas to Louisiana, because that's where my dad was and it happened that my mother was visiting.

I slam the barracks door behind me. Deming has been a hard grind and the mornings, afternoons, and nights were filled with both things to remember and some to forget. I'm leaving forever and parting brings no tears, no feeling of loss. I'm starting a ten-day furlough and after that will report to Hammer Field in Fresno, California. The immediate problem is to catch a hop down to El Paso. In the meantime, I can't help touching those silver wings now and then on the short walk to the flightline. I don't know why. Nobody can take them away now unless I commit some kind of crime. It's all true: those gold bars riding on my shoulders tell the world Jack I. Moore is a Second Lieutenant in the United States Army Air Corps. I am entitled to fly free anywhere in the world that's permitted by my travel orders. It's my Air Corps as much as General Hap Arnold's. Certainly the General would have an easier time finding a seat on any aircraft that tickles his fancy, but I can hope. To the best of my knowledge, in spite of all the petty do's and don'ts that come with a commission, it is not considered unseemly for a 2nd lieutenant to pray silently for a miracle. My pocket rosary has gotten me this far. It seems natural to figure, with the help of a few Hail Marys, some kind of aircraft headed for Louisiana will be waiting on the parking strip at El Paso.

This is Sunday, one of the days when pilots check out planes and point the noses east to El Paso. From there they can walk across the bridge to Juaurez, where the fun is. My prayers are answered and I squeeze into a place on the floor of an AT-11 that is already crowded. There are only four of us, but we're packed in like sardines. The problem is a big round hole that uses up most of the floor space in the back end of the fuselage. The twin engine AT-11s at Deming have been redesigned to carry struggling cadets on bomb runs. There is, therefore, a gaping, bottomless chasm in the floor allowing a fellow cadet to spread eagle himself, lie face down, hold a camera out below the plane and film the success or failure of every bomb his buddy drops. In training we are forced to wear parachutes just in case. It's a big hold and during our night bombing phase we were warned about a cadet in another group who actually fell out of the plane. Fortunately he was wearing a chute and made a safe landing. The nights are very dark out on the mesa but he wandered around until a distant light led him to a remote farmhouse where he knocked on the door. They say the lady of the house almost fainted when she saw the cadet standing there a hundred miles from nowhere holding a parachute in his arms at one o'clock in the morning. In training, we were forced to wear chutes at all times. On this morning's trip, no such amenities are being offered.

As airplane rides go, the distance from Deming to El Paso is not very long. We arrive to find there has been a crash and the runway is strewn with debris. We glance at one another and nod our heads. The site of two green GI meat wagons standing with rear doors half open does not speak well for occupants of the plane. Down below, GI's are throwing many parts of what used to be an airplane onto the back of a truck. We can see that it's not an Air Corps plane, it's more like a little single engine thing, maybe a "grass hopper." The workers have had some trouble moving the fuselage, but now they're bringing in a derrick. It shouldn't be long before we can land. Most of the debris is gradually disappearing. My eyes are drawn to the green GI ambulances parked with rear doors open near the wreckage on the edge of the runway. I wonder what happened to the people who were on board. I get the answer when two men in white coats emerge from the meat wagons and slam the back doors shut. They go forward, climb into the cabs of the meat wagons and move along slowly past the fence that leads away from the airfield. There are no sirens. We are watching a funeral procession.

Our pilot puts us down with a polite bounce on the tarmac and taxis to a parking space. I need to find some sort of transportation but my luck has run out. The air is full of aircraft taking off and landing, but nobody is going to Louisiana and nothing that's destined for Texas has an empty seat. In the end, it's necessary to give up and buy a ticket for a bus trip to Wichita Falls. If connections work out, it will then be possible to board a train for the mile after mile all day rump bumping required crossing the entire state of Texas on a railroad train. Next, if everything goes according to plan about arriving and leaving Wichita Falls, my bruised carcass will be dumped out at Shreveport where it will be possible to board a bus for Alexandria, Louisiana and see my folks again.

I board the train at Wichita Falls, find a seat, remove my brand new officer's blouse and hang it up carefully. In response to an irresistible urge to let the world know the seat is reserved for an officer of the United States Army Air Corps, the blouse is hung with wings and bars glistening. It faces the aisle in the forlorn but possible hope that a pretty young maiden might take notice and decided to occupy the vacant seat next to mine. The engine is puffing and ready to go when I leave the seat to wash my hands.

On my return a beautiful girl my own age sits smiling up from the once empty seat next to mine. She asks if it is taken. I say it isn't and can't help wondering whether this is a dream sequence or reaction from the tequila G.I., Kahler, Bernie and the rest of us consumed last evening in celebrating our liberation from life as aviation cadets. We expected a gradual increase in compatibility with the outside world owning to more freedom and fancier uniforms but wow, can this be real? The answer is "Yes."

The girl is real and after only a few minutes, it is obvious we have many things in common. I had started my sophomore year at the University of Minnesota; she is a freshman at the University of Texas. She is very pretty, qualified to be a pin-up in any barracks. I even find myself willing to overlook her slightly singsong Texas drawl, the kind that has the word 'you' sounding like 'yew.' We talk until lunchtime and then have a sandwich together in the dining car.

The girl I left behind me is no longer writing and has married a sailor who is goofing off the war in a CTD unit at the University. I am free as the breeze and it's a long time since I've enjoyed the company of any young lady let alone one as pretty as this.

314

I don't ever remember having such a satisfying time. The afternoon begins to fade but our concentration and laughter continue until the train begins slowing for her stop at Austin. The end of our meeting will be as short, swift and permanent as an executioner's ax.

We leave the train together, shake hands and say good-bye. I go into the station for a Coke and when I make my way outside she calls for me to come and meet her parents. I do and they seem to be nice people. For a flashing second I think of asking her for her address and volunteering to write now and then. I'm glad I didn't. What would be the point? I have no future that involves v-mail romances or loyal and distant lovers. I can't pretend that the war will end soon or even that I will be there if it does. I'm better off the way I am. It will be a long war and a bona fide unmarried officer in the Air Corps can hope to meet many women along the way. Right now, I can't shake the feeling that it will be a long time before I forget this train ride and the pretty girl from Texas who made me feel like someone special. I shudder to think how long that trip across Texas would have been without her. I wish it had been longer.

I arrived in Louisiana. I knew my dad was there. I knew my mother was there, and I got off at the bus and found a telephone. I don't know if I knew my dad's telephone number, but I knew where he was, so I called and asked for him and they said, "Well, hold the phone."

Then my dad came over and said, "Yes." He didn't know who it was. He said, "This is Colonel..."

I said, "Colonel, I understand that you're having some trouble with some of these lower echelon men."

He said, "What are you talking about?"

And I said, "Well, you've been treating your minor officers..."

and he still didn't know my voice. Then I said, "This is Jack," and he said, "Oh, gee."

So he said, "I'll meet you over at the place." He told me how to get there. The first thing I did was take a shower. I'd been on that thing for 24 hours. He had come back from war college where he was studying, and my mother was staying with him. With my mother and dad I stayed about four days, but I wanted to get home, too. I said, I've gotta go north and stuff. What I will remember and never forget, they came down to the train and I got on the train and sat there a little bit and the train started and I looked out the window and my dad and my mother waved to me as I went by, and I thought *I may never see them again.* Hollowness.

As an aviation cadet in bombardier training, we flew over southern New Mexico and some of the prettiest wonders of the southwest. Later, when we got our silver wings and second lieutenant's commission, it was off to March Field at Riverside, California. I was there for a month while we waited for them to put the crews together.

They kept us there a whole month really without much to do. None of us had any airplanes to be on. They put us through some training we'd done before. You know, that one where you run into a field and drop on your face and they shoot real bullets right over your head. We had a gun and we ran and you would flop down, they warned you all about it, and they'd shoot over your head, and this one time they didn't shoot over the guy's head. We ran and shot at something up ahead.

Eventually, I found myself standing under the wing of a B-24 Liberator on the tarmac at March Field in California with nine other men who would make up our crew. Four of us: pilot, co-pilot, bombardier, and navigator are officers. We studied each other

316

closely, realizing that these are the people with whom we will live or die.

It was my good fortune that our crew worked well together from the very first and progressed to be a lead crew on thirty-six missions over targets ranging from Iwo Jima to the Japanese mainland and Shanghai without a single problem regarding our work together.

We arrived at March Field in the Spring and, in those days, the orange groves were all around. We were there three months while the members of our crew became used to each other and were in the air every day. There is the memory of walking to the flight line feeling good and absorbing the warm morning sun. It was a checkout flight for our pilot, Henry Janeski, so the rest of us were just along for the ride.

In my greenhouse, I was looking down at Los Angeles and wondering exactly where Hollywood might be. Some very famous people were right down there below. Suddenly, a flash of sunlight reflected off the wings of a silvery twin-engine P-38 Lightening. The pilot was doing acrobatics, climbing like a homesick angel, then falling over and dropping slowly, a spinning, falling leaf. Seconds later a blue Navy Corsair with its gull shaped wings burst into the scene spiraling almost straight up in the direction of the lightening. The game was on and we were treated to an Army vs. Navy dogfight that had our crowd cheering when the lightening was on top and groaning when the Corsair managed to come up from behind and stick on the tail of the Army pilot for a minute or two. The P-38 was faster, but the Corsair was more maneuverable. The contest did not last long and nobody won, but it was great to be in the Army, to be a member of an air crew, to be up above the world watching the fun from the best seat in the world.

317

After our training at March Field was completed, we were sent to Oahu, Hawaii by way of San Francisco, Fort Lawton, and a Liberty Ship. At Hickam Field, we saw the evidence of the Japanese attack on Pearl Harbor and knew that, at last, we were approaching the real war. It was there that the greenhouse and I ran into an unusual problem. Because the bombardier was also the armament officer on a B-24, he must be able to fire all the guns and turrets. We were participating in a practice exercise during which enemy fighters, played by Navy fighter planes, attacked us from all sides and we fired back from 50 caliber machine guns loaded with camera film.

When it was my turn on the nose turret, I helped Johnny Scanlan, our nose gunner, out of the turret and climbed in to take his place. Johnny then slammed the turret door and locked it behind me after which he locked a second door which separated the turret from the plane. I quickly saw a fighter coming in and turned the handles to rotate the turret to the right. When I tried to turn the turret back to the front, it wouldn't budge. You can guess the rest: the call to the flight engineer on the intercom, the various advice and scraping and yanking as they tried to unfreeze the turret. Finally, the last word from the engineer, I give it to you verbatim: "Sorry, Lieutenant, I don't think we can get you out up here. Looks like you'll have to land in it."

The angle at which the turret had stopped was one from which I could see no part of the airplane; it was the ultimate ride; just me and the runway coming up at about 150 miles per hour. It might be possible to sustain a claim that I landed before the plane. Janeski set it down easy and they eventually found the used shell cartridge that had stuck in the turret track. I was set free and it was no big thing. However, when I think of it now, I realize that I was coming down on the same runway that the Japanese had bombed two years before.

Then there was the time we flew a practice flight from Hawaii to Midway Island. It was in the Battle of Midway that the tide of the war in the Pacific was in the balance and fell to the United States. It took place long before our crew went there, but it is a most unbelievable island to have so many pages and such an important place in American history.

The flight from Hawaii was eleven hours and every minute was in a raging storm that had those flexible Davis wings on our B-24 flapping up and down while the lightening flashed and St. Elmo's fire, a strange blue halo, was crackling off the propeller tips. A bombsight can also be used to compute drift when it's possible to see the white caps on the water. At one point I noticed enough space in the clouds to get some information and learned that we had sixteen degrees of left drift. I crawled up to the flight deck and found our navigator, Ellis Walker, asleep with his head on the table. When I awakened him and told him we might be heading toward Australia instead of Midway, he made a few computations on his log, gave a new heading to Janeski and that was that. Midway is only a few miles square but we came in right on it. Midway, at least at that time, was a miserable place with gooney birds everywhere and a few marine pilots standing guard. I still don't understand what anybody wanted with it. But it's history and I saw it from my greenhouse.

Our first mission was to Woleai on November 14, 1944. Several of us went out together to this little, little place. We left at 06:15 and it was cold that morning. Believe me, I was kneeling down there in the nose of the plane and I had the guns and stuff but I was just riding there. It was cold, really cold. This was our first mission. It was easy. There was no resistance. I wasn't bothered by it.

(left to right) Father and son: Howard I. Moore and Jack I. Moore

Jack's mother Perrigo Moore (left) and Grandmother Julia Flavin (right).

Jack I. Moore at Edison High School (left) and in the Army Air Corps (right).

CHRISTMAS REUNION FOR VETS

Gathered for their first Christmas together in four years, a Minneapolis father and his two sons, all soldiers, swapped stories and examined each other's souvenirs of action all over the globe in their home at 1036 Thirteenth Av. S.E. Major Howard L. Moore (center) served with the Seventh Army. Lt. Jack L. Moore (left) was with Seventh Air force in the Pacific, and Pvt. William Moore served with the First Infantry division. Jack and William now are students at University of Minnesota. Similar scenes are now being enacted in thousands of other Minneapolis homes this year as servicemen came home for their first postwar Christmas. (...ly Times photo by Merril Palmer.)

Article and photo of Jack, Howard and Bill after the war.

Complete List of Combat Missions of Janeski's Crew

DATE	MISSION	HOME BASE	TARGET	HOURS
1. 11/14/44	Strike	Saipan	Woleai	6:30
2. 11/18/44	"	"	Shipping	10:30
3. 11/24/44	"	"	"	10:00
4. 11/30/44	"	"	Iwo Jima	8:30
5. 12/08/44	"	"	" "	9:00
6. 12/10/44	"	"	" "	8:30
7. 12/14/44	"	"	" "	8:45
8. 12/19/44	"	"	" "	9:15
9. 12/24/44	"	"	Chichi Jima	11:00
10. 12/27/44	"	"	" "	10:50
11. 1/03/45	"	"	Iwo Jima	9:00
12. 1/11/45	"	"	" "	8:45
13. 1/14/45	"	"	Truk	6:40
14. 1/18/45	"	"	Chichi Jima	9:25
15. 1/25/45	"	"	Iwo Jima	8:45
16. 2/03/45	"	"	Chichi Jima	11:00
17. 2/11/45	"	"	Iwo Jima	9:10
18. 2/15/45	"	"	Chichi Jima	10:30
19. 2/19/45	"	"	Iwo Jima	10:00
20. 3/21/45	"	Guam	Chichi Jima	11:30
21. 4/26/45	"	"	Truk	8:00
22. 4/29/45	"	"	Marcus	11:15
23. 5/01/45	"	"	Truk	7:15
24. 5/09/45	"	"	"	8:00
25. 5/13/45	"	"	Marcus	11:00
26. 6/06/45	"	"	Truk	8:00
27. 6/27/45	"	"	"	8:30
28. 7/13/45	"	Okinawa	Byu A/F Kyushu	8:15
29. 7/17/45	"	"	Shanghai	7:40
30. 7/25/45	"	"	Anami O Shima	5:40
31. 7/28/45	"	"	Kure	9:15
32. 7/31/45	"	"	Kyushu	8:00
33. 8/06/45	"	"	"	6:15
34. 8/08/45	"	"	Tsing Tao	9:45
8/09/45	*Nagasaki bombed.*			
35. 8/10/45	"	"	Kumamoto	7:40
36 8/12/45	"	"	Matsuyama	8:00
8/15/45	*Japan surrenders.*			

Janeski's Crew featured as "Crew of the Week"
in the *March Field Beacon*, June 23, 1944

LT. MARION T. GAINES
Co-Pilot

LT. HENRY S. JANESKI
Pilot

LT. JACK I. MOORE
Bombardier

RS SGT. ODMUND T. OLSEN
Radio Operator

CPL. CHRIS S. MULLER
Engineer

LT. ELLIS L. WALKER
Navigator

(left to right) Jack I. Moore, Bob DeLane, Jerry Milner

(left to right) John Scanlan, Jack I. Moore, William Rice, and Ellis Walker.

Janeski's crew: Top row (left to right):Cpl. John W. Scanlan, Lt. Marion T. Gaines, Lt. Henry S. Janeski, Lt. Jack I. Moore, lt. Ellis L. Walker *Bottom row (left to right)*: Cpl. William J. Rice, Cpl Donald L. Olson, Cpl. Robert E. Powers, Sgt. Odmund T. Olsen, Cpl Chris S. Muller.

Below Walker, Gaines, Janeski and Moore.

CHAPTER 20

LOUIE'S FLYING CIRCUS

This is about Major Louis "Louie" Lamb, commander of the 38th Bomb Squadron, 30th Bomb group which was composed of twenty or thirty B-24 Liberator bombers on the 'mystic' isle of Saipan, which was called that because it was a mystery why the Japs kept it for 75 years when they could have left whenever they felt like it. Our duty was to drop bombs on places that the U.S. Marines had decided to take over any way they could, which was usually to slug their way right through the enemy to the far side of the island and then turn around and shoot and hack and chop their way back. They were very good at it. When those guys had made one trip each way and finally chased the enemy up into the hills, the island was declared "secured" and it was time to bring in the Liberators and get started clearing the way for the next invasion. Some of the group came in from the Marshall Islands where they participated in the attacks on Tarawa, Kwagelain, and other places where the gyrines had cleaned up. In our case, it broke up a wonderful vacation at Hickam Field and other watering holes scattered among the orchids and pineapple fields on Oahu. There were actual live girls living there and they were the last we would see for many months.

When our plane landed at Saipan we quickly learned that the island being "secured," as we had been reading in the Honolulu papers, simply meant to imply that the heavy fighting was about finished and the remaining opposing soldiers who were running loose in the woods a couple of hundred feet from our tents were not to be taken seriously. "Secured," we learned, did not mean "We Won!" it just meant that in the long and bloody give and take, the generals had decided that there was no longer a chance that we would lose. Each night, Marine patrols went up into the hills in search of stragglers and the crackle of automatic fire announced that they had rooted some out.

At that time our squadron, the 38th, was an eclectic mixture of veterans with many missions and stories to tell and crews like our own who listened. The big story was not a mission at all and had taken place in the large tent that served as an officers' club, one of the first structures erected. It was there that officers could keep their booze, shoot craps, play card games, and sing dirty songs. It took place the week before we arrived.

By some miracle or political connection, the flight surgeon had arranged for several nurses to visit the "club" and lend their charms to an evening of dancing and good fellowship. Unfortunately, one of the Japanese survivors picked that very evening to wander down from the hills with an empty stomach but a full intent to break up the party. With the mirth and high jinx in full blossom, the determined Jap pulled the pin on a hand grenade, rolled it beneath the canvas, onto the dance floor and escaped into the black night. The grenade exploded wounding two of the nurses and the party was over. The officers who were there at the time seemed very angry, not at the Jap, but at the nurses who were not that badly hurt and didn't have to take off and kill such a promising evening.

Louie had put in a full tour of missions somewhere up in the Alaskan command. The usual weather conditions there in the central Pacific were usually CAVU, airplane talk for "Ceiling and Visibility Unlimited." If you can picture a person who might be a retired boxer but is only slightly and occasionally punch-drunk, you will be imagining Louie. A veteran of many missions in the far North flown from the island of Attu, he was thoroughly educated in the art of weaving snakelike between fog banks, impenetrable clouds and uncharted mountains. Sometimes a weather ship fitted with all the latest gadgets for tracking unpredictable meteorological phenomena was sent ahead to determine the possibility of the lumbering B-24s getting to the target and back. Occasionally, the weather ship itself failed to return. In such a case, and only then, the mission might be called off and the Liberators would turn their efforts toward making a search; roaring blindly down the runway and disappearing quickly into the artificial nether-world that was, in fact, more uninviting that any of the Japanese targets the crews were able to attack occasionally when the elements cooperated.

However, Louie went through an entire tour of missions on that lonely outpost, despite his sparkling credentials for flying blind and surviving social deprivation and terrifying frost. My bridge partner Tom Gill, a navigator who looked like Pete the Tramp, had put in a tour up there and was full of stories about how a bright, shiny sun in your face at the start of the runway could turn into a dirty, gray bank of fog where you lost sight of your own propellers before that Liberator got its wheels off the blacktop. I never met anybody who flew 30 or 40 missions up there who wasn't part way to section eight, which is what they called the psycho ward.

Tom was a truly great bridge player and also knew a bunch of songs that he said they used to sing when there was nothing else to do up there on the frozen tundra of places like Attu Island. Since that was the case most of the time, Tom knew a lot of tunes which he taught us, because it made it possible to sing along and drown Tom out. On occasion, Tom shaved his entire face but usually it was just here or there which nobody noticed particularly because if you looked Tom over at all it was to wonder why his uniform looked like it had been put together with parts of a corrugated box.

According to Tom, sometimes the weather ship would get lost and never be heard from again. Clearly Louis, and probably Tom, too, should have been interned at some snug training base back in the States; at least for a little while. I'll tell you more about Tom later but, for now, I'd like to help you picture Louie.

One thing that must be said about Major Lamb is that his Alaskan experience had not given him any phobias that kept him from accompanying us on missions. We all felt things might be better if it had. As it was, he could not be described as a gibbering idiot because he seldom gibbered. In fact, his speech was profanely precise as it spewed forth the inimitable thoughts and plans that bounced and careened off the rocks within his head. His passion in life was to see, just one time, his squadron get into shape after take-off, fly back over the field in perfect formation, and head out toward the target merrily singing the Army Air Corps song. Actually, he never demanded the singing part, but as for his trying to egg his cohorts into worrying about what the other squadrons thought of our formation as we chugged past the tower, our thoughts were bedeviled by the anticipation of six or more hours out to the target over nothing but water just to fly over some little island where the people disliked us and were certain to try to damage our valuable aircraft and, if possible, shoot it right down into the ocean.

Our indifference while not openly defiant angered the Major more and more until one time, at the briefing the day before the mission, he laid out his plan for how we would act when we returned in triumph from Iwo Jima the next day. We would roar across Saipan as usual and make our usual 180 degree turn to prepare to land. However, this time we would zoom over the island in an echelon of 10 planes; not in a V formation but wing tip to wing tip, side by side. His motivation was clear: "If the other squadrons are gonna call us Louie's Flying Circus, WE'RE GONNA BE LOUIE'S FLYING CIRCUS."

CHAPTER 21

Iwo

We flew to Iwo many times, but we never called it that. We called it *The Mountain*. We were on the way back to Saipan after bombing Iwo Jima for the third or fourth time. We were having trouble with one of the engines and Jan (Henry Janeski, Cudahay, WI.) our first pilot and our co-pilot,(Phil Gaines from Gainesville, FLA) were trying to decide whether to "feather" it. We were almost home and had dropped down close to the ocean to get under a heavy overcast. As usual I (the bombardier) had crawled out of the nose and up on the flight deck as soon as we were low enough to get off the oxygen. The weather could not have been more gloomy; a dancing twilight, like strobe-lights. Jan asked me to go back in the waist and get the gunners ready to drop the ball turret if it became necessary. I hoped there might be some canned turkey left back in the waist. I went through the bomb bay on the catwalk and entered the waist. As expected, the turkey can was empty but the well fed gunners were strangely silent, gazing out the open waist windows. They glanced at me but said nothing.

Shorty Olson left one of the windows and I took his place There it was. The convoy carrying the 1st Marine Division, our next door neighbors on Saipan, was moving out. Moving with the creeping reluctance of a funeral procession and we knew that's what it was.

We knew Iwo! We bombed it many times. Oh how we hated those 120s hidden in the volcano at one end of the little pork chop shaped island that hardly seemed worth fighting over. We knew, all of us; the two Shortys (waist gunners), Johnny Scanlan (nose gunner), Chris Muller (Engineer), Bob Powers (Armorer and Ball Turret Gunner) and Odmund Olsen (Radio Operator). There was not going to be any place to hide. We couldn't know which ones but we knew some would be killed or torn up. It was a doomsday caravan; and nothing would be able to stop it.

I finally broke the silence and told the gunners about being ready to drop the ball turret into the ocean if Jan thought it was necessary. It turned out no drastic action was needed and Jan got us down alright although he had to make a straight-in approach which was complicated because we lost contact with the tower.

He finally said, "Gardenia tower, I can't hear you; hope you can hear me. Coming straight in; blinking the altus lamp."

I crawled into the sack that night thinking about the convoy. It would not be the last time we would see it.

I had received a letter from my brother Bill. He could chose any branch of service upon graduation and he wanted to be a Marine. I jumped up and wrote him right back not to do that, do something else. I was very close to Iwo. We bombed it six times and when we came in to drop, the Japs would shoot form inside the mountain. We talked between missions trying to figure out some way to stop them from shooting at us. Bombers had to fly low and Japs would gun out at them. One guy said we should drop soap down there. We all just looked at him.

The reason I told Bill was we were so sure we needed to get in there. We started bombing them, that didn't help either. We were coming back form a bomb run on a day that the air was funny, half dark. I looked out and off in the distance there were great big boats. You could see the Navy was coming and we knew something was coming. I knew just by the way the air was that it was gonna be bad and a lot of guys would be knocked off. I hate to see where Bill would have been. Some people don't understand, you could see those bad things coming form a long way...the way the air was.

On the morning of the actual invasion, we were to take off at midnight. We'd had our briefing and we're all getting on trucks to go to the flight line. Mackowski and I were standing on a truck and the sun had just about gone down. He leaned over to me and said, "You know, Jack I., we keep doing things like this, we're going to be old men before our time."

What was frightening about that mission, more than anything, was you got all these planes taking off at midnight, and then getting into formation in the dark. We took off and had to climb up to meet each other in the air, in the dark. I'm sitting there looking at a screen with lights flashing green or red, telling me whether the planes out there are coming or going.

It was a long way, and by the time we got there, the sun was coming out. I got all set, opened the bomb bay doors and we were ready to get into the fight when the pilot buzzed me and said, "Jack I., close up those doors. They just called and said we are not going to drop our bombs." So we flew by and didn't drop our bombs.

Jan took us around again, and we flew back. I looked down over the target, and the ocean below us and saw our ships moving toward Iwo Jima. There were men and all kinds of guns. Looking down from the nose of the plane, I was thinking about these guys and I was really crying. These guys had no chance, and I knew that. The Japs had all their guys dug in under the ground and in caves. They had this thing that had bothered us before: a gun they would bring up from underground to shoot at us. The Mountain had no cover, nowhere to hide. They didn't have a chance. It was a long flight back to Saipan.

As soon as we landed, four of us, the officers, could hardly wait to get back to hear what was going on. We ran to the officers' tent and crowded around a radio there. The first thing we heard was, "… proceeding toward Iwo Jima." We had seen this island, we had spent countless hours in the air, hating that thing all the way there and back. We had called it 'The Mountain' and a few other names, but now the four of us looked at each other and said, "What the hell is Suribachi?" Imagine, four voices at once.

After securing Iwo Jima, there was good news. We got a leave starting that same day. The four of us boarded an airplane ferrying people to Hawaii and this was where everything started. Everyone except us was a wounded person. These guys who got on, it was weird, they were injured, they were covered in bandages, but every one of these guys were so happy because they were going home. They were all hurt, but they knew they had won; they were going to live and they were going home.

Across the aisle, an officer was sitting by himself. I can see him now. He was not wounded, but he was going home. I slid over next to him and asked, "How did the guys come out?"

He just looked at me and said, "75 killed in the first ten minutes. 60% lost." He knew this many were lost, and this was only shortly after the fight. There would be many more lost, we found out later.

We knew the guys who were lost. Some of them spent a lot of time running around in their snappy green outfits and looking for stuff they could sell. Then they'd come down to where we were and offer us booze and stuff we wanted to buy. These were the guys who had to lay down the wires for communication when they landed on Iwo Jima. We learned later that they had a difficult time on Iwo Jima. There was no cover on *The Mountain,* and its slopes were slippery so it was difficult to climb; the men would start to gain a foothold and then slide back down. They never had a chance.

CHAPTER 22

LETTERS

December 8, 1944 - Letter to Jack from his mother.

Dearest Jack:

I have been waiting to hear more from you, I am so anxious now that you have a post in the big show. I got a letter from Bill, he can't say much yet. I sent him a box as he got cheated a little by getting an A. P. O. so near Christmas. I sent the nuts and please send another request when you write. It is so much easier if I have some requests in my hand.

I received a letter from Dad today written Nov. 26th. He is so busy and on the go continually. He is watching for Bill. I wonder if he will see him. Our snow is all gone now, but it is quite cold. I am enclosing some snaps. Bob said you'd scream when you saw your sweater. I have had it cleaned and it will be safe and clean for you. The picture of me is terrible, but I'll send it along with the others. Good bye for now darling and write when you can. We have just completed a three day devotion for men in service. It was very nice. Bob and I attended. Take good care of Jack for me.

Lots of love,

Mother

December 21, 1944 - Jack's letter to his sister Pat.

Dearest Paturski:

Pardon the delay in answering your last letter. We have been a little busy lately. As my friend, "Mo" Lund puts it, "We have really been giving those 'push-faces' hell." "Mo" is quite a character and someday I shall write volumes about his witticisms. One night we had an air-raid and the sky was full of flak and trace bullets etc. The action was intense. Airplanes were shooting and bombing and being shot at. Just as the last Jap disappeared I poked my head cautiously out of our fox-hole just in time to see him come wandering sleepily out of his tent asking, "What's all the excitement out here?"

I received the pictures and they are really fine. Whenever you take any snapshots be sure to send me some.

I got a letter from Dad this week. He says he is O.K. and things are going along pretty well. Things here are about the same. The nightly movies have been pretty good lately. So far this week we have had "Watch On the Rhine" and "The Lodger" which were pretty good. I haven't heard any new songs lately. My favorite recording is "It's a Haunted Town." Lena Horne sings it with Charlie Barnet's Orchestra. I don't know whether you have ever heard it or not.

It certainly is swell to get your letters. You don't realize how much it means to get mail out here. By the way, if you know any beautiful girls, between the ages of eighteen and twenty-one, you might sneak up behind them and drop my address in their pocket-book. At any rate, you keep writing those very swell letters and I'll keep my end of the bargain as best I can considering the censor and the lack of news in general.

Love your Brother,

Dusty

December 26, 1944 - Birthday letter to Jack from his sister Pat.

Dear "Dusty,"

Well, here it is the 26th again and both my brothers are a year older. It certainly has been quite a year for all. I just want to take this opportunity to send you birthday greetings, with the hope that your next one will be spent in a far happier way.

Christmas is over and I can't help feeling a little glad. Although it was pleasant it really didn't seem much like Xmas. It was very cold and no sign of snow. We had a very small table tree as ornaments were impossible to get this year. Remember the good old days when I used to get you guys out of bed about 2 in the morning and dad would chase us back to bed and we'd repeat the procedure until he finally fell asleep? I got some very beautiful gifts including a Boliva wrist watch from mother and grandma. I can't tell you how thrilled and surprised I was to get it. Tess and Hugh came over in the afternoon with their family.

We had Mid-nite Masses in all the churches this year. I went to St Helenas, it was very beautiful but I guess everybody and his brother was there. It was the first time in twenty years we've been allowed to have them.

Jerry Milner called up last nite. He's coming over this week, I guess.

I'll close for now as I still want to drop a line to Bill. Take it easy and once again, I'm thinking of you on your birthday and hope you've had as enjoyable a day as possible.

Write when you can --- more later.

Love,

Your Sis,

Patruski

(cartoons/news clippings enclosed)

January 3, 1945 - Letter to Jack from his cousin Colleen.

Dearest Jack,

Well I haven't heard from you in some time. But I suppose you haven't time to be writing to your cousin. Well write if you have time. The weather around here is pretty cold, it is 5 below now but yesterday it was 15 below so you can see we haven't had such nice weather.

Gee all the kids around here are all getting wounded over there. First it was George DeAnglo but he is back in the front now. But Friday Mrs. Smith, Pee Wee's mother, got a letter from the War Dept saying that he was wounded. And today the mailman said that Andy Anderson the boy you used to play basketball with in the back yard. The one who lives on 12th, he was wounded in France. So you can see the people around here have the worry-ies.

Well this is all for now.
Will you please write to me.
With Love and Kisses
Colleen

January 4, 1945 -Letter to Jack from his sister Pat.

Dear "Dusty"

I sent you some clippings yesterday and I just got to thinking you were probably disappointed when you opened the envelope and found nothing but clippings. So here are a few lines to make up for it. Remember Betty Leanard and Stella? Well, they both went to Oregon about 18 months ago to work in the ship yards. Betty came home for the holidays. She's now a blond and Stella is a red-head. I guess the chemicals they were working with turned their hair white around the edges so they both dyed their hair. Betty is still as crazy as ever.

Jerry Milner was over a couple of days ago. He says he's now engaged to Delores Englund. Shirley (Emerson) Noble is "expecting" in a couple of months.

Did you see Bob Hope in "The Princess and The Pirate?" I saw it last week and it really was a scream. If you ever get a chance to see it by all means do.

I've been home from work the last couple of days with a cold. It's going to be awfully hard to tear myself away from the serials and settle down again.

If you're really serious about corresponding with a few of the more glamorous gals in town, I'll start dishing out your address pronto. Have you received any of your Christmas packages? I don't recall you mentioning them.

We've been hearing from dad quite regularly. I guess he's trying to locate Bill by all possible means. I sure hope they do get to see each other.

Bob is sitting next to me doing his homework. He says to tell you they got drubbed last night 34-25.

Ide is also here and says hello. She really isn't able to write and says she hopes you'll write to her sometime soon.

Write to me also as I really enjoy your letters.

Love,

Your Sister,

Patruski

P.S. How do you like this stationary. It was designed by a soldier recuperating in a hospital in England.

January 6, 1945 – France – Letter to Jack from his dad, Howard.
Dear Jack:

I am sorry to have delayed writing for so long a time and assure you that I will do better henceforth. Of course I know that you understand how it is. When things are active you are not in the mood and when there is a period of relaxation you find the period ended without having done half the things intended.

I received three letters from you at about the same time. The most recent was dated Nov. 20th. They were certainly interesting and enjoyed them over and over again.

If it be God's will we will certainly have a great time when we can all get to-gether again and compare notes on our varying experiences. Have covered quite a streak of France, having visited everyplace from Cherbourg to Strassbourg. The gayer days of our rat race across the country in ideal weather is a thing of the past. Right now I am enjoying?? a good old cold Minnesota winter. A lot of snow and the temperature down. So far the winter has not been too hard on me. Have been able to dress according to the weather and find some shelter and a place to keep warm and good food. It has been rugged though. One of the most touching scenes I have seen are refugees trying to get away from active areas to find safer places. Old people and children take off from their homes or what remains of them and take to the highway with a little wagon with their belongings. With the cold and wind sweeping across the road I have seen old people trudging along despairingly with bare hands and suffering from the cold. Although they have endured much during the past four or five years I believe they are finding the present time as rough as they have had.

The Jerry is still as arrogant and fanatical as ever and it looks as though we may have to go into every rat hole and dig them out. I guess the people back in the states got a little shock for themselves when the

Krauts took off recently. I hope that it is their dying kick but don't dare be that optimistic. As a matter of fact I have ceased to guess any further on the ending in this theatre. Lost a couple of bucks by betting last summer that is would end by Nov. 30th.

Am on the look out for Bill as I believe he is headed this way and if good fortune smiles and he should come anywhere near me I believe I can get him into a half way decent spot. Otherwise its pretty rough and the only consoling feature possible is that he has been well trained with his weapons and will be able to take care of himself better than some others. Bob wants to join the Marines. I know how he feels and believe I can make a deal with him to hold off for awhile. At least until either you or I get back which I hope will not be too far into 1945.

Well, Jack, I thought of you and Bill as well as the rest of the family a lot on Dec 26th. I hope you found some opportunity of making it a happy birthday with the age old promise of many happier ones to come. Take as good care of yourself as you can and I'll do the same.

The mail has been irregular but I hear from mother quite regularily and all seems to be well. Have had several letters from the office and they tell me that things there are pretty dead and are anxious for normal times again.

Can imagine that your meeting with Art Erpelding and Joe Kozlak was quite an occasion. Give them my regards if you should happen to see them again.

Will close for now and get this in the mail but will write again soon. With every good wish for you and the crew, I am,
Affectionately
Dad.

January 8, 1945 - Letter from Jack's brother Bill to his mom.

Dear Ma

Well here I am again. I haven't been getting much mail. I have had only two letters since I left Mpls. I wish you'd tell Eddy the next time you see him to get on the ball and write me a letter. I wrote Harry from Ft. Meade and he made arrangements for me to meet him in New York and he had gotten a date with that model and everything was all fixed for a nice time. Well you probably guessed that it all turned out to be an impossibility because of my short stay there. I called again as you know but I didn't call back at night as I didn't get time, and I didn't have anything I could tell you anyway. The book dad sent was really interesting and all of the boys in the hut have read it almost. Veral sleeps above me and he says to say hello. Well I'll close for now but will write soon

As Always

Bill

P.S. Will you send me some candy and some socks?

January 31, 1945 –France –Letter to Jack from his father.

Dear Jack,

Just received your letter of Dec. 3rd with your picture and one of the crew. I appreciate the pictures and wish I had one of myself to send to you but so far haven't been able to find anyone with a camera or any commercial photographers. Hope that one of these days I can get a couple of pictures for you and mother. Expect to see Bill shortly and believe I can arrange for a signa corps photograph to take our picture. Bill is up in Belgium at the moment. I understand he wrote me over a month ago but I have not yet heard from him. Just received his APO from mother yesterday and immediately checked up the location and activity of his outfit. Expect we will be closer to one another before long. I became acquainted with his outfit back in Normandy. They are well seasoned and a good division. Am glad he is just coming over here as the doughfeet over here have had a pretty rugged deal. I have a feeling that it won't last for many more months in this theater and if the little guy can keep his head down and weather out a couple of engagements he will probably wind up in the Army of occupation here which shouldn't be too bad a deal. Guess he likes the Infantry from all I hear. I am going to get to visit him just as soon as I possibly can which I hope will be within the next couple of weeks. Am sort of glad to be here as long as he is here. Not that I can do much for him but if I can see him once in awhile it may help the old morale some for both he and I. As soon as this mess is over I am going to try everything in the book to get back without delay. At present Bill is a rifleman but if his outfit ever comes into the same army I'm in I have the skids all set to get him out of the infantry and into a drivers job at higher headquarters.

Imagine it has been pretty active where you are located. Note what you say of the one incident when the Japs paid you a visit. The Jerry air activity has declined gradually, it being most active on our trip across France last summer. Right now it is practically nil on our sector front. Had an ME109 scare me the other day when it came over at tree top height about a hundred yards away without much warning. It was flying low to get away from some P47's which I don't believe ever saw him. He came so fast and low that he didn't even draw ack ack and was doing no damage himself at the time.

We have been having regular Minnesota winter weather. A lot of snow and low temperatures so that the snow creaked when you walked in it. Have been able to dress according to the weather and have not been too uncomfortable so far. Right now I am very comfortably situated. Being the senior officer in the town that we are in I am the town commander in addition to my other duties. The colonel is in another town. The additional duties are not too burdensome and I have the best quarters that I have ever had in the Army. I have a nice large room with heat, light and nicely furnished. It is with a civilian family and they clean the room amd make the bed each morning. Wash and press my clothes and do everything they can to make me comfortable. Up until recently though lived under canvas and slept on the ground so the present set up is luxurious.

You inquired about the presence of movie stars and whether I see very many. Bing Crosby, Dinah Shore and some others that I don't recall have put on shows very close to the front and endeared themselves to the troopies by the fine job they did. Didn't get to their shows myself so didn't see them but most of our outfit did go. Bing got publicity about his visit to our area because it was pretty active around there at the time and when he heard the firing he remarked to group of GI's that he was talking to that he didn't know that he was up that close. One of the men talking with him told me about the conversation. During his show they had to pull the infantrymen away from the show and send them down the road aways to mop up a pocket of Jerries.

You say that Olson from your crew was with the Coast Artillery in Alaska. Do you remember Gustav Perry Olson that served with me on Leaches' staff? He is a Lt Col and commanded a battalion of Coast Artillery in Alaska.

I hear regularly from mother and all seems to be well back home. Of course it will be better when I can get back which may not be too long from now if all goes well. It will be still better when we are all back there and then there will be some great days. And sure anticipation of those days are mutual. Best wishes to yourself and crew. Will write again in a few days.

Affectionately,

Dad

February 15, 1945 - Letter from Jack's brother Bill to their Mother from hospital after the Battle of the Bulge.

Dear Mom,

How is everything in the residence today? Fine I hope. I'm in England with frostbite and trench foot. About a half and half deal I guess. I'm in good shape, though it might be coming along fine. I didn't know before, if I could say anything about my case, that is why I didn't say much about it in my other letters. I guess I won't go back to the outfit for at least four months, but that's strictly unofficial. Most of the time spent in rehabilitation; I guess I couldn't say anything for sure. I'll give you this address and you and everyone write me here. I suppose everyone else has given up writing to me, but I'll write to Graham, Colleen, and Ida etc. I still haven't received my mail via a core brought us candy bars and cigarettes and generous helpings. So how is the cigarette shortage there anyway? If I'm allowed to send them I'll do it (two cartons). By the way, I'm getting a Purple Heart, which I'll send home. Well, I'll close now, but write soon.

Love

Bill

I'm no letter writer, but I'll keep trying.

PvT. Wm Moore

Detachments of the Patients 4204 U.S. Army Hosp. Plant

February 16, 1945 --France-- Letter from Jack's father to his brother Bill in Paris.

Dear Bill:-

How are you doing old pal? I've had a hell of a time trying to find out where you are at and what it's all about. A few days ago, the Red Cross cabled for mother that you were in a hospital in Paris so I climbed on a truck and drove there. What a job trying to find where you were. Finally traced it to the next place, and finally on to where I got your address. So here you go for a line before you move again. The only address I ever got was your salt water address and I guess even had the wrong company and platoon on that so don't suppose you have ever received them. Have written about eight letters, and I'm now sure that none have yet caught up. Our mail has been slow and so far have had no letter from you. Am leaving Paris today to return to my unit as my pass is up, but at least I now know where you are at and have just asked the Red Cross to give you my address and let me know what's up.

Don't know whether you are headed for the states or back here, but if you ever start back this way, try to get to the second replacement depot and then to the 71st replacement. You can get word to me faster through the Red Cross then by letter, but notify me by letter and Red Cross pulled so it's possible I can locate you.

Don't imagine you have been getting much mail. All is well on the homefront. Had letters from Jack, Bob, Pat and mother. Jack seems quite cheerful despite the fact they are quite active. He was on Saipan Island, the last I heard. Am anxious to hear from you and learn how you are. It's a tough deal but if all goes well I hope you will not feel too badly if you land someplace else other than the infantry. I know I surely wouldn't.

When I get back to my outfit I'm going to see what I can do about getting over to see you, but the chances are probably slim so don't figure on it, but if I possibly can, I will.

Will write more to-morrow. In the meantime I am hoping for the best for you. May have some news of some sort for you to-morrow as this is written in haste.

Affectionately,
Dad

February 19, 1945 –France—Letter from Jack's dad to his brother Bill.

Dear Bill:-

Hi there bub, how yuh doing? O.K. I hope.

Expect the Red Cross is just about reaching you to give you my address. When I got back from Paris I had a letter from Mother in which she told me you had lost my address. I was pretty sure you had when I didn't hear from you and it's easy to understand when you get to bouncing around the way you have been.

Well no mail to-day for me so can't give you any news. Imagine Jack is pretty busy these days as much progress is being made in that area according to the radio news. Say pal, is there anything you particularly wantin' sure you'll let me know if there is and remember I'll stick with you on anything so don't be hesitatin'. Until to-morrow -
Affectionately,
Dad.

March 12, 1945 –France—Letter from Jacks' dad to his mom.
My darling Paree:-

Received a letter from you and one from Pat. Both dated Feb. 19th. Expected another one from Bill but so far only the one of Feb. 20th. Have a hunch that he is probably on his way home although it may be just the slowness of the mail that I don't hear from him. I still continue to write him regularly though.

Col. Hicks dropped in to see me to-day. He had been down to visit the Rest Camp and spoke very encouraging about it. He was recently awarded the French Croix-de-Guerre medal for the work of his battalion. Fredericks is down there now for a couple of days. He hasn't been feeling so good. Maj. Wilmer, who broke his leg in England has rejoined us. He was given an opportunity to go back to the states but turned it down to rejoin the group. Wish I had that spirit but have an idea he won't have it much longer either.

By the time you receive this you will probably have official news releases of our activities.

Well, sweetheart, there isn't any news that I can write about. I'm well and keep hoping and praying that I can get back to you before long. I imagine that you are as lonely as I am but there has to be an end to this thing sometime soon. Days and hours don't mean a thing over here except you figure each morning that it is that much closer to an end. Very seldom do I know which day of the week it is and I have to inquire when I date your letters as to the date. I get up in the morning and am busy until bed time 7 days a week. To be able to relax one day in a couple of weeks would be paradise. At times the old morale gets pretty low but not for long as I have too much to do but it certainly hasn't hit any high mark since I have been with this outfit.

So much for now darling. I miss you so much that I feel like a baby at times. Be good and take care of yourself and I'll do the same. Tell Pat I'll write soon. With all my love.
Howd.

March 31, 1945--Letter from Jack to his mother.

Dearest Mom:

Just a note to let you know everything is O.K. We haven't flown a mission in quite awhile and things are quite slow. I don't go much for all this sitting around doing nothing but then again sometimes we are so busy a guy can't stop to take a deep breath.

I'm enclosing a check for $250.00 which you can put away for me. If at any time an occasion arises where you have to use some of the money I saved, feel free to do so. Be sure and let me know when you receive the check.

I was certainly glad to know that Bill was back in the states. I hope you get a chance to see him soon. He wasn't in combat long, but, as dad put it, "He certainly moved fast."

Tomorrow is Easter Sunday. It will be the third one that I have spent in the Army. Time certainly does fly.

At the rate things are going, I doubt if I'll get home before next fall. I guess as long as I'm here I might as well stay awhile. It might save me the trouble of coming back again.

I saw the movie "Murder My Sweet" tonight. It was quite good.
So much for now.
Your Loving Son
Jack

February 6, 1945--Letter to Jack from his friend Art Erpelding.

Dear Johnny,

Hello Rabbi -- you old son of a gun -- how in the hell are you? Thanks for your swell letter and I was sure glad to see you had about 12 missions under your belt by now you probably have three times that number.

Don't have any news at all except that Joe Bredemus is on this big rock now and I have located him. As yet we haven't got together shall do so in the near future have been down your way a few times but only as a milk run in case you should get this rock -- call #64206 and you can get me any time.

It looks as if Rex will be out this way soon as he is taught man of a group of Baker to nine. His wife is expecting in June, so you know he has been doing a little nite work

That is not the other day when I found out that Ralph Brogdon was killed in California. He was flying the Marine fighter, the F4U "Corsair."

Doing much of anything except to fly a little bit now and then getting a little time in the SBD (A-24) and the F4U to break the monotony of this twin engine stuff. As for the home front -- everything is well as far as I know Glad is behaving and that's about all that matters with me.

Well, John -- please take care of yourself and all the good luck in the world. Remember the big party we had planned and it looks as if you Phil and me will be the only ones without families.

Till next time – all the good luck in the world.

Your buddy,

Art

P.S. Write!

CHAPTER 23

BLACK DRAGONS, PURPLE HEART

We needed to take over Saipan in order to get closer to Japan, but it was not easy. On our 2nd or 3rd mission to Saipan, we encountered the *Black Dragons*. These were little black planes, Kamikaze planes, but we didn't know that term at the time. We had heard about them flying in China, but this was my first experience with them.

We had already dropped our bombs and were heading home when six or seven Black Dragons found us. "I want my mother, " was among the thoughts racing through my head as a Black Dragon neared my plane. He flew right up close to me and then suddenly his plane dropped, rolled over and continued shooting even while upside down. I wanted to get out of there, shooting all the time.

After that mission, back at our base we tuned into Tokyo Rose because we knew she would say something about the incident. I remember so clearly the woman's voice talking about "our wonderful pilots." This was the first time I heard the word Kamikaze and she explained that the boys were not coming back. She called them "wonderful boys."

Purple Heart, Marcus Island April 29, 1945

The day before our plane got shot up, Roy Grice lost his leg when our crew was flying with them. Their plane got hit. It knocked off his leg. Normally you'd expect that they would do something about stopping the blood, but this guy held his hand on it. They should have put a tourniquet on it but apparently that didn't work. Guy must have been tough. Some of the guys were saying they couldn't stop the blood.

The day our plane was all shot up, the time I got hurt…it was like a car crash. No one panicked or yelled. My eyes were caked with blood, glass in them. I climbed up and I was bleeding. I had to pull myself up. Phil was sitting legs wide, wind blowing through a crashed window and hole through the seat. I said "Phil, are you still an atheist?"

Phil says "Yep."

"Hey you guys almost lost your bombardier," I said, just being funny. No one said anything…too busy. The pilot and co-pilot kept it in the air really well. There are all kinds of things you need to fly an airplane. If anything (guns etc.) had been hit, I wouldn't be here today. The day before we'd been hit pretty bad. We gave them all we had. Next day they came back, plane zig-zagging-long flight back. More flak the day before, but they missed us.

People met our plane to help the wounded. We landed, and so many people wanted to see what happened, like a game. I didn't look at the plane. I never checked to see the damage. I said "Hi" to the Doc and walked right past him. We were pretty good friends. I had something to eat. After, we were playing a pretty big card game.

"Jack I. the doc wants to see you."

"I'm not going up there."

"You gotta."

"I'm not." I had money on the table. I didn't go. They came back.

"Doc's really mad, gotta go if Doc wants to see you, and he wants to see you."

I finally went and Doc pulled out little white glass...put on ointment.

"I'm not hurt that bad."

"It's bad enough, now get the hell out of here."

I went back to the game and don't remember if I won. I wasn't so excited. Next day they made me go to this place with other guys that were wounded at the same time.

CHAPTER 24

THE MEN WHO CAME TO DINNER

During World War II, the "grapevine" was a speedy, unconnected and unique means of communication. Rumors flashed from latrines at the speed of light: uncensored and unreliable. However, the grapevine was effective in arranging for me to meet Delane, one of the guys I hung out with before the war. Delane was broad shouldered and happy-go-lucky, somebody you might think would choose to become a paratrooper. Well, that's exactly what he did. His first name was Bob but only his mother ever called him that.

I knew about Delane because a mutual friend of ours, Wade Cole, had written to tell me where he was. Wade, now in Europe with the infantry, learned about what Delane was doing while home on furlough. He wrote that Delane was in the 11th Airborne somewhere out in the Pacific Theater. At the time, our 7th Air Force Group was stationed on Okinawa, bombing China and the Japanese main islands.

The day I received Wade's letter, our crew did not have a mission scheduled and I was enjoying sack time. I held Wade's letter in my hand, thinking about Delane. The afternoon was quiet except for the roar of B-24s taking off from Aslito Airfield and the sound of Jan Janeski, first-pilot and commander of our crew, ransacking shelves and squeezing under cots searching for his copy of Erskine Caldwell's spicy epic, *God's Little Acre.* It was important reading material for those fortunate enough to have the book or nimble enough steal it. Its mysterious disappearances were legendary.

When Jan slowed down to catch his breath, I told him how Delane and I were goalies on opposing high school hockey teams. Jan didn't seem interested until I said my friend was in the 11th Airborne.

"You know somebody in the 11th Airborne?" he asked. "You been down to see him?"

"What do you mean, down to see him? Last I heard the 11th Airborne made a jump in the Philippines."

"Well, they're on Okinawa now, staked out in pup tents on the side of a hill near the turning circle at Naha. I just talked to one getting a drink of water from the Lister bag. Said he was related to somebody on Jeter's crew. You should have seen his boots. Talk about shine. A man could shave looking down at those things."

I gave the matter some thought. "Hey, Jan," I said as he continued his futile search. "How about if you hike down to the infirmary and get Doc Flynn to lend us his jeep? You oughta meet this guy Delane."

"No, I have to find my book, then I'm going to read it."

"You have to find it first." I told him. "I don't think you're going to look in the right place. Besides that, you've already read it twice. Get Doc's jeep and I'll make you a deal."

Jan stopped inspecting Walker's barracks bag. "A deal? What kind of deal?"

"You go get the Doc's jeep, we go down to Naha to find Delane and I tell you where your nasty book is."

Jan studied my face seeking a shred of integrity. "You know where it is? Where is it?"

"Deal?" I asked.

"Deal!" he said. "Where is it? I think Walker's got it again."

"I'll tell you when we get back. Now get going and get that jeep." Walker, our navigator, was not present. Jan looked doubtful. Our conversation was interrupted by the rich and mellow tones of our co-pilot, Phil Gaines, a radio announcer in civilian life.

"Can't you guys ever let anybody sleep?" It was Phil's regular anthem upon being awakened from his early afternoon slumber following his morning siesta. "He's right, Jan. Go get the jeep before Doc starts his afternoon nap. You won't let me sleep anyway. I might as well go along wherever you're going."

Jan left and was soon back with the jeep. Temporarily, at least, he had forgotten about his book. The gloomy sky now began to drizzle. Jan wanted to wait for Walker but Gaines said he wasn't positive that Walker intended to come back so we decided not to wait. The three of us climbed into the jeep and rolled toward Naha, the capital of Okinawa, where we saw debris everywhere and nothing that was recognizable as a building.

The Army had cleaned out the carnage to keep the turning circle open. We joined the traffic and took the exit toward rows and rows of pup tents. They looked like large mushrooms growing on the side of a hill. By now, the drizzle had turned to a downpour, creating tiny rivers running around and through the shelterless shelters. It had to be the 11th Airborne.

A corporal in the headquarters tent directed to us to Delane's tent. Inside, sleeping and snoring, was my old friend from Minnesota.

His tent-mate, who introduced himself as Casey, kicked Delane in the leg and succeeded in bringing him back to life. Delane looked up at me, blinked his eyes a few times and said, "Johnny, either it's you or I've died and gone to hell."

I suggested we all get into the jeep and take a ride back to our squadron area. We lived just off the end of the runway, below a cliff at Aslito Airfield. Bob and Casey were both wearing fatigues and wondered if they would be dressed properly to stroll about our estate and join us for a meticulously prepared repast at the officers' mess. We assured them they would be welcome in our company and not to worry. Janeski stared openly and enviously at the paratroopers' boots which they wore with the cuffs of their fatigues stuffed inside. In spite of the water and mud that surrounded us, the paratroopers' boots were shined to a gloss that reflected light from a bare bulb suspended from the top of the tent.

We all stepped gingerly across the tiny creek that was flowing between the sleeping bags, carving a path on the hard ground. Bob and Casey folded their sleeping bags, placed them on top of green foot-lockers, piled into the jeep and away we went.

They told us they had come up to Okinawa from Manila after making a jump and recapturing Clark Field, which the Japanese had held since the early days of the war. In his version of the story, Casey said Delane had landed on his head and lay unconscious on the concrete runway as the battle raged all around him. Delane told us that Casey let himself get wounded again to earn his third Purple Heart but the Army still would not send him home.

Casey described begging the general awarding the medal to give him something else, maybe a Bronze Star. He tried to explain that each time he received a Purple Heart, the Army telegraphed his parents. The result was a near nervous breakdown for his mother. The general sympathized but pinned the Purple Heart on him anyway.

By the time the jeep reached our home base, we were well aware that these men were a different kind of soldier in a different kind of war than the one we were always griping about. Delane described how the Airborne troopers were told day after day in boot camp that they were the toughest GI's in the service. He said he believed them and the first time he was given a pass from boot camp went into town and picked a fight with a sailor who knocked him silly. "I no longer believe that crap," said Delane.

"Me neither," said Casey.

However, they looked trim to us. In spite of easygoing natures, they had seen plenty of action including hand to hand combat. The difference between them and us was that the last thing we wanted to do was bail out of an airplane. For them, it was the first thing. We asked if they always yelled "Geronimo" as they hurled themselves out into space. Casey said, "Certainly."

Delane said, "If it's good enough for John Wayne, it's good enough for us."

We took them down to the flightline and showed them around. They looked inside a B-24 and said they wouldn't want to be trapped in there when the shooting was going on. We didn't appreciate that phase of our duties either but at least we didn't have to hang there in a parachute while the enemy took target practice. We didn't have to worry about going hand to hand with sumo wrestlers, either.

We were enjoying the afternoon and the company, but sooner or later we would need to take these men to the mess tent. We feared the adventure might, at best, disillusion our friends or, at worst, send them howling to the latrine holding their aching stomachs.

As we approached the mess tent, Bob asked if it was all right for them to eat with us in the officers' mess. We assured them it was just fine while thinking to ourselves that, for a different reason, we often asked ourselves the same question.

The menu was neither better nor worse than usual. It featured Wieners a la Green Skins, Dehydrated Potatoes with Water Base and the "Mystery du Jour," served in a steaming kettle of shredded, red meat. Coffee was served to those presenting canteen cups.

We went ahead of Bob and Casey in the chow line making our usual extremely light and fearful choices and being certain to select plenty of coffee mixed with heaps of sugar. We then gingerly placed our backsides on a bench known to be shedding its slivers. Privately, we considered explanations and alibis.

Bob and Casey arrived shortly and no alibis were necessary. They had heaped their plates to the max and, in a short time, had picked them as clean as a horse player's wallet. The boys had selected some of everything and lots of it. These men were hungry.

The three of us watched in stunned silence. Delane appeared troubled, as if he wanted to ask a question but was embarrassed to inquire. Without doubt the cook's magic was working and one or the other of our paratrooper friends would soon be racing for the comfort station.

When Bob whispered something to Casey who nodded and turned to face us, I got ready to point to the little house just up the hill. "Delane was wondering," Casey said. "Is it okay if we go for seconds?"

Jan was the first to recover his power of speech. "Take all you want," he told them. "Take thirds if you want; take some home to your buddies."

The boys missed the last part of Jan's speech. They were already half way back to the chow line. "These men have cast iron stomachs," I said.

"When you get hungry enough you'll eat anything," said Phil Gaines. "I'm almost there myself." We grew silent, each with his own thoughts. The food was certifiably terrible. We preferred C-rations or even K-rations, which came in little tin cans.

Bob and Casey returned to the table with their plates heaped for the second round. It would soon be dark and there was a curfew so we had to leave before they could go back for a third reprise. The rain had let up a bit but was still dripping on the windshield of the jeep. We gave them a ride back to their pup tent city, shook hands all around, and watched them push their way slowly up the hill.

Jan started the jeep and we headed back home. "You guys see that water coming down the hill through those tents?" he asked. He didn't expect an answer. When we were flying from Guam, most of the tents leaked. There was nothing in our Army Air Corps manual about how to be comfortable when sleeping under water logged blankets. We drove along in silence and arrived back at our base just before dark.

When we entered our tent, Jan looked at Walker's empty cot. "Where the hell's Walker?" he yelled at no one in particular. "I didn't see him in the chow line either. He's got my book. I want that book back on the double!" He was leaving the tent to start a search.

"Hey, Jan," I shouted. "Come back. I know where your book is." I sat down on my cot and waited for what might happen next.

As Jan entered the tent, I reached into my back pocket and pulled out the dog-eared version of *God's Little Acre* which had been passed around the squadron for the past couple of months.

This had been my third chance at it. On the first shot, I finished almost seventy-five pages before it disappeared. The second time, I had it for thirty-five pages more. It was not a thick book but after a month I had finished only a hundred-ten pages and could not even guess when it might pass my way again.

"Here you go," I said, handing Jan the book. "So I wanted to see an old friend and had to con you a little to get the jeep. No way I could walk all the way to Naha."

Jan slapped me on the back. "It was a hell of a day," he said. "We met some real soldiers today, Buddy, and there is not a shred of doubt about that. I mean guys you could drink with but would hate to meet in a dark alley. I wish Walker had been there to see them put down that grub. He could have seen a couple of troopers that don't think we got it too bad."

"Where did Walker go?" I asked Gaines. "He's usually asleep by now, dreaming about turkey and gravy which looks better to him than Betty Grable."

"He's got somebody, an uncle I think, who's on the Missouri anchored out there in Buckner Bay," said Gaines. "The way he tore out of here, he must have been heading for some Navy food."

"I hope he gets a bellyful of it," said Jan. "At least enough to stop him from griping about the food around here. You'd think he was the only man in the squadron who didn't realize it's not fit to eat."

Jan sat down on his cot and put the book under his pillow where it would be safe. Just then Walker came into the tent wearing freshly pressed suntans and a necktie. It was a very unusual costume, one that would indicate he had been participating in a very exceptional situation.

"Good evening, gentlemen," he purred proudly. "I am home from a remarkable dining experience at the officers' mess aboard the USS Missouri where my Uncle Wilbert is an officer. Woo, Woo! How would you like your steak, Lieutenant Walker? More coffee, Sir? Another Tequila Sunrise, Sir? Are you ready for dessert, Lieutenant?"

"Okay, cut it out," Jan was not in a mood to compare the culinary skills of the Navy versus the Air Corps. The swabees brought the food across the ocean and ate well. That was that! Somewhere between ports in the USA and central Pacific, the gremlins were gobbling up our share.

"We are sorry that we were forced to decline your generous invitation to share your remarkable experience but we had no other choice since we didn't know anything about it," said Jan politely.

"It was uppermost in my mind," taunted Walker. "Unfortunately, Uncle Wilbert is an ensign, not an admiral. I felt fortunate and proud to represent the crew on this merry occasion. You will never believe how fine it was to get away from the anonymous slop that we get around here."

Jan rose slowly from his cot and approached Walker. When they were nose to nose, he grabbed Walker's necktie and gave it a tug. "Listen," he growled, "I never want to hear anybody in this crew gripe ever again. Not about flak, not about food, not about anything. We spent the day with some real soldiers, Walker. They thought our food was damn good. Anybody thinks they got it tough, forget it. I'll take 'em down to see the guys we met today. They got plenty to gripe about but they don't think this war is supposed to be a damn tea party. Compared to us, they've got nothing. Would you ever know it? No! The only complaint we got all afternoon was because the Army wouldn't give Casey a Bronze Star instead of his third Purple Heart. I'm telling you Walker, when we go to that mess tent, just eat and keep your mouth shut."

It would be nice to say that Walker never again griped about the food on Okinawa. It would have been too much to expect. But it did keep him quiet for a few days and that was a wonderful relief for which I thank the two paratroopers, the grapevine, and Erskine Caldwell.

CHAPTER 25

THE LONGEST FLIGHT

"I tried seven times to kill myself," Joe Arena, a friend and fellow bombardier, was on the B-24 576 flying a bomb run to tiny Marcus Island. The Japanese damaged eight planes, including 576, which was hit and began smoking near its number three engine.

According to crew members, pilot Lt. Floyd Beanblossom tried to feather the prop but found numerous gas and oil leaks. The plane rapidly lost altitude and the crew commenced jettisoning equipment. Beanblossom and his engineer, Sgt. Guillermo Abrego, discussed their options. If they could sufficiently reduce the weight of the plane, Abrego insisted, they could make it to dry land.

Abrego had wanted to be a pilot. Although he was assigned and trained as an engineer, his passion was flying the plane, and he had studied this extensively. When 576 was suffering, Abrego made the necessary calculations and was correct in his determination about the weight of the plane. However, once every removable object was thrown into the ocean, the plane continued to lose altitude. The crew had to face a tough decision. Their only hope, Beanblossom knew, was to jump.

Abrego had sworn repeatedly to all of us that he would never bail out of an airplane. For one thing, he couldn't swim. According to other crew members, he was persistent with Beanblossom, but eventually agreed to jump. After nine parachutes, including Joe Arena's, opened over the ocean, the remaining crew members in the plane were the pilot and the engineer. Abrego promised Beanblossom he would jump last. Finally, Beanblossom jumped.

When 576 was hit, another crew on the mission, *Wild Ass Ride*, our plane but not our crew this time, detached itself from the formation and escorted the damaged plane to a point about five hundred miles from Saipan where it was decided to leave the crippled craft, which continued to lose altitude. At 3000 feet, the escort witnessed ten parachutes leaving the plane and opening safely. The escort radioed the position to Dumbo, circled the spot and dropped life rafts to the survivors.

Without the weight of ten crew members, the plane was finally light enough to limp home. With full knowledge of how to fly the plane, Abrego took the controls and headed for shore. Bringing a crippled B-24 back single-handedly is a rare accomplishment, but Abrego's heroics were not to be recognized. Coming into Tinian in the dark of night, the engineer knew there were three runways, but chose, unfortunately, the one under construction. The plane touched down safely but crashed into an area between two runways. Abrego died from injuries sustained in the crash.

At dawn, our crew was sent out to find 576's survivors. We flew all day, circling over the blue water of the Pacific. All I could think was, how are we going to find those guys? At dusk, we were forced to turn back.

Back at the base, I said to one of the officers, "I don't know how they're going to find those guys."

He looked surprised and asked, "What are you talking about?"

"576," I told him. "We've been out looking for them all day."

"Well, they got 'em," he told me.

The survivors had been picked up by a submarine. All but one survived, that one being drawn into the propeller of the submarine and drowned. It was days before they arrived back at base and when they did, I was glad to see my friend, Joe Arena.

"What was that like?" I asked him. "What did you do out there?"

"I tried seven times to drown myself," he told me.

There was nothing more to say.

CHAPTER 26

GO RIGHT ON

Editor's note: This chapter consists of excerpts from interviews with Jack I. Moore conducted during the 1990s.

Paul Farnam, from San Jose, California, was a co-pilot on Jeter's crew. He had missed a few missions with a fever or something, and his crew had finished up ahead of him. The first pilot went home, so Paul took his place. They had a celebration...booze. Some others on Paulie's crew had also finished their missions and were going home. When we came to the party, it was raining real hard and the tent was leaking.

At the party, Paul and I were talking and he was so happy because they made him a first pilot (that's a private battle I never got into between pilots and co-pilots, but there was never any love lost). He was so happy because he would be going home as a first pilot and had only five missions left.

It wasn't a week later that I was in this tent that we called the officers' club, just standing there and having a drink. I was probably waiting for the bridge game or poker game to start, that's what we did all the time, when all of a sudden I hear these explosions --BOOM-BOOM-BOOM. I knew then some plane had blown up--I knew something bad had happened.

We didn't live right on the airfield, but we didn't live that far away, and that's the first place we all looked. These bombs are going off one at a time...and that was Paul. That was his new crew. Blew up. Crashed on take off. We all liked the guy. He only had five missions left.

They crashed at night after going on a night snoop. When we took off the next day, there was the wreckage down there. I remember the look on our pilots' faces. Janeski and Gaines looked at each other, because they knew those guys too, but you just go right on.

Another time, I remember the priest getting up and really chewing us all out. A guy named Lights, and his crew had gone down. I think that was on take-off, too. The priest said, "Well, you men missed a beautiful ceremony. We had this ceremony for Captain Lights and his crew, and I don't understand why you don't go down there. Why nobody was there?"

I mean if that priest was too dumb to see that this was denial...I mean, that could be us there. We didn't think of it that way. You always believe that it's never going to happen to you, but you don't care to go down and see what happened to somebody else. Nobody really understands this. These are totally a-typical feelings to anything in civilian life.

I went to Jefferson Barracks, Coe College Cedar Rapids, Iowa with one of my very best friends, George Hendrickson from Minnesota. We went to preflight, bombardier and operational training together but he was on a different crew. Anyway, I remember someone saying, "Did you hear what happened to George?"

I said, "No, what happened?"

He said, "Well, he got it up at Chichi." Chichi Jima is one of the easiest targets in the Pacific. I never saw a fighter, and the flack was always meagre and inaccurate. A mission there was duck soup.

It was a real sad story about George, because he had a buddy named Stew from St. Louis, Missouri (I think he was married to the mayor's daughter or something like that). Stew was a co-pilot and he was made a first pilot, and George had been a bombardier on the crew that Stew was co-pilot on. So, when they made Stew a first pilot, he said "George "I want you go along for luck."

"Well, we're finishing up," George said, "I don't really want to do that. I'll stick to my old crew."

But Stew says, "Come on, George. I really need you there with me, you know." So, George went with him.

On that mission, they got two bursts of flak and one of them went through George's head. Stew was just a nervous wreck after that--he was just out of his mind and shot himself.

I remember on Guam, I was just sitting there in this tent and this enlisted man came in and said, "Is Lieutenant Janeski here?"

I said, "No. I don't know where he is, but he should be back pretty soon."

He says, "Doc thought I should come and see Lieutenant Janeski and explain things to him."

I said, "Explain what?"

He says, "Well, I'm the guy that was dragging his feet out of the bomb bay today." When you taxi down before take-off, they leave the bomb bay doors open, because there are gas fumes in the plane. Then, just before take-off, you close them. Apparently this enlisted man was sitting there dragging his feet. They would stick pretty low to the ground. He was a flight engineer.

So, Jan came back and the guy says, "The flight surgeon told me to give you this envelope and give me a ride over to the hospital."

Jan says "Hey, Jack, why don't you come with?" He didn't know if the guy would start to wrestle or what he was going to do. We rode over to the hospital.

Jan said, "Go ahead, I'll wait for you here."

The guy took his stuff in to the hospital. We waited about ten minutes, and then he came to the door and said, "You guys can go. They want to ask me a few questions."

That was the last I heard of him.

Bob Powers was our turret gunner. He liked to wear guns and sabres and all this other stuff. We were on a search mission looking for a crew that had gone down. We were only flying at 400 or 500 feet above the ocean looking all over for these guys. I smell gas, and I got on the intercom and said "Don't anybody smoke, I smell gas fumes."

Then Janeski got on and said "Yeah, don't anybody smoke." You don't want gas fumes, that's the worst thing you can get. Fumes are worse than the gas. When you have gas in the wing tanks and gas in the bomb bay, generally speaking they'll use up the bomb bay gas tanks first because they've got all that area of wing, and if flak would go into the wings (we had that happen) those are self sealing and so they would just go through, but if you have fumes in there – BOOM– it just ignites.

So I went back toward the bomb bay, and by then the co-pilot was back there. These bomb bay tanks were 500 gallons of gas. They are great big things and they have a big hose that comes out of them for connecting into the fuel system when you need to use the tank. Powers had the hose off and he was trying to fill his little cigarette lighter from this great big tank, and gas was all over his arms. He knew better than to do that. He'd been flying along with us for a year and a half. We took him back, and I never saw him again. We had just about finished all our missions.

One time, we were waiting down to start the engines, just waiting – I think the weather was bad at the target or something and they were delaying our take off. They wouldn't delay it for being bad at the runway, you could go no matter what, but if there wasn't any good weather over the target sometimes you wouldn't do it. The flight surgeon comes along in his jeep. He had a black eye, and I remember we were laughing, telling jokes. We all got on him about the black eye, "What's going on, Doc? What happened to your eye?"

He said, "Well, this is the third one in three weeks. Every time they go off that way they try to beat the hell out of me. If they get another one tonight, that's it. I'm going to be next." Because, he had to handle these guys who kind of lost it.

On election day in 1944, we only had four guys on the crew who could vote, that's how young our crew was. By that time we had about 19 missions or so and only four guys old enough to vote. Youth will be served.

Our navigator was Ellis Walker from the University of Indiana. We called him 'Squaker' Walker. He was 27. He'd been working at an ad agency before the war. He was married to the daughter of a guy that owned a large diesel company. When we were on Saipan we only flew missions about every three or four days so we had to kill some time in between. We had a little singing group called *The Foxhole Serenaders*, a quartet. It was Walker, Makowski, Francis Belt from Maryland, and me. We were not too bad. Our navigator, Ellis Walker, was in that. The guy [Erwin Makowski] that was writing the arrangements graduated from Loyola. This was strictly for our own pleasure, but one time the 20th Air Corps Band was going to come to play and they asked us to play with them. It was going to be our big debut. It was going to be a big party, but at the time we were supposed to sing, one of our members had gone off somewhere with a nurse, so we never got to sing.

Walker was a good guy, but he was just old. We were 21, but this guy was 27. He wanted to go home. I think the biggest argument I ever saw him have was with these ATC pilots. These pilots would come in and carry the USO out there and then they'd go back to the states and come back in C-46s and fly them as cargo. Sometimes they'd stop in and say "Who wants to be in a locker front?"

In a 'locker front' anybody who wanted could give them $100 or so and then when they would come back, they'd bring booze. Well, Walker gave this guy his money, I don't know how much. Jan, Phil and I gave them money for booze, but Walker didn't give them money for booze, he gave money for "condiments." He wanted to have ketchup. I mean the food was so terrible, you can't believe it. It was horrible. The Navy had all the good food. So, Walker wanted "condiments," that's just what he called them. Salt and ketchup. What would he put them on? The runny eggs?

Well, the guy turned up later and he brought us the booze, and Walker said "Where are my condiments?"

"Ah, damn, Walker, I forgot them. I'll give you your money back," the guy said.

"I don't want my goddam money back. I want the condiments!" Walker said. He called the chaplain, and he was just pacing. He was out of his mind. Maybe it was a month between the time these guys went and came back. Walker just dreamed about the condiments that whole time. He hated the Army. The singing saved his life, I think. He loved to do that.

Walker was a very good navigator. One time we flew a practice flight from Oahu down to Midway Island. It was about 11 hours, and it's all over water. From the time we left Hickam Field until we landed at Midway Island, it was storming. It was rain, lightening, St. Elmo's Fire (a blue static electricity that comes off the sticks of the propellers).

After about an hour, I realized we had 12 degrees of left drift. You can redrift on the bombsight. You take the bombsight and put in the direction of the waves, that's the direction the wind is coming from, and it will tell you how much drift your airplane has. In other words, how much the wind is taking the plane this way or that. I saw we had about 12 degrees of left drift. That's a lot in an hour. I just wanted to see where we were at and what was going on. Walker was sitting with his head on the desk, just snoring.

I said, "Walker, wake up" and I shook him.

He said, "What do you want?"

I said, "We've got 12 degrees of left drift. We've been going quite a ways. Says 12 degrees."

"Yeah? Geez," he said.

So, Walker did a few figures, called the pilot and said, "Hey, Jan, better change the heading to about 2-7." Jan said ok and changed it.

I thought, 'Oh boy, I hope he knows what he's doing, because we are going to be heading for Australia and we don't have enough gas to get there.' Then I went back down, sat around some more, and pretty soon Walker said, "Well our ETA is..." so and so, and we broke out of the clouds and there was Midway Island, about as big as your back porch.

There are two things I remember about Midway Island. One is when you come in on the final approach, there's a water tower right in the middle of the runway, so the pilot has to go out a little bit and come back and then land. I've never seen anything like it, but I guess the island isn't big enough and they needed water. The other thing I remember is that it is populated by Marine pilots and by gooney birds, these crazy, funny, little birds. That's all there was on the island. It was like Siberia almost, except it was nice, warmer weather, and they gave them all the booze they wanted. You've never seen so much booze. So, when we landed, the weather was so horrible, we thought we'd never have to fly back to Oahu tomorrow, so we might as well drink it up. I was playing poker and things like that. I remember that by the time I got in bed, it was very, very late. It seemed like I just turned out the light and I wasn't even beginning to fall asleep, when the light came back on. There was an enlisted man and he said, "Well, it's time to go Lieutenant."

"Go where?" I said.

"Well, the CO says we have to fly back. That they need these planes on Oahu. I don't know why," he said.

It was seven-thirty in the morning, and you don't ask questions. You just do what they tell you to do. I got on a truck and Walker and Gaines and Janeski were already at the plane. I climbed in through the bomb bay doors and the first thing I see is that Walker and Janeski are hurling into the bomb bay doors, just throwing up. The co-pilot Gaines, he's siting up there in the co-pilot's seat but he's on full oxygen...we were still on the ground. So, I just thought, "Well," and I went up in the nose and curled up and went to sleep.

Our airplane showed a picture of a bucking donkey and a beautiful girl on the back wearing a cowboy hat and boots and the name of it was *Wild Ass Ride*. This was the plane we flew on most of our missions. We liked it.

On Saipan we had air raids every once in a while. Mostly they were trying to blow up the B-29s which were a little ways from us, so we weren't directly in line. Being a bombardier, I knew they weren't always going to fall where they aimed them. So, they got a lot of guys together to dig foxholes.

Our tents had four cots in them. The sides of the tent were

often rolled up and then we'd have mosquito netting and the cots and the footlocker underneath. Actually, I didn't have a footlocker, I had a B-4 bag, a bombardier bag that you'd put your personal belongings in, and that was all you had in the world. So, anyway, a lot of the guys began to dig foxholes on Saipan because of the air raids. They told us we should do that.

Walker was the only guy on our crew out there in the hot sun. On Saipan it got hot, and Walker's out there digging this foxhole. Jan, Phil and I are laying on our cots reading or talking and every once in a while looking out at Walker laughing, making fun of him, you know: "Here they come, Walker! Air Raid! Air Raid!" Anyway, he dug this foxhole outside our tent. God, I felt for him sweating and perspiring. It took a couple of days at least. The ground was kind of hard.

Well, the night after Christmas, on my birthday, we had this air raid and it was a big deal. We'd had a mission that day, and then a big air raid that night. Everything was going off. The Navy flak just filled the sky and the bombs were falling and they had two or three little Japanese airplanes up there in the search lights, but they couldn't hit them. They were going click-click-click-click-click-click-click and our planes were going chuck-chuck-chuck. They called our planes 'washing machine Charlies' because that's what they sounded like. They couldn't hit the Japanese planes, but they had them in the search lights. What happened was, you get the air raid sounds and everything, a lot of flak, but by the time Walker gets out of bed and goes for his foxhole, we're all in it--and there's no room for Walker.

The foxhole was right near my bed. I was the first one in it. The others jumped on top of me. Nobody wore pajamas during the service, we wore underwear. Anyway, after we're pushing Walker out and everything, I look over at the tent and Elmo Lund from Salt Lake City, Utah, is standing there (and Elmo is the one guy in the United States Air Corps who wore pajamas apparently), he's standing in the door of his tent, looking around and saying "What's all the excitement out here?" That's the way he was. One time we were sitting there talking and we got on the subject of religion and I said "Do you believe in God?" and he said, "Well, you gotta believe in something. You can't believe in Benny Goodman."

Let me tell you about the food. Oftentimes, they gave you one of these big cans of turkey. That was good. Whenever we had turkey though something would happen. We'd finish the bomb run, we'd get back down to a lower altitude, take off the oxygen masks. You're starved. You've been up in the air six hours already. You go back to the waist to have some of that turkey...and it's all gone.

"It's all gone, Lieutenant, sorry, it's all gone." The enlisted men were eating it on take off. The enlisted men in the back of the plane weren't taking any chances. They gave you these things they called D rations, which was a chocolate bar. You'd take that thing up to 25,000 feet and it freezes. So you go back in the plane and you're hungry and all the enlisted men ate the damn turkey.

After each mission they'd give you two ounces of scotch or rye whiskey. When you'd get back from a mission, you'd have what they call a critique, and then you'd go to the flight surgeon and he'd give you two ounces of rye. We made a deal with him to keep the whiskey so when we finished our missions they'd give us however much we had for the celebration. When we finished our missions we made a deal with the enlisted men, because they couldn't get any whiskey, 'you guys get the food someplace and we'll get the whiskey.'

The Navy had great food. They had these new rations with all this good stuff in it. So when we first thought we had finished our missions, Scanlan, Shorty Olsen and I think Rice, went down to the dock and they crawled under the barbed wire. They grabbed some of this food, and as they were crawling out, the Navy started shooting at them, but they escaped.

CHAPTER 27

A Lazy Sunday In Okinawa

From the island of Okinawa, we flew bombing missions to China and the Japanese mainland. One day was like another and nobody cared whether it was Tuesday or Saturday. When the chaplain tossed a couple of blankets over inverted cartridge cases, that was Sunday because it felt like Sunday even if it was really Thursday. We went wherever the altar was set up and a service was going on.

Our first pilot, the captain of our crew, was Henry Janeski from Cudahy, Wisconsin, and a very good man to have in that left hand seat. Jan was married and very much in love with his wife who had traveled from Wisconsin to California to be with him at March Field. Our crew trained there for four months and the Janeski family made no secret of their plan to have a child on the way before Jan shipped out.

Providence was kind, Jan and I and Phil Gaines, our co-pilot, emptied most of a fifth of Scotch at the Hickam Field officers' club the evening he gave us the news. Ellis Walker, our navigator, came in late and finished the bottle. Walker was married, but restricted his fervent wishes to getting home alive and eating well. Now, months later, on Okinawa, his aspirations were for one decent meal anywhere.

Jan, Phil, and I were twenty-one and Walker was twenty-seven, the maximum age for flight duty. We thought of him as being very old and cranky. In fact, we called him "Squawker Walker," but since he was a very good navigator we forgave him a few peccadilloes linked to old age.

All of us sparkled with good humor at Hickam Field where we dined on steak and lobster. When we went "down under" to Saipan, we enjoyed fresh baked bread, but balked at powdered eggs and green wieners. By the time we had been transferred to the 11th Bomb group on Guam, Walker was reduced to building a small fire on the floor of the tent, punching holds in the top of a tin of K-rations, and tossing it into the flames. We laughed at first but when he was eating the dehydrated ham and eggs, it looked like a good idea. We also received a pair of cigarettes plus two sheets of toilet paper in each package. At Okinawa, loud and angry voices, including Walker's, shattered the midnight air, wagers were made as to whether that red stuff in the pot had been goat or horse meat in real life.

It was a long trail from March Field to Oahu to Saipan to Guam to Okinawa. We had been in combat for just less than a year but it seemed like forever. There were church services for most faiths now and then but the schedule was sporadic. I went to the Catholic mass whenever I saw the notice, which was once in a while on no particular day.

So, one day the bulletin board announced that there would be a Catholic service out in the back of our area. Jan had gone to mail call, one of the big events of the day. I didn't go; the girl who used to write had married a sailor. Gaines and Walker were at the officers' club. I decided to go to mass and met Jan at the door as I was leaving.

"Where you going?" he asked, raising the mosquito netting and tossing some letters on his cot.

"They're having mass out in back. I think I'll go over there and say a prayer for you guys."

Surprisingly, he slapped me on the back and said, "Hey, maybe I'll go with you." I knew that he had changed religions because his bride to be would not change hers. I remembered sitting in a little bar in San Bernardino as he told Gaines and I about it for no reason at all. As if we cared one way or another. I understood and Gaines was an atheist. We happened to like the guy. He could have worshipped baboons as long as he kept getting us out there and back.

"How come?" I asked him. "You having chest pains or something?"

"Well," he said, "I notice sometimes you go when there's a Lutheran padre."

"Sure," I said. "Why not. It's the same God."

We dropped the subject and walked silently toward the makeshift benches in front of the altar. I noticed the two Shorties and Johnny Scanlan sitting across the way. Jan and I waved and after a pause, they waved back. I noticed they put their heads together in a heated discussion.

The mass was short. The priest didn't have to spend time telling us to pray. Struggling down the runway in a B-24 Liberator with 2,700 gallons of gas in the wing tanks, 500 gallons in the bomb bay tank, and eight five hundred pound bombs hanging on the racks will inspire more prayers in a shorter time than the Baltimore Catechism. At communion time, Jan remained on his chair and appeared thoughtful. I felt good that he had gone with me. I did not think he was dissatisfied with his own religion anymore than I was with mine. I'm certain he wasn't. There was something special about his sitting there beside me. It was as if he was saying "Hey, this is a hard way to go and I'm glad I've got you for my bombardier. If we die out here together we'll go to heaven and bomb hell." He was an excellent pilot and very proud of his crew. As we arrived at our tent, Johnny Scanlan and the two Shorties caught up with us. Johnny asked if he could talk with me for a minute.

I followed him over to where the other two were waiting. Jan had ducked into the tent. I wondered what they might want to talk about. Shorty Olson took the lead. "What," he asked, "is the matter with Jan?"

"What do you mean *what's the matter with Jan*? Nothing! He was just at mass with me," I said.

"Is he worried or something?" demanded Shorty Olson. "Is he getting, you know, like fatigue or something?"

I couldn't believe my ears. "What's the matter with you guys? Sure he's tired. He's tired of eating that goat meat and green egg special they serve up at the mess tent just like you are!"

Johnny Scanlan finally got to the point. "Well, O.K., Jack, explain this: How come he was in church? Jan never goes to church. Why now? Is something wrong? Is he afraid of something?"

"Well, boys, I hate to tell you this but the reason you don't see him is because he isn't there. The reason he isn't there is that he's not a Catholic, he's a Lutheran and that's when he goes. He went with me today because I asked him to." That part was a bit of a fib, but who did it hurt?

"Well," said Shorty Olson, "we just wanted to know."

"Yeah," Shorty Rice chimed in, "we just wanted to know."

Johnny Scanlan suggested they mosey on and they soon disappeared down the path toward the enlisted men's area. They did not seem convinced.

When I got back to the tent, Jan was sitting on the side of his cot holding an open letter and wearing a smile from ear to ear.

"Eight pounds, six ounces," he said. "It's a boy!"

"You knew about this before, right? Why didn't you tell me? This is great!"

"I read it at the post office. I wish I had some cigars."

"Why didn't you tell me before? I would have rounded up the crew for a little celebration."

"No, Jack I. We can celebrate later. I felt so good that it didn't seem fair. I just wanted to go over there and say a few prayers for you guys."

It was a great day for Jan and the rest of us, too.

I think it was a Sunday.

CHAPTER 28

THE IRISHMAN'S BOAT

Today, July 28th, 1945, it is warm and windy, a nice afternoon on the island of Okinawa. Jan and I are winding down a wooden path to the large pyramidal tent that will host a hastily called briefing. It is for pilots and bombardiers of lead crews only. We glance up indifferently as a roaring B-24 lifts off above the steep cliff at the end of the Aslito Field runway. We have heard rumors, but don't know what to anticipate.

Jan and I take seats on one of the rough wooden benches lined up to provide a good view of the huge map covering most of the front wall. Someone in the back shouts, "Attention!" We all rise and stand at attention as a colonel whom we do not know marches swiftly down the aisle.

Arriving at the front he reveals, in a deep southern accent, that he is from 7th Air Force Bomber command headquarters. He tells us that we are being trusted with a mission that might shorten the war. The Navy's 5th fleet has bottled up all that remains of the Emperor's sea power in the bay at Kure Harbor. We will be part of a massive air attack to apply the knockout punch. He then calls on our commander, Colonel Miller, to explain what part of the action includes us. Colonel Miller takes his place before the map.

"Gentlemen," he announces. "Here is your target for tomorrow." He taps the pointer three or four times at a dark circle in the center of the bay.

"We have been given the honor of being the key element in the success of this plan. Your target for tomorrow is (hesitation for effect) the battleship Haruna."

I cannot believe my ears. Colin Kelly destroyed the Haruna at the beginning of the war. The headlines were huge, page after page detailing how the handsome West Point graduate gave his life to maneuver a damaged B-17 straight down the smokestack of the battleship Haruna. He had, in a single blow, eliminated the pride of the Japanese fleet. Colin Kelly was a hero to every American, but none more than those of us with an Irish heritage. We were taught to love God and all his children, but it was no mortal sin to show pride and offer a cheer for a deserving fellow Celt upon occasion. However, at the present moment, the prospect of flying over a battleship is not appealing. Deep in my Irish heart I wish that Kelly had finished the job. I wonder, what next?

I find out quickly. Colonel Miller is telling us that our bombing altitude over the battleship will be nine thousand feet. The facial expressions of his audience silently ask the rhetorical question, "Whose idea was this?"

A B-24 can get away with a deck level attack using surprise and moving fast enough to get in and out in a hurry. At a medium altitude, such as nine thousand feet, we will be hanging over the target like balloons in front of a used car lot. I study the huge map on the wall. It doesn't show any red dots indicating the locations of anti-aircraft guns near the town on the left side of the harbor. At least we will be able to break away over dry land. Miller is not finished.

"Listen closely, gentlemen. What I tell you now is of maximum importance. I say it again, maximum importance. You will break away from the target by banking right and exiting the area by passing over the two aircraft carriers stationed at this point." He thumps his pointer hard against the map several times for emphasis.

"One more thing," says Miller. "Over on the left you can see a town. Do not fly over that town, do not bomb it, do not strafe it. Don't ask me why. They don't tell me half of what I'd like to know. I got those orders from the big brass and I'm giving them to you. Just do as I say. That's all, men. Full crew briefing at 1800 hours right here."

The briefing is over and I walk up to the blackboard where the colonel with the Texas accent is checking his notes. I salute. He salutes back and says, "Can ah help y'all?"

"Yes, sir," I say. "I'm confused. I don't understand why we're breaking away over those carriers. Why can't we turn left over the land? I don't see any anti-aircraft over there."

His friendly smile straightens into the firm lip line that high-ranking officers exhibit to first lieutenants when asked a discomforting question. "Ah feel Kunnel Milluh made hisself cleah, Lieutenant."

He notices that I am not convinced; his voice softens, becomes confidential. "Look heah, Moah. Y'all a good bombadeah. Ah strongly suggest y' just take y'self a nahse long bomb run and hit that sum'bich and not go back theah no moah."

I salute and walk away surprised that he knew my name. I'm thinking, "You come along and sit beside me in the nose when that flak is puffing, Colonel. Then you can tell me how long we should go straight and level to give those 120's time to line us up."

There is something strange about this trip. Breaking away over aircraft carriers seems foolish when there is plenty of unprotected real estate available.

I go to chow and return to the tent for a little sack time before the next briefing. However, in walks Erwin Makowski, my best buddy. We met at preflight at Santa Ana and since our names both started with 'M' the Army keeps sending us to the same places. Now he's up at 7th Air Forces Headquarters. Mack makes himself at home on an empty cot, but appears troubled. He uses his thumb to move his properly crushed Air Corps hat back off his forehead. I say, "What's up?"

After a short silence he asks, "Jack I., are you on that thing tomorrow?"

I answer, "We're leading it."

"Damn," he says. "I probably shouldn't tell you this. I don't think you want to hear it anyway."

"C'mon, Mack, let's hear it. I tell you one thing, it's going to be a rough ride."

"Really rough," says Mack. "They think up at Command they might lose half the 7th Air Force."

"Thanks, old Buddy," I tell him. "Thanks a lot. I needed that."

Truthfully, I am not particularly frightened by any 7th Air Force predictions. After thirty missions, it is clear that some tough missions turn out to be easy and easy ones can be really tough. Somehow, a mission the next day always seems far away in time. The ruling powers might change their plans, bad weather could cancel the mission. It is too early to feel that big knot in the stomach, to pay attention to the little voice that whispers, "Why are you doing this, you idiot? Why are you putting your neck on the block while movie stars and athletes play it safe?"

I have to leave for the second briefing which is for the full crews, so Mack heads down to the officers' club. While I'm walking along the path, I run into Captain Creasy, our S-2, also known as intelligence officer. 'Crease,' as we call him, stands about six feet six and weighs less than an empty footlocker. He appears to sway in the light breeze as we talk.

"Crease," I ask, "what are the odds of a B-24 going over a battleship at nine thousand feet?" He peers at me for a moment through his thick glasses after which he runs a hand nervously through his thinning hair. Finally he looks down at me in disbelief.

"What the hell, Moore!" he shouts. "You're an old timer out here. You're not about to do that, are you?"

"Yup," I say. "I know I am because they told me I am."

Crease shakes his head sadly and continues his shuffle toward the officers' club for a leisurely evening with Jack Daniels. I go on to the briefing, which is short and sweet. Ellis Walker, our navigator, myself, and the six gunners then hop a truck and bounce down to the flightline to wrestle four, two thousand pound semi-armor piercing bombs into the bomb bay. We are not allowed to load bombs on the plane until dark because there have been several air raids at the field.

After that we sit on overturned cartridge cases and shoot the bull waiting for a truck to pick us up. A stranger hearing our conversation might wonder who are the officers and who are the enlisted men. Everything is on a first name basis and there is little, if any, formality. The respect you get is what you earn. What might be apparent is that we are proud to be in each other's company.

Eventually, a truck stops by to pick us up and drop us off at our area. It's sack time. Some will not sleep well, but most will strip down to their khaki shorts, pull up the mosquito netting that forms a canopy over the cots, spray mosquito poison inside the net and settle down for the night.

Before crawling in, each crew member scheduled for the mission places a white towel on the foot of his cot. In the early morning an orderly from operations tiptoes into the tent, a living alarm clock. The towel tells him who he must awaken to face an uncertain sunrise. When he shines his flashlight in my eyes and says softly, "Time to go, Lieutenant." The clock begins to run, ticking toward problems and possibilities that must be resolved before sundown.

The cooks are already working in the kitchen to the rhythms of Tokyo's Hit Parade. It's the only radio they can get at this early morning hour. The music is suggestive of thirty out-of-tune guitars and fifty amplified ukuleles playing in different keys while kindergarten kids bang spoons on the table. In spite of the clatter, the cooks are trying to prepare a decent breakfast for the crews on the mission. There may be real eggs and pancakes, things like that.

A visitor would not find an aura of fear at the breakfast tables. He would find more than a hundred young men who have made peace with their mortality and are able to perform their duty under extreme stress. Their crew is their family and the squadron is their social circle. If you cannot do what they do, you can never be one of them. They are polite young men, mostly of college age. If you are a paddle foot (ground officer of any rank) they feel superior to you and no matter how hard you try or how much they enjoy your company, you will feel the difference. Usually, before a mission, the only sound in the mess hall other than the radio is the clicking of knives and forks on the plates.

We finish breakfast and take trucks to the flightline. Jan and Phil Gaines, our co-pilot, run down the checklist to preflight the plane.

The take-off of an overloaded B24 is always critical. We do not have a bomb bay gas tank today because the two thousand pound bombs will take up so much space. We will have twenty-five hundred gallons of gas in the wing tanks. I am standing on the flight deck when I hear Jan tell Muller, our engineer, to start the putt-putt motor. It chatters and begins pumping life into the number three engine.

The engines growl and roar as Jan runs them up one at a time. When Jan gets the word from Gardenia Tower, we taxi out to the runway. We are first in line. The twelve other planes in the squadron crawl behind us and wait. We completely ignore the rules for position of the crew during take-off. Jan wants as much weight as possible in the front of the plane. He needs the weight forward to hold the nose down and allow the ship to get maximum speed before leaving the ground. I stand between the pilot and copilot beside the engineer. The navigator and radio operator are seated on the flight deck. The nose gunner and top turret gunner are on the catwalk below. The time is 07:30.

We start to roll and are almost at the end of the runway before the wheels leave the runway. Then Jan slaps Phil on the back of his hand and Phil throws the lever to lift the gear up. We are on our way to visit the Japanese homeland. For the next five hours we will each be alone with our thoughts. The day is clear and sunny as we make our way along through the puffs of white cumulus clouds. They will seize the sunlight and grow into towering alabaster castles by the time we are returning.

One of the nice things about a low altitude mission is that we don't have to wear our oxygen masks. They itch and are very uncomfortable. I think about the mission and how much responsibility we bear for the success or failure of it. Walker will have to navigate us to the Initial Point where we will start toward the target. Other planes will follow us in formation. When I open the bomb bay doors on our plane, they will open theirs. When the cross hairs on my bombsight meet and our bombs tumble out, they will follow our lead and drop theirs.

Janeski is a great pilot and we have a very good crew. My mind is clear about the bomb run. I feel we have to be straight and level for at least fifteen seconds on the run. The battleship is a large target, fifteen seconds should be enough. I keep wondering why they won't let us turn left from the target and avoid the carriers. As we approach the harbor, even before we see the Haruna, even though we are far out of range, erratic fire from some of its big guns creates small black puffs in the sky. Maybe they are telling us they are ready and waiting.

When we hit our IP (initial point) and turn toward the target, I take a momentary look at the town down below. It's just another city. Why would Bomber Command care whether we broke away over it or even strafed it? Quickly I shift all my attention to the bomb run. The Haruna begins to loom in front of us like an impregnable fort. We take some evasive action until I get on the intercom to tell Jan I'm opening the bomb bay doors and remind him to keep it level. Any quick, sharp turn or drop can tumble the gyroscopes in the bombsight and make it useless. I throw the lever to open the bomb bay doors.

The sky is filled with flak. I can see it in the bombsight as I focus on the deck of the ship. We are vulnerable, straight and level. We have never seen colored flak before: red, green, orange, blue. It's a short bomb run but seems to last forever. Finally, the cross hairs in the bombsight meet, the B-24 lurches and I call, "Bombs away!"

My work is finished. I do not put my head out the window to see whether the bombs hit the target. Somewhere in the formation someone is taking pictures to be analyzed later at Bomber Command.

I huddle behind the bombsight for protection. Looking up, I see two of our P-51 fighters criss-crossing in the sky. I think to myself, "Those are some very special flyboys."

Jan drops a wing and makes a tight turn to the right. We zoom up and over the carriers. Later, the flak will be estimated at ten thousand bursts in fifteen minutes. Somehow we avoid it and break free. We are out of the harbor and on our way back to Okinawa. John Scanlan, our nose gunner, tells us on the intercom that he saw our bombs hit the deck of the Haruna. I am just happy that we made our run and are going home in one piece.

A few days after the mission, Doc Flynn, our flight surgeon, comes over to our tent for a visit. We have a wooden floor in the tent and I am sitting on the stoop. Doc comes over, reaches down and shakes my hand.

"Well," he says. "I see it took an Irishman to get the Irishman's boat."

That's really all I ever heard about the mission for the next fifty years, until five of our crew members had a reunion in Dayton, Ohio. Nose gunner Johnny Scanlan brought a book about the 11th Bomb Group that related that there were many failed attempts to hit the big ship, but the 42nd Squadron of the 11th Bomb Group had succeeded in putting four bombs on its deck during an attack on Kure Harbor.

Time did not take so long to reveal why we had been ordered to break away from the target by perilously passing over two aircraft carriers instead of taking a safer path over land. The big brass had a different plan for that mission. The town that I looked down at just before we started the bomb run was Hiroshima. A few days after our visit, it was blown out of existence.

By the time we again passed Nagasaki, the day after the bomb hit there, we knew well that we were experiencing a series of events that somehow would change the world forever. Before takeoff that morning, I talked to Walker, our navigator, and asked him to make sure that he notified the crew just before we would pass Nagasaki. It was less than 24 hours after the bomb fell and we hoped to be able to see the damage.

As we neared Nagasaki, Walker told us on the intercom it was coming up. We were at about 20,000 feet up and just off the coast. I looked out the bombardier's window beneath the nose turret and made out the small boats in the bay. However, the air seemed to be filled with shimmering heat waves and visibility was difficult. I cannot honestly say that I saw the damage that the blast had caused. The view was very much like that on an August afternoon in Minnesota; the kind that hovers above a lake, or meadow, or asphalt playground.

CHAPTER 29

IT AIN'T OVER 'TIL IT'S OVER

According to the laws of chance and rules of the 7th Air Force, we have earned the right to party tonight. Tomorrow a C-54 ATC transport will lift us up and carry us home. We have just completed our thirty-fifth and last required mission. Cooperation has produced the trimmings for our celebration. The flight surgeon, Doc Flynn, has presented Janeski a fifth of rye whisky. We earned it. At our request, Doc has saved the shot of rye that is usually given to flying officers after each mission.

There will be real food on the table. Our enlisted men have, as promised, visited the boondocks where, in a totally uncharacteristic lapse of prudence, the Navy has stored large cans of new and better tasting C-rations enticingly near its barbed wire perimeter. We do not ask how four gleaming cans with labels promising bacon, chicken, eggs and other delights has been liberated. We are all gathered in the tent. Now, why is somebody yelling on the P.A. system from the operations tent?

"Now hear this! Now hear this!" The voice betrays hysteria. We wait for the next sentence attentively. It will reveal to us the direction in which we must flee.

If he shouts "TYPHOON" we strike the center pole of our tent and await the worst. The pilots and co-pilots will hustle to the trucks for a fast and furious ride to the flight line. They will spend the next few hours taxiing B-24s into the wind.

If he hollers "AIR RAID" we will all race for foxholes on the perimeters of the squadron area. To me, his voice indicates "AIR RAID!" Okinawa, especially the ships in Buckner Bay, has been a dartboard for suicidal Kamikaze pilots many times. Therefore, we are in no way prepared for his next words. In a mere instant, they change the life of every person in uniform, Japanese or American, and of all those who pray for them nightly.

"The Japanese government has agreed to the terms of the Potsdam Conference." He shouts. "The war is over men! World War II is over! The War is over!" We are stunned. We slam down our rye, push the food aside and scramble out to join the tumult. It is increasing by the second.

A soldier rushes out of the tent opposite ours carrying an elephant gun that looks like an oversized musket. I watch him aim at the sky and fire. It knocks him flat on his back. He jumps up whooping and hollering and fires again with the same result. The Navy fleet in Buckner Bay sends crimson ribbons of tracer bullets arcing gracefully toward the man in the moon.

The men are euphoric, shedding the premonition of death, trying to absorb quickly, in one miraculous instant, the gift of a life that can be seen beyond tomorrow. There will never be another time for them exactly like this.

We feel their elation. It is what our crew felt a few hours earlier as our wheels touched the runway and our tour was completed. The celebration goes on, but eventually we return to our food and rye.

I see Al Jarvis from operations enter the tent and start chatting with Jan. Jan does not look happy, but with all the noise, it is difficult to know what they are saying. Our crews have flown several missions together; Jarvis and Jan are good friends, but when Al leaves, he and Jan do not shake hands. Apparently, Jarvis had more on his mind than offering congratulations.

"Hey, you guys. Knock it off." Jan yells, trying to be heard above the bedlam outside. Jan seldom raises his voice, the silence is immediate. "Listen up! I got some news for you guys you won't like."

We wonder, "What can we not like on a night like this?" He is given all the silence he could ever want.

"You won't believe this! Jarvis just told me they're giving us a mission tomorrow." He maintains a perfectly straight face. We laugh. It's a totally appropriate joke, very typical of Jan who is waving his arms, asking again for quiet. "I'm serious," he says. "We are being screwed by the fickle finger of fate." We understand the expression and realize that for whatever reason, things are about to be as bad as they can get.

There is a dead stillness in the tent. Jan swallows his anger and breaks the silence by explaining that the mission is scheduled and the bomb group is short of lead crews. This is understandable because most of the first pilots in the squadron are right outside our door, lit up like lightening bugs, and leading the unending hilarity with the furious gymnastics of a symphony conductor bothered by an insatiable itch.

There are ten of us in the tent and nine are trying to ask Jan if he is aware the war is over? Jan waves us off. "Jarvis says the treaty is not official because the Japs haven't signed the papers yet. We're supposed to stay tuned to command. Once the papers are signed they'll call us back." There was resignation in Jan's voice and no use arguing.

The Seventh Air Force says, "You go!" We go! We figure, war's over, missions finished. Well, not quite. *They* don't think so. The big party is ended before it began. I screw the cap back on the bottle of rye, which is still almost full; the shiny cans of food remain unopened. Johnny Scanlan, Shorty Olson, Shorty Rice, Odmund Olson, and Chris Muller are crestfallen. I watch them file silently out of the tent to be swallowed by the darkness on the path to the enlisted men's area.

Jan, Phil, Walker and I have nothing to chat about. The idea of having to fly an extra mission makes a man jumpy. The scenario drips with possible melodrama. One minute, we are winners, the lucky ones who beat the wheel and won our lives. Now, when the battle has ended for the rest of the world, we are ordered to roll the dice one more time. Can such a thing really happen?

As usual, each of us puts a white towel on the foot of his cot to signify we are anxious to be awakened at 0400 hours for a delightful all expense paid trip across the blue Pacific to Japan; returning same day if possible. We slip through the mosquito net protecting our cots and allow such thoughts as may occur to wander where they will. How could we be so unlucky?

Trying to sleep, I toss and turn remembering stories of star crossed soldiers who lost their lives after the cease-fire in other wars. This is too bizarre! I remember *All Quiet on the Western Front*. There is Lew Ayres reaching out of the trench for a flower. The sniper raises his rifle and fires. Our hero dies one minute before the end of World War I. Some of the tales are no doubt true. I trust this time they will not be about us. Sleep comes eventually but it seems only minutes before the orderly shines his flashlight in my eyes and says, "Time to go, Lieutenant."

Today is August 12th, 1945. History will probably say that World War II was already over, finished and done with. Not for us. We are going to breakfast and then attend the briefing. After that, we have been given the privilege of leading eleven B-24s on a bombing mission to the island of Shikoku. We have plainly been awarded the booby prize of World War II.

Shikoku is a place we have never visited. The paddlefoot doing the briefing tells us that it is separated from Honshu by water and can be reached only by ferryboat. We could care less. Perhaps he's forgotten we'll be traveling by air.

For the first time in thirty-six missions my mind wanders during a briefing. What does the guy doing all the talking know about it? He's never been there before and he's not going this time either. He rambles and I wonder if he's half hung over from the big celebration.

There is no enthusiasm in the room. We know all we need to know which is that Shikoku is one of the main islands of Japan, that our P-51 fighter escort is indisposed and will not be joining us today, and that we cannot be sure whether the enemy will be tuning up their cannons in hope of bagging a couple of Liberators and going out in style.

Our payload consists of anti-personal fragmentation bombs to be dumped on the runway at Matsuyama Airfield. Shikoku is across Kure Harbor from Hiroshima where the atomic bomb was dropped just six days ago. Our crew knows about Kure Harbor where we led the 42nd Squadron through an estimated ten thousand bursts of flak in a low-level attack on the Battleship Haruna less than two weeks ago. The Navy credited the 11th Bomb Group with hitting the big boat and the 11th Bomb Group credited our squadron, the 42nd, with four hits on the deck. Today, unless the Japs are holding a track meet, running up and down the middle of the airstrip, it is certain we will inflict no serious damage.

We ride the trucks directly from briefing to the flight line. I pull myself up through the open bomb bay doors and crawl down to the nose to go over the bombsight while Jan and Phil complete their preflight checklist.

The crew is not thinking of this as just one more mission. Right now, it is, first of all, one more take-off in an airplane filled with bombs and carrying twenty-seven hundred gallons of high-octane gas weighing six pounds per gallon. Fortunately, Aslito Airfield offers plenty of room to get some speed and we do not anticipate trouble. However, in combat, every take off is an adventure and we have lost good friends under such circumstances.

We sit at the head of the runway followed by the other eleven planes in our 42nd Squadron. They will follow us down the runway at intervals of forty-five seconds. Jan revs the engines and pushes the throttle forward while holding the brakes. Most of the crew members are on the flight deck or below it to keep as much weight as possible toward the front of the plane. Jan wants to hold the nose down in order to attain maximum speed before allowing the plane to lift off. Aside from meeting fighters or flak, this is the most critical moment of the day.

Jan releases the brakes and our ship, *Wild Ass Ride*, starts to creep, then to roll slowly, then faster and faster until the nose lifts and our B-24 climbs slowly, patiently with the lumbering uncertainty of an elephant struggling up a flight of stairs. When Jan slaps the back of Phil's hand, he pulls the lever and the landing gear comes up but Jan leaves full power on until he considers we have reached a safe altitude.

We circle as the rest of the squadron drifts into formation with us and we lead them back over the Aslito Tower on the way to Japan.

Standing between the pilot and co-pilot glancing through Jan's window I see the B-24 on our left wing. It is only a few feet away and I can look into their flight deck. The war may be over but the pilots know the brass will be staring up from the tower making notes and praying for one more chance to yell and scream about any open space in the formation.

The sun has risen and sparkles off the wings and fuselage of the silver Liberators. It is nice to think the war is over; at least for everyone else. Again, as always, it is a marvel and wonder to watch our B-24 bombers, uglier than Cinderella's sisters on the ground, become sleek and graceful in the sky. The long, thin Davis wing stretches one hundred ten feet from tip to tip and waves ever so slightly. With the blue sky, bright sun and a clean take-off behind us, it seems, for the moment, that this is the only place to be.

Once out of sight of Aslito tower, the other planes in our squadron loosen the formation and flip to auto pilot. For most it will be a very short flight. Long before we reach the target, all but two will have fabricated an excuse to abort the mission, dropped out of the formation and returned to Okinawa. Our crew has never turned back for any reason and Jan is not about to do so now.

We keep the radio on command and wait for word that the Potsdam Agreement has been signed and we can return to base. The message never arrives. It is a long, uneventful flight. We have been in the air since 0550 hours and have an ETA over the target of 0930 hours. The total flight will be about eight hours.

All of our missions are entirely over water. The main scenery is the Pacific Ocean and the white tops on its waves. Occasionally there are also towering white cumulus clouds for those who might prefer such an alternative. Since radio silence must be observed, we often cannot even speak with each other.

My ears begin to pop signaling we are climbing to our bombing altitude, which will be nine angels. Angels are a specified number of feet above a base altitude, which changes with each mission. If the base altitude is ten thousand feet and each 'angel' is one thousand feet, an altitude of seven angels is seventeen thousand feet. The Japanese gunners are wise to the system and will sometimes ask, in perfect English, "Hey, Joe, I'm lost. Where are you? What are your angels?" It is only one of the reasons why we maintain complete radio silence when anywhere in range of the target.

As the altimeter goes up past twelve thousand feet, it's time to grab the little green constant flow oxygen mask and strap it tight over my mouth. As time passes it collects saliva and begins to itch but most people can only stay conscious without oxygen for ten minutes or less at seventeen thousand feet. Today we are bombing at nineteen thousand. As we near that altitude, it's time to pull the forty pound flak suit over my head and hang it on my shoulders. An iron flak helmet completes the costume, which doesn't feel any better than it looks.

Johnny Scanlan, our nose gunner slides around the nose wheel and enters the nose. He opens the two doors to the nose turret and I help boost him inside. The nose turret pivots on a circular track, which is actually outside the plane. When Johnny is ready, I close the outside door to the turret, lock it and slam the inside door shut. It is not the place for sufferers of claustrophobia. Once again, I vow to remember not to bail out in any emergency without first pulling Johnny out of the nose turret.

In my earphones, Walker, the navigator notifies me that the IP, initial point for starting the bomb run, is coming up. I tell Jan I am opening the bomb bay doors and he says, "Roger!" I pull the lever and in a few seconds hear Jan again. "Bomb bay doors open."

We lead our two remaining wingmen on the bomb run. I can see flak in the bombsight as I concentrate on the airfield. It is all white phosphorous, no black flak. We fly straight down the airstrip and drop our anti-personnel bombs on the airfield runway. Since we do not see any anti-personnel, we feel certain no one has been hurt. We think the Japanese were sending us a message with that white phosphorus We believe it was their way of saying, "We surrender, the war is over; why are you doing this?" The simple truth is we don't have the least idea.

A weight has been lifted, our spirits rise. Jan drops down to twelve thousand feet and it is a pleasure to rip off the oxygen mask and rub my chin. For the thirty-sixth consecutive time, I crawl around the nose wheel door, tiptoe down the catwalk in the bomb bay and enter the waist hoping to find at least a mouthful of the canned turkey that has been provided for the crew. For the thirty-sixth consecutive time it is all gone. Usually the gunners turn their backs to hide their guilt. Today, they are waiting to present me with the empty can after which they laugh and slap me on the back. Oh, well! It says something about the privileges of rank in the U.S. Army Air Corps. We all feel great.

It remains only for Jan to get the wheels down on the runway and, finally, even for us, the war will be ended. We have flown day after day with Jan since February of 1944. It is now August of 1945 and he has brought us home safely from thirty-five missions. Our crew is credited with more than seven-hundred combat hours and Jan has put us down safely with props feathered, gas running out, engine on fire, and wings, fuselage, nose, and flight deck filled with jagged holes ripped by flak. Why should we be worried?

I stand between the pilot and co-pilot, Jan and Phil. Chris Muller, our engineer and Ellis Walker, our navigator, join us. Gardenia Tower clears us to land and the squadron roars above the runway, we do a steep 80 degree turn and make the final approach. Muller says, "Put 'er down like a crate a eggs, Jan."

Jan does not turn his head but we can see him smile. No way will he blow this landing. We know that. The landing is entirely routine but it's the last one, the most important of all. The ten of us who have trusted our lives to one another will never fly together again. We will slip away, one by one, and return to our other lives and, God willing, forget the unrelenting loneliness and uncertainty that hung above us like a Sword of Damocles every morning, noon and night.

Jan taxis up to the hardstand and a truck is waiting. It drops Jan, Phil, Walker and I off at our tent. Things begin to improve quickly. Our distress at having our party destroyed last night now becomes a blessing. The bottle of rye stands at attention on a small table as if faithfully awaiting our return. The cans of C-rations are virtually untouched. We have it made. We enjoy some of the food and quite a bit of the rye as we ponder, weak and weary, whether we might be the only crew ever to complete their last mission twice.

CHAPTER 30

The Dominator

It was the middle of the night, August 28, 1945, and it knocked me out of my bed. The base where we slept was beneath a 100 foot cliff, right on the ocean. Guys were running around hollering, guns were going off, people were screaming. I jumped out of the tent and saw guys running around in circles. A lot of them were naked, it was weird. In a place like Okinawa it is very hot in August so a lot of the guys preferred not to wear anything to bed at night. I ran out to see what was going on and heard people screaming, "Get me out of here!"

Normally, if a plane was taking off and something happened, people would run out in jeeps to see what they could do to help. But this time, with the Dominator, there was all that distance. I understand they were test flying. There were newspaper people aboard and they were going to Japan. They got to the edge of the runway and they couldn't get the engines going and the whole thing fell off the cliff. This was maybe 100 feet that they fell into the ocean in front of us.

At this time, the war was over. They had been developing a huge plane, bigger even than the big ones that they had already. I had heard about the Dominator, but I never did see one, even though it was right up there above us on the island.

When they first brought one to Okinawa, they pushed us off and we had to move to a different runway which was much tougher to take off from. Bill Daney, our head guy, had heard about this plane. He got some guys and jeeps and drove up to see it. As he neared the plane he saw that there were ropes all around so he could not get through. There was also a big sign posted that gave the name of the plane and warned that no one was allowed past that point.

Daney felt bad about that; he felt it was a bad deal to tell a guy you can't go there. He came back down to our base and got some guys together. They made their own sign and put it at the entrance to our base. If featured a picture of a B-24 and the words: *Best God Damned Plane in the World -Everybody Welcome*.

We felt bad about getting kicked off our runway because we had to go to the other end of the island. At the end of that runway was a precipice that just fell off so you had to fly to the end of that thing and rev 'em up. We could not take off unless we had a certain level of power and the right wind. Most times, I'd stand between the pilot and co-pilot during takeoff and look out over the front and help them determine their speed. Near the end of the runway, they'd put on the power. As we went over the edge the plane would drop down...and then it would start to crack. The plane would jump around a little bit, catch the wind and shoot out over the ocean.

Around this island was some of the deepest water in the world. Sometimes we would take off when the rain was coming down so thick that, standing between the pilot and co-pilot, I could not see out the

406

front. We were a good crew so often we were leading. But those times we didn't lead, if there was anybody ahead of us they would just disappear from sight as they dropped over the cliff. We'd see them go over and then looking way out ahead, we would see them come up again.

I don't remember hearing the Dominator fall. Really, there was no reason to hear it fall, because without the engines there was no noise. Even if there had been a sound, well, there were planes flying all the time, day and night, so it was in our heads. You don't get up every time you hear an airplane.

When we heard men screaming "Get me out of here," we flew out of the tents. As I remember guns were going off, so maybe they had guns on the plane. I did not know anyone on that crew, but they were all killed. That was the end of that plane.

CHAPTER 31

Going Home

Soon we receive orders to proceed to a replacement depot in Manila, Philippine Islands. The orders tell us where to go but offer no hints as to how we get there. They suggest the "first available means of transportation." Because planes are being used to transport returning prisoners of war, catching a flight will be difficult. I hitch a lift up to Yonaburu Airport and succeed in scheduling a ride for the next morning on a C-46.

I show up early in the morning to find I'm the only passenger on board who is not a returning POW. To see these men is to understand one of the most brutal horrors of war. They all appear tired and emaciated as could be expected but they are surrounded by an aura of hopelessness. There is no light in their eyes; they sit motionless, speechless, on bucket seats lining both sides of the plane. As we leave Okinawa for Clark Field, I would like to talk with the ex-POW next to me but do not feel I should unless he talks first. I look at him and nod as if to say, "Hello." He looks at me briefly then turns his head away.

When we are in the air, several of the men light cigarettes and seem relieved. I notice the auxiliary gas tank across the aisle from where I'm sitting. There is no question that smoking should not be permitted under these conditions. I am the only officer in the passenger section and could easily tell the men to stop smoking and put out their cigarettes. Instead, I go through the door to the flight deck and explain the situation to the pilot. He tells me to go back and tell them to stop. I go back and sit down. The chances of the plane blowing up are really not very great. It's not my crew. If the pilot wants to take the cigarettes away from these guys he can do it himself. I don't have the heart for it.

In an hour or so I see the flight engineer come through the door from the flight deck. He goes to the gas tank and works at it with a wrench and screwdriver. After a short time, he utters a few choice descriptive adjectives at the tank and goes back to the flight deck. He soon reappears with a different wrench and a hammer. He twists and pounds and finally kicks the tank after which he goes back to the flight deck. Soon, the co-pilot comes through the door and announces that they are unable to transfer gas and will have to return to Yonaburu. The POWs greet the news without expression, as if one place is as good as another because, wherever and whatever it is, it will be a thousand times better than where they've been.

When we land, I wander around Yonaburu Airfield like a Mendicant friar begging for a lift on anything that flies. It is difficult to get a ride but the situation will become worse as each day more people receive the same orders. I want to go home so I plead tearfully and finally arrange a flight with a B-24 crew going to Clark Field. I feel jinxed, very jinxed. I go back to Aslito and rejoin Janeski, Walker and Gaines in the tent. So far, they have had no luck finding a hop. I think they are a bit jealous so I explain they should split up. None of the crews I talked to had extra spots for more than one person. We ate some more C-rations, finished the rye and slept comfortably;

completely indifferent to anything that might have taken place on *The Western Front*, quiet or noisy. I did say a little prayer for those POWs. I would never feel unlucky again. At least that's what I thought.

Next morning we take off and I wish I were with my old crew. I already miss the confidence that I had with Jan doing the flying. We are all strangers; there is virtually no conversation. I lean back against my barracks bag and try to catch some zzzs.

I wake up about the time we are passing Formosa. Somebody has told me once that Formosa is swarming with headhunters. I shudder slightly at the thought of being forced to parachute into the jungle. The way my luck is running, such an event does not seem out of the question.

As if on cue, while gazing out the window, I notice oil streaming out from beneath the number two engine. I walk through the catwalk up to the flight deck and inform the pilot. He takes a look and talks with the flight engineer. They decide to feather it, which means the pilot will shut the engine off and stabilize the propeller by turning it to the proper angle against the airstream. It's a simple procedure that almost always works. However, in those cases where the propeller refuses to be still and windmills out of control, it creates drag and vibrations that make the situation very serious, even dangerous. In this case it works fine and I return to my place in the waist. I am not concerned but there is always a sense of foreboding looking at a propeller standing starkly still when it should be spinning and pulling you home.

Experience has taught me that a B-24 can fly like a homesick angel on three engines and it is a great relief to see the home of the headhunters fading further and further behind us.

However, as we near the north end of Luzon, still some miles from Clark Field, I notice that the number four engine is also feathered.

410

This isn't my first time in a B-24 with two engines out. We still have the fan turning on number three, which means we have the hydraulic system working and will have brakes when we hit the runway. My mind tries to block out thoughts of the problems we will face if we lose another engine. I do not want to see our ride end in the trees and brush of northern Luzon.

As we near Clark Field, a very busy place, the pilot succeeds in contacting the tower, which clears him for a straight-in approach. Turning or banking a plane with one engine out is tricky. With two out the problem is greater, especially if both bad engines are on the same side. In our case, with one engine working on each side, the pilot made a straight approach and put the plane down very nicely. The runway was filled with fire engines and ambulances but thankfully they were not needed.

Clark Field is packed with people from everywhere wearing all kinds of uniforms and everybody in a hurry. My first thought is, *Here is where it started.* They hit Hickam Field hard and temporarily weakened our Navy and Air Force but Japan was never able to capitalize on its surprising first success. By contrast, the poorly equipped, under-manned troops on Luzon were over run and made to suffer the bloody consequences of total defeat including the Batten Death March. In the bay we can see Corrigador. Clark Field is where our two buddies from the 11th Airborne, Casey and Delane, made a jump and fought hand to hand to secure the runway on which we have just landed.

I am able to hitch a ride in a jeep and find the replacement depot. Manila has been pretty well shot up but is functioning. The streets are filled with horse drawn pom-pom wagons and old ladies smoking cigars. The pom-pom wagons now serve as public transportation but I am told that, at one time in the past, they conveyed prostitutes on their various pursuits, hence the name.

The people seem understandably happy to be liberated from the merciless domination of the Japanese. This morning a little boy came through the tent area selling bananas, which he carried on his head. "One Centavo," he says when I ask the price. I hesitate, "My brudder was Gureela," he tells me. "He keel twenny-five, fourteen, thirty-seven Japs."

"How about one for victory?" I ask.

"O.K. Joe. For veektory, two for one centavo. Only green, not yellow."

I take the two green. We have learned that bananas are the only edible food in the camp and one color tastes the same as another. They are never in short supply as the vendors, usually young kids, come through the rows of tents constantly.

We have also learned, the hard way, to be careful of what we drink in the category of alcoholic beverages. Two or three times during the middle of the night we are awakened by hysterical screams of men who have been made blind by inexpensive bathtub concoctions available all over town.

Those of us who have been in combat almost two years, working our way up the central Pacific chain, recognize, once again, the thick, rancid smell that persists like an invisible fog on these islands. Since we always arrive on the scene after weeks and months of gruesome fighting, for all we know, it may be the odor of death and carnage. It hangs in the air always.

I have a cot in a very large pyramidal tent holding twenty-five or thirty officers. Although it is September, the weather is hot and the sides of the tent are rolled up to the roof. This makes for a nice breeze blowing through, but becomes a problem when the monsoon sweeps in. The rain comes down sideways and soaks sleepers up and down the line.

I occupy the cot next to Gordy Hart, a co-pilot from St. Louis, Missouri who plays clarinet and was once a member of the Chico Marx Orchestra. Gordy said his most important role with the band was to stand up at the end of a set in the middle of the evening, raise his clarinet and shout, "Wow, what a band." That was the cue for Chico to come out from the wings and play the piano with an orange.

Gordy is accomplished in the art of deadpan humor. One morning I am shaken out of sleep by a howling wind blowing a horizontal Niagara Falls through the tent. I look over at Gordy and he is wide-awake, staring straight up with a blanket pulled under his nose. He turns his face toward me, fixes me with an angry look and growls, "I'm going into town today and drink myself to death and you can't stop me either!"

A few days after my arrival at the replacement depot, Janeski, Gaines, and Walker straggle into the tent, throw down their barracks bags and tell us about the gigantic typhoon that smashed into Okinawa. The wind knocked down tents, blew away airplanes on the flightline and sunk ships in the harbor the day after I left. They say our tent, which contained a floor made with two by six redwood lumber held up but was moved about a foot on the foundation.

Gaines and I, the unmarried officers on the crew, decide to go into town. Although Rizal Stadium has a huge hole in the roof, a boxing card is scheduled for the evening. Walker and Janeski decide to join us.

The fights are a disappointment. We watch a couple of three round waltzes which lack only the proper musical score by one of the Strauses so we decide to visit a huge dance hall that is talked about at the replacement depot. It turns out to be an old dirigible hanger, which is so big it features a large swing band at each end.

The place is packed with Air Force, Navy, Marines, and regular GI's as well as a large variety of Filipino girls who would like to dance. Unfortunately, we have forgotten how to dance so we listen to the bands for a few sets. We don't trust the booze, so we don't drink. We know that the Japanese left poisoned rice wine where the GI's would find it on Saipan. Since we are close to getting home, we would like to arrive without further damage, so we hire another Pom Pom wagon and return to the base. It concludes our only excursion to explore the nightlife of Manila.

As time moves along, the bridge and poker games start again with the same people playing except we now play for Centavos and Pesos. On Saipan and Guam we used American money; on Okinawa we used Yen. We are surviving almost entirely on bananas. Our travel plans are now definite. We will not be able to fly home because all available air travel is being reserved for prisoners of war. We will be floated home on a Liberty Ship, *The Robin Wentley*, and the trip will take about thirty days.

I suddenly realize that all my dress uniforms are in my footlocker, which is stored in Hawaii. Unfortunately, we will not be stopping there on the way home. My Bridge partner, Tom Gill, will be on the boat so I feel optimistic about being able to raise the $125.00 it will cost for new uniforms. Tom is a walking enigma. A navigator, he had already finished a tour up in Alaska before joining the 30th Bomb Group at Saipan. He earned his degree and was teaching Math at St. Thomas University in Pennsylvania at the age of nineteen. Tom seldom shaves, but does comb his hair occasionally. His suntans are usually wrinkled and moderately soiled, but he is a fantastic bridge partner.

Actually, he is more than a partner; Tom is the controlling half of our team. The game of bridge as played in an officers' club tent on an island in the central Pacific is not of a variety found in tea rooms. On Guam and Okinawa, when Tom and I were involved in a game, it would usually draw ten to thirty kibitzers generously armed with currently fashionable or cleverly original epithets. Failing in a daring finesse was certain to provoke a Greek chorus of "I told you so" accompanied by various instructions on removing one's head from one's anterior orifice.

Tom and I have played together for a year and a half and my job is to make certain the power comes from his side of the table. We seldom lose. I am confident Tom and I will find some people on the boat ready to play us. It should not be difficult to win $125.00 in the thirty days we expect to be at sea. The amount of $125.00 is my estimate of the cost of a complete set of new uniforms.

When the word comes down that the Robin Wentley is waiting at the dock, we scramble to pack our B-4 suitcases and stuff the overflow into a barracks bag. Most of us have left our dress uniforms and trench coats back in Hawaii and do not care whether we ever see them again. On the other hand, we will not be stopping on Oahu and my final destination, by way of San Francisco, is Minnesota. They tell us we may not reach the states until late October or November. When the trucks that will take us to the dock arrive, we grab our belongings and rush out to pile on for the ride around Manila Bay to the liberty ship, *Robin Wentley*, which will be our limited playground for the next month or more.

As the engine of the battered green GI truck coughs pitifully and begins to roll, the thought occurs that this will probably be our last bouncing ride on one of these loyal old kidney-shaking gas-guzzlers. We should soon be going aboard for the first part of the last leg of our journey home. The reality is difficult to believe.

Our lives have changed drastically in just a short time. Thirty days on the boat will offer time to think, to put our ducks in a row. I say this to Phil and he says, "What is there to think about? We get on the boat and go home. That's it."

Jan hears what Phil says and smiles. Without question he is counting the days, hours, minutes, and seconds until he gets to see his new son.

It is easy to envy Jan; his future will be dictated by what is best for his family. Whatever he finds to do there in Cudahy, Wisconsin, he'll be good at it. Our crew was the best wherever we went, from training through the toughest kinds of missions because Jan was a terrific pilot. We believed in him because he made the rest of us look good.

Walker doesn't pay us any attention as he tries to keep *God's Little Acre* from bouncing out of his hands. He says he's reading it for the fifth time although Phil says the last four times Squawker only goes over the spicy parts. It hasn't been easy for Walker because Phil, Jan, and I are all six years younger and tend to enjoy many of the things that happen.

Squawker despises anything in anyway connected to military service, especially the food. Amazingly, he navigated the big wide Pacific as if it were his backyard swimming pool. In thirty-six missions and all kinds of other flights, he managed to grab a few Z's now and then but always showed us the way to find our targets no matter how small and then, more importantly, point us right down Main Street for the trip home. He was a different person harmonizing with Makowski, Belt and I; *The Foxhole Serenaders*. It must be said, however, that to get to know him was to understand why he was sometimes called Squawker.

For two years my mind has disciplined itself to deflect daydreams of returning home alive, to dismiss random thoughts about tomorrow. My brain has taught itself to nourish hope while minimizing negative possibilities. Without those capabilities, it would not be possible to perform tasks under the stress of combat.

What happens now? Those bothersome negative possibilities have evaporated; it will be necessary to change my entire world. To look at tomorrow, to think about the future is like staring into a chasm.

Jan goes home with a rating as a multi-engine pilot tested under the most trying circumstances. If he so desires, some lucky airline should snap him up in a minute. Phil had already started a career as a radio announcer before entering the service. With his great tones, network producers should come looking for him. Walker is married to a girl whose daddy owns a huge factory known nation wide. Squawker, himself, is a graduate of Indiana University although he never revealed his major.

So there I stand with my bombsight. The ancient art of sacking large cities, especially by dropping explosives on their factories, appears headed for extinction. During my first year at the University of Minnesota, I picked up a little French, some math, and played catcher on the freshman baseball team. It struck the Army Air Force as expert preparation for an emerging bombardier. They could have added, "And little else!" I really don't have any idea where I want to apply my time and effort.

I am surprised to be weighing such things at this time when they have no relevance. The bus clatters and rattles throwing pebbles in all directions from the yellow hardened clay road. The ride to the boat seems endless. We have no idea of how far we must go. We have seen Corregidor and Bataan but there's no sight of the Robin Wentley. We can see Manila Bay all around us.

Pictures of home flash in and out of my thoughts. If we don't arrive there until November or even later, I will need to purchase new uniforms and a trench coat. A man in shirtsleeves at that time of year might be converted into an ice sculpture quicker than Lot's wife turned to salt.

A certain amount of ready cash will be necessary because officers' uniforms are not government issue. Calculating and speculating it appears $125 will be enough for what I need. It seems reasonable that Tom Gill and I, aided by our customized version of the Blackwood system, can reel in the necessary amount in one or two sessions of contract bridge. I will be able to defy fiendish Old Jack Frost at his worst. Let him huff and puff across the countryside plastering icy covers over frozen ponds and lakes. Let him try forcing the mighty Mississippi, king of all rivers, to stop and stand still. I'll show him.

Thoughts of cold weather remind me of how fortunate our crew has been in regard to weather. In any branch of the service, where you go and what you do, even whether you live or die, depends on what all service men call, "The Fickle Finger Of Fate." For transition training we could have been to Tonapah, Nevada, or Muroc Dry Lake but the finger pointed to March Field, a regular Army country club in Riverside, California. After finishing training at March, we were rushed to Seattle, Washington, without the furlough usually given to crews going overseas. The rush was to get us to replace crews lost in the D-Day invasion. Once again, the finger saved us. Not as many crews as anticipated were lost in the invasion of Europe. Replacements would not be necessary. The result was a boat ride to the Island of Oahu, in Hawaii, for a three-month stay in Paradise. The finger was not so obliging when it sent us "down under" to join the 30th Bomb Group on Saipan. No sane or objective person could ever call Saipan, in the condition in which we found it, a paradise. A fair assessment might put it closer to purgatory. However, the weather was perfect and the beach the most beautiful anyone could imagine; several times as large and more pristine than Waikiki. After the Marines captured Iwo Jima, the finger pointed toward Hawaii again for a two-week rest leave. We spent one week on Oahu and Phil and I spent the other week with the family of a plantation owner on the big island, Hawaii. The finger did us a small favor when it called for us to return to Guam rather than Saipan. Guam, which had belonged to us, was taken from us at the beginning of the war but recaptured by the Army. It had been occupied by Americans for many years and smelled better than Saipan. Of all the islands we were on, Guam was by far the most beautiful, with the exception of Hawaii.

Guam had a tendency to rain a bit more than the others did but days were sunny and beautiful. It was possible to sit outside the tent and watch a squall line approach in the distance. We could usually play a few more hands before it reached the island. We would then go inside the tent, play a hand or two while the rain passed over and then go outside to finish the game. Living conditions were not always five star but we are spoiled rotten after almost three years of sun, fun and balmy evenings where the climate was cloned in heaven.

Our final stop was at Okinawa, which had been the scene of a horrible, battle on land and at sea. It witnessed the final suicidal gasps of the Kamikazes. We flew in from Guam on a Sunday afternoon to land in an eerie white cloud. Everything was covered with white coral dust. Airplanes poised on their hardstands, people working on the flight line, boxes of shells and piles of bombs; a ghostly sight for our crew which had just finished the long flight from Guam. Within two weeks the Seabees had paved the runway and turned Aslito into a first class airfield. Okinawa was not a pretty place to be but it was summertime, and the sun shined every day. Only when faced with impending disasters such as earthquakes, typhoons and Kamikaze attacks do people in warm climates think about the weather.

At home, in the Midwest, the weather is always topic number one. People sit by their radios waiting for the weather before attending to the bathroom, eating breakfast, or reading the morning paper. In the evening, they wait for weather on the six o'clock news and listen again to the ten o'clock report before retiring. An alarm clock is set to awaken them for the early morning forecast. Pilots flying at night mention the phenomenon of lights all across Minnesota turning off simultaneously immediately after the final evening report.

If we arrive in October we may catch some of Indian Summer, a wonderful season. We will find a few weeks of warm afternoons and cool evenings, a time for wiener roasts and sweater golf. It means watching leaves turn gold and brown and flaming scarlet as well as indescribable colors that artists try vainly to capture. The air will be filled with footballs and the acrid perfume of burning leaves. It may even be possible to take in a Golden Gopher Big Ten game in Memorial Stadium. In any case, it will be home and the family will be together again. I'll have a bed without mosquito netting and my mother's cooking. It occurs to me that now, when I am almost home, I have become homesick.

The truck rolls on toward the dock but I remain in my private world, totally indifferent to the conversation around me. The words seem distant; humming and buzzing, meaningless. It is a chorus of detached voices straining mightily to anesthetize inescapable boredom. My mind kicks back to real time when Anatole Babykin, Jeter's bombardier, asks if anyone has heard about the GI who fell to his death yesterday while walking up the gangplank to board a ship for home. "Splattered all over the sidewalk," is how Anatole put it.

Well, there it is; pure irony, the switch that triggers great stories, plays, movies, and legendary tales. A young man survives the horrors of war only to fall off a gangplank and land on his head. How ironic can it get? Here is irony that cries out for empathy and embellishment, a chapter right out of my dreams the night before our mission to Shikoku. Extra! Extra! Read all about it! I wonder if he had any premonition. How is it possible to fall off a gangplank?

Because we now have something to talk about, we discuss the matter until the truck pulls up at the dock where the *Robin Wentley* is sitting. It presents a totally unexpected crisis more frightening and crucial than any single moment on any of our missions. The aspect is terrifying and there is no reasonable avenue of escape. The side facing us is very high and reminds me of the left field fence at Fenway Park in Boston where the Red Sox play. The distance to the regular fence is so short that they put a second fence on top of the first to prevent scores from hitting triple digits. It appears to be thirty or forty feet high.

We take our first glimpse at the floating concentration camp that will be our home for the next month or so. We all try to drop off the back of the truck at the same time, which has barracks bags swinging in circles, like a horseless carousel. Shortly we reclaim our baggage and move toward the looming wall of the ship. We stop to stare.

What stops us is an ascending wooden walkway less than four feet wide inclining steeply toward the topside of the wall. It will mean carrying our bags up those shaky looking boards forty feet in the air. From our angle, on the sidewalk, it looks more like a hundred and forty. It's rickety, as if it were thrown together hastily by a committee of drunken carpenters.

There are no sides or railings; there are gaps in the planks. The landing area beneath this monstrosity is concrete in all directions. Each of us is carrying a B-4 bag, the military version of a large suitcase, in one hand and a full barracks bag slung over the other shoulder. I am holding my breath and notice that the men around me are doing the same. This is not fair. We are trained as air crews not acrobats or high wire daredevils.

Over the course of many missions we have learned to manage fear and get the job done. It is not fashionable to wear medals on sun tans and fatigues, but the men looking skeptically at the sagging combination of wood, rope, and nails have innumerable awards ranging from Air Medals, and Distinguished Flying Crosses to Purple Hearts somewhere in their barracks bags.

Right now there is fear in our eyes. One reason we have survived this far is that we have avoided doing something stupid. Right now, to us, the idea of carrying our luggage up these sloping boards seems very stupid.

No one will be forced to climb those planks and get on the ship but the alternative means another month at the replacement depot eating bananas for breakfast, lunch, and dinner. In the end, we will go up that plank because we are tired and want to go home and this is just one more damn thing. Somebody says, "Hey, I forgot to wear my chute harness!" It brings forth a nervous laugh. We are standing silent in a circle, but the extra sensory perception is coming over at R/5 S/5 (meaning loud and clear). Somebody has to start the show, has to be the first one to play mountain goat on those treacherous slopes.

Our fear has some basis in fact. There is little margin for error. We are not worried about height; it's the bags we are carrying that pose the problem. If they start to sway and affect balance there is not enough room to recover and no kind of railing to use as a grab-bar. We have no choice. Jan says, "Let's go gents." And our crew falls in behind him. I say a Hail Mary. Phil follows Jan. The other crews are silent spectators.

A little voice says, "Don't look down, don't look down," and keeps repeating it. The thin boards shake under our weight. My eyes are firmly fixed on a point between Phil's shoulders and just below his neck. Phil reaches the top and disappears over the wall. I throw my bags over the side, pull myself up and fall in a heap with a thump. Walker appears and does the same. Next come our enlisted men; Scanlan, the two Olsons, Shorty Rice and Muller. We do not move away from the deck until they are all on board.

Soon we are summoned by the public address system to listen up. They tell us about the rules that will be in effect, when meals will be served, and where we will sleep. They tell us there are 2,500 men on board and no showers. They explain that one of their turbines is not functioning properly, which may add travel time to our journey. We wonder what else is new!

We, the four officers, go down in the hold of the ship to stake out our beds. The bunks are in tiers of six from bottom to top. No one wants the top bunks for some reason but my experience whispers that it is better to climb a few feet than have the bottom of the bunk above touching my nose. Thanks to the involuntary dietary regimen practiced at Saipan, Guam, and Okinawa my weight is down to 128 from 160. However, I'm lithe as a monkey and swing up to that sixth bunk like Jane is in it and Tarzan is out of town.

There are military personnel of all ranks and branches of service on the boat. The hold is moldy and stuffy which leads some people to sleep under the stars on the hardwood deck. The weather is very hot but, true to the captain's word, there are no showers. Thirty days of this and the smell alone may cause a mutiny.

Tom and I have already arranged a game tomorrow against some guys from the 5th Air Force. They flew most of their missions down in the South Pacific, wear skull and cross bones on their t-shirts and call themselves *The Jolly Rogers*. We are anxious to get started. If they are not better pilots than they are bridge players, it's a wonder they're still alive. Tom and I took home $25 each so my guess of winning enough to buy clothes is well ahead of schedule.

If the Robin Wentley limps along at the predicted speed, we may not arrive in San Francisco until Christmas or even Easter. However, Phil Gaines, who is something of a celebrity in his role as the ships regular newscaster, has talked with the captain who maintains stoutly that the ailing turbine will soon be healed. He predicts we will be in Frisco at the end of October or first of November. Phil was a radio announcer before the war. He has a great voice and will probably have a career in radio if that's what he wants. I am not seeing much of Walker although I know he got on the boat. Mack (Makowski) did not leave Okinawa with us because he was with 7th Air Force Headquarters. Frances Belt is on the boat but Mack was the backbone of the "Foxhole Serenaders" and we can't do much without him. He not only supervised the singing but also made the arrangements. I'll never hear *What a Difference a Day Makes* or *The Very Thought Of You* without thinking of our quartet. We sang together almost any day one of us was not on a mission. We never sang in public, which may or may not have been a blessing.

The days go rolling by, but are consistently dull. Last night, there was no movie; something went wrong with the projector. It is the only entertainment for all these guys and the engineers worked until the projector was fixed at which time the sound went out. For lack of anything else to do, I hung around and watched. The crowd thinned out but there were about ten of us left when it was decided by one of the mechanics that we might as well watch the picture without sound. Someone produced a handkerchief and they showed the movie on that little screen only about a foot square. If there had been sound, it would have been neat. We seemed to be close to the picture. I wondered if someone would ever invent such a thing as that where the family could sit and watch at home instead of going to a theater. It's hard to see how there would be any money in it.

Today, Tom and I have a game with some friends of the Jolly Rogers who we took to the cleaners our first day out. They said their friends are really good and wanted to challenge us. They should have stayed down in the hold. We let them get vulnerable and ate them alive. My treasure chest for uniforms is now over $100 and we've only been out a week. Just $25 more to go but it's already getting difficult to find opponents. We have a game tomorrow with some people from our own squadron. They know us and we know them. After playing each other every week for a year or more, there is little we can do to surprise them. We will need to be lucky to get my remaining $25 from these people.

The movie tonight was a miserable Van Johnson epic where he was a smiling P-38 pilot who did tricks with a Lockheed Lightening that could shatter the basic principles of aviation. At one point, he turned a square corner without ever dipping a wing. We loved it but it should have been sent to Tokyo. Van would have had those Zero pilots choking on their rice.

I swing into my upper bunk and wonder where Hollywood gets this stuff. We know they mean well, but they could be a bit more accurate. For instance, we have had some good laughs at movies where the hotshot power-diving pilots are old enough to be our fathers. The maximum age to enlist for air training in the Army Air Force is twenty-seven. On our crew of ten only four are old enough to vote. The pilot, co-pilot and bombardier are all twenty-one. The navigator, who seems very old, is twenty-seven.

You should have heard the boys howl the other night at a Cary Grant movie. He played a Navy pilot on leave with a couple of buddies. When they are notified that their beloved aircraft carrier has been sunk they shout, "We gotta get back out there right now!" The final scene shows the boys taking off into the sunset as their wives and lady friends wave tearfully from the dock. The rest of us are left to wonder, "How are they going to land on a sunken aircraft carrier?"

My dreams should be sweet tonight. This afternoon Tom and I picked up another $25 each which means I will get new uniforms and be prepared to meet the family dressed in the height of military fashion. Nobody wants to play us anymore so Tom and I may have to split up and play against each other. We really don't want to do that so we'll have to see what happens.

We really don't have any idea where we are other than somewhere on the Pacific Ocean. It's a very exciting day when a whale is spotted now and then. They are a very big fish and spout water high into the air but when you see one you have seen them all. Mostly, we hang around shooting the bull and catching a few rays. Some men hang over the rail all the time as if they're counting white caps on the waves. At first I thought they were sick, but they say they're just bored.

If we don't get home until November it can be cold, perhaps brutally cold. I do not like biting wind, driven snow and the kinds of problems they create but right now, as I stand next to the rail on the bow of the Robin Wentley watching white capped waves dancing in the bright sunlight, I can hardly wait to feel winter in the air.

The big events of the day are chow and the movies. The food is good and if there was water for showers this could be a nice trip. We have heard of so-called "sand baths." For the adventurers who have tried one, there is no encore. They don't try it again. Their advice, "Forget about it!"

I went down to the galley (Navy talk for kitchen) early and had a nice breakfast. Who should I meet there but Bob Myers who was with us at CTD, College Training Detachment, at Coe College in Cedar Rapids, Iowa. He was one of the people in our dorm, an alumnus of Jefferson Barracks College of Pneumonia and Encephalitis. Bob went into pilot training after Santa Ana Preflight School and ended up as a fighter pilot flying P-38s in the South Pacific. He really hadn't changed but looks tired. Maybe we all do.

My chat with Bob made me wonder why Hollywood always portrays fighter pilots as devil may care playboys. The fighter pilots we know are not like that at all. For one thing, based on those we've had a chance to meet, they are younger and much less flamboyant. On Saipan we lived close to Ease Field where Thunderbolt and Lightning fighter pilots lived. On the few occasions we visited them, their officers' club was sedate. Compared with the full throttle, bawdy singing and non-stop poker at our club, theirs had the hush-hush atmosphere of a public library.

They are to be admired. The sight of two P-51 Mustangs weaving just above us through the heavy flak at Kure Harbor will be in my memory forever. They did not have to do that. Normally, when the flak starts, the fighters on both sides find somewhere else to play. Those Mustang pilots were up there alone with all their faith placed in just one engine. At least on a B-24 we have four engines and somebody to talk with. Doing their job without being an introvert would be very uncomfortable. It was nice to see Bob but he didn't have any news to offer about other people from our three months at Coe College.

Life goes on aboard the Robin Wentley but it is repetitive, boring, and some days it seems the ship makes no progress at all. However, we know we are getting close to the mainland when we begin hearing commercials on the radio. It is amazing how intrusive the hard selling announcers and cutesy-pooh singing commercials can be when the listeners have been enjoying commercial free programs for a long time. Neither Saipan Sam nor Tokyo Rose had commercials and they were the only two stations we could get. As the days go by we become more accustomed to the programming. In fact, being a Nat King Cole fan I enjoy his "Use Wildroot Hair Oil, Charley" commercial.

I don't know what day of the week it is; they all seem the same. The time is sunset as we sail under the Golden Gate Bridge and see the lights of San Francisco begin to wink from the shore. There is a crowd on the dock as we await our orders. They are mostly young girls, probably volunteers of some kind. I don't know what to say or do. I notice a girl looking at me from the steps of the gangway. She smiles up at me and I smile back. This is the real world. She moves down the line and dutifully smiles at the next guy. I feel good anyway. I feel fine. We are all ticketed to go to Camp Stoneman for the night. Tomorrow we will be put on the trains for various places close to home with facilities to take care of a nice military honorable discharge. Camp McCoy, Wisconsin is where Jan and I will go.

The trucks take us to Stoneman where we are each given a nice room and take our first showers in almost a month. We have a nice meal and chat with the hostesses whose job it is to chat with the soldiers. Walker has disappeared. He said he was meeting his wife in San Francisco and, as we predicted all along, he managed, one way or another, to set a world record for getting out of the Army. It looks as though he didn't bother to get out; he just went.

I do not feel good about the way I look. Earlier, when I stepped out of the shower and looked in the mirror the reflection was the image of a prisoner of war, a 128-pound bag of bones. I am looking at ribs that would make a very nice washboard and hips that look like I'm wearing a pair of football pads under the skin.

The thing that bothers me most is that my skin is a weird ugly yellow color from head to toe. I owe it all to Atabrin, the anti-malaria drug that we were required to take every day to prepare for our move from Guam to Okinawa. It does not prevent Malaria but does suppress the symptoms. The truth of this scenario is that we may or may not actually have malaria. We will find that out in a month or so when the effect of Atabrin wears off. Not everyone who took Atabrin changed color. Unfortunately those who did, like myself, may have to remain quasi Charlie Chans for the immediate future.

Now that I am finally going home, I don't want the family to see me like this. There is no way out! What they see is what they'll get. It's just one more damn thing.

Jan and I say goodbye to Phil who will be on a different train tomorrow since he's going to Florida. Now that we're splitting up I begin to appreciate how lucky I was to get on a crew with these guys. There is a distinct possibility we will never see each other again.

In the morning, Jan and I get on the train bound for Camp McCoy. It is a routine trip except for a single experience that makes us all angry. The train stops in Denver and we are told we have about half an hour to get a sandwich and cup of coffee. As we start to get off the train, the military police stop us and say we are out of uniform and cannot go outside. In particular, they say we are not wearing ties. We can't believe it. Most of us have not worn a tie in at least two years. Plainly this paddlefoot sergeant is determined to show these smart-ass officers who's in charge here.

We are, to be perfectly candid, a sorry looking outfit even though we've had our first shaves and showers in thirty days. Our sun tan shirts and pants, wrinkled from four weeks of being stuffed in the bottom of a barracks bag, would have earned us enough demerits (called gigs) to be walking tours for six months when we were aviation cadets. Several of us are a funny yellow color that the MP's note suspiciously. So they restrict us to the train for not wearing neckties when we don't know where we could get one and have forgotten how to tie one if we found it. It was another one of those damn things.

We go back to our seats and sit down with the certain knowledge that this kind of crap will soon be behind us. The train chugs along, the miles pass, the sun sets. We have not been given sleeper bunks so we put our seats back and try to shrug into a position that will allow at least a fitful sleep. It does but at a painful price. We greet the dawn with stiff necks and aching backs.

Jan and I have a decent breakfast in the dining car and sit back to wait for Shangri-la. Early in the afternoon the train begins to slow and drifts up next to the depot platform. Jan and I trade smiles as we gaze through the coach window and see the sign, *CAMP McCOY WISCONSIN.*

Jan's wife is there to meet him at the station with Henry Jr. in her arms. We shake hands and pat each other on the shoulder but Jan never turns his eyes away from the son he is seeing for he first time. I know it is time to leave these people alone.

I turn to go inside the building but Jan's voice stops me. "Hey, Jack I." I stop and turn back. Jan is still holding his son but looks me in the eye. "I know one thing. I had the best bombardier in the whole damn Air Force."

"Well," I said. "I had the best pilot." The nice thing is that I knew we both meant it. I moved quickly to get into the building before I began to choke up. I was ready to buy some uniforms, fill out my papers, and leave this part of my life behind.

It's the 26th of October and the early afternoon breeze is mild but nippy, as it tends to be at this time of year. The sun goes down early. I'll need to buy a trench coat to go with my new regalia. It will fit inside the amount budgeted for the purpose. I go inside a large room crowded with people as frantically anxious as I to finish the trip and go home. This is still the Army and there is a line waiting.

I decide to telephone my mother to tell her where I am and that I expect to arrive at the Milwaukee Depot at about seven-thirty. I cut the conversation short because I want to get back in line. It's been a long time and there will be plenty to talk about but not on the phone and not until things are taken care of here at McCoy.

When I finally reach the front desk, I give my file to a thin young red-haired man wearing thick glasses and a nametag bearing the word Jim. He looks through the file with a few page flips back and forth. In no time at all, he closes the file, reaches into a basket on his desk and gives me a paper to fill out and take to the doctor who will give me my final physical. He then points out which hallways to follow and doors to open to find the place where I will be examined.

As was to be expected, there is a line. However, it is not a long one and I am soon disrobing and stepping up on the scale. The doctor looks at me, balances the weights, looks at me again and says, "My God, fella, you're thin!" The scale registers one hundred twenty-nine pounds, one more pound than I thought. He pokes and prods a bit and tells me to cough. He puts the cold stethoscope on my chest and protruding ribs to check my lungs and heart. He says, "You're OK. When you get home you'll eat more."

While I'm getting dressed, he says he notices I've been taking Atabrin. I say, "Yeah, Doc. How long before that stuff goes away?"

He looks thoughtful for a moment, then says, "Hell, I don't know. Half the men who come in here are the same way. I always tell them, find a nice girl; get her to take some, too. You'll make a lovely couple."

I take the paper he hands me and start back to the main desk. Soon again I'm at the end of the line, waiting my turn.

After about fifteen minutes I am able to hand the doctor's report to Jim who looks at it up closely through his thick glasses and puts it in the file I had given him previously. He tells me it looks like everything is in order and hands me my discharge papers which he typed while I was being examined. "Sign it," he says. "Sign it and get out of here before they start another war."

Suddenly, I remember that my MOS (Military Occupational Specialty) should be changed. I am listed as a regular bombardier with the MOS-#1035. In reality, because I am checked out on radar, the number should be changed to reflect that fact. I inform the man of the situation and he turns very serious.

"Listen, Lieutenant," he says. "Why don't you leave things the way they are? If you put radar on that rating, you'll be one of the first ones called if there's ever any trouble. It's up to you; I can change it if you want."

It sounds like good advice. I can't imagine what trouble there could be but, if there ever is any, my position will be a traditional, "Don't call me, I'll call you!"

I thank him, he wishes me luck, and I head for the PX to buy some uniforms. I have an hour before my train leaves and within a half-hour I have purchased a pair of "pink" slacks, a green shirt, a green blouse and trench coat. I show the clerk my discharge papers and he examines them to see what medals I am entitled to wear.

He unlocks the glass showcase under the counter and takes out a Purple Heart, Distinguished Flying Cross, an Air Medal with Five Oak Leaf Clusters, and several other ribbons of less meaning. He slides the ribbons into little brackets that can be pinned on a shirt or blouse. There are three rows and he arranges them in order of importance with the Purple Heart at the top right. I pin the medals over my upper left-hand pocket. The time has come. I don my new trench coat, pick up my bags and am out the door. The train for Minneapolis should be along shortly.

On the platform, I put down the bags and seat myself on a bench next to one occupied by a pair of elderly ladies. They smile pleasantly and I smile back. The train appears in the distance, grows closer, slows gradually and coasts to a stop immediately opposite my bench. I take a bag in each hand, take two steps toward the open door of the coach and WHAM! I am blindsided by the two senior ladies who had smiled tenderly only moments earlier. As I stagger a step or two, they push past me and scurry up the steps and into the coach trailed by an overwhelming scent of cheap perfume.

I have just had my wake up call. "Time to go, Lieutenant. Today's target will be another world, safer but much less orderly than you and your friends have known in the last few years. Briefing will be at 1950 hours this evening when you kiss your mother, shake hands with your father, and hug your brothers and sister. Thank God, it will be over. Your guardian angel wishes you good luck and says good-bye."

Epilogue

Excerpts from an interviews conducted during a reunion of Janeski's crew in Dayton, Ohio in 1997.

We were needed and it's something you carry with you and people who weren't there are never going to understand. You make a deal with your mortality: "I'm never going to get home, so whatever happens is going to happen to all of our crew and that's the way it's going to be." You don't really get uneasy until you get up there around thirty missions and you think, "Hey I might make this," and then you start thinking about home.

There's something else I want to add to this. We never aborted. We flew every mission. We went to the target if we took off. And that was because of Chris Muller. I remember sitting in driving rain at the end of the runway and Jan running up the engines, with a full load of bombs and everything, and Jan turns around and hollers, "Muller, the mags are falling off, what is this?" And Muller said, "Ah, the leaves are a little wet, let's go." So we did. It shows we were absolutely dependent on each other. Muller said "Go." The pilot didn't say, "Well, let's take

435

another look at it." Nobody on the crew argued with anyone else. We all had our jobs to do. We did feel well trained and relied on each other. They talk about team spirit. It's something we never talked about, but it was there.

[After the war] we went from one world into another. We had lived together for a year and a half, two years, gone through a lot of things, and at that point were more of a family than you would expect to experience at any other time. But that had its uncertain elements, too. It wasn't all pleasure. So once it was over and we had survived it and went home, we went to a completely different world. And those people weren't really in that world. We didn't forget them, but we were busy, doing things, going to school, getting married. And so while you thought of these guys sometimes, you were too busy doing other things to take the time to go phoning around the country to see if one of these guys caught a cold or something.

There was really never any rank. After the war Shorty Olson came and stayed with my family, two or three months. He had that ambition to own a bar in California. I saw Shorty quite a bit and then he went to California and started a bar. Just the year I was married he came back with his wife and we visited awhile. Unfortunately he's not here anymore. Janeski, the pilot, was a really good pilot and a really good guy. He only lived in Milwaukee and I live in Minneapolis and I wish I could do it over again. It's such a short run down there. But I did talk to him just a couple of times on the phone. I was really shocked to learn that he had passed away several years before.

It's hard for me to explain. We did not expect to get through 36 missions. You hope to, and you don't think really, down in your heart that anything is going to happen, but you're ready for it. You see it happen and you're ready for it. You've made a deal with your own mortality. It's no big deal. We're all going to die sometime, so I'm not going to worry about that. I used to think, so I go down here over the ocean and the guys that goofed off at home are only going to live another 30, 40, 50 years and they're going to end up where I am, so I'm not going to worry about that.

I was talking to a flight surgeon over on Okinawa one day. We had almost finished our missions by then. He said, "Well, you know, Jack, once you guys get home you're going to be really easy to please; a dish of ice-cream, some good food, meet some interesting people." And that's exactly right. I feel so grateful to God every day. I'm here and enjoying life to this point. I never thought that I'd live to be 30 or 40 or 50, but I did feel that once I'd lived to be 22 there was a good shot I'd live a lot longer.

As far as flying the missions, we didn't realize that at the time, because it was an everyday thing, but we were a good crew. They kept picking us to lead things, and so what I learned from that was an absolute interdependence that we have on everybody, and it's true all through your life. I've owned businesses and you have to depend on other people. You have to believe other people and try to find people around you that are there for you and good in a crunch and I think we had that on this crew to a greater extent than we realized when we were doing it.

As far as the young people now, we had eleven children. One died when he was 18, but the rest are all out doing well. The youngest one just graduated from law school. I do think this, and I think it very sincerely, that the younger generation is very, very much underestimated. It's just full of good, young people. They're meeting obstacles we didn't have to meet, doing more difficult things, trying to fathom technologies, trying to get into a position where you can really survive in what's a very competitive world. Sure the economy is good now, but as they say in the Air Force, anybody can fly an airplane when it's straight and level, but what do you do when it flips on its back? And I think if the same situation arose, under the same circumstances I have no doubt they would be really good, that they would perform in national life excellently. I think they're maturing a lot, the young people, and I hope we're not going to have any more elections where only 50% of the registered voters vote. I think they're going to have to take control. They're getting ripped off, and have been one way or another for years. I'm not talking about political parties. They're going to have to focus on that, because it's their money. But I think they're great. I think the young people are just great.

Seeing these guys is emotional to a certain extent. You know what it makes really clear to me, and I think it's something that's bothered all of us in the same boat for a long time, is that we lived in a different world. It was not a real world at all. We had experiences in that world that you can't understand. Nobody can understand if they weren't there. It's just that unless you were there, you know, been there done that, and leaned on these guys and put your life on the line, and come out on the right side instead of the wrong side, you're a different person. Sometimes people say to me, "Nothing ever bothers you." Well, what can bother me? What worse can happen that could have happened already and it didn't happen? So it gives you a kind of – it levels you out. If you went into it and you got through it, it's better than a college education. It taught you how to live with people, it taught you how to meet yourself face to face. But like some other people say, 'War is a few million other men's hard luck'...and I weep for them.

438

ABOUT THE AUTHOR

After earning a Purple Heart, a Distinguished Flying Cross, and five Air Medals during world War II, Jack I. Moore began a career in radio. In 1961, he built and managed WAYL FM, and produced the first FM stereo broadcast between Chicago and the West Coast. During the 1970s and 80s on KTWN-FM, he developed the "Smooth Jazz" radio format which *Radio & Records* called "the first pop jazz station ever launched." He launeched the first Twin Citeies-based cable radio in 1983, and in 1987 he created teh market's first satellite-delivered radio network, *The Breeze Radio Network*. He founded CAFE 105 in the 1990s. For his innovations and accomplishements as a broadcasting pioneer, he was inducted in to the Minnesota Museum of Broadcasters' Hall of Fame in 2004. Married to his wife Emily for over 56 years, he is the father of eleven children, and grand-father to many, many more. Jack passed away on December 19, 2012 in Northeast Minneapolis, only a few minutes away from the home he writes about in *We Never Said Good-Bye*.

Made in the USA
Las Vegas, NV
05 December 2022

61267938R00249